THE ART BOOK

New Edition

Phaidon Press Limited
Regent's Wharf
All Saints Street
London, N1 9PA

Phaidon Press Inc.
65 Bleecker Street
New York, NY 10012

www.phaidon.com

First published 1994
Reprinted 1994, 1995, 1996,
1998, 1999, 2000, 2001, 2004,
2006, 2009, 2010, 2011

Second edition (revised,
expanded and updated)
published 2012
This edition © 2014 Phaidon
Press Limited

ISBN 978 0 7148 6796 0

A CIP catalogue record for this
book is available from the
British Library

Designed by Alan Fletcher
Jacket designed by
Javier Mariscal

Printed in Singapore

Note

Abbreviations:

c=circa
b=born **d**=died
h=height **w**=width **l**=length
diam=diameter
dur=duration

The publishers have made
every effort to include
dimensions wherever
possible. As some frescos
illustrated are part of
large cycles, covering
entire rooms, the correct
measurements have been
impossible to acquire and
are therefore omitted.

THE ART BOOK presents a whole new way of looking at art. Easy to use, informative and fun, it's an A-to-Z guide to the greatest painters, photographers and sculptors from medieval times to the present day. It debunks art-historical classifications by throwing together brilliant examples from all periods, schools, visions and techniques. Only here could Carracci be seen alongside Cartier-Bresson, Duccio be found beside Duchamp, Mondrian be considered with Monet, or Warhol contrasted with Waterhouse. Each artist is represented by a full-page illustration of an exemplary work, accompanied by an illuminating text on the piece and its creator. The entries are comprehensively cross-referenced and glossaries of artistic movements and technical terms are included, together with an international directory of galleries and museums to visit. By breaking with traditional classifications, **THE ART BOOK** presents a fresh approach to art: an unparalleled visual sourcebook and a celebration of our rich and multi-faceted culture.

Abramović Marina

The House with the Ocean View

In November 2002 Marina Abramović spent twelve days and nights living in the Sean Kelly Gallery in New York. The artist's accommodation consisted of three specially constructed living units built on raised platforms. With each unit on open view, visitors to the gallery were invited to watch the artist's every move (a telescope was provided), their voyeuristic presence forming an integral part of the work. For the duration of the event Abramović did not eat or speak. Her self-imposed imprisonment was emphasized by the presence of three ladders with rungs made from upward-facing butcher knives. A pioneering figure in the Performance art movement since the early 1970s, Abramović's work has often involved the enacting and ritualizing of everyday activities. Audience participation has also been central to her art. In one infamous performance of 1974 she sat passively as people were invited to manipulate her body with a selection of items, including a whip, rose, scalpel, feather, gun and a single bullet.

► Cahun, Kruger, A Piper, Rist, Sherman

Marina Abramović. b Belgrade, 1946. **The House with the Ocean View.** 2002. Performance at the Sean Kelly Gallery, New York, NY

Abts Tomma

Sculptural shapes seem to float on planes of teal blue and green, their impossibly interlocking forms silhouetted by shadow, highlights and line. Like all of Abts's work, this painting is determinedly non-representational. Its strict geometries do not symbolize or describe anything else, nor are we given any hint of emotion or information. It is an exploration of colour and space, in which subtle shifts of both create unexpected effects: movement, stillness, depth. Abts was born in Germany, and the titles of her works derive from German first names. She creates small canvases, always the same size, using a labour-intensive technique in which thin layers of paint are laid like strata, over-painted again and again as she changes her mind and works intuitively, often for months, on a single canvas. Like the American painter Jasper Johns, she is interested in a painting as both image and object, representing nothing but itself.

▶ Hayter, Johns, Marden, Noland, Popova

Tomma Abts. b Keil, 1967. Uphe. 2011. Acrylic and oil on canvas. h48 × w38 cm. h18¾ × w15 in. Private collection

Adams Ansel

View South from Manzanar to Alabama Hills

In 1943 Ansel Adams visited the internment camp for Americans of Japanese descent in Manzanar, California. Mostly he documented its residents and their life there, but he also photographed the landscape of the central California site. The most popular photographer in America, Adams was sometimes criticized for his 'inhumane' work, in which people, with their messy suffering and joy, have no place. His Manzanar photographs refute that accusation – in addition to his portraits of internees and documentation of camp activities, his empty landscapes reveal a subtext of human injustice and despair. A key achievement of Adams's work was to reconcile landscape photography with twentieth-century Modernism. Capturing a transient moment in a chaotic world of light and shadow, he produced images that are almost abstract in their graphic boldness, blending emotion with rigorous artistic discipline and technical precision.

► Atget, Cartier-Bresson, Le Gray, Spilliaert, Steichen

Ansel Adams. **b** San Francisco, CA, 1902. **d** Carmel, CA, 1984. **View South from Manzanar to Alabama Hills**. 1943. Gelatin silver print. **h**18.5 × **w**23.4 cm. **h**7¼ × **w**9¼ in. Library of Congress, Washington, DC

Agasse Jacques-Laurent

The Nubian Giraffe

A giraffe leans its long, slender neck to reach the bowl held by its Arab keepers. Two Egyptian cows can be seen in the background. With the development of communication links, traders of the early nineteenth century were able to travel farther and farther afield and return with increasingly exotic gifts. Giraffes, lions and leopards were given to wealthy landowners and Agasse, being renowned for his acute attention to detail, was often commissioned to paint them. King George IV paid Agasse £200 for 'a picture of the

Giraffe and Keepers'. The gentleman depicted wearing a top hat is Edward Cross, a well-known importer of foreign birds and animals for the royal menagerie. Born in Switzerland, Agasse lived in England from 1800 where he achieved considerable success painting sporting scenes and exotic animals. He also painted a number of portraits of noblemen on horseback.

► Audubon, Landseer, Longhi, Stubbs

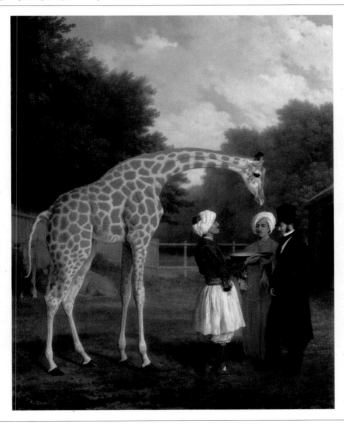

Jacques-Laurent Agasse. b Geneva, 1767. **d** London, 1849. **The Nubian Giraffe.** 1827. Oil on canvas. **h**127 × **w**101.5 cm. **h**50⅛ × **w**40 in.
The Royal Collection, Windsor Castle, Windsor

Ai Weiwei

Template

In 2007 Ai Weiwei's monumental sculpture was unveiled at documenta 12, a large contemporary art event held every five years in Kassel, Germany. Shortly after its installation the work – constructed of wooden doors and windows salvaged from destroyed Ming and Qing dynasty houses – was knocked over by a strong wind. Appreciative of nature's intervention, the artist announced that the sculpture was now more beautiful than before. During the exhibition he also arranged for 1,001 people – farmers, street vendors, students – to travel to the German town from his native China. Well known for his political views, Ai Weiwei is considered to be one of the world's most powerful artists. Inspired by the work of Duchamp, Rauschenberg and Johns, his modification of found objects raises subtle questions relating to changing cultural and financial values in the globalized world.

► Alÿs, Deacon, Duchamp, Perry, Rauschenberg, Zhang Huan

Ai Weiwei. b Beijing, 1957. **Template**. 2007. Wooden doors and windows from destroyed Ming and Qing dynasty houses. **h**422 × **w**1106 cm. **h**116¼ × **w**435½ in. As installed at documenta 12, Kassel

Albers Josef

Homage to the Square

Four squares of yellow nest together. Despite a rigid format, they float freely, creating an optical illusion of another dimension. Each area has been painted in a single colour. The paint has been applied with a knife, directly from the tube. Albers' most famous series of paintings, of which this is one, shows squares created from pure colour. The optical illusion created in this picture means it is related to the Op Art movement. Yet the way the paint has been applied and the use of colour link it with the Post-Painterly Abstraction movement. Between 1920 and 1923 Albers studied at the famous Bauhaus school. He joined the staff in 1923. A Dutchman by birth, Albers moved to the USA in 1933, where he taught many established artists at the Black Mountain College and Yale University. His influential book *The Interaction of Color* was published in 1963. In this he explores the perception of colour, which was a dominant theme throughout his life.

► Andre, Van Doesburg, Kelly, Klee, Reinhardt, Vasarely

Josef Albers. b Bottrup, 1888. d New Haven, CT, 1976. **Homage to the Square.** 1964. Oil on panel. h76.2 × w76.2 cm. h30 × w30 in.
Tate, London

Algardi Alessandro

Bust of Cardinal Paolo Emilio Zacchia

The cardinal's fine robes, lace cuffs and distinctive moustache and beard tell the viewer immediately that this is a distinguished individual. The marble portrait has a spark of life that shows Algardi's close observation of the cardinal's features. As was customary at the time, Algardi originally sculpted this bust in terracotta. This would have been used as a study before making a final version in the more expensive medium of marble. Although an artist of the Baroque period, Algardi's style is more reserved than the flamboyant approach of his contemporary Gianlorenzo Bernini. This may be because he trained in Bologna under the painter Lodovico Carracci (the cousin of Annibale) before embarking on a career in Rome. One of the century's foremost Italian sculptors, Algardi was commissioned to make many important works while in Rome, including the tomb of Leo XI in St Peter's and a bronze statue of Innocent X.

► Bacon, Bernini, Carracci, Houdon, Manzù

Alessandro Algardi. b Bologna, 1595. **d** Rome, 1654. **Bust of Cardinal Paolo Emilio Zacchia**. c1625/30. Marble. **h**121 cm. **h**47⅔ in. Museo Nazionale del Bargello, Florence

Allston Washington

Landscape with a Lake

A path with a figure by a lake leads the viewer into a stark landscape that has a haunting sense of emptiness. The plants in the foreground, the trees and gnarled trunks are all carefully rendered in great detail. Allston was the greatest of North America's Romantic painters. His landscapes glorify the natural wonders of the New World. As a young man he studied in London (where he was a pupil of his compatriot Benjamin West) and Rome. His early landscape paintings were directly inspired by the French artist Claude, who was much admired in England at the time. However, he soon developed a more sublime, melodramatic conception of the landscape in the manner of J M W Turner and John Martin. Allston's portraits and canvases on scriptural themes won him great acclaim, while the poetry he wrote was somewhat less enthusiastically received.

▶ Bierstadt, Claude, Cozens, Hodler, Martin, West, Turner

Washington Allston. b Charleston, SC, 1779. **d** Cambridge, MA, 1843. **Landscape with a Lake.** 1804. Oil on canvas. **h**96.5 × **w**130.2 cm. **h**38 × **w**51¼ in. Museum of Fine Arts, Boston, MA

Alma-Tadema Sir Lawrence

A Coign of Vantage

Three Roman women watch the return of galleys from a corner, or 'coign'. This charming work conveys a sense both of height and of warm sunlight. The fabric of the women's clothes, the marble ledge and the bronze beast are all rendered in great detail. In the handling of the women and the sea far below, the artist shows his great skill with complicated perspective. A Dutch painter who moved to England in 1870, Alma-Tadema had a successful career and was lavished with personal and professional honours in his lifetime. His

Neo-Classical portrayals of ancient Roman, Greek and Egyptian life were highly popular with Victorian society. They also showed the artist's knowledge of archaeology and social history. On several occasions Alma-Tadema was commissioned for theatre designs, in particular Sir Henry Irving's 1901 production of *Coriolanus* at the Lyceum Theatre in London.

► Carpaccio, Gérôme, Leighton, Poussin, Waterhouse

Sir Lawrence Alma-Tadema. b Drontyp, 1836. **d** Wiesbaden, 1912. **A Coign of Vantage**. 1895. Oil on canvas. **h**64.2 × **w**45 cm. **h**25¼ × **w**17¾ in. Private collection

Altdorfer Albrecht

Battle of Alexander at Issus

A sweeping Alpine landscape dominates this dramatic painting, emphasizing the enormous scale of the swirling battle taking place in the lower half. A monumental panel floats high above the soldiers, informing the viewer that Alexander the Great has gained a decisive victory over King Darius III of Persia (who can be seen fleeing in his chariot to the left of the scene) at the Battle of Issus in 333 BC. The representation draws comparison between this great historical victory and contemporary battles of

Altdorfer's day. The action itself is shown in vivid detail with hundreds of individual figures depicted. Altdorfer is known to have taken a tour of the Danube and the Austrian Alps in 1511, and the scenery he encountered there no doubt confirmed his inclination towards the landscape. He produced a large number of drawings and engravings, many of them depicting landscape without any narrative.

▶ Dossi, Dürer, Leonardo, Patinir, Uccello

Albrecht Altdorfer. b Regensburg, c1480. **d** Regensburg, 1538. **Battle of Alexander at Issus**. 1529. Oil on panel. **h**158.4 × **w**120.3 cm. **h**62⅜ × **w**47⅜ in. Alte Pinakothek, Munich

These film-stills capture moments from the artist's nine-hour journey pushing a block of ice through the streets of Mexico City. As the melting ice becomes lighter, the decreasing size of the block appears to add to the awkwardness of the task. Eventually Alÿs resorts to kicking the ice as he walks along. The Belgian-born artist moved to Mexico City in 1986, and since then has produced a number of works commenting on the country's economic and cultural situation. The arduous but essentially futile act of pushing a block of ice through the hot streets acknowledges the daily routines of the city's poorest paid workers; moving goods from place to place with little reward. In a more recent work, *When Faith Moves Mountains* (2002), the artist enlisted five hundred volunteers to move, shovel by shovel, a complete sand dune near Lima, Peru. Alÿs documents his performances in a variety of media, including video, photography, painting, animation and writing.

► Abramović, Ai Weiwei, Matta-Clark, Rist

Francis Alÿs. b Antwerp, 1959. **Paradox of Praxis I (Sometimes Doing Something Leads to Nothing)**. 1997. Video with sound. **dur** 5 min.
Private collection

Amigoni Jacopo

Juno Receives the Head of Argus

Juno, the wife of Zeus, asked the hundred-eyed giant Argus to watch over Io, whom she rightly suspected of being her husband's lover. Argus was murdered at Zeus' command by Mercury. Juno set the giant's eyes into the tail of her peacock in his memory. The picture here shows Juno receiving the head of Argus. The soft, sensual style, light colours and graceful lines of the painting are typically Rococo. Amigoni was a fashionable and successful painter of portraits and of historical scenes. Like many Rococo artists, he worked all over Europe, particularly in England. It was probably he who, upon returning to Venice after a highly profitable trip to London, persuaded Canaletto to travel to England in 1746. In England he painted decorations for Covent Garden and Moor Park. Thereafter he lived comfortably by painting elegant portraits of the royal family and of nobility.

► Boucher, Fragonard, Gentileschi, Luini, Tiepolo

Jacopo Amigoni. b Venice, c1685. **d** Madrid, 1752. **Juno Receives the Head of Argus.** c1730. Oil on canvas. **h**396.2 × **w**304.8 cm. **h**156 × **w**120 in. Moor Park, Rickmansworth

Andre Carl

Zinc Magnesium Plain

Thirty-six industrially produced square plates of pure magnesium and zinc have been alternately placed flat on the floor. Contrary to the traditional concept of sculpture, these separate parts are not bound together in any way; each can be picked up and interchanged with another. Nor are they built up to create a vertical structure; they simply sit on the ground. They do not stand upright in space like traditional sculpture; they are not crying out to be seen, but merge with the floor to be trodden on and walked over. Originally influenced by the work of Frank Stella and Constantin Brancusi, from 1960 to 1964 Andre worked on the Pennsylvania Railway, which involved using standardized, interchangeable units. From the mid-1960s he assembled groups of bricks, styrofoam planks and cement blocks, extending them horizontally on the floor. The configurations of these identical shapes are determined by simple mathematical principles.

► Albers, Brancusi, Judd, LeWitt, Long, Serra, Stella

Carl Andre. b Quincy, MA, 1935. **Zinc Magnesium Plain.** 1969. Zinc and magnesium. **h**182.9 × **w**182.9 cm. **h**72 × **w**72 in. Baltimore Museum of Art, Baltimore, MD

Andrea del Sarto

Madonna of the Harpies

In one of the best-known works by this Renaissance painter, the Virgin and Child stand on a pedestal, with two putti grasping the Virgin's knees. On the left St Francis (patron saint of the convent of San Francesco dei Macci, who commissioned the painting) looks at us over his shoulder, while St John the Evangelist glances up from his writing at the right. The harpies on the pedestal may represent the Virgin's triumph over evil, as described in the Revelations of St John. Andrea del Sarto was the leading Florentine painter of the early sixteenth century, he combined Leonardo's *sfumato* technique with a richer range of colours in works that deeply impressed his contemporaries, from Michelangelo to Pontormo. Giorgio Vasari, however, damned him with faint praise by writing that his technical perfection was blighted by his lack of spirit. Nevertheless, Andrea del Sarto was highly influential, and his practice of making preparatory drawings before a painting became standard for later artists.

▶ Fra Bartolommeo, Leonardo, Perugino, Piero di Cosimo, Pontormo

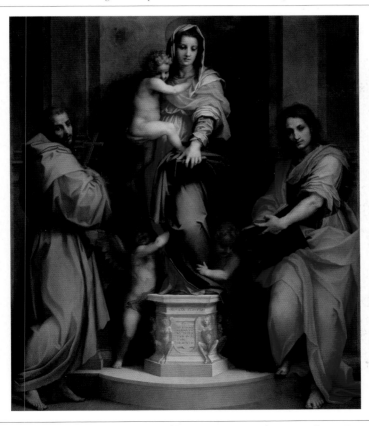

Andrea del Sarto. b Florence, 1486. **d** Florence, 1530. **Madonna of the Harpies**. 1517. Oil on panel. **h**208 × **w**178 cm. **h**81¾ × **w**70 in.
Galleria degli Uffizi, Florence

Fra Angelico

The Annunciation

The Archangel Gabriel tells the Virgin Mary that she is to give birth to the Son of God. Calmness, order and simplicity are the outstanding features of this painting. Mary kneels and bows her head as she humbly accepts Gabriel's message. The fresco is painted on a cell wall in the monastery of San Marco where Angelico was a friar. (He became a Dominican monk in 1407.) On the left, St Peter the Martyr prays as he watches the scene; he is included in the picture to encourage the viewer to contemplate the Annunciation as he is doing.

Fra Angelico's powerful and simplified forms and his sensitive treatment of light and colour are indicative of the recent developments in Florentine art. A celebrated religious painter in his lifetime, he earned the nickname Angelico ('Angelic') from his visionary, harmonious paintings on many Christian themes. He died while painting a private chapel at the Vatican.

▶ Martini, Piero della Francesca, Tintoretto

Fra Angelico (Guido di Pietro). b Vicchio di Mugello, c1387. **d** Rome, 1455. **The Annunciation.** c1441–3. Fresco. **h**187 × **w**157 cm. **h**73⅔ × **w**61⅞ in. Museo di San Marco, Florence

Anguissola Sofonisba

Self-portrait

The artist has portrayed herself as an honest and devout woman: she looks at us with a frank gaze as she fingers the cross around her neck. Anguissola was a leading portraitist in Genoa and Palermo – an extraordinary feat for a woman in the sixteenth century. Of noble birth, Anguissola began a three-year apprenticeship when she was quite young. The Duke of Alba in Spain drew her to the attention of the Spanish Court, and she went on to become Court painter and lady-in-waiting to the Spanish Queen. A letter from the Queen of Spain said of Anguissola that she was 'an excellent painter of portraits, above all the painters of this time'. Anguissola painted numerous self-portraits and portraits of her family. All of these have a special tenderness, as well as a direct approach. Towards the end of her life the young Anthony van Dyck became her friend, and painted her likeness as an old woman.

▶ Van Dyck, Ramsay, Sittow, Verrocchio, Vigée-Lebrun

Sofonisba Anguissola. b Cremona, c1532. **d** Palermo, 1625. **Self-portrait.** c1600. Oil on canvas. **h**22 × **w**17 cm. **h**8⅔ × **w**6⅔ in. Private collection

Antonello da Messina

Saint Jerome in his Study

Stealing a look through the open window of St Jerome's study, the viewer sees the saint absorbed in his reading. Only the lion on the right pauses in his tracks to acknowledge the outside world. It is possible that Antonello was influenced by aspects of Netherlandish painting; details such as the objects on the shelves, the tiled floor, the birds perched on the windowsill and the quality of the light are reminiscent of the intense realism of paintings by Robert Campin and Jan van Eyck. There is no proof that Antonello ever left Italy,

but he seems to have been familiar with the techniques of the Netherlandish masters. Several authorities believe he was taught oil painting techniques by the master Van Eyck himself, and then brought the 'secret' method to Italy. More likely, Antonello was influenced by Flemish artists in Milan. In 1475-6 he was in Venice, where his innovative technique greatly influenced Giovanni Bellini.

► Giovanni Bellini, Campin, Van Eyck, Patinir, Reni

Antonello da Messina. Active 1456. **d** Messina, 1479. **Saint Jerome in his Study.** c1475-6. Oil on panel. **h**46 × **w**36.5 cm. **h**18 × **w**14¼ in. National Gallery, London

Appel Karel

Phantom with Mask

The central figure fixes his eyes and teeth on the viewer with a demonic expression. The paint is applied with characteristic force in thick, sweeping strokes, creating a harsh and brutal image – but there is also humour, and a childlike quality. Appel found the very act of applying paint a liberating, almost sensual experience. He delighted in combining raw energy, expressed through slashes of wild colour, with savage, challenging subjects. The painting is a representative example of the work of the Cobra movement, which was formed in 1948 by a group of artists from Copenhagen, Brussels and Amsterdam. Cobra rejected the abstraction of post-war European painting, considering it lifeless and too passive. Instead, it turned to children's paintings and mythological tales for its inspiration. Appel lived in New York, where he continued to paint exuberant, representative images in dazzlingly lurid colours.

► Baselitz, Dubuffet, De Kooning, Pollock

Karel Appel. b Amsterdam, 1921. **d** Zurich, 2006. **Phantom with Mask**. 1952. Oil on canvas. **h**116 × **w**89 cm. **h**45¾ × **w**35 in.
Private collection

Araki Nobuyoshi

Yoko (from *Sentimental Journey*)

With her eyes closed, seemingly sleeping, a young woman lies before us in a foetal position. Although the composition of the image is somewhat awkward, this is an intimate moment captured by Araki of his recent bride Yoko. Part of the artist's ongoing autobiographical documentation – or 'i-photography' – in 1971 the photograph was included in *Sentimental Journey*, a privately published book that recorded the couple's honeymoon. Thirty years later the artist published *Winter Journey*, this time including photographs that captured Yoko's life in the period leading up to her death from a terminal illness in 1990. In his photographs Araki repeatedly captures the mundane, such as meals that he has eaten, as well as the erotic. It is in relation to the latter, in particular his 'Kinbaku' series, which explores the Japanese art of bondage, that his art has received a degree of notoriety.

► Cartier-Bresson, Evans, Kertész, Utamaro

Nobuyoshi Araki. b Tokyo, 1940. **Yoko (from *Sentimental Journey*)**. 1971. Gelatin silver print. **h**16.4 × **w**12.1 cm. **h**6½ × **w**4¾ in. Private collection

Archipenko Alexander

Walking

At first glance this sculpture seems to be abstract. Looking closer, it is possible to see a walking woman, who has been made out of bronze with a green surface. Archipenko created the figure by using gaps and by hollowing out sections. Her head, for example, is made from the space created by the bronze around it. This is possibly the first work in the history of Western sculpture to introduce such concepts of construction, representing a radical departure from the Classical tradition. Archipenko was associated with the Cubist movement, which challenged and redefined the traditional approach to portraying the human form. His use of holes and spaces to create a new way of looking at the human figure paralleled the Cubists' method of fragmenting the subject, portraying a number of views of the same object simultaneously. Archipenko developed his sculptural techniques further by mixing together different materials.

► Braque, Giacometti, Lipchitz, Picasso

Alexander Archipenko. **b** Kiev, 1887. **d** New York, NY, 1964. **Walking**. 1912. Bronze. **h**67.3 cm. **h**26½ in. Private collection

Arcimboldo Giuseppe

Summer

Up close, this painting looks like a greengrocer's dream. Moving away from the picture, a human head emerges. It has been made entirely of the fruits and vegetables of summer – pears, peaches, cherries and plums can all be found. While he often used fruits and vegetables to create his portraits, Arcimboldo was also known to use pots, pans and even workmen's tools to create his weird images. His most important works were painted in Prague, where he was employed by a series of Hapsburg emperors. Arcimboldo had other courtly duties besides painting, such as designing decorations for festivities, purchasing works of art for the Emperor's collection and, strangely enough, designing and constructing waterworks. Arcimboldo's paintings were looked upon as slightly silly, although they were imitated often enough. It was not until the Surrealists recognized a fellow artist who loved visual puns that he became popular.

► Dalí, De Heem, Koons, Magritte

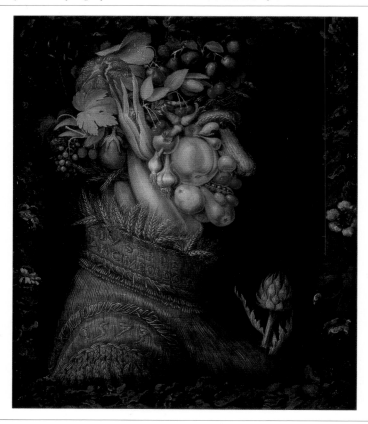

Giuseppe Arcimboldo. b Milan, 1527. **d** Milan, 1593. **Summer.** 1573. Oil on canvas. **h**76 × **w**63.5 cm. **h**30 × **w**25 in. Musée du Louvre, Paris

Arp Jean

Leaves and Navels, I

Small circular forms punctuate the stillness of this work, the shadows of their shapes in relief distinguishing them from the white painted wood background. They are arranged in a harmonious pattern with no logical order, evoking the fluttering of leaves in the wind or the natural randomness of drops of rain falling on glass. Arp's work is characterized by its use of sensuous sculptural shapes recalling organic forms, which are highly poetic and suggestive in their delicacy. He was intimately involved with several of the major art movements of the first half of the twentieth century, particularly the Dada movement. The Zurich Dadaists were formed in 1916 and Arp participated in many of their riotous and infamous 'happenings' at the Cabaret Voltaire. In his quest for a spontaneous, elementary art he wrote poetry, created collages, made wood reliefs (such as the one shown here) and experimented with automatic writing.

► Cornell, Hepworth, Mondrian, Schwitters

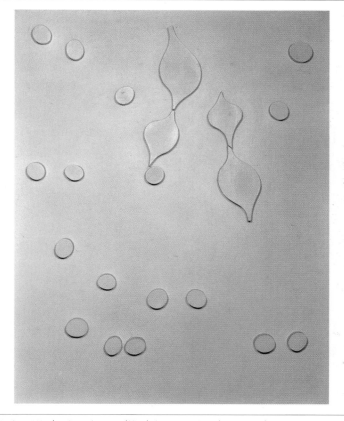

Jean Arp. b Strasbourg, 1886. **d** Basel, 1966. **Leaves and Navels, I.** 1930. Painted wood. **h**101 × **w**81 cm. **h**39¾ × **w**31¾ in. Museum of Modern Art, New York, NY

Atget Eugène

Saint-Cloud

In this photograph of the large pond at Saint-Cloud, outside Paris, the conventional solidity of lawns, trees and stone sculpture is transformed into an almost surreal illusion of surface and void, silhouette and space. The vast trees billow like symmetrical clouds, starkly highlighting the white marble statues silhouetted against them. The atmosphere of the still composition, peopled only by frozen statues, is beautifully eerie. Atget began making documentary photographs of Old Paris in his middle age, eventually compiling a vast collection of saleable visual references for painters, designers and craftsmen. The most important feature of his images of street scenes, architecture and parks was clarity. From 1914, however, he began to produce photographs imbued with an existential mood and metaphorical power that set them apart from his earlier work. It was this sense of elegiac disquiet and strange uncanniness that so appealed to Surrealists such as Man Ray and Jean Cocteau, who championed Atget's work.

► Evans, Man Ray, Sander, Steichen

Eugène Atget. b Libourne, 1857. d Paris, 1927. **Saint-Cloud**. 1920. Gelatin silver print. **h**16.7 × **w**21.5 cm. **h**6½ × **w**8½ in.
George Eastman House, Rochester, NY

Audubon John James

Roseate Spoonbill

From its odd, spoon-shaped bill to each feather, this bird has been depicted with immense care. Audubon's desire to classify the birds he observed in North America, coupled with careful scientific research, resulted in the splendidly illustrated book *Birds of America* which included 435 plates. Audubon trained to be a painter alongside the famous French Neo-Classicist Jacques-Louis David. He coupled his skills as a painter with a passion for ornithology to create a practical use for his training. Even though the book on birds concentrated on

North America, Audubon had to travel to Britain to find funding for his work. Ultimately it was published in America and Britain, and remains both a beautiful work of art and an important scientific document. He spent the last seven years of his life compiling a companion volume, *The Quadrupeds of America*, which also combines exquisite illustrative skills with naturalistic knowledge.

► Agasse, Catlin, J-L David, Stubbs

Auerbach Frank

J Y M Seated in the Studio VI

The surface of this picture, which is a portrait of one of the artist's regular sitters, looks like wet newspapers compressed into ridges and gullies. Auerbach is well known for his technique. Brushfuls of paint are dragged in violent swirls across the picture surface, creating arms and eyes, legs and cheeks. These are not restful, comfortable works to look at; instead they invite the viewer into a world of squashy movement, as thick and sensuous as peanut butter. Auerbach is a member of the School of London, but uses paint in a different way to the others in this loose grouping of artists. He adds thick layers and then scrapes them back, creating the subject through his manipulation of the paint and the surface. Auerbach is known to work with great discipline, regularly from morning till night, every day. His studio has remained unchanged since 1954, when he inherited it from his friend Leon Kossoff.

► Bacon, Kitaj, De Kooning, Kossoff, Sutherland

Frank Auerbach. b Berlin, 1931. J Y M Seated in the Studio VI. 1988. Oil on canvas. h55.9 × w50.8 cm. h22 × w20 in. Private collection

Avercamp Hendrick

A Scene on the Ice Near a Town

An entire town full of people seems to be enjoying itself on a frozen lake. The picture wonderfully evokes the chilly skies of a northern winter. The attention to detail in many of the figures, such as the woman with her red sash at the lower left, brings the scene to life, giving it a joyful feeling. (It is said that Avercamp was deaf, hence his acute visual sense and the almost anecdotal quality of his minutely detailed paintings.) Seventeenth-century Holland witnessed a rise in the middle classes and a decline in church patronage because of

Protestant reform. This led to painters specializing in small-scale easel paintings for the new market of private collectors. Avercamp was well known for his wintery scenes, which are similar in style to those of Jan Bruegel, and his careful observation of lighting effects made his paintings highly prized. He was also one of the originators of realist landscape painting in seventeenth-century Holland.

► J Bruegel, Cuyp, Van Goyen, Lowry, Raeburn, Ruisdael

Hendrick Avercamp. b Amsterdam, 1585. d Amsterdam, 1634. **A Scene on the Ice Near a Town**. c1615. Oil on panel. h58 × w90 cm. 22¾ × w35½ in. National Gallery, London

Bacon Francis

This terrifying image, based on Diego Velázquez's famous portrait, depicts the tortured expression of a blood-spattered Pope, imprisoned in a tubular construction resembling an unpadded throne. The background, painted in dramatic vertical strokes, cruelly blurs out the screaming figure as he sits helplessly with clenched fists. While Bacon's sources and subject matter were often based on real or traditional images – Old Master paintings, newspaper photographs, film stills or X-rays, for instance – his treatment of them is shockingly perverse. As in this painting, he highlighted the distasteful, and sometimes the disgusting, depths of the human psyche with nightmarish intensity. Although his early works have been likened to those of the artist Graham Sutherland, Bacon progressed to develop his own particular idiom, remaining best known for his often horrific distortions of the human form.

► Bosch, Manzù, Soutine, Sutherland, Velázquez

Francis Bacon. b Dublin, 1909. **d** Madrid, 1992. **Study after Velázquez's Portrait of Pope Innocent X**. 1953. Oil on canvas. **h**153 × **w**118 cm. **h**60¼ × **w**46½ in. Des Moines Art Center, Des Moines, IA iconic work by the Conceptual artist John Baldessari only expresses his mischievous and subversive sense of our, but also as his lifelong interest in language and his sity about the potential significance of everyday things. photographs of a pencil, first dull, and then sharp, are nted above a handwritten caption that creates a narrative nd the work. By magnifying the importance of this lane object, and constructing a story around it, the forces us to look at the world – not just at the pencil –

differently, or, as he said, to 'look between things rather than at things'. Baldessari began his career as a painter, but in 1970 he burned most of his canvases in a performance called *The Cremation Project*, which announced his transition to text-based art and photography. Blending influences from Dada, Surrealism, Pop and Conceptual art, his subsequent works explored the interrelationships between language and visual art, always interrogating the nature of art itself.

► Cornell, Duchamp, Gonzalez-Torres, Kawara, Wool

I HAD THIS OLD PENCIL ON THE DASHBOARD OF MY CAR FOR A LONG TIME. EVERY TIME I SAW IT, I FELT UNCOMFORTABLE SINCE ITS POINT WAS SO DULL AND DIRTY. I ALWAYS INTENDED TO SHARPEN IT AND FINALLY COULDN'T BEAR IT ANY LONGER AND DID SHARPEN IT. I'M NOT SURE, BUT I THINK THAT THIS HAS SOMETHING TO DO WITH ART.

Baldung Hans

The Three Ages of Man and Death

These four figures are an allegory of the three ages of man. Death is portrayed as a skeleton holding an hourglass. Around him are a sleeping baby (infancy), a youthful maiden (youth) and a haggard old woman (old age). Baldung was a productive draughtsman, and the realism of the bodies in this picture shows that he studied the nude figure closely. Like his teacher Albrecht Dürer, Baldung was both a painter and a printmaker. He created many fanciful engravings, and also designed stained glass and illustrated books. Like Hieronymus Bosch,

Baldung was one of a group of artists that expressed the terror and suffering of their times through the use of fantasy. One of Baldung's most important commissions was for the panels over the altar at Freiburg Cathedral, which he made in 1516. He died in Strasbourg, a wealthy and influential member of the community.

► Bosch, Cranach, Dürer, Ribera

Hans Baldung. b Schwäbisch-Gmünd, c1484. **d** Strasbourg, 1545. **The Three Ages of Man and Death**. 1539. Oil on panel. **h**151 × **w**61 cm. **h**59½ × **w**24 in. Museo del Prado, Madrid

Balla Giacomo

Flight of the Swallows

A flock of swallows swirl and dive outside the artist's window. Balla has recreated their speed and movement by placing them in precise sequence, one after another. He appears to have included the rigidity of the shutters to contrast their motionlessness with the birds' continuous movement. Balla painted a series of swallow paintings during a visit to Düsseldorf from 1912 to 1913. The picture is a good example of the work of the Italian Futurists, who were primarily concerned with depicting motion as a symbol for the dynamism of the modern world. Balla publicly declared his affiliation to the Futurist movement in March 1910. With Gino Severini, Umberto Boccioni and Carlo Carrà he developed the notion of depicting movement by presenting the same form over and over again, like the stills from a video tape. From 1931 Balla moved away from this style of painting, and developed a more figurative approach.

► Boccioni, Carrà, Catlin, Feininger, Gris, Severini

Giacomo Balla. b Turin, 1871. **d** Rome, 1958. **Flight of the Swallows**. 1913. Tempera on paper. **h**50.8 × **w**76.2 cm. **h**20 × **w**30 in. Museum of Modern Art, New York, NY

Balthus

Girl and Cat

A simple scene presents itself: an adolescent girl sits in a stark and gloomy interior, a contented cat at her feet. Yet the image is somehow disturbing, perhaps because of its erotic overtones: are we looking at an innocent girl, or a sexually sophisticated young woman? In fact, what Balthus has captured is the disturbing quality of adolescence, when the innocence of childhood, portrayed by the cat, is pushed aside by the new, sexual feelings of adulthood. This is emphasized by the fact that the only light in the picture is directed at the girl's thighs. Although Balthus received no formal art training, he studied the Old Masters extensively and was encouraged by such artists as Pierre Bonnard and André Derain. He is known particularly for erotically charged paintings such as this, featuring young girls sleeping, daydreaming or reading within a darkened interior.

► Bonnard, Derain, Foujita, Rego, Schiele, Sherman

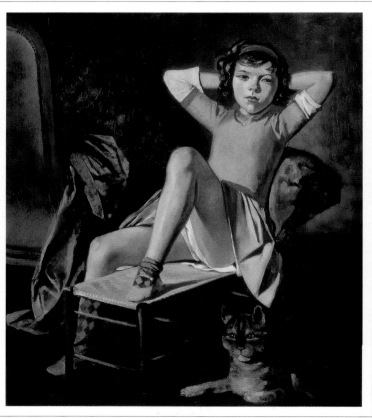

Balthus (Balthazar Klossowski de Rola). b Paris, 1908. d La Rossinière, 2001. **Girl and Cat.** 1937. Oil on panel. **h**88 × **w**78 cm. **h**34½ × **w**30¾ in. Private collection

Barney Matthew

Cremaster 4

In these images we are introduced to a number of the fantastical characters from Matthew Barney's film *Cremaster 4*. The figure on the left – played by Barney – is the Loughton Candidate. As he combs his hair a socket is revealed, one of four that will eventually grow into the horns of the Loughton Ram – shown on the right – an ancient breed native to the Isle of Man, where the film is set. The androgynous character in the centre is one of three fairies that accompany the Loughton Candidate on his journey. Although thematically

the penultimate episode in Barney's epic series, *Cremaster 4* was the first of the films to be made, the last, *Cremaster 3*, appeared in 2002. The title of the series is derived from the cremaster muscle, the function of which in the human body is to raise and lower the testes as a protective response to changes in temperature. Although a coherent narrative remains allusive, themes of biological change and sexual development resurface throughout the series.

► Abramović, Beuys, Hesse, Sherman

Matthew Barney. b San Francisco, CA, 1967. **Cremaster 4**. 1994. Video with sound. dur 42 min. Private collection

35

Fra Bartolommeo

Resurrected Christ with Saints

The billowing drapery, the raised arm of Christ, the pointing arms and turned heads contribute to the overwhelming sense of movement in this painting. The powerful figure of Christ dominates the composition, inspiring worship and contemplation in the viewer. Fra Bartolommeo studied painting in Florence. Here he was profoundly influenced by the preaching of the charismatic and controversial Dominican priest Savonarola – so much so that he entered the Dominican Order when Savonarola was burnt at the stake in 1498. At this point he took the name Fra Bartolommeo – before this he was known as Fra Baccio della Porta – and allegedly destroyed all his paintings and drawings of the nude figure, considering them sinful. A friend of Michelangelo and Raphael, Fra Bartolommeo studied the works of Leonardo da Vinci and created brilliantly vivid paintings on religious subjects.

► Carracci, Leonardo, Michelangelo, Raphael

Fra Bartolommeo (Baccio della Porta). b Florence, c1474. d Florence, c1517. **Resurrected Christ with Saints**. 1516. Oil on canvas. **h**284 × **w**204 cm. **h**111¾ × **w**80¼ in. Palazzo Pitti, Florence arsh finger and brush strokes have been used to depict is upside-down female nude, imprisoned by a heavy black order. The strong impact of the thick black paint was chieved by the artist actually walking on the canvas. Baselitz as portrayed the woman crudely, without compassion or ubtlety. Muted in colour, her image is stark and simple, with o distracting detail. This avant-garde artist likes to paint eatrical sets with a shouting or gesticulating figure which repeated from canvas to canvas. He paints violent and

distinctive images with topsy-turvy figures and colourful and liberated brushwork. He also makes sculpture by fiercely cutting away at a massive chunk of wood leaving a hacked figure, which he often daubs with red pigment. Baselitz's work is aggressive and expressive to the extent that one of his paintings was seized by the public prosecutor who claimed that it might 'arouse sexual desire among certain kinds of viewers'.

► Fautrier, Van Gogh, Kiefer, De Kooning, Polke

eorg Baselitz. b Deutschbaselitz, 1938. **More Blondes**. 1992. Oil on canvas. **h**162 × **w**130 cm. **h**63¾ × **w**51⅛ in.   37
thony d'Offay Gallery, London

Basquiat Jean-Michel

Untitled

Crudely drawn figures, handwritten phrases and scientific formulae are jumbled together on a multi-coloured background, forming a visual cacophony of colour and shapes. The primitive and childlike images reflect Basquiat's links with graffiti art. The painting seems to be a distillation of the New York underworld of the artist's roots, evoking its multi-ethnic, hip-hop culture and reflecting the fast-moving, chaotic reality of the city's street life through a series of disconnected images and written fragments. Basquiat was part of a loosely associated group of so-called graffiti artists, some of whom worked in New York's subways, and indeed he started his own short-lived career by daubing graffiti on public walls. His international reputation was rapidly established and rose with meteoric speed – fuelled by the art boom of the 1980s – until his death from a drugs overdose at the age of 28.

► Dubuffet, Gaudier-Brzeska, Rauschenberg, Twombly

Jean-Michel Basquiat. b New York, NY, 1960. **d** New York, NY, 1988. **Untitled**. 1984. Acrylic, silkscreen and oilstick on canvas. **h**223.5 × **w**195.6 cm. **h**88 × **w**77 in. Estate of Jean-Michel Basquiat

Bassano Jacopo

The Animals Entering the Ark

Two by two, Noah and his family usher a crowd of animals on to the Ark before the break of dawn. The boat is not an important part of the picture, as the artist shows only its side and door. Instead, he has focused on the parade of wonderful beasts. They almost spring off the canvas, so real and alive do they seem. To create this wonderful menagerie, Bassano must have studied all kinds of animals – dogs, cats and even turkeys. A prolific draughtsman, Bassano often used bright chalks to help him in designing his colourful paintings. His early works appear somewhat provincial, but over the years his style evolved into a sophisticated synthesis of the colouring of Venetian masters such as Tintoretto and Veronese, coupled with the vibrant figures of central Italian masters such as Francesco Salviati. All four of Bassano's sons followed in their father's footsteps, although only one of them, Francesco, achieved distinction as a painter.

► Hicks, Salviati, Savery, Tintoretto, Veronese

Jacopo Bassano (Jacopo da Ponte). b Bassano del Grappa, c1510. d Bassano del Grappa, 1592. **The Animals Entering the Ark**. c1590. Oil on canvas. h207 × w265 cm. h81½ × w104⅜ in. Museo del Prado, Madrid

Batoni Pompeo

Thomas William Coke

A sumptuous silk suit, trimmed with lace and bows and topped by a fur cape, makes up the exquisite outfit worn by the man in this portrait. The statue of Venus, the colonnade and the broken pediment give the viewer clues that the setting is Rome. Thomas Coke was the quintessential eighteenth-century wealthy gentleman, who completed his education by going on the traditional Grand Tour of the European continent. Batoni himself was one of the most wealthy and successful painters of the eighteenth-century Roman school

of painting, and many of his commissions were from eminen foreigners. He was best known for his smooth portraits of popes, monarchs and the British upper classes. The latter considered his portraits a 'must' to bring home as a souvenir from the Grand Tour. Batoni was curator of the Pope's collection of art, and his house became a centre of artistic, intellectual and social debate.

► Dobson, Hilliard, Kneller, Moroni

Pompeo Batoni. b Lucca, 1708. **d** Rome, 1787. **Thomas William Coke**. 1774. Oil on canvas. **h**245.8 × **w**170.3 cm. **h**96¾ × **w**67 in. Holkham Hall, Norfolk

Large egg-shaped blots of colour appear on the surface of this picture. Their relationship to each other – both formalistically and colouristically – is unclear, creating a disjointed feeling of tension and uneasiness. The small appendages are connected to the parent blocks with delicate, fragile lines that make them seem like mathematically induced organic growths. Baumeister's early works were influenced by Fernand Léger and others, but he went on to develop a personal form of expression that has been termed 'abstract Surrealism'.

He was much concerned with the philosophy of art, believing that freely imagined forms could provide images relating to the deeper, primitive roots of humanity – ideas which he set out in his 1947 book *Das Unbekannte in der Kunst* ('The Unknown in Art'). His paintings are not entirely subjectless, but are intended as representations of 'other' realities.

► Arp, Dali, Heron, Léger, Matisse, Miró

Willi Baumeister. b Stuttgart, 1889. d Stuttgart, 1955. **Mortaruru with Red Overhead**. 1953. Oil on board. h100 × w81 cm. 39¼ × w31⅞ in. Private collection

Bazille Frédéric

The Artist's Studio on the rue de la Condamine

Inside his studio, Bazille is showing one of his pictures to fellow artists Claude Monet and Édouard Manet (with the hat). To the left is Pierre Auguste Renoir (seated), deep in conversation with the writer Émile Zola (standing on stairs). It is a fascinating glimpse into the world of the artist at that time, his friends and everyday surroundings. The picture itself also shows Bazille's bold modelling of figures, and the broad handling of colours that became his hallmark. Although he died four years before the first Impressionist exhibition, Bazille is closely linked with the movement as he executed a radically new kind of painting that recorded his observations of everyday life. The number of paintings that he produced is small as he was killed in battle in the war with Prussia at the age of only 29. His death occurred shortly after this painting was rejected by the French academy, known as Le Salon.

► Manet, Monet, Renoir, Sisley, Teniers

Frédéric Bazille. b Montpellier, 1841. **d** Beaune-la-Roland, 1870. **The Artist's Studio on the rue de la Condamine.** 1870. Oil on canvas. **h**97 × **w**112 cm. **h**38⅛ × **w**44⅛ in. Musée d'Orsay, Paris

Beauneveu André

Saint Philip

St Philip sits on an elaborate Gothic throne. The artist has paid particular attention to his bearded face, and to the folds of his robe where it has spread out on the ground. The throne itself recedes into the background in an attempt at realistic perspective, but the saint seems to be floating awkwardly in his seat, not solidly fixed to anything, or held by gravity. The picture comes from a page in a psalter or Book of Psalms that was made for Jean, Duc de Berry. The duke was a great patron of the arts, who prided himself on his large collection of manuscripts. This included the wonderful book of hours, the *Très Riches Heures du Duc de Berry*, by the Limbourg brothers. Psalters were made very small so that they could be carried about easily. At the time that Beauneveu was working on this manuscript, the illustration of religious works was experiencing a revival in Renaissance France.

► Antonello, Van Eyck, Fouquet, Limbourg

André Beauneveu. Active in Valenciennes, 1361. **d** Valenciennes, c1402. **Saint Philip**. c1380/5. Illumination on vellum. **h**12.7 × **w**10 cm. **h**5 × **w**4 in. Bibliothèque Nationale, Paris

Beccafumi Domenico

Tanaquil, Wife of Lucomo

The contemporary appearance of the sitter's gown and hairstyle belie the fact that she is an Ancient Roman; she is pointing to a tablet which identifies her as Tanaquil, who persuaded her husband to move to Rome where he reigned as King Tarquinius Priscius from 616 to 578 BC. During the Renaissance, Tanaquil was greatly admired for her fortitude and perseverance and was thus seen as a notable historical figure. The soft colours and elongated forms show Tanaquil in an elegant and sensitive style. These elements were to

become hallmarks of Mannerism. An imaginative artist and draughtsman, Beccafumi is famous for decorating the churches of Siena with many paintings and frescos. He was able to combine the ideas formalized in the work illustrated here with the bright and decorative colours typical of Sienese painting. He is particularly famous for designing an elaborate marble pavement inside Siena Cathedral, decorated with scenes from the Old and New Testaments.

► Cranach, Goya, Parmigianino, Pontormo, Rosso Fiorentino

Domenico Beccafumi. b Valdibiena, c1486. **d** Siena, 1551. **Tanaquil, Wife of Lucomo.** c1520. Oil on panel. **h**92 × **w**53 cm. **h**36¼ × **w**21 in. National Gallery, London

Becher Bernd and Hilla

Water Towers

Nine black-and-white images of different water towers have been arranged in a 3 × 3 grid. In these exquisite photographs anonymous industrial structures take on a sculpture-like presence. The composition of each photograph follows the same rules: the tower is captured against an overcast sky; the structure fills the frame of the image. Working as a husband and wife partnership, the Bechers started to photograph industrial architecture in the late 1950s. Through the selection and isolation of different functional types – grain silos,

gas tanks, blast furnaces etc. – they revealed not only the structural elements and forms shared by each type, but also the subtle design variations that appear across periods and locations. The objective and scientific approach taken by the Bechers would influence a younger generation of photographers including Andreas Gursky and Thomas Struth. Themes of repetition and standardization in their work can be seen to parallel the interests of Minimalist artists.

► Gursky, Judd, LeWitt, Struth

Bernd Becher. b Siegen, 1931. **d** Rostock, 2007. **Hilla Becher. b** Potsdam, 1934. **Water Towers**. 1980. Nine gelatin silver prints, **h**155.6 × **w**125.1 cm. **h**61¼ × **w**49¼ in. Solomon R. Guggenheim Museum, New York, NY

Beckmann Max

Departure

Horror and brutality are juxtaposed in stark contrast with serenity and peace in this triptych. The left and right panels depict nightmare scenes of torture and degradation, in which men and women are subjected to terrible pain, while the centre panel portrays spiritual figures in the blue of an apparently infinite sea. The work is considered to be the most powerful in a series of nine triptychs Beckmann painted. It mirrors the political turbulence of Germany during the early 1930s, when the rise of Nazism and the consequent constricting atmosphere put the future of art into question. Although the painting evokes with powerful force the artist's own feelings, and could therefore be considered as an example of Expressionism, Beckmann did not ally himself to any particular movement. In 1938 political persecution drove him to Amsterdam. He spent the last three years of his life in the USA, where he helped to spread the influence of contemporary German art.

► Bosch, Ensor, Heckel, Kokoschka, Siqueiros

Max Beckmann. b Leipzig, 1884. **d** New York, NY, 1950. **Departure.** 1932–5. Oil on canvas. **h**215.5 × **w**314 cm. **h**84⅞ × **w**123⅝ in. Museum of Modern Art, New York, NY

Renaissance Venetians took great pride in their city and it was common for works of art to be commissioned to depict special events. The 'miracle' shown here is used as an excuse for the artist to show off everyday life in Venice, and his skill as well. The gondoliers, monks, society ladies and gentlemen, palaces and canal are all part of the beautiful city in which Gentile lived and worked. The scene is full of delightful details: ladies' jewellery and the bricks in the chimneys are painted with equal skill and concern. In addition, Gentile has

infused the scene with a soft light that picks out the figures in the crowd and illuminates the buildings. Gentile came from an important dynasty of Venetian painters, which included his father Jacopo and his younger brother Giovanni. In 1479 he travelled to Constantinople where he worked in the Court of Mohammed II and painted his portrait.

▶ Giovanni Bellini, Bellotto, Canaletto, Guardi, Hiroshige

Gentile Bellini. b Venice, c1429. **d** Venice, 1507. **The Miracle of the True Cross near the San Lorenzo Bridge**. 1500. Oil on canvas. **h**323 × **w**430 cm. **h**127¼ × **w**169¼ in. Galleria dell'Accademia, Venice

47

Bellini Giovanni

Young Woman at her Toilet

With its idealized face and distant landscape, this painting recalls some of Bellini's paintings of the Virgin Mary. The aim of this work, however, was certainly not to create an object of religious devotion; this nude presents us with a secular ideal of feminine beauty. Giovanni was the most famous member of the Bellini dynasty and did much to popularize the new technique of oil painting. In fact, he takes much of the credit for transforming Venice into an important centre of the Renaissance. The major influence on his early years was his brother-in-law Andrea Mantegna. However, Bellini's pictures tend to be romantic and imaginative, where Mantegna's are sharp and precise. Bellini led an active workshop, with Titian and Giorgione among his pupils. As was common at the time the master would sign the workshop paintings as his own. Today Bellini's own paintings are considered to be superior, but at the time, any workshop paintings would have been valued as the master's work.

► Gentile Bellini, Giorgione, Ingres, Mantegna, Titian

Giovanni Bellini. b Venice, c1434. **d** Venice, 1516. **Young Woman at her Toilet**. 1515. Oil on panel. **h**62 × **w**79 cm. **h**24¼ × **w**31 in. Kunsthistorisches Museum, Vienna

Bellmer Hans

The Spinning Top

A whirling skeletal female form spins on a top which she is holding in her bony hand. This peculiar image symbolizes woman turning the hearts and heads of men, as she spins in defiance of gravity. Relating to an unrealized project for a sculpture, conceived in 1936–9, it is certainly one of Bellmer's most haunting images. The painting was reworked over several years, and only signed when Bellmer had found a buyer in 1956. Polish-born, Bellmer became an active Surrealist when he moved to Paris in 1938. This painting reflects many of the movement's preoccupations – its distorted, phantasmagoric imagery appears to have emerged directly from the artist's subconscious fantasies. Bellmer's central theme was that of the female body, often treated in an obsessively erotic manner. He is known particularly for his disturbingly fetishistic 'Dolls', a series of articulated female mannequins, and for his drawings and lithographs, executed with superb technical precision.

► Brauner, Delvaux, Ernst, Matta, Tanguy

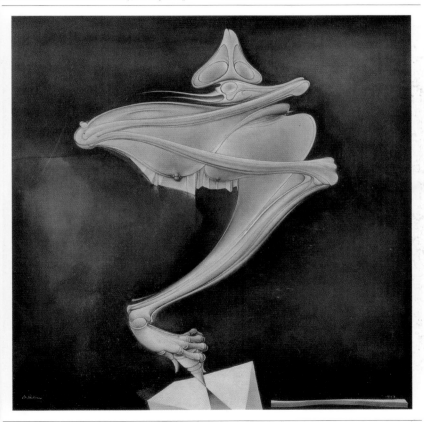

Hans Bellmer. b Katowice, 1902. d Paris, 1975. **The Spinning Top**. c1937-56. Oil on canvas. h65 × w65 cm. h25⅝ × w25⅝ in. Tate, London

Bellotto Bernardo

View of the Ponte delle Navi, Verona

With splendid visual accuracy the artist has evoked the crusty plaster and brickwork of buildings, and the bright play of sunlight on the city skyline. Bellotto was the nephew and pupil of Canaletto, and for a time worked with the master as an assistant in Venice. Bellotto's style is very much like his uncle's – in fact he sometimes signed himself Canaletto, which caused much confusion. However, Bellotto's works are cooler and crisper, and he was more interested in clouds, shadows and foliage. Bellotto's paintings also include more figure groups than Canaletto's – as can be seen in this picture, with its strolling couples, running children, and so on. In 1746 Bellotto left Venice and visited other Italian cities. He then travelled to Munich, Dresden and, finally, Warsaw. Bellotto's views of the Polish capital were considered of such accuracy that they were used in its reconstruction after the Second World War.

► Gentile Bellini, Bonington, Canaletto, Guardi, Pannini

Bernardo Bellotto. b Venice, 1721. **d** Warsaw, 1780. **View of the Ponte delle Navi, Verona.** c1745. Oil on canvas. **h**132 × **w**233.7 cm. **h**51 × **w**92 in. Private collection. On loan to the National Gallery of Scotland, Edinburgh

Bellows George

On the right of the pier a child is frozen in a half-completed dive. The children have been caught as if in a photograph, at the split-second of action. The artist has used rapid brushstrokes to simplify the bodies in order to give the impression of a fleeting moment. Bellows turned his back on the formality of the artists who came before him, with their posed portraits and idyllic landscapes. Instead, he aimed to capture real life as he saw it. He was influenced and inspired by a group known as The Eight, who believed that art should reflect reality, particularly the gritty reality of the city. Bellows often painted subjects that evoked the vitality of city life such as crowded neighbourhood streets. He painted portraits as well as landscapes, and later in life experimented with different subjects and techniques. Bellows personified the American spirit of enthusiasm and eagerness both in his painting and in his life.

► Eakins, Hopper, Vuillard, Wyeth

George Bellows. b Columbus, OH, 1882. d New York, NY, 1925. Forty-two Kids. 1907. Oil on canvas. h107.6 × w153 cm. h42⅜ × w60¼ in. Corcoran Gallery of Art, Washington, DC

Bernini Gianlorenzo

The Ecstasy of Saint Theresa

In a vision, St Theresa of Avila sees an angel thrusting a golden spear into her heart. Swooning in physical and spiritual abandon – symbolic of her love of God – she expresses the intensity of her mystical experience for all to see. This marble group is a perfect example of the Baroque spirit – full of drama, emotion and movement. Bernini was an outstanding artist of the Italian Baroque. The virtuosity and delicacy of finish of his statues is reminiscent both of Michelangelo and of Antique statuary, although it also combines the styles of his contemporaries Caravaggio, Annibale Carracci and Guido Reni. An accomplished architect as well as a sculptor, Bernini virtually monopolized papal commissions during Rome's 'golden age'; no other single artist has left such an indelible imprint as he has on the city. The layout of Rome's St Peter's Square is one of his grandest architectural achievements.

► Caravaggio, Carracci, Michelangelo, Reni

Gianlorenzo Bernini. b Naples, 1598. **d** Rome, 1680. **The Ecstasy of Saint Theresa.** 1646–52. Marble. **h**350 cm. **h**138 in.
Santa Maria della Vittoria, Rome

Beuys Joseph

Felt Suit

This stitched felt suit expresses the idea of human physical warmth. It symbolizes and evokes a sense of safety and shelter because felt is an insulating and life-protecting fabric. Beuys was at one stage connected with Fluxus, a movement dedicated to organizing anarchistic events and 'happenings', and this suit was copied from one he wore at an anti-Vietnam event. Beuys considered art as a medium for social and political change. He also saw it as having a spiritual dimension, and believed that commonplace materials (felt and animal fat were among his favourites) could be invested with an intense healing power. He saw the role of the artist as parallel to that of the shaman, channelling energy from objects and giving them new powers and new meaning. Beuys achieved cult status in his native Germany, and many of his works, including this suit, were produced in large editions.

► Broodthaers, Duchamp, Oldenburg, Schwitters

Joseph Beuys. b Krefeld, 1921. d Düsseldorf, 1986. **Felt Suit**. 1970. Stitched felt. **h**170 × **w**100 cm. **h**67 × **w**39⅜ in. Private collection

Bierstadt Albert

The Rocky Mountains

During the early nineteenth century the passion of the American nation was stirred by the peaceful forests and wide open spaces of its own lands. This occurred at a time when America was becoming rapidly industrialized. The threat of the railroad and of the Machine Age was a real one, and in response, the nation desired to protect its places of natural beauty. Bierstadt was a master at creating romanticized visions of the American wilderness. His canvases were usually huge and painted in great detail. They showed nature at her most remote and unassailable, from the distant splendour of the Rocky Mountains to the magnificence of the Yosemite Valley. Bierstadt was born in Germany but moved to the USA as a child. His work represented a nation's last gasp of romanticism before the railroad ate into the countryside. The need to believe in the existence of a New World, at least in spirit if not in reality, remained strong for a long time.

► Church, Cole, Cozens, Daubigny, Hobbema, T Rousseau

Albert Bierstadt. b Solingen, 1830. **d** New York, NY, 1902. **The Rocky Mountains**. 1863. Oil on canvas. **h**180 × **w**306 cm. **h**73¼ × **w**120¾ in. Metropolitan Museum of Art, New York, NY

Bingham George Caleb

Fur Traders Descending the Missouri

In a misty peacefulness, two trappers and their cat glide down the Missouri. A warm light, shimmering across the still river, creates a dreamy sense of timelessness. The two figures will soon be out of sight. In many of his early pictures Bingham used carefully balanced horizontals and diagonals, with figures placed at right-angles to create a solid structure. The artist, one of the most important of the early North American Frontier Painters, painted the landscapes and settlers of the American West. At a time when the camera was not widely used, it was left to artists to show the world what this new and strange land was like. Gradually, Bingham moved off the river, onto the land, and into politics (he was elected to the Missouri legislature in 1848). However, he is best remembered as a popular chronicler of a bygone American way of life, and a painter of great skill and sophistication.

▶ Allston, Bierstadt, Cole, Friedrich

George Caleb Bingham. b Augusta County, VA, 1811. **d** Kansas City, MS, 1879. **Fur Traders Descending the Missouri.** 1845.
Oil on canvas. **h**74 × **w**92 cm. **h**29 × **w**36½ in. Metropolitan Museum of Art, New York, NY

Blake Peter

On the Balcony

The figures sitting on a park bench are surrounded by and display four paintings executed by Blake's fellow students, together with various expendable commercial items including cigarette packs, magazines and food packaging. The painting's simple arrangement pays little attention to perspective, as the represented objects are the most important ingredients of the composition. At the time it was considered Blake's most important work in its direct visual impact, and it now also conveys a sense of the escalating culture of the 1950s by confronting the viewer with an unordered riot of popular imagery. It is this depiction of commercial memorabilia that helped pave the way for the British Pop Art movement. During the 1970s Blake moved towards a more naturalistic style and in 1975 he became a founder member of the Brotherhood of Ruralists, whose ideal was to work together in the countryside, as artists had in the nineteenth century.

► Hamilton, Hockney, Jones, Rauschenberg, Schwitters

Peter Blake. b Dartford, 1932. **On the Balcony**. 1955–7. Oil on canvas. **h**121.3 × **w**90.8 cm. **h**47¾ × **w**35¾ in. Tate, London

Blake William

Pity

An apparently lifeless woman lies on the ground. Above her two female figures rush by on horses, the wind lifting their hair. One of the women looks down, and is holding a tiny child. The work illustrates a passage from Shakespeare in which Macbeth contemplates the results of the murder of Duncan: 'Pity, like a newborn babe, striding the blast of heaven's cherubin, hors'd...'. Blake's precisely delineated forms, rejecting traditional composition and ideas of perspective, evoke an enigmatic otherworldliness. His style reflects his uniquely personal, mystical vision, in which imagination and reality become one. Originally a book engraver by trade, Blake's genius expressed itself through his poetry as well as his striking symbolic paintings. He believed that the spiritual was more important than the material world, and that the true artist is a prophet because he or she is given divine insight.

► Etty, J Martin, Moreau, Redon, Turner

William Blake. b London, 1757. **d** London, 1827. **Pity**. c1795. Watercolour heightened with ink on paper. **h**42 × **w**54 cm. **h**16¾ × **w**21¼ in. Tate, London

Boccioni Umberto

Elasticity

The dynamic movement of a horse and rider is captured in a mass of bright colours and swirling, fragmented forms. The man and animal appear machine-like as they speed through a landscape of factories and electricity pylons. A co-founder in 1910 of the Italian Futurist group, Boccioni was fascinated with the depiction of motion through time and space. With great bravado the Futurists rejected the conventions of Western art since the Renaissance, instead looking towards science, technology and the city for inspiration. With a pictorial style that owed a certain debt to Cubism, Boccioni aimed to present simultaneously the new impressions and sensations of the modern world. Boccioni was a sculptor as well as a painter. In line with the militarism of the Futurists, in 1915 Boccioni volunteered to fight in the First World War. He was killed falling from a speeding horse.

► Balla, Feininger, Gertler, Popova

Umberto Boccioni. b Reggio di Calabria, 1882. **d** Sorte, 1916. **Elasticity.** 1912. Oil on canvas. **h**100 × **w**100 cm. **h**39⅜ × **w**39⅜ in. Private collection

Böcklin Arnold

Centaurs' Combat

A suggestion of horror, rather than its explicit reality, is portrayed in this painting. Set in an otherworldly landscape, the animated, heroic figures of the centaurs dominate the canvas with their dramatic choreography. Much of the tension of this painting derives from the contorted poses and haunted expressions of the centaurs, loosely painted in rich tones, which convey a sense of heightened drama and emotion. Böcklin spent much of his career in Italy. This inspired him to take up Classical and mythological themes which

he interpreted in a poetically Romantic manner, influenced by Eugène Delacroix and Théodore Géricault. The artist's dream-like settings, menacing tones and haunting emotional undercurrents brought him popularity in his day, and later inspired the work of the German Expressionists and the French Symbolists. His allegorical paintings were particularly admired for their strong impact and their challenging demands on the emotions.

► Delacroix, Géricault, Giulio Romano, Schmidt-Rottluff

Boetti Alighiero

Alighiero Boetti inserted an 'e' (meaning 'and') between his names in 1973, symbolizing the dichotomy between the private person and the formal surname that identified him civically and professionally. The double self-portrait in *Twins* functions in the same way. One becomes two, creating a 'dialectic exchange between these two selves' and questioning the very uniqueness of the Self. Walking hand-in-hand the two figures are not mirror images, but rather reflect the relationship between two equal but separate things – reason and creativity, the individual and society, order and chaos. Boetti was part of the movement of Italian artists called Arte Povera (Poor Art), and though he disassociated himself from the group in 1972, he retained the Arte Povera ethos in his use of mundane materials, such as cardboard, fabric, cement blocks. His later work, often collaborative, is characterized broadly by an interest in classification systems, in finding order within disorder, pattern within randomness.

► Beuys, Cahun, Close, Merz, Sherman

Alighiero Boetti. b Turin, 1940. d Rome, 1994. **Twins.** 1968. Gelatin silver photomontage postcard. **h**15.2 × **w**11.2 cm. **h**6 × **w**4½ in. Private collection

This large-scale installation consists of two walls of metal biscuit boxes and a series of black-and-white photographs taken from obituaries in a local newspaper, poorly illuminated by clamp-on electric lamps. Powerful sensations of life and death are evoked by this shrine to the memory of the dead, with its almost religious atmosphere of perpetual stillness and peace. In previous works, Boltanski had used photographs of Jewish children. Here, by using images of the Swiss – a race associated with neutrality rather than a specific and terrible

fate – Boltanski lays greater emphasis on the universality of mortality. His unique style, medium and subject matter focusing on themes of death have made Boltanski one of the most acclaimed artists of our time. His other works include glass display cabinets containing memories of childhood, 'Shadow' sculptures made of scrap materials which are illuminated by candles, and rooms filled with clothes which he also calls 'Reserves'.

► Andre, Kiefer, Poussin, Teniers

Christian Boltanski. b Paris, 1944. **Reserve of Dead Swiss**. 1990. Photographs, metal tins and electric lamps. **h**203 cm. **h**80 in.

Marian Goodman Gallery, New York, NY

Bomberg David

The Mud Bath

At first, this might seem to be a completely abstract picture. In fact, it shows a vapour bath, used by the Jewish community of Whitechapel in London. Blue and white figures jostle and leap around the bath's red rectangle shape, throwing themselves around the central dark pillar. The son of a Polish immigrant, Bomberg used angular and semi-abstract forms to express the vitality and dynamism of the twentieth century and the excitement of the Machine Age. He was a founder member of the London Group, an exhibiting society formed in 1913. Although Bomberg kept his distance from the Cubists, Futurists and Vorticists, which were all active at the time, he did identify with some of their theories. In the 1920s he moved away from geometric forms and turned to a more representational style, often using vibrant colours and expressive brushstrokes.

► Bellows, Boccioni, Braque, Lewis, Nash, Picasso

David Bomberg. b Birmingham, 1890. **d** London, 1957. **The Mud Bath**. 1914. Oil on canvas. **h**152.5 × **w**224 cm. **h**60 × **w**88¼ in. Tate, London

Bonington Richard Parkes

Rouen from the Quais

The steeple of the great Rouen Cathedral and the tall masts of the boats create strong verticals in this picture. Watercolour is a lively, immediate medium, which has allowed the artist to capture the activity of the busy quays. Bonington's watercolour style is characterized by a small range of colours applied to highly textured paper. This work was painted while he studied under the artist Baron Gros at the École des Beaux-Arts in Paris. He was close friends with the Romantic painter Eugène Delacroix, who wrote of him, 'no one in the modern school, perhaps no earlier artist, possessed the lightness of execution which makes his works, in a certain sense, diamonds, by which the eye is enticed and charmed'. Bonington spent most of his life in France and, in addition to city views, he also painted landscapes and historical scenes. Shortly before his death Bonington began to paint in oil; he is best remembered, however, for his skill as a watercolourist.

► Gentile Bellini, Bellotto, Cozens, Delacroix, Gros

Richard Parkes Bonington. b Arnold, 1802. d London, 1828. **Rouen from the Quais**. 1821. Watercolour on paper. **h**40.5 × **w**27.5 cm. 15⅞ × **w**10¾ in. British Museum, London

Bonnard Pierre

The Open Window

The interior and open window, the sleeping girl and the kitten are barely visible in a rich riot of colour. The viewer is encouraged to enter the room and join the scene, looking out of the window at the trees beyond. Bonnard successfully conveys the atmosphere of heat and tranquillity of the South of France by using warm and bright tones of colour. Known particularly for his intimate domestic interiors, Bonnard was a member of the group known as Les Nabis whose aim was to simplify the outline and colour of their paintings.

The Nabis rejected the idea of engaging the viewer purely through subject matter. Instead, they aimed at expressing feeling through form, often using broad areas of flat colour. As well as a painter Bonnard was a master of lithography, using shapes, colour and line to great effect. He was one of the few foreign artists to be elected to the Royal Academy in London.

► Caillebotte, Denis, Hassam, Matisse, Vallotton, Vuillard

Pierre Bonnard. b Fontenay-aux-Roses, 1867. **d** Le Cannet, 1947. **The Open Window.** c1921. Oil on canvas. **h**118 × **w**96 cm. **h**46½ × **w**37¾ in. Phillips Collection, Washington, DC

Ter Borch Gerard

Dancing Couple

stylish and rather mischievous-looking courtier in military uniform asks a demure-looking young lady dressed in a sumptuous white silk gown to dance. Light falls on the couple as he takes her hand; the rest of the sparsely furnished interior and the seated onlookers fall into shadow. Ter Borch, an early Dutch portraitist and painter of genteel genre paintings, achieved recognition for his intimate, homely scenes of well-to-do family life and for the expertise with which he captured fine fabrics such as silk and satin. The detail of his paintings

and the curious doll-like charm of his figures appealed to the tastes of the Amsterdam and Haarlem middle classes. Ter Borch travelled extensively throughout Europe and must have had first-hand knowledge of almost all the great seventeenth-century artists, including Rembrandt and Diego Velázquez, yet his style of painting bears no hint of their influence.

► Dou, Metsu, Rembrandt, Velázquez, Vermeer

Gerard ter Borch. b Zwolle, 1617. d Deventer, 1681. **Dancing Couple**. 1660. Oil on canvas. **h**76 × **w**66 cm. **h**30 × **w**26 in.
Polesden Lacey, Dorking

Bordone Paris

Presentation of the Ring to the Doge of Venice

A fisherman who had been rescued by St Mark is giving the saint's ring to the Doge of Venice. The artist has depicted the figures in contemporary dress, even though the incident is said to have happened hundreds of years earlier. Portraits of prominent Venetians, including the Doge of the time, were used as models. Elaborate columns, arcades and apses dominate the work, which is a good example of Renaissance Venetian art. Bordone was a leading portraitist as well as a painter of landscapes and anecdotal and mythological scenes.

He originally studied under Titian, and in fact rivalled his master in popularity. The painting shown is very much in the style of Titian. Bordone was invited to France by François I, who was a great admirer of Italian Renaissance artists. While in France, Bordone painted several portraits of the prominent political figures of the day.

► Gentile Bellini, Clouet, Guardi, Sassetta, Titian

Paris Bordone. b Treviso, 1500. **d** Venice, 1571. **Presentation of the Ring to the Doge of Venice.** 1534. Oil on canvas. **h**370 × **w**300 cm. **h**145⅔ × **w**118 in. Galleria dell'Accademia, Venice

Bosch Hieronymus

The Tribulations of St Anthony

The pious hermit St Anthony is subjected to all the temptations and tortures that Bosch's ghoulish imagination can muster. Evil lurks around every corner – a seductive temptress hides in a cleft tree, a monster bursts forth from a huge, over-ripe fruit, and the scene is rife with menacing, supernatural-looking creatures. The raging inferno in the background hints at the fate that awaits all those who succumb to evil. Bosch's style is unique, and unparalleled in the Netherlandish tradition of painting. His work is not at all similar to other artists of the time, such as Jan van Eyck or Rogier van der Weyden. Most of the subjects of Bosch's paintings revolve around scenes from the life of Christ, or a saint confronted by evil and temptation, or allegories or proverbs about the folly of human beings. Bosch's work seems strangely modern: four hundred years later, his influence emerged in the Expressionist movement, and still later in Surrealism.

► Beckmann, Dali, Elsheimer, Van Eyck, Van der Weyden

Hieronymus Bosch. b 's-Hertogenbosch, c1450. d 's-Hertogenbosch, 1516. **The Tribulations of St Anthony**. c1505. Oil on panel. 31.5 × w172 cm. h58 × w67 in. Museu Nacional de Arte Antiga, Lisbon

67

Botero Fernando

Our Lady of Cajica

The universal image of the Madonna is portrayed here as an inflated, rotund figure in Botero's unique style. He has created a sense of the Madonna's monumental hugeness by contrasting her with tiny figures that peep out of the clouds behind – a device frequently employed by the artist. In addition, the snake at the bottom of the picture has been made unnaturally long, in order to emphasize her largeness. Botero was born in Colombia and the religious subject of this painting is largely a response to his upbringing.

In most Catholic Latin American countries the Madonna is worshipped as the most important religious figure. Botero's works are characterized by their simplicity of form and exquisite application of paint. He has been living in Paris since 1971, where he continues to paint and sculpt. His later work includes a series of monumental sculptures of the female nude, which were displayed down the length of the Champs-Elysées.

▶ Bouts, Fouquet, Lochner, Spencer

Fernando Botero. b Medellín, 1932. Our Lady of Cajica. 1972. Oil on canvas. h234.4 × w181.8 cm. h95¾ × w71⅝ in. Private collection

Botticelli Sandro

Spring

The diaphanous gowns of the Three Graces, the elegant hands of Venus and the flowered dress worn by Flora combine to make this one of the most beautiful paintings of the Italian Renaissance. The painting reflects the fine draughtsmanship that was fundamental to Florentine art at that time, and Botticelli's graceful line creates a sensitive, almost feminine atmosphere. Botticelli began his training under Fra Filippo Lippi and went on to move in the intellectual circles that flourished during the Florentine 'golden age'. Many of his paintings involve philosophical and allegorical meanings; *Spring* in particular has sparked much debate as to its symbolic significance. Later in life he came under the influence of a charismatic priest called Savonarola, and painted fewer paintings with mythological themes. Botticelli died in obscurity. He was rediscovered in the nineteenth century by the Pre-Raphaelites, who particularly admired the Renaissance artist's delicate linework.

► Filippo Lippi, Millais, Pontormo, Rubens

Sandro Botticelli. b Florence, 1445. d Florence, 1510. **Spring**. c1478. Tempera on wood. **h**203 × **w**314 cm. **h**79⅞ × **w**123⅝ in. Galleria degli Uffizi, Florence

Boucher François

Odalisque

A young girl lies naked on a bed with lavish draperies all around her. Blatantly provocative, she flirts with the viewer as she looks out from her boudoir. Boucher's paintings epitomize the frivolous excesses of the mid-eighteenth century, making him one of the truest exponents of the Rococo style. In his youth he was closely connected to Antoine Watteau, whose pictures he engraved, and in the 1740s obtained the patronage of Madame de Pompadour. Through her influence he became chief painter to Louis XV.

Boucher was one of the most sought-after decorators in Paris and his charmingly coquettish pictures of naked nymphs and goddesses, usually in mythological and allegorical scenes, pandered to the taste of the Parisian upper classes whose elegant houses he decorated. Epitomizing the artifice of the Rococo age, he allegedly said of nature that it was 'too green and badly lit'.

▶ Drouais, Fragonard, Ingres, Moore, Watteau, Wesselmann

François Boucher. **b** Paris, 1703. **d** Paris, 1770. **Odalisque**. c1745. Oil on canvas. **h**53 × **w**64 cm. **h**20¾ × **w**25¼ in. Musée du Louvre, Paris

Boudin Eugène

The Beach at Trouville

A crowd of formally dressed Parisians is seen basking in the sun at the fashionable seaside resort of Trouville on the Normandy coast. Boudin came to be known as 'the painter of beaches' and frequently travelled to this particular beach throughout his career. An exceptionally gifted observer and recorder of nature, he was able to capture the characteristic gestures of people. Using a subtle and free brushwork, speckled with flecks of pure colour, he could make the surface of his paintings sparkle, evoking a glowing sky or a glittering sea. As in seventeenth-century Dutch landscape painting, the sky in Boudin's paintings plays an important role. It often takes up two-thirds of the picture, forcing the viewer's eyes to focus on the tiny figures below. Boudin was a major source of inspiration for the Impressionists, particularly Claude Monet, who painted this very beach some years later.

► Avercamp, Van Goyen, Krøyer, Monet

Eugène Boudin. b Honfleur, 1824. d Deauville, 1898. **The Beach at Trouville**. 1864. Oil on wood. **h**26 × **w**48 cm. **h**10¼ × **w**18⅞ in.
Musée d'Orsay, Paris

Bourdelle Antoine

Herakles

Power, strength and tightly coiled energy seem about to burst forth from the impressive form of Herakles. The sculptor has used muscular shapes and bold, expressive features to create a sense of vitality. The tension is clearly shown in the bowstring, which is being pulled back by a huge, powerful hand. Further tension is created by the archer's leg which, with its bulging tendons, strains against a boulder. Bourdelle was a pupil of Auguste Rodin. Rather than following his master's loose style, however, Bourdelle studied Gothic and Ancient Greek sculpture. Inspired by the images of Antiquity, Bourdelle aimed to create a similar feeling of density and volume. This was very different from the popular sculpture of the time, which was usually concerned with graceful forms. Taut and heroic, this sculpture epitomizes Bourdelle's quest for the monumental in his art.

► Böcklin, Giambologna, Rodin, Rosso Fiorentino

Antoine Bourdelle. b Montauban, 1861. **d** Vesinet, 1929. **Herakles**. 1908. Plaster. **h**248 cm. **h**97⅔ in. Musée Bourdelle, Paris

Bourgeois Louise

Here I Am, Here I Stay

Encased within a glass casket, a pair of truncated human feet are firmly placed on a roughly hewn block of marble. Perhaps alluding to the triumphant order man has created out of the disordered chaos of nature, the elemental qualities of the material – marble, glass, metal – evoke the timeless world articulated by human endeavour. Great attention has been paid to the sensual surfaces, ranging from the roughness of the stone hewn from the earth to the smoothness of the man-made glass. Bourgeois' work is frequently suggestive of the human form, often in a remote, abstracted context. The dynamic tensions of opposing materials and finishes raise provocative responses to the physical presence within the natural environment. Bourgeois moved to New York from Paris in 1938 where she had worked with the Surrealists. Initially a painter and engraver, she turned to sculpture in the late 1940s.

► Brancusi, Canova, Dali, Noguchi, Rodin

Louise Bourgeois. b Paris, 1911. d New York, NY, 2010. **Here I Am, Here I Stay**. 1990. Marble, glass and metal. h88.9 × w102.8 cm. h35 × w40½ in. Galerie Karsten Greve, Cologne

Bouts Dieric

Virgin and Child

This image of the Virgin and Child is painted with neither austerity nor pomp. The Virgin is seen tenderly cradling the Christ Child as any mother would her new-born baby. The result is a picture that is both spiritual and human. Small, half-length images of the Virgin and Child were popular in Netherlandish art. They were treated as objects of private devotion, and were kept at home. Such works were often made of two panels, the second being a portrait of the owner looking over at the Virgin, as if in prayer. The sleepy cast to the eyes of the figures in this picture is a quirky characteristic of Bouts' way of painting faces. Bouts was undoubtedly influenced by Rogier van der Weyden's angular, sharply defined and sculptural approach to painting, although some of his works hint at an understanding of a more sophisticated form of perspective.

► Campin, Fouquet, Schongauer, Van der Weyden

Dieric Bouts. Active in Louvain, 1457. **d** Louvain, 1475. **Virgin and Child.** c1460–5. Oil and tempera on panel. **h**27.9 × **w**24.1 cm. **h**11 × **w**9½ in. Private collection

The swirling, radiant colours of the sky converge at the bright sun. In the foreground, a scraggy black beast, a hint of a tear falling from its sad eye, looks longingly at a dead, upturned ray as if he were the cause of its demise. A man in an unnatural pose holds the goat; perhaps he is a farmer, perhaps a fisherman. The shallows of the sea in which they appear to stand reflect the red of the sky, clashing violently with the yellow coat of the man who, like the goat, sticks out his tongue at the sun. The fiery, passionate colours and

visionary nature of this picture give it an expressionistic quality. In fact, many of his paintings are concerned with the emotions of sexual passion, guilt and betrayal. Born in Australia, Boyd belonged to a family of artists – his father was a sculptor and potter, his mother a painter. He moved to England in 1959 where he gained a high reputation as an artist both there and in his native land.

► Burra, Heckel, Kitaj, Nolan, Schmidt-Rottluff

Arthur Boyd. b Murrumbeena, 1920. d Melbourne, 1999. **The Australian Scapegoat**. 1987. Oil on canvas. **h**259 × **w**442 cm. **h**102 × **w**174 in. Art Gallery of New South Wales, Sydney

Brancusi Constantin

The Kiss

Tightly entwined, two lovers embrace in a passionate kiss.
The elemental power of this work is expressed by the bulk of
the stone from which the forms are only sketchily emerging,
as if roused from a timeless slumber. Brancusi reduced his
sculptures to their most basic, most abstract, lending them
a primordial vitality. Eschewing all surface decoration, nothing
but pure form remains. Brancusi had an immense effect on
twentieth-century sculpture and abstract art in general.
The simple grandeur of his works evokes a sense of freedom

and strength. In 1904 he walked from Romania (the country
of his birth) to Paris, a feat which gained him widespread
admiration. His celebrity was further fuelled by the law case
he brought against US Customs, who wanted to charge
duty on an imported bronze sculpture which they considered
as nothing more than raw material, thus liable for tax.

► Bourgeois, Gaudier-Brzeska, Moore, Noguchi, Rodin

Constantin Brancusi. b Hobitza, 1876. **d** Paris, 1957. **The Kiss**. 1907. Stone. **h**28 cm. **h**11 in. Muzeul de Arta, Craiova

Braque Georges

The Round Table

A selection of commonplace objects, including a guitar, a knife, fruit and a bottle, are arranged on a round table situated in the corner of a room. The tabletop is tilted forward, and the whole space of the interior is pushed forwards towards the viewer. Unlike traditional perspective, which creates the effect of looking through a window into a three-dimensional world, Braque's composition draws attention to the surface of the canvas. This is further enhanced by the artist's application of sand, which introduces an unexpected texture. Along

with Picasso, Braque is credited as the joint inventor of Cubism, one of the most important artistic developments of the twentieth century. Although his later paintings are compositionally much looser than his early pioneering works, as is evident in the present example, in its subject matter and the inclusion of non-art materials, elements of Cubism still remain.

▶ Davis, Gris, B Nicholson, Picasso

Georges Braque. b Argenteuil-sur-Seine, 1882. **d** Paris, 1963. **The Round Table.** 1929. Oil, sand and charcoal on canvas. **h**144.7 × **w**114 cm. **h**57⅜ × **w**44¾ in. Phillips Collection, Washington, DC

Brauner Victor

Fascination

Muted browns and ochre tones decorate a spartan room with a table – part furniture, part wolf – at which a featureless naked lady sits nonchalantly as if calmly waiting for a meal to be served. Her hair curves up and forms a bird with a swan-like neck which viciously confronts the wolf's head growing out of the table. His tail and genitals are at the other end. Brauner produced a series of paintings such as this inhabited by strange hybrids of women, animals and objects. These absurd, hallucinatory fantasies spring from the enigmatic world of Surrealist art, in which the visual imagination is freed from the constraints of reason and logic. The Surrealists' vision aimed to harness the unconscious to produce revelatory, stimulating images. Born in Romania, Brauner worked mainly in France. In 1931 he painted his *Self-portrait with Extracted Eye*; the work proved to be prophetic, as the artist lost his left eye in a bar brawl in 1938.

▶ Bellmer, Dali, Ernst, Magritte, Matta, Tanguy

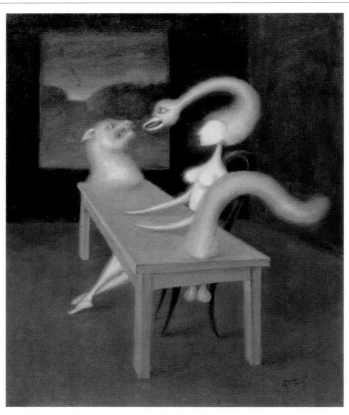

Victor Brauner. b Piatra Neamt, 1903. **d** Paris, 1966. **Fascination**. 1939. Oil on canvas. **h**65 × **w**54 cm. **h**25½ × **w**21¼ in. Private collection

Bronzino Agnolo

An Allegory with Venus and Cupid

Venus turns to kiss Cupid, who fondles her breast. A bearded Father Time pulls a curtain over the scene. Jealousy clutches her head in her hands, and a masked figure looks on the scene from above. A girl who is part furry beast and part reptile holds a honeycomb in one hand and the stinging end of her tail in the other. The painting is obviously some kind of allegory, but what is it about? No one is certain. The cool light that bathes this bizarre scene and the smooth handling of the paint are typical of the artist's style. Bronzino's work is a wonderful example of Mannerism, in the way he distorts natural poses, exaggerates expressions and emphasizes movement. A successful portrait painter in his day, Bronzino often placed his models in oddly rigid poses. His sitters' somewhat cold, detached expressions compel the viewer to look closely for a glimmer of emotion.

▶ Michelangelo, Parmigianino, Pontormo, Vouet

Agnolo Bronzino. b Florence, 1503. d Florence, 1572. **An Allegory with Venus and Cupid**. c1550. Oil on ponel. h146 × w116 cm. h57½ × w45¾ in. National Gallery, London

Broodthaers Marcel

Casserole and Closed Mussels

A tall pile of mussel shells is held together with green-tinted resin, evoking the sea. The shells seem to be surging upwards in an explosion of vitality. The image uses a pun on the words *la moule* ('the mussel') and *le moule* ('the mould'). The work is intended as a metaphor for the artist's home country of Belgium, where mussels are a national dish; it is also a satire on the Belgian bourgeoisie. It is probably Broodthaer's most famous image. The artist's sculpture can be categorized as Conceptual Art, in that the ideas behind his works are more important than the works themselves. Broodthaers was also greatly influenced by his compatriot, the Surrealist painter René Magritte. Like Magritte he often delights in incongruous juxtapositions and the creation of visual paradoxes through the combination of words, everyday objects and printed material.

► Beuys, Duchamp, Magritte, Oldenburg, Rauschenberg

Marcel Broodthaers. b Brussels, 1924. **d** Cologne, 1976. **Casserole and Closed Mussels**. 1964-5. Mussel shells, polyester resin and iron casserole. **h**30.5 cm. **h**12 in. Tate, London

Brown Ford Madox

Work

It is impossible not to get the artist's message in this action-packed picture crammed with detail. What is perhaps less obvious is that the painting is also meant to celebrate the relationship between art and work. It was therefore painted in a style to mimic the great Italian masters of the early Renaissance. The idea of combining art and work later became the central theme of the Arts and Crafts movement. Brown settled in England in 1845 after training at Antwerp, Paris and Rome. He became associated with the Pre-Raphaelite Brotherhood, but never joined them. Although he shared their desire to return to the simple vision of the early Renaissance painters, Brown was more interested in social issues than in purely artistic matters. In 1844 and 1845 he entered a competition to paint frescos for the Houses of Parliament, which he lost. Instead, he won a commission to paint frescos for Manchester Town Hall.

► Burne-Jones, Hunt, Léger, Filippo Lippi, Millais, Rossetti

Ford Madox Brown. b Calais, 1821. **d** London, 1893. **Work**. 1852–65. Oil on canvas. **h**134.6 × **w**196 cm. **h**53 × **w**77⅛ in. Manchester City Art Gallery, Manchester

Bruegel Jan

The Garden of Eden

Exotic and everyday animals mingle in this Garden of Eden, richly and meticulously endowed with a profusion of lush plants and flowers. Bruegel's main concern in this picture was the creation of a mystical, imaginary landscape, and the figures of Adam and Eve have been reduced to insignificance in order to emphasize their setting. The limited selection of flora and fauna may seem comical to the modern eye, but Bruegel has successfully imbued this sylvan glade with a dream-like quality. His breadth of feeling and sensitivity to natural surroundings helped to develop the great tradition of seventeenth-century Dutch landscape painting. His highly finished manner of painting flowers, landscapes and Garden of Eden subjects earned him the nickname 'Velvet' Bruegel. Jan came from the great Bruegel dynasty of Flemish painters; his father was Pieter Bruegel the Elder.

► Bassano, P Bruegel, Hobbema, Patinir, Ruisdael

Jan Bruegel. b Brussels, 1568. **d** Antwerp, 1625. **The Garden of Eden**. c1620. Oil on panel. **h**53 × **w**84 cm. **h**20¾ × **w**33 in. Victoria and Albert Museum, London

Bruegel Pieter

Peasant Wedding

The viewer is invited into an animated feast to celebrate the wedding of two peasants. The painting is rich in detail – the figure filling the jug of wine at the left, the pies being brought to table on a door, and the bagpipe player hungrily staring at the food. All show Bruegel's ability to capture the peasants' earthiness. The drunken, bumbling characters who animate Bruegel's lively scenes are the very opposite of the Italian ideal of refined perfection. Yet it is Bruegel's work, based on real-life observation, that is the more real and human.

Legend has it that Bruegel would put on disguises in order to take part in the peasants' rollicking gatherings; this led to his being given the nickname 'Peasant Bruegel'. His technique, however, was far from crude; his carefully applied thin layers of paint express a wonderful sense of the richness and variety of colour. Pieter Bruegel headed a family of painters which flourished in the sixteenth and seventeenth centuries.

▶ Bosch, J Bruegel, G David, Ostade

Pieter Bruegel. b Brögel, c1525. **d** Brussels, 1569. **Peasant Wedding**. c1568/9. Oil on panel. **h**114 × **w**164 cm. **h**44⅞ × **w**64⅝ in.   83
Kunsthistorisches Museum, Vienna

Ter Brugghen Hendrick

The Flute Player

A young dandy dressed in a striped brocade shirt with baggy sleeves is playing a flute, his dark velvet hat setting his profile into relief. This painting appears to be free from all literary overtones – a pure evocation of a light, joyful subject. Dutch painting of this time generally held a wider symbolic meaning, however, and this picture may represent a personification of Music, or may illustrate Hearing, one of the five senses. The design of the picture is unusual: the boldly painted figure, outlined against a plain background, is viewed close-to and almost fills one-half of the picture space. This directness of composition, and the dramatic use of light and shade, show the influence of the early work of Caravaggio. Ter Brugghen studied in Rome and together with Gerrit van Honthorst and other members of the so-called Utrecht School was instrumental in transporting Caravaggio's ideas to northern climes.

► Caravaggio, Greuze, Honthorst, Lotto

Hendrick ter Brugghen. b Deventer, 1588. **d** Utrecht, 1629. **The Flute Player.** 1621. Oil on canvas. **h**71.3 × **w**55.8 cm. **h**28⅛ × **w**21⅞ in. Staatliche Kunstsammlungen, Kassel

Buren Daniel

Two Levels

What is seen here is only a small part of a spectacular, colossal sculptural installation which was created especially for the Cour d'Honneur of the Palais-Royal in Paris. Each column is constructed of black and white strips of marble and is placed in a rigid, uniform sequence in the central square. The work's impact is entirely governed by the surroundings, as Buren creates his own interpretation of an existing architectural space (the traditional columns are visible in the background). A leading light in French Conceptual Art,

Buren acknowledges that meaning is determined by context. He demonstrates this by reproducing his trademark – vertical stripes – in a variety of settings. Although neither his idea nor his form of expression have changed over the years, he did at one time apply his paint to different materials, including flags, sails, stone steps and walls.

▶ Andre, Christo, Heizer, Judd, Long

Daniel Buren. b Boulogne-Billancourt, 1938. **Two Levels**. 1985–6. Black and white marble. surface area 67 × 50 m. 220 × 164 ft. Palais-Royal, Paris

Burne-Jones Sir Edward

King Cophetua and the Beggar Maid

A lost age of chivalry and romance is rediscovered in this elegant painting. It tells the story of a king who searched far and wide for the perfect woman, and finally found her disguised as a simple beggar. She is the brightest object in the picture, and appears to glow with heavenliness. Burne-Jones was deeply affected by artists of the early Italian Renaissance, such as Sandro Botticelli and Andrea Mantegna, and was also inspired by his association with Dante Gabriel Rossetti. Although he was not one of the original members of the Pre-Raphaelite Brotherhood, his work reflects many of the ideas associated with those painters. Burne-Jones' rich colours, poetic subject matter and meticulous attention to detail give his paintings a mystical, spiritual quality. At the time, William Morris' Arts and Crafts movement had swept the country, and its influence can be seen here in the leaves, fabrics and designs on the staircase.

► Botticelli, Brown, Mantegna, Millais, Rossetti

Sir Edward Burne-Jones. b Birmingham, 1833. **d** London, 1898. **King Cophetua and the Beggar Maid**. 1862. Oil on canvas. **h**76.2 × **w**63.5 cm. **h**30 × **w**25 in. Tate, London

Burra Edward

Cornish Landscape with Figures and Tin Mine

The artist has captured the spirit of the formidable and depressed figures in this haunting Cornish landscape, with its ruined tin-mine workings in the background. It is known that the man in the striped coat (who is painted twice) was seen by Burra in a pub, and the two tattooed figures are direct copies from a book. The strange, ghostly head, just visible in the top left-hand corner, may reflect Burra's interest in Surrealism. Although he knew a number of the Surrealists while living in France, he never really allied himself with them or any other

movement. Burra's work during the 1930s became satirical, recalling that of George Grosz. Towards the end of his life his work developed into his own peculiar style. Most of his famous works are watercolours of women, or of people enjoying themselves. These were done in Burra's sharp, slightly exaggerated style, which changed little throughout his life.

► Boyd, Dali, Grosz, Kitaj, Tanguy

Edward Burra. b London, 1905. d Playden, 1976. **Cornish Landscape with Figures and Tin Mine**. 1975. Watercolour on paper. h78.1 × w135.9 cm. h30¾ × w53½ in. Private collection

Burri Alberto

Sacco

Materials that have been ravaged by time and discarded as waste, lacerated and unravelled, have been stitched back together and painted. Burri's early experiences as a doctor, handling blood-stained bandages and sewing up wounds during the Second World War, provided the inspiration for this work. The coarseness of the material used, and the violence with which it has been torn, creates a powerful tension between beauty and decay. The picture reflects the philosophy of the Art Informel movement, a post-war school of abstract art that rejected conventional ideas of composition and turned to new materials for inspiration. Burri's works demonstrate his fascination with surface texture and different media. He has made a series of pictures using charred wood, iron plates and plastic sheets, burnt into gaping holes with a blowtorch, which are highly sought after by collectors.

► Dubuffet, Fautrier, Riopelle, Still, Tàpies

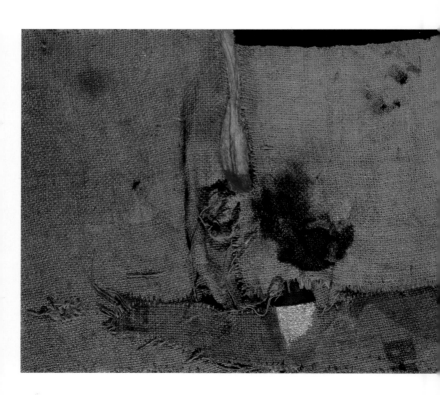

Alberto Burri. b Città di Castello, 1915. **d** Nice, 1995. **Sacco.** 1954. Burlap, linen, oil and gold paint on board. **h**33 × **w**38 cm. **h**13 × **w**15¼ in. Private collection

Cahun Claude

Untitled (Self-Portrait)

figure looks towards us, confronting our gaze; their reflected image looks away. Is this a man or a woman? The photograph is in fact a self-portrait. Born Lucy Schwob, in 1919 the artist adopted the sexually ambiguous pseudonym Claude Cahun. Central to both Cahun's life and art was questioning and destabilizing of established models of gender identity. During the 1920s and 1930s Cahun lived in Paris, where the subversive nature of her work led to loose association with the Surrealist group of artists.

In 1937 she settled in Jersey with her lover, stepsister and artistic collaborator Suzanne Malherbe (Marcel Moore). Following the German occupation of the island in July 1940, the sisters, as they were known, began to produce and distribute anti-Nazi leaflets. In 1944 they were arrested and sentenced to death. Although the sentence was not carried out, much of Cahun's work was destroyed.

► Abramović, Boetti, Man Ray, Sherman, Zhang Huan

Claude Cahun (Lucy Renée Mathilde Schwob). b Nantes, 1894. d Jersey, 1954. **Untitled (Self-Portrait)**. 1928. Gelatin silver print.
8 × w24 cm. h7 × w9½ in. Jersey Museum and Art Gallery, St Helier

Caillebotte Gustave

Young Man at his Window

The artist's younger brother René stands with his back to us, looking out from the window of the family home at 77 rue de Miromesnil, Paris. The huge stone balustrade creates a strong division between the inside of the house and the world beyond, as our eyes are drawn to the streets below following René's gaze. This device of drawing the viewer into the picture via the window-frame view makes it one of Caillebotte's most compelling images. Caillebotte specialized in views of Paris and its surroundings, and images of working-class life. An intimate and supportive friend of Claude Monet, Pierre Auguste Renoir and Alfred Sisley, Caillebotte not only organized exhibitions of the Impressionists' works but also bought many of the paintings they found difficult to sell. In his will Caillebotte left his collection, including 65 Impressionist paintings, to the state. The collection was refused, and only after three years of negotiations were 38 pictures finally accepted.

► Bonnard, Matisse, Monet, Renoir, Sisley, Vuillard

Gustave Caillebotte. b Paris, 1848. **d** Paris, 1894. **Young Man at his Window**. 1876. Oil on canvas. **h**116.2 × **w**80.9 cm. **h**45¾ × **w**31⅞ in. Private collection

The delicate balancing and twisting of the metal shapes create an image of a lobster trap, while the stylized brightly coloured fish and nine black elements suspended below give us the impression that we are looking at a fish skeleton. The metal elements gracefully swing independently of each other in slow circles, set in motion by currents of air. Calder combines the humour of the marine images with the sense of beauty and grace of a construction which continually rises, falls and turns at varying speeds and in different directions. The element of motion in the work makes it a prime example of Kinetic Art, a term applied to works of art in which actual movement, or an impression of movement, plays an integral part. Calder was the inventor of the mobile, and made his first one in 1932. His mobiles have ranged in height from around 4 cm (1½ inches) to over 5 metres (12 feet); an example of the latter can be seen at JFK Airport in New York.

► Caro, Lissitzky, Miró, Tinguely, Vasarely

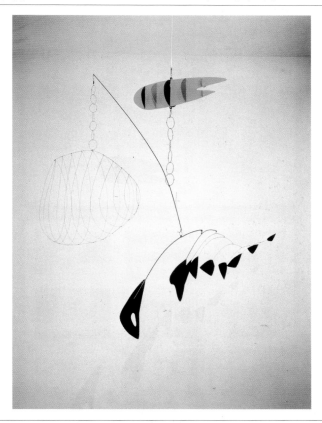

Alexander Calder. b Philadelphia, PA, 1898. d New York, NY, 1976. **Lobster Trap and Fish Tail**. 1939. Steel wire and painted sheet aluminium. w289.5 cm. w114 in. Museum of Modern Art, New York, NY

Calle Sophie

The Hotel: Room 24, March 2, 1981

Sophie Calle's conceptual projects examine identity, emotion and intimacy, using a voyeuristic method that scrutinizes not only friends and strangers but also, in an exhibitionistic way, the artist herself. In 1981 Calle was employed for three weeks as a chambermaid in a Venice hotel. As she cleaned, the artist recorded and scrutinized the personal possessions that belonged to the hotel guests occupying each room. In addition to photographing the items, the artist created diary entries in which she wrote down her thoughts and

observations as she rifled through letters and rummaged through the discarded contents of the waste paper basket. The project resulted in twenty-one diptychs, each specific to a room, in which text and image were presented along side each other. As with much of her work, 'The Hotel' series centres on the artist's interest in the interface between public and private lives – her own and those of others – and her fascination with unconscious patterns of behaviour.

► Baldessari, Holzer, A Piper, Rist

Sophie Calle. b Paris, 1953. The Hotel: Room 24, March 2, 1981. 1981. Gelatin silver print with ektachrome print collage. h105 × w145 cm. h41¼ × w57 in (each panel). Private collection

Campin Robert

The Virgin and Child before a Fire Screen

Despite her rich and elaborate fur-lined gown, the Virgin is shown in a homely setting. She looks as though she has just put down her book to nurse her child. Minutely observed details appear throughout the work; the townscape in the background is as clear and precise as the figures in the foreground, while the pages of the Virgin's book, the decoration along the hemline of her dress and the rushwork of the fire-screen have been painstakingly rendered. The artist's technical skill and inventiveness invite comparison with his contemporary, Jan van Eyck. Robert Campin's identity is shrouded in mystery. It is generally thought that he is the same person as the so-called Master of Flémalle, a name given to the painter of a group of pictures that were (wrongly) supposed to have come from Flémalle. It is thought that Rogier van der Weyden may have been one of Campin's pupils.

▶ Bouts, Van Eyck, Fouquet, Schongauer, Van der Weyden

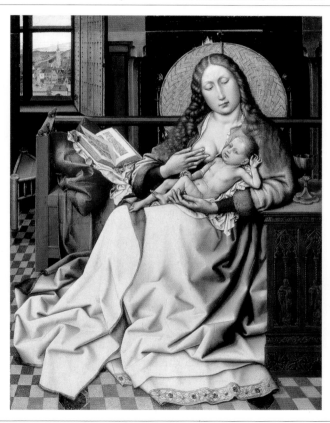

Robert Campin. Active in Tournai, 1406. d Tournai, 1444. **The Virgin and Child before a Fire Screen**. c1425/30. Oil and tempera on panel. **h**63.5 × **w**48.5 cm. **h**25 × **w**19 in. National Gallery, London

93

Canaletto

The Basin of San Marco on Ascension Day

Seen from across the Basin of St Mark's, the Doge is about to embark on the magnificent state barge, the *Bucintoro*, to celebrate Venice's symbolic Wedding to the Sea, one of the great events of the Venetian calendar. On Ascension Day each year, the Doge would throw a ring into the Adriatic Sea. The event presented the artist with a grand opportunity to show all the pomp and splendour of his native city's festivals. As the leading Venetian landscape painter of his day, Canaletto's works were very popular, especially with the English nobility. Canaletto's acutely observed paintings of Venice's canals and palaces, with their shimmering wealth of detail, even today evoke a romantic view of this beautiful city. Canaletto visited England in 1746, and while there painted a group of landscapes, including views of Warwick Castle, Eton College and Whitehall.

► Gentile Bellini, Bellotto, Bonington, Guardi, Pannini

Canaletto (Antonio Canale). b Venice, 1697. **d** Venice, 1768. **The Basin of San Marco on Ascension Day**. c1740. Oil on canvas. **h**122 × **w**183 cm. **h**48 × **w**72 in. National Gallery, London

Canova Antonio

Cupid and Psyche

With wings not yet folded, Cupid lands to revive his dying over Psyche with a tender embrace. The focus of the sculpture is created by their interlocking arms and gaze of love. Their smooth bodies and delicate limbs create a sense of young passion in all its innocent purity; the entire scene is one of effortless, spiralling grace. Canova's sculpture is a fine example of the Neo-Classical ideal of perfection of form and finish. However, he also was able to express the ardour that pulsates beneath the lovers' thin marble skin. Canova had

a distinguished career in Venice, where he was commissioned to create public monuments, tombs and statues. He also established a school for young artists. As an emissary of the Pope, he travelled throughout Europe, demanding the return of works of art that were looted during the Napoleonic wars.

► Bernini, J-L David, Etty, Powers, Prud'hon, Rodin

Caravaggio

Doubting Thomas

It is just after the Crucifixion. St Thomas is touching Christ's wounds to see if they are real. The heads of Christ and the three Apostles are the focus of the composition. The moment is intense, as the Apostles look on St Thomas who, with deeply furrowed brow, plunges his finger into Christ's side. The drama of this shockingly realistic detail is heightened by the harsh lighting and dark shadows (known as *chiaroscuro*); the background is non-existent. Caravaggio was renowned for his vivid realism and rejection of idealization, an approach that was revolutionary at the time. He often used coarse peasant types for his models of saints and Apostles, and is even said to have painted one of his Virgins from a drowned prostitute fished out of the River Tiber. Despite a somewhat dubious personal reputation (he was frequently in trouble with authority), Caravaggio almost singlehandedly brought about a revolution in art. Even today his paintings have the power to astonish us.

▶ Bernini, Ter Brugghen, Hals, Jordaens, Rembrandt

Michelangelo Merisi da Caravaggio. b Caravaggio, 1571. **d** Porto Ercole, 1610. **Doubting Thomas.** 1599. Oil on canvas. **h**107 × **w**146 cm. **h**42¼ × **w**57½ in. Stiftung Schlösser und Gärten Potsdam-Sanssouci, Potsdam

A selection of steel sheets, i-beams and tubes has been bolted together and painted with a uniform coating of red. The resulting sculpture is a lyrical arrangement of lines and forms; the heavy materiality of the sculpture appears deceptively light. In the early 1960s, *Early One Morning* represented a challenge to conventional sculptural practices. Sitting directly on the gallery floor, its open horizontality marked a notable departure from the traditional carved block. By fabricating his sculptures in steel, Caro was able to create a more linear form of work, evoking qualities more often associated with abstract painting. During the 1950s Caro worked as an assistant to Henry Moore. In 1959 he visited the USA where he met Kenneth Noland, Morris Louis and the sculptor David Smith. The art he experienced on this trip had a considerable impact on his decision to abandon the traditional sculptural materials of clay and bronze, and develop a more gestural form of abstract sculpture.

► Deacon, Louis, Moore, Noland, Smith

Anthony Caro. **b** New Malden, Surrey, 1924. **d** London, 2014. **Early One Morning**. 1962. Painted steel and aluminium. 289.5 × w619.5 × d335.25 cm. **h**114 × **w**244 × **d**132 in. Tate, London

Carpaccio Vittore

Two Venetian Ladies on a Balcony

The pearl-covered gowns worn by these two ladies are typical of Venetian nobility in the fifteenth century. The two sit on a balcony, idly toying with the birds and animals around them. The point of the picture is not clear – it is neither a portrait nor a story. It has probably been cut from a larger panel, which would have put it in context and made it more understandable. Carpaccio has a straightforward style. His paintings are not as realistic as those of some of his Florentine counterparts, however, favouring picturesque

story-telling over the balanced intellectualism that was gaining ground in that city. His bright colours have all the charm and vibrancy associated with Venetian Renaissance painting. He probably trained with Gentile Bellini and like him often used historical or religious subjects as an opportunity to depict everyday Venetian life.

► Alma-Tadema, Gentile Bellini, Canaletto, Giorgione

Vittore Carpaccio. Active in Venice, 1472. **d** Venice, 1526. **Two Venetian Ladies on a Balcony**. c1495/1500. Oil on panel. **h**164 × **w**94 cm. **h**64½ × **w**37 in. Museo Correr, Venice n a low-ceilinged room, the main character is a plaster-cast of a female tennis player with a mannequin head. She stands next o a map of Trieste and Istria; in the background, a brightly oloured geometric cone stands behind a canvas painted with actories. The irrationally juxtaposed and dream-like images re curiously disturbing, and link this painting with the Pittura Metafisica ('metaphysical painting') school. Founded y Carrà and Giorgio de Chirico, Pittura Metafisica used isconnected and mysterious images to create a magical

and often weird atmosphere. Carrà had met De Chirico in 1917, and swiftly adopted his imagery of mannequins set in claustrophobic spaces. His work had earlier passed through a Futurist phase; Carrà was one of the signatories to the 1910 Futurist manifesto. From 1924 he turned away from 'Metaphysical' painting towards a more heightened realism, inspired by the Italian masters of the early Renaissance.

► Balla, Boccioni, Brauner, De Chirico, Kahlo, Wadsworth

Carracci Annibale

Christ is shown bearing the Cross as he appeared in a vision to St Peter. Upon being asked where he was going, Christ said to St Peter, 'I am going to Rome to be crucified again'. The artist shows great sensitivity to detail in this painting, particularly in the landscape. The harmonious composition and the beautiful figures recall the work of Raphael and Michelangelo, and represent the artist's desire to bring back the Classical spirit to seventeenth-century Rome. His style is characterized by a fusion of naturalism and Classicism. In a letter he spoke of his admiration for Correggio and Titian: 'I like this straight-forwardness and this purity that is not reality and yet is life-like and natural, not artificial or forced.' With his brother Agostino and cousin Lodovico, Annibale Carracci founded an important academy of fine arts in Bologna in 1595. The academy trained a number of artists, many of whom were to form the great school of seventeenth-century Baroque Bolognese painting.

▶ Correggio, Raphael, Reni, Titian, Vouet

Annibale Carracci. b Bologna, 1560. **d** Rome, 1609. **Christ Appearing to Saint Peter on the Appian Way.** 1601–2. Oil on panel. **h**77.4 × **w**56.3 cm. **h**30½ × **w**22 in. National Gallery, London

Four people, more than likely two married couples, picnic on the bank of the Seine. Below them is a small rowing boat; attached to it are numerous fishing rods. Although they have not responded to the photographer's presence, the image has been taken from close up. The shallow and flattened space of the composition creates the effect of pushing the group even closer towards the viewer. Taken two years after the French government passed a law guaranteeing workers two weeks of paid vacation a year, Cartier-Bresson's photograph can be seen to capture an important moment in the country's social history. The son of a wealthy textile manufacturer, Cartier-Bresson studied painting at the private art school of the Cubist artist André Lhote. Inspired by his association with the Surrealists, in the 1930s he turned to photography. Using a handheld Leica camera, he became a pioneer of an informal, candid style of modern photography that looked to capture the 'decisive moment'.

► Araki, Evans, Frank, Sander, Tissot

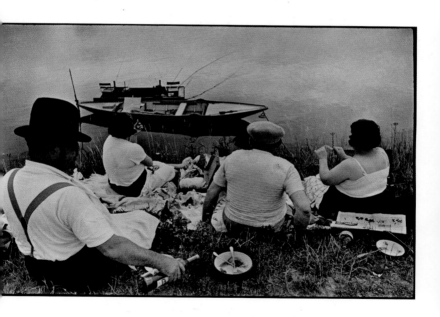

Henri Cartier-Bresson. b Chanteloup-en-Brie, 1908. d Montjustin, 2004. **Juvisy, France**. 1938. Gelatin silver print . h23.3 × w34.8 cm.
h9⅛ × w13¹¹/₁₆ in. Museum of Modern Art, New York, NY

Cassatt Mary

Woman Sewing

The woman here has been caught in a quiet moment as she does her sewing. It is not a portrait, but a study in the interplay of colour and light in an outdoor scene, which would have been painted from life. The artist's realistic approach stems from her studies at the Pennsylvania Academy under Thomas Eakins. Later, in Europe, Cassatt formed a close association with Edgar Degas, who had a great influence on her style. Cassatt exhibited with the Impressionists at their 1874 show and although an American, she is classified as part of the French Impressionist movement. Many of her paintings show mothers with children, painted with a feminine tenderness not found in other Impressionist work. Cassatt was very influenced by Japanese woodcuts, and excelled in making woodcut prints. She is widely credited with popularizing Impressionism in North America.

► Chase, Degas, Eakins, Hiroshige, Monet, Morisot

Mary Cassatt. b Pittsburgh, PA, 1844. **d** Mesnil-Théribus, 1926. **Woman Sewing.** c1880/2. Oil on canvas. **h**92 × **w**63 cm. **h**36¼ × **w**24⅞ in. Musée d'Orsay, Paris

Castagno Andrea del

The Young David

Bold power and strength characterize this image of David with the head of Goliath. These were qualities that were highly valued by Florentines at the time; they identified with the young, spirited warrior who overcame the huge giant with a sling-shot. The image is painted on a leather shield, to be carried through the streets of Florence during festive processions. Artists in fifteenth-century Italy made such decorations regularly. However, because they were not made to last, most examples have not survived to the present day. Castagno is known for his strong, powerful figures. He painted a number of frescos, which in particular reflect his sculptural approach to painting. He did not pay much attention to either landscape or nature, choosing to focus on the human form. Castagno was at one time thought to have brutally murdered his teacher. We now know this story to be untrue, but it may reflect the artist's violent nature.

▶ Botticelli, Donatello, Ghiberti, Ghirlandaio, Signorelli

Andrea del Castagno. b Castagno, c1421. d Florence, 1457. **The Young David**. c1450/7. Tempera on leather mounted on panel. h115.6 × w76.9 cm. h45½ × w30¼ in. National Gallery of Art, Washington, DC

Catena Vincenzo

The artist has used a straightforward composition to highlight a simple meal. The table, glassware and setting have all been kept to a minimum. All, that is, except the cloth that hangs behind Christ. The simplicity of the picture contrasts with the elaborate cloth, drawing the viewer's attention to the Saviour. The Cloth of Honour, as it is known, is a feature of other Venetian Renaissance paintings and can be found, for example, in many works by Giovanni Bellini, particularly in his paintings of the Virgin. As with many Venetian paintings of the time, colour and light are as important to this picture as its composition: the play between the blue and yellow of the servant's clothes and the yellow and purple of the man on the right shows the artist's inventive colour sense. Catena appears to have entered into some kind of partnership with Giorgione at one stage in his career. His works show the influence not only of Giorgione but of other Venetian artists such as Titian and Palma Vecchio.

► Giovanni Bellini, Champaigne, Giorgione, Titian

Vincenzo Catena. b Venice, c1480. **d** Venice, 1531. **The Supper at Emmaus**. 1520/30. Oil on canvas. **h**130 × **w**241 cm. **h**51 × **w**94¾ in. Galleria degli Uffizi, Florence

Creating a pretty red-and-white pattern along a plain stretching out to the horizon, a flock of flamingoes attend to their nests. Overhead a group of birds fly in a looping formation across the sky. A hunter and his servant lurk behind a bush, waiting for the perfect moment to shoot. The hunter is meant as a reminder of how the beauty of nature can so swiftly be destroyed by man. Catlin has taken great care in presenting the flamingoes in different poses, so as to express variety and movement and to create rhythm in a painting

that is otherwise fairly rigid. A lawyer by training, Catlin turned to portrait painting and spent many years studying and living among the Indians of North and South America. He painted many portraits of native American Indians, and was an early campaigner for the preservation of Indian tribes. In 1841 he published *Manners...of the North American Indians*, illustrated with some 300 of his engravings.

► Allston, Audubon, Bingham, Cole

George Catlin. b Wilkes-Barre, PA, 1796. d Jersey City, NJ, 1872. **Ambush for Flamingoes**. c1857. Oil on canvas. h48.3 × w67.3 cm. h19 × w26½ in. Carnegie Museum of Art, Pittsburgh, PA

Cattelan Maurizio

La Nona Ora

When *La Nona Ora* (The Ninth Hour) was first exhibited, it provoked an incendiary response. The lifelike image of Pope John Paul II struck down by a meteorite, and the broken glass from an imagined window or ceiling littering the red carpet, was read as an attack on the aged and reactionary pontiff – and so it was. Now, however, the life-sized figure of the pope, dressed in silken ecclesiastical robes and clutching a crucifix, has a tragicomic quality – the representation of universal knowledge and infallibility felled by a completely random cosmic accident. Cattelan follows in the tradition of Marcel Duchamp, the Dadaists and the harlequin jokers of his native Italy to use humour and satire as a means of challenging contemporary society. He delights in cultural insubordination, playing the role of the jester or trickster to question authority and to reveal uncomfortable contradictions at the heart of modern life.

► Broodthaers, Dali, Duchamp, Hirst, G Orozco

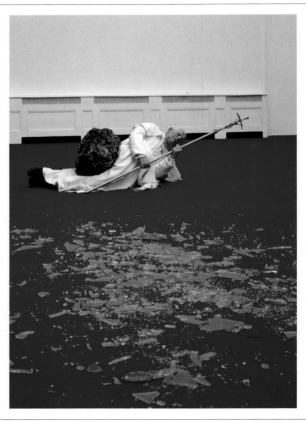

Maurizio Cattelan. b Padua, 1960. **La Nona Ora.** 1999. Wax, clothing, polyester resin with metallic powder, volcanic rock, carpet, glass. Dimensions variable. Private collection

Cellini Benvenuto

Salt Cellar

This beautiful salt cellar is made of two figures – Neptune and Ceres, who represent Water and Earth. Their intertwined legs symbolize the combination of these elements, which together produce salt. Cellini was a celebrated goldsmith, sculptor and engraver. He worked for emperors, kings, popes and princes; this particular object was made for King Francis I of France. The splendour and grace of Cellini's work is a perfect example of the Mannerist school. The aim of these artists was to appeal to the emotions through aesthetic effect. This led to the use of elongated figures and sharp colours, as can be seen in the work of late sixteenth-century artists. A great deal is known about Cellini's tempestuous life from his autobiography, which is full of racy anecdotes such as an account of his imprisonment for stealing the papal crown jewels. Unfortunately, most of Cellini's smaller works – medals, cups and daggers – were melted down. Many of his larger masterpieces, however, have survived.

► Clouet, Giambologna, Parmigianino, Rosso Fiorentino

Benvenuto Cellini. b Florence, 1500. d Florence, 1571. **Salt Cellar**. 1540/3. Gold, enamel and ebony. **h**26 × **w**34 cm. **h**10¼ × **w**13⅛ in.
Kunsthistorisches Museum, Vienna

Celmins Vija

Web #3

Vija Celmins' gossamer cobweb glows with light against a receding darkness. The white centre draws the eye inexorably, like a black hole, the strands of the web radiating out and circumscribing their hub. This is not a metaphorical conception, however. Like all Celmins' work, it was created with the dispassionate view of a photographer and attention to the quality of light. Celmins began her career in New York, in thrall to the dynamic painting of the Abstract Expressionists, but she gradually came to make art that recorded what she could see, rather than reflecting her own internal emotions. Nevertheless, her cobweb works combine the organic geometry of the natural world, precisely and impartially observed, with a melancholy imagination, conjuring up ghost stories and dusty rooms. Her painstaking working method, creating multi-layered images in graphite, charcoal or oils over many months, results in a fragile luminosity that is mesmerizing in its detail.

► Close, Marden, Richter, Weston

Vija Celmins. b Riga, Latvia, 1939. **Web #3**. 2000-2. Oil on linen. **h**38.1 × **w**45.7 cm. **h**15 × **w**18 in. Museum of Modern Art, New York, NY

Cézanne Paul

Purples, blues, yellows and reds create this mountain in the South of France. Rather than altering the tones of the colours as they changed with the light and shade, Cézanne changed the colours themselves. The mountain and surrounding landscape have been simplified into geometrical shapes and planes of colour. The result is a painting that may not faithfully reproduce the scene, but which evokes its tones and volumes through the interplay of light and shade. Cézanne said that he 'wanted to do Poussin again, from

Nature'. He achieved this by combining direct studies of the landscape with a Classical sense of form. Mont Sainte-Victoire, near the artist's home town of Aix-en-Provence, was Cézanne's favourite subject. He returned to it again and again throughout his career, producing paintings that were increasingly radical in conception. His reduction of nature into simple geometric shapes, and his use of bold colours, point to the later work of the Cubists and the Fauves.

► Braque, Derain, Hodler, Picasso, Poussin, Vlaminck

aul Cézanne. b Aix-en-Provence, 1839. d Aix-en-Provence, 1906. **Mont Sainte-Victoire**. 1885/95. Oil on canvas. h72.8 × w91.7 cm. 28⅜ × w38⅛ in. Barnes Foundation, Merion, PA

Chagall Marc

Above the Town

Above a town made up of simple wooden houses and barns, two fantastical figures fly across the sky. The man's hand gently cups the woman's breast. They seem to be lovers, perhaps eloping. The quaint and naively ordered town, painted in blocks of colour, with its pretty wooden fencing and warmish tones, shows Chagall's interest in fairy-tales and fantasy. Chagall was born in Russia and much of his imagery is firmly rooted in the Jewish folklore of his early years. His style is both sophisticated and childlike, blending reality and dreams into colourful compositions. He was compelled to leave Russia because the state demanded a certain type of art, and came to divide his time between the US and France. He was a very productive artist, painting and designing mosaics, stage sets and tapestries. His works can be found in many public buildings, including the Paris Opéra and the UN Headquarters in New York.

► Gontcharova, Hodgkin, Rodin, Soutine, Utamaro

Marc Chagall. b Vitebsk, 1887. **d** Saint Paul-de-Vence, 1985. **Above the Town.** 1914-18. Oil on canvas. **h**141 × **w**197 cm. **h**55½ × **w**77½ in. Tretyakov Gallery, Moscow

Chamberlain John

Balzanian

Balzanian, inspired by Rodin's sculpture of the French writer Honoré de Balzac (1898), stands with balletic poise and strength, the heavy drapery of its crumpled automobile parts expressing the idea not only of Rodin's sculpture, but of Balzac himself. Chamberlain was an artist of Hemingwayesque proportions – his sculpture is the instinctual, broad-gestured, three-dimensional equivalent of Abstract Expressionist painting and, like his contemporaries Pollock and Rothko, he lived his life 'like going into a spin in a car'. His main inspiration was the abstract sculpture of David Smith, from whose example he learned to manipulate car parts into sculptures. Chamberlain eventually broadened his media to incorporate steel, Plexiglas, foam and aluminium foil, but he returned to metal car parts in the mid-1970s. The idea of an innate connection between the elements of his sculptures is central to his work, the pieces themselves dictating their positions and the eventual form of the whole.

► Caro, Deacon, Pollock, Rodin, Smith

ohn Chamberlain. b Rochester, IN, 1927. d New York, NY, 2011. **Balzanian**. 1988. Painted and chromium-plated steel.
227.3 × w157.5 × d123.2 cm. **h**89½ × **w**62 × **d**48½ in. Pace Gallery, New York, NY

111

Champaigne Philippe de

The Last Supper

Christ announces to the Apostles that one of them will soon betray him. A mysterious air pervades the scene. The only light in the picture falls from the window, barely illuminating the back wall. This sets the figures in relief and heightens a feeling of drama and tension. While Christ consecrates the bread, the Apostles express their feelings without words. The rich colour of the draperies and the rhythmic folds of the tablecloth help the viewer's eye move across the picture. Champaigne did not paint dramatic scenes like his contemporary artists of the Italian Baroque, but the dignified, restrained emotions expressed in his work are rich and powerful. Of Flemish origin, Champaigne became a naturalized Frenchman, working as a portrait painter at the Court of King Louis XIII of France. One of his most well-known paintings is a full-length, austere study of Cardinal Richelieu.

► Catena, G David, Domenichino, Guercino

Philippe de Champaigne. b Brussels, 1602. **d** Paris, 1674. **The Last Supper.** c1652. Oil on canvas. **h**158 × **w**233 cm. **h**62^1/$_3$ × **w**91¾ in. Musée du Louvre, Paris

Chardin Jean-Baptiste-Siméon

The Young Schoolmistress

The subject is simple: a young woman teaching a child to read. Painted with great honesty, in a simple and direct style, the artist conveys a strong emotional link between the two figures. There is little background detail, and the thickly layered but carefully planned brushstrokes create depth and solidity. It is a silent painting, similar in its timelessness to the work of Jan Vermeer. Only the key of the cabinet breaks the magical spell of serenity and repose. Chardin was a leading painter of genre and still-life scenes in eighteenth-century France.

His simple, unsentimentalized compositions are rich in feeling; with their calm, balanced tonal range they embody an acute analysis and understanding of form. In this century, Chardin's work has regained popularity because of its almost abstract nature. He is widely considered to be the greatest still-life painter of his day.

► De Hooch, Lancret, La Tour, Metsu, Vermeer

Jean-Baptiste-Siméon Chardin. b Paris, 1699. d Paris, 1779. **The Young Schoolmistress**. c1736/7. Oil on canvas. h62 × w66 cm. h24¼ × w26⅛ in. National Gallery, London

Chase William Merritt

A Friendly Visit

Two elegant women sit on a sofa exchanging chit-chat. Sunlight fills the room, lightening the tone of the artist's bright palette. This is not a formally posed scene, but one typical of everyday life. Like the Impressionists, Chase used loose brushwork and pastel colours to portray the world around him. The informality of his subjects and the vigour with which he painted them may be particularly North American characteristics, but they have been injected into an essentially European style. Chase worked in North America throughout his long and active career. He was particularly influenced by the painter James Abbott McNeill Whistler, and for a time adopted that artist's flat, decorative style. He even painted Whistler's portrait when he met him in London in 1885. Chase was particularly admired for his portraits, landscapes and the type of everyday scene shown here. He was also a highly influential teacher.

► Cassatt, Manet, Sargent, Tissot, Whistler

William Merritt Chase. b Williamsburg, IN, 1849. **d** New York, NY, 1916. **A Friendly Visit**. 1895. Oil on canvas. **h**76.8 × **w**122.5 cm. **h**30¼ × **w**48¼ in. National Gallery of Art, Washington, DC

De Chirico Giorgio

The Uncertainty of the Poet

A pile of bananas and a Classical plaster-cast of a female torso appear in front of an arcade. The horizon is defined by a wall. Behind this, a train disappearing into the distance can just be seen. Such a collection of objects may appear arbitrary and nonsensical, but each has a symbolic meaning: the plaster cast symbolizes a human presence; the bananas represent exoticism; the train, a voyage. The outlines of all this strange imagery are drawn with vigour. However, it is the shadows, monumental and menacing as they sweep across

the picture, that add power and mystery. De Chirico and Carlo Carrà founded a movement called Pittura Metafisica ('metaphysical painting') that was known for its imaginative and mysterious imagery. De Chirico's enigmatic, dream-like paintings profoundly influenced the Surrealists of his day. From 1925, however, he adopted a more traditional style and his later paintings included portraits, horses on the seashore and still lifes.

► Carrà, Dalí, Delvaux, Magritte, Tanguy, Wadsworth

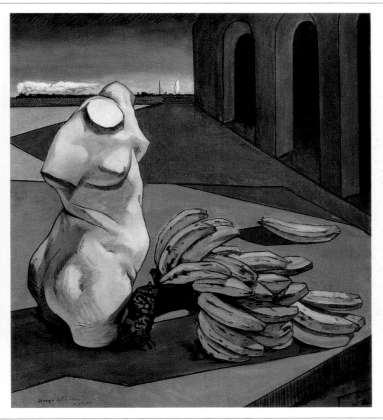

Giorgio de Chirico. b Volo, 1888. d Rome, 1978. **The Uncertainty of the Poet**. 1913. Oil on canvas. **h**106 × **w**94 cm. **h**41¾ × **w**34 in. Tate, London

Christo & Jeanne-Claude

The Pont Neuf Wrapped, Paris

Partners in both art and life, Christo & Jeanne-Claude became world-famous for their sculptural use of fabrics on a grand scale. Shown here is a work they created by wrapping one of the great landmarks of Paris – the Pont Neuf – in woven nylon, secured by rope. The temporary transformation of the bridge into a work of art was an exciting new way of creating sculpture. By covering it in fabric, the artists drew people's attention to the sculptural details of the bridge, while also creating a majestic and mysterious object of beauty.

It also served to emphasize the importance of preserving such historical monuments. Their work encourages us to look at objects in a new and different way. This notion of transforming familiar objects is typical of the New Realists, a movement founded in 1960. In 1976 they completed *Running Fence*, comprising 40 km (25 miles) of white fabric running over the Californian hills. Christo & Jeanne-Claude first collaborated together as artists in 1961.

► Gentile Bellini, Buren, Hiroshige, Klein, Long, Matta-Clark

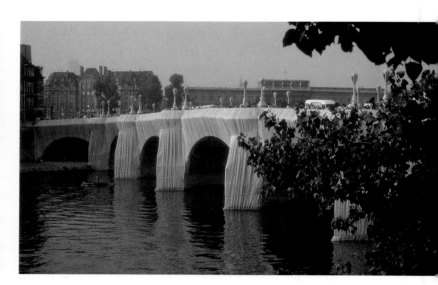

Christo & Jeanne-Claude. Christo Javacheff. **b** Gabrovo, 1935. Jeanne-Claude de Guillebon. **b** Casablanca, 1935. **d** New York, NY, 2009.
The Pont Neuf Wrapped, Paris. 1985. Woven nylon and rope. Now dismantled

Church Frederick

Twilight in the Wilderness

The sun sets over the distant horizon, leaving behind a blood-red and orange sky reflected in a wide river. Gnarled tree branches stand out against the background like skeletons. Church has revealed the power of nature in all its glory. The only pupil of Thomas Cole, Church chose to banish man from his compositions and concentrate on nature in its purest state. After exploring his native New England, he went in search of dramatic and panoramic landscapes further afield. He explored the length and breadth of the American continent: he painted the volcanoes of Mexico, the tropical jungles of South America, the snow-covered peaks of the Andes and the icebergs of Labrador. Church recorded the uncharted marvels he saw with amazing skill, changing the texture of his paints, for example, according to the different natural forms he described. The epic grandeur and sublime drama evoked by his work epitomize the ideals of the Romantic movement.

▶ Cole, Friedrich, Grimshaw, J Martin, Turner

Cimabue

Originally gracing the high altar of the church of Santa Trinità in Florence, this image was intended to inspire contemplation and devotion. The Virgin and Child sit on an ornate throne flanked by graceful angels. Below, four bearded prophets look out from an arcade as they, too, contemplate the divine image. The picture's simplicity and abundance of gold leaf would have helped to make it more visible in the dark church. The fine gold lines in the Virgin's robe are reminiscent of the rigid Byzantine style, yet the artist's attempt to put the figures in some kind of three-dimensional space points towards developments that were to flower during the Renaissance over a century later. Cimabue's origins are obscure. He is also known for his magnificent figure of St John – part of a large mosaic in the apse of Pisa Cathedral. Legend has it that he taught Giotto, who in turn developed Cimabue's naturalistic approach to painting the human form.

► Campin, Duccio, Giotto, Lochner

Cimabue. Active in Florence, 1272. **d** Florence, 1302. **The Santa Trinità Madonna**. c1260/80. Tempera on panel. **h**385 × **w**223 cm. **h**151½ × **w**87¾ in. Galleria degli Uffizi, Florence

A Vanitas Still Life

human skull dominates this odd array of objects. Bathed
warm tones, with a ray of sunlight sweeping across them,
e objects are painted in shades of pale brown. The artist was
enowned in the Netherlands for still lifes such as this. These
ere often painted in almost monochrome tones, lending
sense of mystical harmony to the objects he depicted. The
eme of this work is the transience of earthly life: the skull
presents death; the overturned glass symbolizes life flowing
way; the watch reminds the viewer that time is forever

moving on. Dutch seventeenth-century painters delighted
in the depiction of everyday objects, often treated with
great illusionistic skill. Such paintings were not overtly
moralizing in tone, but would often be rich with symbolic
meanings that would have been readily understood at the
time. Today, these paintings are more commonly admired
for their sheer virtuosity.

► Hals, De Heem, Hirst, Kalf, Ruysch, Snyders

eter Claesz. b Burgsteinfurt, 1590. d Haarlem, 1661. **A Vanitas Still Life**. 1645. Oil on panel. **h**39 × **w**61 cm. **h**15¹⁄₃ × **w**24 in.
ivate collection

Claude Lorrain

Landscape with a Sacrifice to Apollo

This magnificent, spacious scene is an example of Classical landscape painting at its best. It is carefully constructed, using a balance of strong horizontals and verticals, while areas of light and shade help to move the viewer's eye across and into the scene. Claude has captured the solemn grandeur of the Roman countryside. The delicate atmosphere is developed from a careful colour-range of greens, blues and browns. The figures, representing a scene from Classical mythology where Psyche's father makes a sacrifice to invoke Apollo's help in

finding a husband for his daughter, are almost incidental to the setting. Claude was a Frenchman, but spent his long creative life in and around Rome. His pastoral scenes and the poetry of his vision were a source of great inspiration to English eighteenth- and nineteenth-century landscape painters. Upon seeing the painting shown here, J M W Turner remarked that it seemed 'beyond the power of imitation'.

► Allston, Constable, Cozens, Poussin, Turner

Claude Lorrain (Claude Gellée). b Chamagne, 1600. **d** Rome, 1682. **Landscape with a Sacrifice to Apollo.** 1662. Oil on canvas.
h176 × **w**223 cm. **h**69 × **w**87¾ in. Anglesey Abbey, Lode

Clemente Francesco

Self-portrait: The First

he naked artist fixes his penetrating gaze on the viewer, ho feels compelled to return his look. A host of different rds rest on the artist's shoulders. The first in Clemente's ries of large, calligraphically rendered drawings of himself, is picture illustrates the artist's almost erotic drive towards lf-exploration and self-exposure. The figure is treated an expressive manner, while the birds symbolize the premacy of subjectivity and imagination over reason. The ork is an example of the Neo-Expressionist trend known

as Transavanguardia, which focuses on expressive figurative work done on a large scale. Towards the end of the 1970s Clemente and other Italian Neo-Expressionists largely led the way in reviving figure painting. This revival may be seen partly as a reaction to non-figurative Abstract Expressionism, which dominated the art scene for many years.

► Baselitz, Dürer, Kirchner, Pollock, Schiele, Schnabel

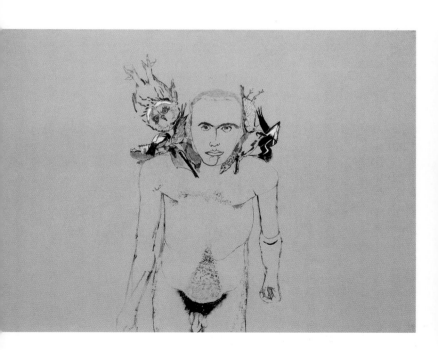

ancesco Clemente. b Naples, 1952. **Self-portrait: The First**. 1979. Gouache, **w**atercolour and ink on paper mounted on canvas.
12 × **w**147 cm. **h**44⅛ × **w**57⅞ in. Private collection

Close Chuck

Big Self-Portrait

The artist, his hair bedraggled and a cigarette held between his lips, fixes our gaze. His position in relation to ours is somewhat unclear. Does he stand above us looking down? Or is it he who is below us? In actuality the viewer occupies the position of the camera held in the artist's hands. In 1967 Close moved to New York. Abandoning the abstract paintings of his youth, the artist committed himself to the creation of large-scale photorealist portraits, of which the current work is the earliest example. By working from photographs – which the artist overlays with a grid in order to transpose accurately the image to canvas – Close creates portraits in which the gestural contribution of the painter is denied. Whilst this was an approach that presented parallels with the systematic working methods of the Minimalist artist, the meticulous detail of his finished portraits imbues them with psychological intensity.

► Cahun, Leyster, Rembandt, Richter, Rosa

Chuck Close. b Monroe, WA, 1940. **Big Self-Portrait.** 1967-8. Acrylic on canvas. **h**273 × **w**213 cm. **h**107½ × **w**83½ in. Walker Art Center, Minneapolis, MN

Clouet François

Portrait of François I on Horseback

Sitting astride an ornately decorated horse and dressed in an equally splendid suit of armour, François I of France looks at us with a slightly bemused expression on his face. Clouet is renowned for his powers of observation and detailed technique. Here he has rendered the intricate patterns of the King's attire with dazzling precision, especially the heads on his kneecap and elbow and the figures on his arms and chest. Clouet has not only paid homage to his master by depicting him in all his finery but has placed the horse and rider on the top of a hill with a landscape stretching behind him to imply that his King was ruler of an extensive kingdom. Clouet was a prolific painter of royal portraits. He was Court painter to four Kings of France – François I, Henri II, François II and Charles IX – and achieved great fame for his ceremonial portraits and striking drawings.

► Van Dyck, Van Eyck, Géricault, Holbein, Lawrence

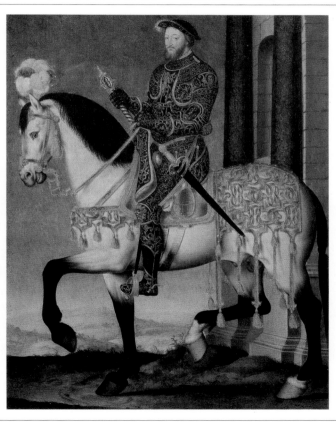

Cole Thomas

Scene from Last of the Mohicans

Massive outcrops of rock overwhelm a circle of small figures in this craggy, mountaintop scene bathed in an autumnal glow of warm colours. The artist has taken great care to show every natural detail, evoking the awe-inspiring vastness of the American wilderness. The picture illustrates a scene from James Fenimore Cooper's *The Last of the Mohicans*. Cole is considered the leading painter of the Hudson River School. This group of painters, who worked mainly around New England, were fond of river and mountain scenes untouched by man – particularly by Europeans. Cole aimed to bring religious and moral meaning to his paintings. He once wrote that 'the wilderness is yet a fitting place to speak of God', and after converting to Anglicanism, his painting became increasingly religious in feeling. He visited England, France and Italy, but was not greatly influenced by what he saw there. His paintings had a strong Romantic quality, full of drama and grandeur.

► Allston, Bierstadt, Church, Cozens, Friedrich

Thomas Cole. b Bolton-le-Moors, 1801. **d** Catskill, NY, 1848. **Scene from Last of the Mohicans**. 1827. Oil on canvas. **h**64.5 × **w**89 cm. **h**25⅜ × **w**35¹/₁₆ in. Wadsworth Atheneum, Hartford, CT

Constable John

The Lock

man struggles to open a lock, as his companion tries to old a barge still in a current of surging water. With its silvery ghlights and rich colouring, this picture is a celebration of e freshness and beauty of nature. Perhaps more than any her landscape painter, Constable sought to express his love the open countryside. Through an apparently spontaneous e of colour and rapid brushstrokes he was able to capture e fleeting mood of a scene. Behind these speckled, flecked ts of paint, however, lies a carefully composed structure.

Constable enrolled at the Royal Academy in 1799 and for the first decade of his painting career he failed to sell any work in England. This was not the case in Paris, however, where his paintings were accepted with enthusiasm. Constable's landscapes had a strong influence on French landscape painting, and his swift gestures and use of light to create a particular mood were an inspiration to the Impressionists.

► Corot, Daubigny, T Rousseau, Ruisdael, Turner

hn Constable. b East Bergholt, 1776. d London, 1837. **The Lock**. c1824. Oil on canvas. **h**142 × **w**120 cm. **h**56 × **w**47½ in.

ndación Colección Thyssen-Bornemisza, Madrid

Copley John Singleton

The Death of Major Pierson

The limp body of Major Pierson is held by his generals as his life slowly ebbs away. His furious black servant fires back at the enemy. The painting portrays the English repelling a French invasion on Jersey in 1781. A truly dramatic scene, it is symmetrically composed, clearly lit and described in great detail. Copley colourfully chronicles the heroism of the young officer killed in the service of a country whose flags are patriotically waving overhead. Copley first established his reputation as a portrait painter, becoming known for his direct, precise style and ability to capture the essence of his sitters. In 1774 he left America and settled in England, embarking upon a career as a history painter. Copley was among the first to treat subjects from modern history – such as *The Death of Major Pierson* – in the grand manner usually reserved for Classical subjects.

► J-L David, Delacroix, Uccello, West

John Singleton Copley. b Boston, MA, 1738. **d** London, 1815. **The Death of Major Pierson.** 1782–4. Oil on canvas. **h**252 × **w**366 cm. **h**99 × **w**144 in. Tate, London frugal assortment of stamps, newspaper cuttings and other objects with no particular relevance to each other is placed in a wooden box. This container acts as a metaphor for the whole world, inhabited by these strange items. It is also a treasury of curiosities that is compelling to explore and evokes a mood of nostalgia. The fragments of once ornamental or beautiful objects come together in a magical and dream-like way. This is Cornell's genius, and why he has proved so popular over the years. The randomness of

these 'assemblages', as they are known, reflects Cornell's interest in the irrationality of Surrealism. Nevertheless, a sense of order and precision pervades pieces such as this. Of his own work Cornell once said, 'Shadow boxes become poetic theatres or settings wherein are metamorphosed the elements of a childhood pastime.'

► Blake, Brauner, Rauschenberg, Schwitters

Joseph Cornell. b Nyack, NY, 1903. d Flushing, NY, 1972. **Untitled**. c1950. Mixed media in a wooden box. h38 × w27 cm. h15 × w10½ in. Private collection

Corot Jean-Baptiste-Camille

Ville d'Avray

In this landscape of great delicacy, soft pastel tones and feathery trees evoke a dreamy, dewy, early-morning atmosphere. A pale, silvery sky is reflected in the lake, and the sun shining on the houses to the left recalls Corot's oil sketches of Italian buildings. Corot's father bought a country house in 1817 at Ville d'Avray near Paris, the site of this painting. Throughout his long career he continued to paint the scenery in the area. Corot was one of the greatest landscape painters of the nineteenth century. His work

spanned practically the entire century, and he was inspired by and inspired generations of painters. His grounding in the academic tradition, together with his clear, fresh vision, have led him to be called the 'last of the Classical landscapists, and the first of the Impressionists'. Indeed, aspects of his later paintings can be seen in the work of Alfred Sisley and Claude Monet. Corot is thought to have painted around 3,000 canvases during his career.

► Boudin, Claude, Daubigny, Monet, Pissarro, Sisley

Jean-Baptiste-Camille Corot. b Paris, 1796. **d** Paris, 1875. **Ville d'Avray**. c1867/70. Oil on canvas. **h**49 × **w**65 cm. **h**19½ × **w**25½ in.
National Gallery of Art, Washington, DC

...hrist illuminates this painting with a divine light, a light so ...right that the woman at his feet has to shield her eyes from ...s glare. The asymmetrical composition of the scene is full of ...ovement. The staff of the shepherd leads the viewer's eye ...to the composition, directing it up towards the angels, who ... turn point down towards the child. This vibrant picture is ...pical of Correggio's late style. The movement and drama ...f the work look forward to the seventeenth-century Baroque ...yle. Best known for his paintings executed in cupolas and the

ceilings of churches, Correggio aimed to give the viewer the sensation of looking up into the glory of Heaven. One of his greatest works is a fresco on the inside of the dome of the church of St John the Evangelist, Parma, which is a dizzying mass of swirling figures. Correggio worked for most of his life in Parma, where he was one of the city's outstanding painters.

► Caravaggio, Carracci, Elsheimer, Parmigianino

...orreggio (Antonio Allegri). **b** Correggio, c1489. **d** Correggio, 1534. **The Nativity**. 1530. Oil on panel. **h**256 × **w**188 cm. ...00¾ × **w**74 in. Staatliche Kunstsammlungen, Dresden

129

Del Cossa Francesco

May

It is May. Apollo the sun god sits atop a chariot, presiding over courtiers, cherubs and gentlemen. The nudes below represent the astrological sign of Gemini. This pageant is one in a series of 12 frescos that cover the walls of the Sala dei Mesi ('room of the months') in the palace of the Duke Borso d'Este in Ferrara. Cossa was commissioned with other artists to depict the activities of the Court throughout the year by using astrological signs and deities. The fresco is painted in bright colours, in a slightly unrealistic style that is typical of Cossa and his fellow artists of that area. The principles of perspective, important to Florentine art of that time, do not seem to have been used. We know that Cossa, upset that he had been underpaid for his work on the fresco cycle, lodged a letter of complaint with the Duke. He subsequently left Ferrara and spent the rest of his days in Bologna.

► Limbourg, Mantegna, Piero della Francesca

Francesco del Cossa. b Ferrara, c1435. **d** Bologna, c1478. **May.** 1470s. Fresco. **h**216 × **w**320 cm. **h**85 × **w**126 in. Palazzo Schifanoia, Ferrara

In May 1854 Courbet arrived at Montpellier as the guest of Alfred Bruyas, an important patron and collector of the arts. Courbet has shown himself with a walking-stick and knapsack at the moment he was met on the road by his host, his servant and dog. Courbet's choice of subject, painted with stark realism and honesty, caused a great stir when the painting was exhibited at the Paris World Exhibition of 1855. Soon Courbet was heralded as the champion of a new, anti-intellectual type of art that was free from the shackles of academic history and religious painting. In turning away from literary subjects to the natural world around him, Courbet was an important influence on Édouard Manet and the Impressionists. When asked to include angels in a painting for a church, he is said to have replied, 'I have never seen angels. Show me an angel and I will paint one.'

► Daubigny, Manet, Millet, T Rousseau

Gustave Courbet. b Ornans, 1819. d Tour de Peitz, 1877. **Bonjour, Monsieur Courbet**. 1854. Oil on canvas. h129 × w149 cm. 50¾ × w58¾ in. Musée Fabre, Montpellier

131

Cozens John Robert

Between Chamonix and Martigny

A traveller on horseback and his companion cross a pass above the tree-line in the French Alps. Their diminutive size and inconsequence are stressed by the overhanging rock above them and the monumentality of the spiked, snowy summit of the Aiguille Verte. From 1776 to 1779 Cozens travelled through Switzerland to Italy via the Alps and was overawed by the all-powerful presence of these mountains. A melancholy and poetic painter, Cozens' restricted palette of subdued colours evokes the magnitude of space and the unassailability of nature. Cozens is considered one of the most talented English landscape painters of the eighteenth century. He had a marked influence on J M W Turner and John Constable; the latter claimed that he was the 'greatest genius that ever touched landscape'. Cozens painted landscapes in watercolour almost exclusively; he is known to have executed only two works in oil, one of which is now lost

► Church, Constable, Friedrich, J Martin, Turner

John Robert Cozens. b London, 1752. **d** London, 1797. **Between Chamonix and Martigny**. c1776/9. Watercolour on paper. **h**43.5 × **w**61.6 cm.
h17⅛ × **w**24¼ in. Private collection

Cragg Tony

Eroded Landscape

The artist has concocted an urban landscape out of a collection of containers of frosted glass. The group of objects has been arranged to evoke feelings of both familiarity and strangeness. The glass shelf could be found in any home. It too might be displaying objects that mean something to their owner, but not to the viewer. The two large vases at the bottom right and left support the structure and give the composition amazing symmetry and stability. The entire composition takes on the feel of a Greek temple, so stabilizing is their influence. Cragg has specialized in the arrangement of industrial objects. His works are an exploration of the space between reality and the imagination. His compositions frequently evoke the idea of consumer waste, yet they are often arranged with a delicate sense of poetry, and a sensitivity to the beauty of still life.

► Bourgeois, Caro, Deacon, Morandi, Smith

Tony Cragg. b Liverpool, 1949. **Eroded Landscape**. 1992. Glass. **h**43 × **w**132 cm. **h**16⅞ × **w**51⅞ in. Lisson Gallery, London

Venus wears only an elaborately jewelled hairnet and necklaces. She is coyly holding a diaphanous veil and looks out seductively at the viewer. Her body is idealized, perhaps because artists at this time rarely used live female models. Nude women were not often shown unless they appeared in a narrative scene or as mythical goddesses. Cranach seems to have ignored the Classical spirit of the day, and for this reason his nudes sometimes seem almost primitive. The choice of a mythological rather than a religious subject for this picture may have been because the patron was Protestant. We know little about Cranach other than that his influence in Protestant Germany was widespread. He seemed to appear suddenly, and produced his best work early in his long career, thereafter leading the easy life of a Court painter. He is called Lucas the Elder because he was the first in a dynasty of artists who carried on his traditions and style.

► Baldung, Dürer, Grünewald, Leighton

Lucas Cranach the Elder. b Kronach, 1472. **d** Weimar, 1553. **Venus**. 1532. Oil on panel. **h**37 × **w**25 cm. **h**14½ × **w**9⅞ in.
Städelsches Kunstinstitut, Frankfurt

Cuyp Aelbert

Peasants and Cattle by the River Merwede

This peaceful country scene is bathed in the golden glow of evening sunlight. The warm light permeates every detail of the composition and creates a luminous effect, very different from the cool blues and greens of Cuyp's contemporaries such as Meindert Hobbema. The apparently random placement of the animals was in fact closely studied by the artist in order to show the play of light and shade on the cows, which almost appear to radiate the light of the sun. Cuyp is considered one of the most important seventeenth-century Dutch landscape painters and was influenced by Jacob van Ruisdael and Jan van Goyen in their close scrutiny of nature. He is particularly admired for his river and town views, which he painted mainly in and around his native Dordrecht. Cuyp's landscapes were first appreciated and bought by British collectors in the late eighteenth century. As a result he has since then had an incalculable effect on British art.

► Bierstadt, Claude, Van Goyen, Hobbema, Ruisdael

Aelbert Cuyp. b Dordrecht, 1620. **d** Dordrecht, 1691. **Peasants and Cattle by the River Merwede.** c1658–60. Oil on panel. **h**38.1 × **w**50.8 cm. **h**15 × **w**20 in. National Gallery, London

Dalí Salvador

Lobster Telephone

A plaster lobster has been attached to the receiver of a telephone; a slight modification has turned an everyday object into something ludicrous. An incessant showman, and outspoken member of the Surrealist group, Dalí promoted the idea of absurdity and the role of the unconscious in art. He also drew close analogies between food and sex, and in the current example he intentionally positioned the genitalia of the lobster in line with the mouthpiece of the receiver. Whilst he made a variety of Surrealist objects, the artist is best known for his meticulously worked paintings in which dream-like scenarios become unnervingly vivid. Dalí was also involved in the production of a number of films, working on projects with Luis Buñuel, Alfred Hitchcock and Walt Disney. The artist produced several versions of the *Lobster Telephone*. The example below belonged to Dalí's important English patron, Edward James.

▶ Broodthaers, Cattelan, Duchamp, Magritte, Oldenburg

Salvador Dalí. b Figueres, 1904. **d** Figueres, 1989. **Lobster Telephone**. 1938. Mixed media, including steel, plaster, rubber and resin. **h**17.8 × **w**33 × **d**17.8 cm. **h**7 × **w**13 × **d**7 in. Tate, London

Daubigny Charles-François

The Lock at Optevoz

In this quiet contemplation of nature, a shepherdess with her dog is attending to a herd of cows by a lock. It is painted with a smooth, creamy technique and predominantly cool tones. This dreamy landscape retains its freshness by Daubigny's close observation of nature; indeed, he executed a full-sized sketch of the scene on site. In this way, he was one of the earliest to paint outdoors (*en plein air*), a method that the Impressionists were later to adopt and to develop to its furthest extreme. Daubigny's ideals and manner of painting were that of the Barbizon School, who favoured simple, rustic scenes, painted with vigour and immediacy. However, in changing this scene into one of atmospheric nostalgia Daubigny shows the influence of Camille Corot, who was a great friend. It was Daubigny's vision that later helped to pass on Corot's genius to the Impressionists.

► Bingham, Constable, Corot, Pissarro, T Rousseau

Charles-François Daubigny. b Paris, 1817. **d** Paris, 1878. **The Lock at Optevoz.** 1855. Oil on canvas. **h**92 × **w**162 cm. **h**36¼ × **w**63¾ in.
Musée des Beaux-Arts, Rouen

Daumier Honoré

The Print Collectors

Two elderly gentlemen are looking through a folder of prints in an art dealer's gallery. It is clear they are only pretending to be knowledgeable. The picture may have been the artist's own bitter comment on his inability to sell his works to the newly rich middle classes. Daumier was a supreme satirist, able to capture a person's character with a single stroke of his pen. He was well known and feared for his biting, sarcastic portrayals of leading figures of the day, as well as for his comments on political issues. Daumier had the rare gift of being able to express in pictures what would take hundreds of words. He was also a fine painter and sculptor. His cartoon lithographs, of which he produced around 4,000, were collected by artists such as Edgar Degas and may be compared with the work of Japanese calligraphers in their marvellously free handling.

► Degas, Hogarth, Hokusai, Toulouse-Lautrec, Utamaro

Honoré Daumier. b Marseille, 1808. **d** Valmondois, 1879. **The Print Collectors**. c1878. Ink and wash on paper. **h**35 × **w**32 cm. **h**13¾ × **w**12½ in. Victoria and Albert Museum, London

David Gérard

The Marriage Feast at Cana

This picture depicts an episode from the Bible, but all of its characters wear contemporary dress. The intricate details of their garments have been executed with minute precision. The donors who commissioned the painting have been included as guests at the feast, and can be seen kneeling at either side of the composition. It was usual in the Netherlands at this time to include the patrons in the painting, usually positioned as if kneeling in front of the altarpiece. David's rich colours and meticulous attention to detail are typical of northern painting

of the fifteenth and early sixteenth centuries. He was one of the masters of the time, and his compositions were copied repeatedly. His domestic scenes from the life of Christ were very popular, and he excelled in painting landscapes. Although the city of Bruges was in decline, David's workshop continued to be successful, supplying paintings to other countries.

▶ Bouts, P Bruegel, Van Eyck, Van der Goes, Memling

Gérard David. b Oudewater, c1450/60. **d** Bruges, 1523. **The Marriage Feast at Cana.** c1511. Oil on panel. **h**100 × **w**128 cm. **h**39¼ × **w**50½ in. Musée du Louvre, Paris

David Jacques-Louis

The Death of Marat

Jean-Paul Marat, one of the most passionate leaders of the French revolution, was a personal friend of David. He was stabbed to death in his bath, and this powerful image commemorates his murder. David has included only the most important elements to tell the story: the limp body, the bloody wound, the murder weapon and the letter which the murderer used to gain admission to the house. The bright lighting and contrasting plain, dark background highlight these details. David denounced the flowery Rococo style of the previous generation and led a return to Classical ideals. These were expressed with realism, a strong sense of composition and crisp handling of paint. David was also an active political revolutionary. He voted for the execution of Louis XVI and was an ardent supporter of Napoleon, whom he painted a number of times.

► Canova, Delacroix, Géricault, Ingres, Powers, Prud'hon

Jacques-Louis David. b Paris, 1748. **d** Brussels, 1825. **The Death of Marat.** 1793. Oil on canvas. **h**165 × **w**128.3 cm. **h**65 × **w**50½ in.
Musées Royaux des Beaux-Arts de Belgique, Brussels

Davis Stuart

Egg Beater No. 4

Ambiguous colours and shapes stand together in this delightful interplay of form, line and depth. Individual elements have been crystallized into an abstract whole created from blocks of flat colour and precise shapes. These invite the eye to zip around the canvas, following the angular movements of the egg beater. Much of the artist's work shows the influence of Cubist fragmented shapes, although Davis has developed these through the humour, zest and zany sounds of jazz, which he was passionate about. Painted

in 1927 and 1928, the 'Egg Beater Series' was based on the shapes of an egg beater, a fan and a pair of rubber gloves and demonstrated the first abstract compositions to be created by an American artist in ten years. Davis used contemporary American life as his subject matter, painting everything from petrol stations to landscapes.

► Braque, Feininger, B Nicholson, Picasso

Stuart Davis. b Philadelphia, PA, 1894. d New York, NY, 1964. **Egg Beater No. 4**. 1928. Oil on canvas. h68 × w97 cm.
27 × w38¼ in. Phillips Collection, Washington, DC

Deacon Richard

Fish Out of Water

Although this sculpture wears its construction on its sleeve – glue seeps out between layers of bent hardboard, and hundreds of rivets keep the whole from springing apart – its bulging, rib-like structure makes it distinctly organic, like a skeleton blown dry by a desert wind. One of a generation of sculptors who emerged in Britain in the 1980s, Deacon shares with them an interest in the objects of everyday life. His works use the construction techniques of boat-building or aviation. Like drawings in space, they trace outlines that expose frameworks, echoing engineering structures, and form curvilinear skins that enclose volumes, evoking pots and vessels. The body is also a constant motif. Often room-sized in scale, these sculptures suggest a repertory of body parts – from ribcages to genitalia. Rather than representing anything specific, Deacon's forms suggest images, emotions and memories which are, of course, different for each viewer.

► Bourgeois, Calder, Cragg, Serra, Smith

Richard Deacon. b Bangor, 1949. **Fish Out of Water**. 1986/7. Laminated hardboard. **h**245 × **w**350 cm. **h**96½ × **w**137¾ in.
Hirshhorn Museum and Sculpture Garden, Washington, DC

Degas Edgar

The Rehearsal

The artist is giving the viewer a secret glimpse into a rehearsal studio. We hide with him, in the shadows, watching the fluid movement of the slim, supple limbs and graceful bodies of the young ballet dancers. Degas has depicted the dancers from unusual angles and viewpoints. The composition appears totally random: the figure on the far right is cut off by the edge of the canvas, and truncated legs appear at the top of the stairs – had he waited only a few seconds more, it seems, another dancer would have walked into the picture. The painting is executed with vibrant, rapid strokes of pastel and some areas have merely been sketched in. The cool tones and lack of formality are refreshing. Degas' real interest was not in the ballerinas or ballets themselves; what fascinated him was the movement of abstract forms and shapes and the colours' graceful harmonies.

► Hiroshige, Laurencin, Toulouse-Lautrec, Whistler

Edgar Degas. b Paris, 1834. d Paris, 1917. The Rehearsal. 1873–4. Pastel on canvas. h59 × w83.8 cm. h23¹⁄₃ × w33 in. e Burrell Collection, Glasgow Museums and Art Galleries, Glasgow

143

Delacroix Eugène

The Battle of Taillebourg

So real is this scene of the historic victory of Louis IX over Henry III of England that the battlecries can almost be heard. Despite its vast size, the painting is compactly composed. A whirling mass of figures brings our attention to the focal point at the centre, dominated by Louis on his white horse. Executed with great gusto and passion in warm tones, it shows the Romantic spirit of Delacroix, who managed to free himself from the stiff Classicism that dominated French early nineteenth-century art. He was much inspired by Peter Paul Rubens' colour and loose brushwork, as well as by the landscapes of John Constable and Richard Parkes Bonington. At the Paris World Exhibition of 1855 Delacroix showed 36 canvases in one room. His journals provide a vivid commentary on the social, intellectual and artistic world of Paris in the first half of the nineteenth century.

► Bonington, Constable, Copley, Géricault, Rubens

Eugène Delacroix. b Charenton-St-Maurice, 1798. **d** Paris, 1863. **The Battle of Taillebourg**. 1835/7. Oil on canvas. **h**485 × **w**555 cm. **h**191 × **w**218½ in. Musée National et Domaine de Versailles, Versailles

Delaunay Robert

Homage to Blériot

In this apparently abstract composition, swirling spirals and rotating discs of colour form a lyrical pattern across the surface of a sheet of paper. On closer inspection we can see the Eiffel Tower on the right and the wings and propeller of an aeroplane on the left. These combine with the floating forms in the sky to celebrate the first flight across the English Channel, undertaken by Louis Blériot in 1909. Artists often used paper to jot down ideas and work out compositions. This watercolour is a preliminary sketch for a large collage of the same title that hangs in the Kunstmuseum in Basel. Delaunay developed his use of colour to create purely abstract paintings whose shapes and forms originated from his imagination and bore no relation to the tangible world. This style of painting, which was closely related to music, was called Orphism, a term invented by the poet Guillaume Apollinaire.

▶ Klee, Kupka, Marc, Nash, Seurat, Signac

Robert Delaunay. b Paris, 1885. d Montpellier, 1941. **Homage to Blériot**. 1914. Watercolour on paper. h78 × w67 cm. h30¾ × w26⅓ in.
Musée d'Art Moderne de la Ville de Paris, Paris

Delvaux Paul

Venus Asleep

In a moonlit town Venus lies asleep, watched over by a skeleton and a dressmaker's dummy. She lies with her legs open, dreaming of the seduction of Death. Perhaps it is the combination of youthful female beauty and death, of desire and horror, that makes this painting so disturbing. It was the hallmark of Surrealists like Delvaux to depict such strange, often beautiful, images that were inspired by dreams and the subconscious. Delvaux came late to Surrealism, after experimenting with Impressionism and then Expressionism.

He was popular in fashionable art circles after the Second World War, when Surrealism was in its heyday. Delvaux visited Italy in 1939 and was deeply impressed by Roman architecture. He is known for his dream-like images of beautiful, often naked, young women, usually positioned in front of meticulously rendered buildings.

► De Chirico, Cranach, Kahlo, Magritte, Tanguy

Paul Delvaux. b Antheit, 1897. **d** Knokke, 1994. **Venus Asleep.** 1944. Oil on canvas. **h**173 × **w**199 cm. **h**68 × **w**78⅜ in. Tate, London

The subject of this photograph appears to be the corner of a normal, albeit somewhat untidy, kitchen. There is however something peculiar about this scene. Everything is surprisingly untarnished and rather sterile. There are no numbers on the dials of the cooker, or words on the packaging of the bottle and carton. This is in fact a life-size cardboard-and-paper reconstruction of the kitchen belonging to the house where US troops discovered Saddam Hussein in hiding in 2003. The artist, who originally trained as a sculptor, based the carefully crafted three-dimensional model on an image that was published widely in the press. After it was photographed, the model was destroyed. Whilst the artist's process of working raises questions relating to our common acceptance of photography as a conveyor of reality, the current work also emphasises the banality of the setting for a historically important and politically charged event.

► Eggleston, Oldenburg, Struth, Wall

Thomas Demand. b Munich, 1964. **Kitchen**. 2004. Chromogenic colour print. h133 × w165 cm. h52⅜ × w65 in. Private collection

Denis Maurice

Portrait of Yvonne Lerolle

Three images of the same slender figure dominate this painting. The folds of her dress, and tree trunks, combined with the straight walkways, emphasize the vertical lines of the composition. Denis was a member of the Nabis, a group of painters who associated themselves with Paul Gauguin's expressive use of colour and rhythm. At the age of 20 Denis made the following statement, which is often considered the key to contemporary painting: 'Remember that a picture – before being a war horse or a nude woman or some anecdote – is essentially a flat surface covered with colours assembled in a certain order.' This way of looking at art eventually led to abstraction. The painting shown here confirms the artist's belief that a picture's subject matter is not as important as its composition. Paradoxically, Denis later attempted to revive religious painting – which is very dependent on subject matter – and in 1939 he published a history of religious art.

▶ Bonnard, Gauguin, Maillol, Mucha, Vallotton, Vuillard

Maurice Denis. b Granville, 1870. **d** Paris, 1943. **Portrait of Yvonne Lerolle**. 1897. Oil on canvas. **h**166 × **w**78 cm. **h**65⅜ × **w**30¾ in.
Musée Départemental du Prieuré, Saint-Germain-en-Laye

ight colours dance and shimmer on a dock on the River ames. The unmistakable silhouette of Tower Bridge is the distance. Derain has transformed the scene into a nbow of primary colours, which have been applied in ld blocks. His use of colour distorts the perspective and es the painting's surface a pulsating, vibrating unity. The ontaneous brushwork shows the artist's understanding of e techniques of Impressionism. Derain has made colour e picture's subject; the setting has become nearly irrelevant.

Along with a group of like-minded artists, Derain's inspiration came from a desire to work only with strong colours. This, plus the primitive power of the artists' style, caused a public outcry when they first exhibited. They were given the nickname 'Fauves', or wild beasts, as an expression of their 'wild' use of colour and unusual subject matter.

► Van Dongen, Van Gogh, Matisse, Signac, Vlaminck

Diebenkorn Richard

Ocean Park No. 67

Geometric lines define different sections of colour, evoking the local tones and light of the sea, sky and tawny hills of Ocean Park, California. The artist has created an illusion of space by making his canvas appear like a window through which to view the space contained within it. The painting hovers between a purely abstract composition of lines and colour, and a representation of sea and sky. This may be because up until this and similar paintings of the same subject, Diebenkorn's work was largely representational. The painting is close in feeling to the work of the Abstract Expressionists who were popular in the 1950s and whose use of expressive paint and colour would have had a great influence on Diebenkorn. There is also a tranquil, mystical quality to the picture, which is often found in Abstract Expressionist work, notably that of Mark Rothko, with whom Diebenkorn taught at the California School of Fine Arts in San Francisco from 1947 to 1950.

► Albers, Louis, Marin, Noland, Pollock, Rothko

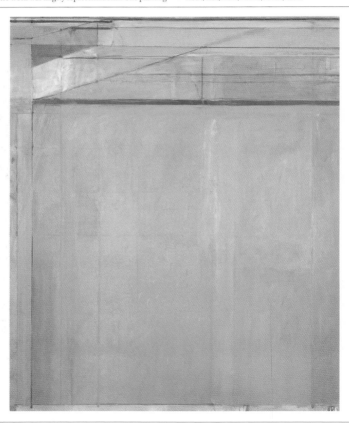

Richard Diebenkorn. b Portland, OR, 1922. **d** Berkeley, CA, 1993. **Ocean Park No. 67.** 1973. Oil on canvas. **h**254 × **w**205.5 cm. **h**100 × **w**81 in. Private collection deep red heart pulsates on a background of iridescent patchwork colours. This glitzy image glows with a strange appeal. It brightly captures the viewer's attention, despite looking like a lurid birthday card. Dine's roots lie in Abstract Expressionism, evident in his loose, free brushwork. He sometimes used real objects such as lawnmowers and toothbrushes, which he would attach to painted canvases. He often emphasized these objects with painted shadows, would write the name of the object beside it to draw attention to its everyday existence. Dine has experimented with a host of different styles and media, but is best known as a prominent figure of American Pop Art, a movement characterized by its irreverent use of familiar and banal images. His 'Heart' series of paintings, executed from the early 1980s, are said to represent the artist's personal expression and his belief in the ability of paint to convey feeling.

► Hamilton, Klee, Oldenburg, Rauschenberg, Warhol

Dine. b Cincinnati, OH, 1935. **My Name is Jim Dine 2.** 1992. Oil and enamel on canvas. **h**91.4 × **w**127 cm. **h**36 × **w**50 in. Pace Gallery, New York, NY

151

Dix Otto

Portrait of the Journalist Sylvia von Harden

The eccentric, severe-looking journalist Sylvia von Harden is portrayed with the essential accoutrements of a café society woman – a gilt chair, a marble-topped café table, elegant Russian cigarettes and a glass of Spritzer, the most fashionable drink in Berlin at the time. A feeling of tension and suspense is created by the use of vibrant colours, while a sexual element is hinted at by the stocking slipping down the journalist's leg. Considered to be one of Dix's finest, this portrait encapsulates the decadent glamour of Germany's

Weimar Republic. Its harsh, almost grotesque portrayal of its subject makes the painting an excellent example of New Objectivism (*Neue Sachlichkeit*). Dix's other renowned paintings form a protest against the horrors of war, and the often depict working people, cripples and whores. Because of his penetrating social criticism, Dix was suppressed by th Nazis. He began to paint again after the Second World War.

► Beckmann, Ensor, Grosz, Schad

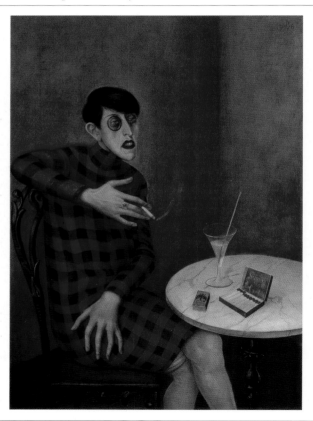

Otto Dix. b Gera, 1891. **d** Singen, 1969. **Portrait of the Journalist Sylvia von Harden**. 1926. Oil on panel. **h**120 × **w**88 cm. **h**47¼ × **w**34¾ in. Musée National d'Art Moderne, Paris

s through the intricate lace collar and cuffs, pearl buttons d gold embroidery, all topped by a proud gaze, that the portance and flamboyance of this person are conveyed. addition, the bust of Apollo and the rifle and dead hare w that this is a cultured man, known for his gentlemanly suits. Endymion Porter was Groom of the Bedchamber Charles I and can be seen to represent all of the elegance the English Court in the years before the Civil War. At his me, Dobson was considered to be the most accomplished

portrait painter in England. His contemporary Aubrey described him as 'the most excellent painter England hath yet bred'. His style was vigorous, with a strong English character. Dobson's ability to evoke sumptuous fabrics in paint is a hallmark of his style. Said to have been 'somewhat loose and irregular in his way of living', he was imprisoned for debt and died soon after his release.

► Batoni, Van Dyck, Hilliard, Kneller, Lely, Moroni

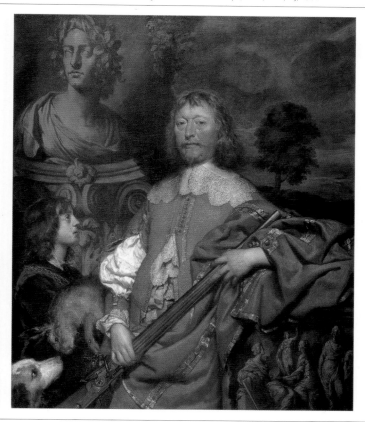

Van Doesburg Theo

Arithmetic Composition

A sense of movement and perspective is created in this picture by the sequence of black squares starkly painted against a white background. In fact, the artist has used a simple mathematical calculation – the sides of each square, and the distance between them, are half the size of the preceding square. Through the use of this simple square motif Van Doesburg was able to create a three-dimensional effect on a two-dimensional surface. The use of a mathematical formula perhaps reveals Van Doesburg's interest in architecture. The artist Piet Mondrian strongly influenced his work. In 1917 the two artists founded *De Stijl*, a magazine representing the work and ideas of that same group. De Stijl artists tended to use flat, primary colours which were arranged geometrically. Van Doesburg devoted much of his life to promoting De Stijl's ideas through his writing, lecturing, art and architecture.

► Albers, Lissitzky, Malevich, Moholy-Nagy, Mondrian

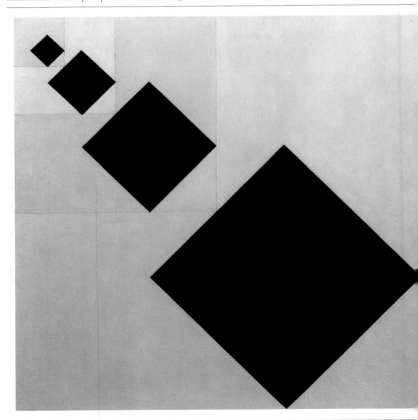

Theo van Doesburg. b Utrecht, 1883. **d** Davos, 1931. **Arithmetic Composition**. 1930. Oil on canvas. **h**101 × **w**101 cm. **h**40 × **w**40 in. Private collection

a canoe sits the ghostly figure of a long-haired, bearded
n. He looks towards us. The sea around him is impossibly
, the sky a vivid pink. On the horizon we see an island.
his the place from where the man has travelled? Was he
adrift? The eerie, spectral feeling of the composition is
anced by the artist's application of thin washes of paint.
some areas, the paint has been left to run down the canvas.
ilst the image of the canoe – a recurring motif in Doig's
ntings – has associations with his upbringing in Canada,

the artist recalls that he was first inspired to include it in his
work after watching the horror film *Friday the 13th*. The source
for the figure in this painting is taken from the cover of the
1972 album *Duane Allman: An Anthology*, which included
a photograph of the band's bassist sitting in a canoe. The
background is derived from a separate photograph depicting
Carrera, a prison island off the coast of Trinidad; a country
where the artist lived for a short time as a child.

► Bingham, Monet, Ruscha, Waterhouse

r Doig. b Edinburgh, 1959. **100 Years Ago**. 2000. Oil on canvas. **h**200 × **w**296 cm. **h**78⅞ × **w**116½ in. Museum of Contemporary Art,
ngeles, CA

155

Domenichino

The Sacrifice of Isaac

Abraham has been instructed by God to sacrifice his son Isaac as a test of his faith. The naked youth bravely accepts his fate as his father wields his sword in blind obedience. An angel intervenes, indicating that Abraham should offer the ram instead of Isaac. This dramatic scene is played out in the foreground of the picture so as to enhance the sense of immediacy. Abraham, the most important figure, dominates in his rich blue and red robes. Domenichino trained at the Carracci Academy in Bologna. He became a popular artist who was often commissioned to decorate the many palaces, villas and chapels that surrounded Rome. Although he worked within the Baroque period, with its characteristic swirls and painterly effects, Domenichino remained firmly Classical in his style. For this he met with hostility in Naples and had to leave the city, his many works unfinished.

► Carracci, Poussin, Reni, Vouet

Domenichino (Domenico Zampieri). b Bologna, 1581. **d** Naples, 1641. **The Sacrifice of Isaac.** c1620/1. Oil on canvas. **h**147 × **w**140 cm. **h**57¾ × **w**55 in. Museo del Prado, Madrid

Donatello

David

This statue of David shows the young hero in a dreamy, contemplative mood after slaying Goliath, whose head lies at his feet. The flowing naturalism of David's pose, his shy demeanour, and the sensual surface texture of the bronze combine to bring the statue to life. This ability to instil human emotion in Classical statues was Donatello's greatest gift. As one of a group of remarkable sculptors, architects and painters who brought about an artistic revolution in Florence, he is considered a founder of the Renaissance style. Donatello was a favourite artist of the famous patron Cosimo il Vecchio de' Medici. He was by far the leading Florentine sculptor before Michelangelo, and possibly the most innovative and influential of all Renaissance artists. His *David* was the first full-sized bronze nude to have been cast since Ancient times.

► Canova, Castagno, Ghiberti, Michelangelo, Powers

Donatello. b Florence, c1386. d Florence, 1466. **David**. c1433. Bronze. h159 cm. h62½ in. Museo Nazionale del Bargello, Florence

Van Dongen Kees

Portrait of Dolly

The artist's daughter is painted in flat, decorative sections of intense colour. The beauty of the child is conveyed in an exotic style. Her sensuality is evoked by her blackened, almond eyes and fiery red lips, echoed by the colour of the ribbon under her hat. Van Dongen was a master colourist, as demonstrated for instance in the delicate green tones used to construct Dolly's face. He was born in Holland but settled in Paris and took up French nationality in 1929. He was a member of various movements, including the Fauves and the Expressionists. The influence of both can be seen in his vibrant use of pure colour. Young, talented and precocious, from his early thirties Van Dongen enjoyed an extravagant lifestyle supported by the success he achieved. Some feel his great artistic talent was abused when he began to paint portraits of fashionable women, which soon became somewhat superficial.

► Gontcharova, Jawlensky, Matisse, Rouault, Vlaminck

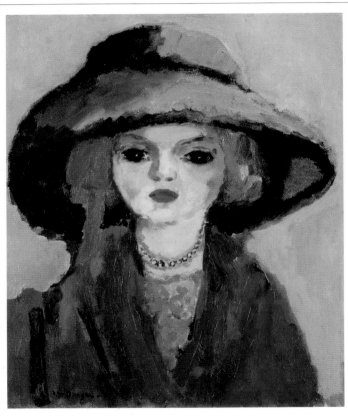

Kees van Dongen. b Delfshaven, 1877. **d** Monaco, 1968. **Portrait of Dolly.** c1911. Oil on canvas. **h**55 × **w**46 cm. **h**21⅔ × **w**18⅛ in. Private collectic gleaming armour and battalions of troops reinforce this image of a great military leader. As Duke of Ferrara, Alfonso led his troops in many battles against Papal and Venetian aggressors. In addition to controlling his army, Alfonso was also an enlightened patron of the arts who attempted to rival the Pope in his ambitious commissions from the greatest artists of the time. (Despite all his efforts, however, Alfonso was never able to secure Raphael or Michelangelo to fulfil any of his requests.) Dosso Dossi was principal Court painter

for the Este family and together with his brother Battista provided mainly mythologies, portraits and decorative frescos. The style of this portrait is reminiscent of Venetian art; it is in fact a derivation of a portrait of Alfonso by Titian. Influenced by the Venetians and by Correggio, Dossi later chose to paint mysterious exotic landscapes suffused with an unearthly, glowing light.

► Altdorfer, Correggio, Michelangelo, Raphael, Titian

Dosso Dossi (Giovanni Luteri). b Ferrara, c1490. d Ferrara, 1542. **Alfonso I d'Este**. After 1528. Oil on canvas. **h**147 × **w**113.5 cm. **h**57⅞ × **w**44¾ in. Galleria e Museo Estense, Modena

Elaborately composed, this small, intimate scene shows a young woman servant pouring water from a brass jug over a balustrade which also serves as a window framing the picture. The artist has paid meticulous attention to details such as the fraying cloth, the terracotta pot and the birdcage, giving the painting a gem-like quality. Dou was a pupil of Rembrandt, and it is possible to see the master's influence in some of Dou's earlier pictures. He delighted in depicting everyday or 'genre' scenes, which he filled with a wealth of closely observed detail – he would sometimes even use a magnifying glass to work. This interior, with its theatrical setting, recalls a type used in the Netherlands in the fifteenth century by Jan van Eyck, and was to be a starting point for Jan Vermeer and Pieter de Hooch. Dou was a prosperous and respected artist for much of his life. His workshop was filled with students, who continued producing works in his style until well into the eighteenth century.

► Van Eyck, De Hooch, Metsu, Rembrandt, Vermeer

Gerrit Dou. b Leiden, 1613. **d** Leiden, 1675. **Maidservant at a Window.** c1640. Oil on panel. **h**37 × **w**28 cm. **h**14½ × **w**11 in.
Museum Boymans-van Beuningen, Rotterdam

bright circle of colour, representing the moon, dominates his composition. A series of lines and tones surround it like the rings around the moon, or the layers of the imagination. Dark, brooding colours create an air of melancholy nostalgia flowing across this landscape of the soul. The canvas richly evokes feelings for the beauty of nature. Dove's work often suggests nature in a metaphysical, rather than a literal sense; the forms of natural objects are transformed into abstract representations. He wrote: 'I should like to take the wind and water and sand as a motif and work with them, but it has to be simplified in most cases to color and force lines just as music has done with sound.' Born in New York state he visited Europe in 1907–9 where he saw the work of the Fauvists. On his return to the USA he was to paint some of the first abstract paintings in modern art, certain aspects of which are similar to the work of Wassily Kandinsky.

► Heckel, Heron, Kandinsky, O'Keeffe, Vlaminck

Drouais François-Hubert

Madame de Pompadour at her Tambour Frame

Painted during the last year of her life, King Louis XV's mistress is shown as a cultured, matronly figure, her small dog testifying to her loyalty to the king. The books, prints and lute beside her indicate her sophisticated refinement, while her embroidery frame and the box of threads suggest she is a simple, uncomplicated woman, happiest at her sewing. Madame de Pompadour was anything but simple, however, and she controlled every aspect of her representations, commissioning portraits throughout her life that reflected

the way she wished to be seen. At the time Drouais was painting this likeness, she had been the king's mistress for almost twenty years, and while the relationship was no longer sexual, she still exercised considerable influence on Louis XV and, through him, on French politics. Acting as unofficial gatekeeper to the king, she often interviewed those who had business with him while working at her embroidery, a meaning that would not have been lost on contemporary viewers.

► Batoni, Ramsay, Reynolds, Rigaud, Romney, Stuart

François-Hubert Drouais. b Paris, 1727. d Paris, 1775. **Madame de Pompadour at her Tambour Frame**. 1763–4. Oil on canvas. h217 × w156.8 cm. h85½ × w61¾ in. National Gallery, London

Dubuffet Jean

Jazz Band (Dirty Style Blues)

The members of a jazz band line up across the picture in a static frieze. Apparently random colours have been applied in an unusual manner with a brush, and the surface of the painting has then been smeared, rubbed and incised to create the outlines of the players. The graffiti-like effect is amusing and enchanting, giving the picture a naive, childlike simplicity. Loosely allied to the Art Informel movement, Dubuffet believed there was more truth in the unspoiled, creative art of the insane and amateur than the professional artist. Indeed he coined the term Art Brut ('raw art'), to describe the kind of art created by psychotics, children and untrained people. Dubuffet's pieces were often mocked by both the public and art critics, and were even physically attacked in an exhibition in Paris in 1946. Despite this adverse reaction, he has become a widely respected artist.

► Appel, Basquiat, Fautrier, Tàpies, Twombly

Jean Dubuffet. b Le Havre, 1901. d Paris, 1985. **Jazz Band (Dirty Style Blues)**. 1944. Oil on canvas. h97 × w130 cm. h38¼ × w51⅛ in. Private collection

Duccio

The Rucellai Madonna

The traditional subject for altarpieces was an image of the Virgin and Child enthroned, surrounded by angels looking upon them with devotion. Duccio has used this same image, but has included a degree of tenderness that is unusual in paintings of the thirteenth century. Sienese paintings of this time were characterized by their attention to line and colour. Here, the line is expressed by the elongated forms and the gold edge of the Virgin's drapery. The angels' gowns, in particular, exhibit the artist's skilled application of colour.

Duccio was the leading painter of Siena during the thirteenth and fourteenth centuries. He was unequalled in the art of panel painting, in which he excelled as a narrator. The fact that this painting was commissioned by a Florentine confraternity when Florence and Siena were traditional enemies attests to Duccio's high reputation outside his native town.

► Campin, Cimabue, Giotto, Lorenzetti, Martini

Duccio di Buoninsegna. b Siena, 1255. **d** Siena, c1319. **The Rucellai Madonna**. 1285. Tempera on panel. **h**450 × **w**290 cm. **h**177⅛ × **w**114⅛ in. Galleria degli Uffizi, Florence

Fountain

This work is a replica of a porcelain urinal which was originally purchased by the artist in 1917 from a plumbing supply firm in New York. Duchamp simply signed the object with the pseudonym R Mutt, then entered it for an art exhibition. The bizarre item exemplifies the notion of taking a commonplace object out of its customary setting and placing it in a new and unfamiliar one. It was through this work that Duchamp first defined the concept of the 'ready-made' or 'found object' – an idea which has influenced countless artists since. In defending the original sculpture in 1917 Duchamp challenged traditional preconceptions of what art is. He stated that it was not important whether or not 'Mr Mutt' had *made* the work with his own hands; what mattered was that he had chosen it. Therefore the creation was not important but the idea and selection was.

► Beuys, Broodthaers, Johns, Koons, Oldenburg

Marcel Duchamp. b Blainville, 1887. d Neuilly, 1968. **Fountain**. 1917/64. Porcelain. **h**33.5 cm. **h**14 in. Indiana University Art Museum, Bloomington, IN

Dufy Raoul

The Paddock

The colourful atmosphere of the racecourse has been captured in this paddock scene. Dufy has painted elegant ladies with parasols, gentlemen in top hats, jockeys on horseback and a sailor propping his bicycle against a tree. In the background, a deep blue sea is littered with cruise-liners and yachts. This is the world of riches and relaxation. From the beginning of the 1920s Dufy visited racecourses regularly with the famous dress designer Paul Poiret. It was Poiret who urged Dufy to study the smart clothes of the fashionable

ladies who came to the racecourses to be seen. Although he had earlier been influenced by the Impressionists, the Fauvis and the Cubists, this painting illustrates Dufy's personal mode of expression in the light strokes of outline and vibra colours. His palette often recalls the French Riviera and Mediterranean. Dufy also designed textiles and painted one of the largest murals ever, for the 1938 Paris Exhibition.

► Derain, Van Dongen, Laurencin, Matisse, Vlaminck

Raoul Dufy. **b** Le Havre, 1877. **d** Forcalquier, 1953. **The Paddock**. c1926. Oil on canvas. **h**81 × **w**125 cm. **h**31⅞ × **w**49¼ in. Private collection

his volcanic portrait, shown in extreme close-up – larger
an life, like a face on a movie screen – seethes with
xpressive power. Only the mouth and eyes are fully realized;
ae face that frames them is rendered almost abstract, as the
ewer's gaze is drawn to these symbols of female sensuality.
a colours as unrealistic as those of the early twentieth-
entury Fauve artists, the portrait is confrontational. The
oman's gaze is direct, and her finger touches a plump
o suggestively. Marlene Dumas has been described as an

'intellectual expressionist', her style a mixture of strongly
gestural painting and the cerebral detachment of Conceptual
art, of unapologetic eroticism and profound feminism.
Her depictions of women are often based on magazine
photographs or Old Master paintings, re-processed through
a contemporary view and represented in fluid, loosely applied
paint, mixed with translucent washes. Using bold contours,
the boundaries are blurred between painting and drawing.

► Close, Derain, Van Dongen, Jawlensky, Warhol

Dürer Albrecht

Self-portrait with Gloves

The technique of placing the sitter's arm on a sill was a well-known method of creating the illusion of proximity between the viewer and the artist's model. Dürer may have learned this visual trick from works such as Leonardo's *Mona Lisa*, which he would have seen while travelling in Italy. Dürer painted many self-portraits, a subject that was not common at the time and which can be seen as a promotion of the artist's status in society. If a patron can be reproduced in paint, why not an artist? The landscape seen through the open window (as on the right here) was a feature often used by northern artists such as Jan van Eyck and Robert Campin. An extraordinary and prolific artist, Dürer revolutionized northern European art by combining different aspects of Netherlandish and Italian art. He is also well-known for his woodcuts and engravings which spread his fame far and wide in sixteenth-century Europe.

► Campin, Van Eyck, Grünewald, Leonardo, Rosa

Albrecht Dürer. b Nuremberg, 1471. **d** Nuremberg, 1528. **Self-portrait with Gloves**. 1498. Oil on panel. **h**52 × **w**41 cm. **h**20½ × **w**16⅛ in. Museo del Prado, Madrid spotless armour, a steady gaze and a regal demeanour – it is apparent that this is a man of great importance. As painter to Charles I, the artist was commissioned to convey the king's majesty to all who saw it. After studying with Peter Paul Rubens in Antwerp, Van Dyck went to London and then on to Italy. Here he adopted a more elegant manner of painting, which he kept all his life. It was in Italy, too, that Van Dyck created a style that began the great tradition of English portrait painting. These works were usually of noblemen

with proud postures and slim figures. He was often accused of flattering his sitters, but not all were pleased. The Countess of Sussex reacted to her portrait by saying she felt 'very ill-favorede', and 'quite out of love with myself, the face is so bige and so fate that it pleases me not at all. It lokes lyke on the windes puffinge – but truly I think tis lyke the originale.'

► Clouet, Dobson, Gainsborough, Lely, Rigaud, Rubens, Titian

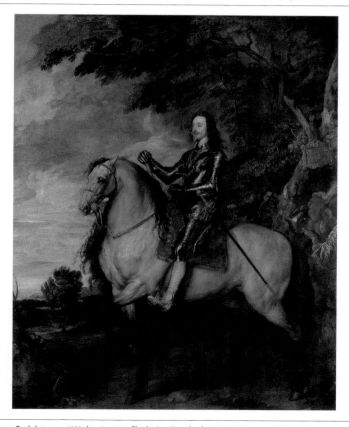

Eakins Thomas

Between Rounds

It is almost impossible not to witness the cheers of the crowd, the smell of cigar smoke and the sweat of the boxer coming from this painting. The fighter, caught in the few moments between rounds, is the focus of the work. Eakins was fascinated with the human form. He often used sporting events such as boxing and rowing to capture the nude in motion. As a teacher he caused an uproar by insisting that his art students should draw from the nude. He had travelled in Europe, and was influenced by the Spanish Realists Diego

Velázquez and Jusepe Ribera. It was through these artists in particular that he learned to paint with such vibrant realism. He also often exploited the effects of light and dark to produce a feeling of drama, much as Rembrandt had. Eakins paintings were largely unappreciated during his lifetime, but he received recognition for his realist approach from the generation that followed.

► Bellows, Rembrandt, Ribera, Velázquez

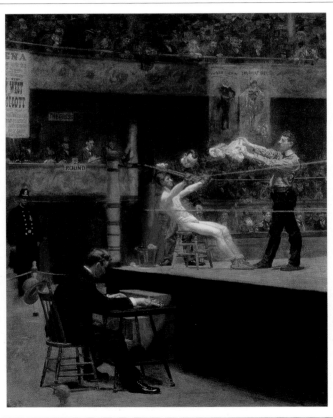

Thomas Eakins. b Philadelphia, PA, 1844. d Philadelphia, PA, 1916. **Between Rounds**. 1899. Oil on canvas. h127 × w101.5 cm. h50⅛ × w39⅞ in. Philadelphia Museum of Art, Philadelphia, PA

From the ceiling of a red room hangs a light bulb, white cables spread outwards towards the walls. Eggleston considers this photograph to be one of his most difficult and powerful works. The subject could hardly be more mundane. Yet there a painting-like quality to the composition, reminiscent a canvas by Henri Matisse or Barnett Newman. Although was inspired early in his career by the black-and-white photographs of Robert Frank and Henri Cartier-Bresson, the mid-1960s Eggleston started to experiment with colour photography. An important development came with his adoption of dye-transfer printing – a technique that had been predominantly used in commercial design. This enabled him to produce prints with an intense saturation of colour. Often discovering an aesthetic value in the banal and the commonplace, Eggleston's images have helped to establish colour photography as a recognized fine art medium.

► Cartier-Bresson, Frank, Gursky, Matisse, Newman

lliam Eggleston. b Memphis, TN, 1939. **Greenwood, Mississippi**. 1973. Dye-transfer print. h32 × w48.3 cm. h12⅝ × w19 in.
seum of Modern Art, New York, NY

Eliasson Olafur

The Weather Project

In a vast interior, groups of people are drawn towards a large solar disc suspended on the wall high above them. An orange glow radiates throughout the room. This vision of a futuristic industrial landscape is in fact a large-scale optical illusion installed in the Turbine Hall of London's Tate Modern. To create the sun-like effect, Eliasson positioned a semi-circular arrangement of powerful monochromatic lights below hundreds of mirrors – these were carefully offset to produce a slightly jagged reflected image. An atmospheric mist was also pumped into the room. The work was inspired by the artist's realization that, in the urban environment, people's experience of weather was one of the few direct encounters that they still have with nature. Employing architects, artists, technicians and art historians, in 1995 Eliasson established a studio in Berlin to act as a laboratory for spatial research.

► Graham, J Martin, Monet, Turner, Vasarely

Olafur Eliasson. b Copenhagen, 1967. **The Weather Project**. 2003. Mixed media. **h**35 m. **h**115 ft. Tate, London (now dismantled)

Elsheimer Adam

The Stoning of Saint Stephen

St Stephen died without resistance to demonstrate that his devotion to Christ was more important than his own life. Martyrs can be killed in many different ways; this martyr was stoned to death. Here, a ray of heavenly light shines down on him, encouraging him in his plight. Elsheimer has paid great attention to detail, particularly to the musculature of the human body. The flying figure on the left and the standing man on the right gave the artist an opportunity to paint figures in action. A German painter and printmaker, Elsheimer travelled to Italy in 1598 where he was strongly influenced by Venetian artists. He combined their use of colour with his own understanding of light and emphasis on realism to create such works as this. Many of his paintings were copied by other printmakers and his influence stretched well into the seventeenth century.

▶ Altdorfer, Bosch, Caravaggio, Dürer, Michelangelo

Adam Elsheimer. b Frankfurt, 1578. d Rome, 1610. **The Stoning of Saint Stephen**. c1603-4. Oil on copper. **h**34.7 × **w**28.6 cm. **h**13⅝ × **w**11¼ in. National Gallery of Scotland, Edinburgh

Ensor James

Two skeletons fight in futile combat for the body of a hanged man suspended above them. Masked figures stare at the wretched and pitiful scene. We are invited to gaze with astonishment at this extraordinary and dismal spectacle. The grotesque nature of this painting reflects the artist's own vision: a world ruled by absurdity, in which disconnected thoughts and futile actions play too large a part. With its strong emotional impact and dramatic imagery, Ensor's art was much admired by artists of the German Expressionist movement. He exerted a particularly powerful influence on Emil Nolde, who visited him in 1911. His works often included masks, skeletons, and gruesome and grotesque figures. His paintings and graphic works were very satirical, with a biting, sometimes bitter, humour. Born of English parents, Ensor lived in isolation in Ostend, becoming a Belgian national in 1929.

► Beckmann, Bosch, Kokoschka, Nolde, Pechstein

James Ensor. b Ostend, 1860. **d** Ostend, 1949. **Skeletons Fighting for the Body of a Hanged Man**. 1891. Oil on canvas. **h**59 × **w**74 cm. **h**23¼ × **w**29⅛ in. Koninklijk Museum voor Schone Kunsten, Antwerp

Epstein Sir Jacob

Elemental

The pent-up energy of primitive man is conveyed by the tense, compact form of this hunched-up body and by the way the head is positioned as though in surrender to the unknown powers above. The sculpture embodies a poignant juxtaposition: of terror or death, suggested by the frozen grip of the hands, and unborn life, suggested by the figure's foetal position. The strength of the sculpture lies in its deliberately unfinished state, with the chisel and file marks still visible on the unveined alabaster surface. Epstein developed his own unique style, which illustrates direct inspiration from the Ancient and primitive sculpture which he would have seen during visits to the Louvre museum in Paris. Throughout his life Epstein worked in two ways, carving in stone and executing portraits in bronze of a more descriptive nature. His most renowned bronze is a bust of Sir Winston Churchill.

► Brancusi, Gaudier-Brzeska, Moore, Rodin

Sir Jacob Epstein. b New York, NY, 1880. d London, 1959. **Elemental**. 1932. Alabaster. h81 cm. h31⅞ in. Private collection

Ernst Max

Forest and Dove

The all-enveloping and stifling nature of this forest, in which the only sign of life is a solitary bird trapped in a cage, evokes a feeling of simultaneous enchantment and fear. The tangled trees seem petrified and loom over the bird in wild and irrepressible growth. Like many artists of his time, Ernst worked in many media. He produced an enormous collection of collages and introduced a technique called *frottage*. Similar to brass-rubbing, this involved laying a sheet of paper on a rough surface and drawing on the paper so as to reveal the relief of the object beneath. Because the artist had no control over the picture he was creating, *frottage* was also seen as a method of gaining access to the subconscious. The 'chance' element of this technique, together with the hallucinatory quality of the image it has created, make the picture a fine example of Surrealist preoccupations.

► Dali, Gorky, Lam, Miró, H Rousseau, Tanguy

Max Ernst. b Bruhl, 1891. d Paris, 1976. **Forest and Dove**. 1927. Oil on canvas. h100 × w81.5 cm. h39½ × w32 in. Tate, London

Is it real – or is it art? This street scene, complete with advertising billboards, is a celebration of American popular culture. Its startling realism is a surprise and delight. Estes did not invent the subject matter – he simply chose it, photographed it, and then reproduced it exactly as it appeared in the photograph. Estes' hyper-real art was in many ways a reaction to Abstract Expressionism, a movement that had dominated the American art scene since the 1950s. The New Realism and Photorealism movements, born in the late 1960s,

said something very different. Gone was emotion, colour, poetry – and in came reality. By using photographs, Estes and other artists perfected their work to the point where reality and illusion became one. What Estes chose to portray, was a world familiar to millions of Americans. In this way the everyday was transformed into fine art.

► Hamilton, Lichtenstein, Richter, Ruscha, Sherman, Warhol

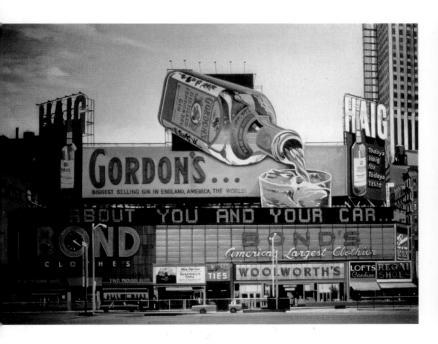

Richard Estes. b Kewanee, IL, 1936. **Gordon's Gin**. 1968. Oil on board. h62.2 × w81.3 cm. h24½ × w32 in. Private collection

Etty William

Hero and Leander

Each night Leander would swim across a stretch of sea to meet his lover Hero, a priestess of Aphrodite. She would guide him by holding up a lighted torch. One night, during a storm, Leander drowned. The grief-stricken Hero threw herself from a tower. Here, the two dead lovers are shown in their tragic, final embrace, as their lives drift away. The tones of their glowing, sensual skin are set off against a sombre sea and storm clouds. The black hair and drapery of Hero seem to merge into the dark shadows. Etty's imagination was fired by an obsession with the nude, which he studied and painted throughout his career. His paintings often evoke the sensuous poses and rich colouring of Titian and Peter Paul Rubens. Etty frequently used Classical mythology and allegory as a means of expression. His works were particularly admired by Eugène Delacroix and other Romantic painters.

► W Blake, Delacroix, Géricault, Rubens, Titian

William Etty. b York, 1787. **d** York, 1849. **Hero and Leander.** 1828-9. Oil on canvas. **h**77 × **w**95 cm. **h**30½ × **w**37¼ in. Private collection

This study of a poor sharecropper's cabin exhibits the careful lighting and superb framing of Evans's documentary oeuvre. The photograph was taken during the summer of 1936, when Evans (then employed by Farm Security Administration) and the journalist James Agee spent several weeks with three sharecropper families in the American south. The resulting images and essay were eventually published as a book, *Let Us Now Praise Famous Men*, which influenced generations of Depression-era and later photographers and artists, from William Eggleston and Stephen Shore to Andy Warhol. The picture recalls Agee's observation that household objects 'are set very plainly and squarely discrete from one another', giving each possession value and strength. Evans insisted that his purpose as a photographer was to reveal, not to comment, and he refused to politicize or patronize his subjects. He took them on their own terms, without vanity or self-pity, and gave them a dignity and grace.

► Atget, Eggleston, Frank, Shore, Struth

Walker Evans. b St Louis, MO, 1903. d New Haven, CT, 1975. **Kitchen Corner, Tenant Farmhouse, Hale County, Alabama**. 1936. Gelatin silver print. **h**19.5 × **w**16 cm. **h**7¾ × **w**6¼ in. Metropolitan Museum of Art, New York, NY

Van Eyck Jan

The Arnolfini Portrait

An Italian merchant living in Bruges, Giovanni Arnolfini, holds the hand of Jeanne de Chenany, his young bride. The small dog, the slippers on the floor, the fruit on the window sill, the single candle, the rosary hanging on a nail, the floor boards and carpet have all been painted with jewel-like precision. Van Eyck was probably asked to paint this picture to commemorate this happy union and, like a witness in a wedding ceremony, he has written the words *Johannes de eyck fuit hic* ('Jan van Eyck was present') on the far wall. In the

mirror beneath, the backs of the betrothed couple are visible and a third figure, who is possibly the painter, witnesses the event. The painting's smooth, enamel-like surface was achieved by applying numerous glazes of pigment mixed with linseed oil. It was then coated with varnish. Using this technique, Jan van Eyck and his brother Hubert are traditionally credited with having 'invented' oil painting. The Van Eycks' style was often imitated, but never surpassed.

► Campin, Limbourg, Memling, Van der Weyden, Wood

Jan van Eyck. Active in The Hague, 1422. **d** Bruges, 1441. **The Arnolfini Portrait**. 1434. Oil on panel. **h**81.8 × **w**59.7 cm. **h**32¼ × **w**23½ in. National Gallery, London

Fabritius Carel

The Goldfinch

Set against a creamy background, a little goldfinch rests on a green perch. The goldfinch seems so real, it is tempting to reach out and touch it. The simplicity and intimacy of this small painting almost cloud the skill with which it is painted. Fabritius was the most brilliant of Rembrandt's pupils. However, he reversed his master's technique of painting light against dark, and instead painted dark objects on a light background. Fabritius paid special attention to visual accuracy. This particular feature of his work may have influenced the artist Jan Vermeer, who was his student. The careful composition of this work and its startling simplicity also give a foretaste of Vermeer's work. Tragically, Fabritius died during the explosion of a gunpowder store in Delft while working on a portrait. The painting shown here is one of a small number of his works that have survived.

► Audubon, Claesz, De Heem, Kalf, Rembrandt, Vermeer

Carel Fabritius. b Middenbeemster, 1622. **d** Delft, 1654. **The Goldfinch.** 1654. Oil on panel. **h**34 × **w**23 cm. **h**13¼ × **w**9⅛ in. Mauritshuis, The Hague

181

Fantin-Latour Henri

White and Pink Roses

The roses in this picture seem to glow against the dark background. These are cut flowers that because of their short lives are often seen as symbols of mortality. Each petal has been formed by a thick stroke of paint. The variation of colour has been created by the artist applying pink and white colours to the brush without blending. Fantin-Latour began his career as a traditional painter, accepted by the Parisian Salon. His romantic vision, however, caused him to move away from the academic approach. By 1863 he was exhibiting along with his Impressionist friends, including Édouard Manet. Besides his still lifes, Fantin-Latour is well known for his groups of figures. One such picture shows Manet and his artist friends grouped around a portrait of Eugène Delacroix. Fantin-Latour also did a series of lithographs illustrating the music of Wagner and other Romantic composers.

▶ Bazille, Courbet, Delacroix, Manet, Ruysch, Whistler

Henri Fantin-Latour. b Grenoble, 1836. **d** Buré, 1904. **White and Pink Roses.** 1890. Oil on canvas. **h**37 × **w**32 cm. **h**14½ × **w**12½ in. Private collection

Fautrier Jean

Sarah

The irregular-shaped, thickly textured central section of this picture shows a distorted female form. The painting was made from paper glued to the canvas, over which the artist applied a thick paste with a spatula. He then coated these areas with coloured powder bonded to the surface with varnish. Fautrier began to work in this unique way during his most creative period, during which his images were largely of the horrors of war. Perhaps he developed this time-consuming and problematic technique in order to express more forcefully his

feelings about the state of the world. The free brushwork and the heavily textured surface illustrate the artist's connection with the Art Informel school of painting. Born in France, Fautrier spent his childhood in London and enrolled at the Royal Academy School at the age of 14. He was very active throughout his career and his varied work includes drawings, etchings and sculptures.

► Burri, Dubuffet, Ingres, Modigliani, Poliakoff, Tàpies

Feininger Lyonel

Sailing Boats

Overlapping triangles of colour echo the sails of the boats creating a rhythmic pattern and sense of speed and space. Although born in New York, Feininger's development as an artist took place mainly in Europe. While in Paris he exhibited several paintings and became aware of Cubism. He met the artist Robert Delaunay, who became a major influence on his work. The two artists shared an interest in the emotional effects of colour, as well as in urban architecture as a subject for painting. In 1913 Feininger exhibited with the Blaue Reiter group, which included Wassily Kandinsky among others. A few years later he joined the Bauhaus school, which was closed by the Nazis in 1935. At this point Feininger returned to the USA. He was interested in many aspects of modern life, but favoured architectural and marine views for their geometrical quality.

► Balla, Delaunay, Gris, Hodler, Kandinsky, Picasso

Lyonel Feininger. b New York, NY, 1871. **d** New York, NY, 1956. **Sailing Boats**. 1929. Oil on canvas. **h**43 × **w**72 cm. **h**17 × **w**28¼ in.
Detroit Institute of Arts, Detroit, MI

Flavin Dan

Red, white and blue: the colours of the French Republic glare at us from industrially manufactured fluorescent tubes which have been assembled into a three-dimensional, pillar-like construction. The work was executed to celebrate the bicentenary of the French revolution. Its full name is *Untitled (To the Citizens of the Republic of France on the 200th Anniversary of their Revolution), 3*. By using objects with the same shape, the sculpture takes on the appearance of a fragment of a monument, or a 'pseudo-monument',

as Flavin called his works. The use of coloured light instead of paint adds another dimension. There is neither a frame nor any hard edges to mark its limits. The light radiates beyond the work, redefining the space in which it is shown and posing the question, where does the art begin and where does it end? This use of light, space and identical, geometric objects, connects Flavin's work with the Minimalist movement.

▶ Buren, Judd, Kelly, LeWitt, Merz, Nauman, Viola

Dan Flavin. b New York, NY, 1933. d Riverhead, Long Island, NY, 1996. **Untitled (To the Citizens of the Republic of France...)**. 1989.
Blue, red and white fluorescent light. Height dependent on location. Leo Castelli Gallery, New York, NY

Fontana Lucio

Spatial Concept

After painting the canvas in monochrome blue the artist has slashed it vertically seven times with a sharp knife. A dramatic image – but what does it mean? Fontana was primarily concerned with the concept of space. By slashing the canvas he relieved it of its tautness, and allowed the viewer to see the space behind. The painting's primary significance lies in the fact that the artist has rejected the traditional picture format. It represents a symbolic and physical escape from the usual flat surface stretched tightly over a wooden frame.

In allowing us to look through the canvas the artist creates another dimension and conveys a sense of infinity. Fontana was a member of the Spatialism movement which stressed that space, movement and time were as important as colour, perspective and form. Born in Argentina of Italian parents, his family returned to their native country in 1905 where Fontana lived for the rest of his life.

► Kelly, Klein, LeWitt, Lissitzky, Malevich

Lucio Fontana. **b** Santa Fé, 1899. **d** Comabbio, 1968. **Spatial Concept**. 1962. Waterpaint on canvas. **h**52 × **w**52 cm. **h**20½ × **w**20½ in.
Private collection

Foujita Tsugouharu

Young Girl in the Park

This nostalgic and enchanting scene of a young girl holding a cat was created when the artist was 71 years old. The outline is painted with a fine Japanese brush dripped in black paint. The image was then delicately filled in using only a small amount of colour. This is especially noticeable in the girl's pale flesh tones. Foujita was a master of drawing, and this painting demonstrates how he used simple lines to convey a sense of childlike innocence and purity. The Japanese tradition of art is mainly graphic, and Foujita continued this tradition by exploiting the use of line, while absorbing Western artistic influences. Born in Tokyo, the artist settled in Paris in 1913, where he joined a circle of artists including Marc Chagall, Chaim Soutine and Amedeo Modigliani. His work includes landscapes, nudes and book illustrations. In 1959 he converted to Catholicism and changed his name to Léonard in homage to Leonardo da Vinci.

► Chagall, Hokusai, Laurencin, Modigliani, Soutine

Tsugouharu (Léonard) Foujita. b Tokyo, 1886. d Zurich, 1968. **Young Girl in the Park**. 1957. Oil on canvas. h50.8 × w65.4 cm.
h20 × w25¾ in. Private collection

Fouquet Jean

Virgin and Child

Apparently a religious image of the enthroned Queen of Heaven and her Child, this painting also appears to represent a more earthly subject. It is rumoured that the Virgin is actually a portrait of Agnès Sorel, the mistress of Charles VII of France. This woman was also adored by a man named Chevalier who was Fouquet's first patron. As this painting was executed the year Agnès died it is possible that it was commissioned as a memorial to her. Well known as a draughtsman and for his illuminated manuscripts, Fouquet, one of the leading French painters of the fifteenth century, travelled to Italy where he would have seen works by Piero della Francesca and other Renaissance artists. His acute attention to detail – as seen in the jewelled crown and the different textures of the cloth, fur and transparent veil – demonstrate his debt to northern artists such as Jan van Eyck.

► Botero, Bouts, Campin, Van Eyck, Piero della Francesca

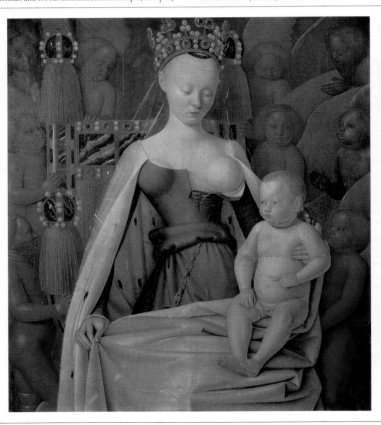

Jean Fouquet. b Tours, 1425. **d** Tours, before 1481. **Virgin and Child**. 1450. Tempera on panel. **h**95.3 × **w**86.4 cm. **h**37½ × **w**34 in.
Koninklijk Museum voor Schone Kunsten, Antwerp

Fragonard Jean-Honoré

The Swing

ith an air of flirtatious abandon, a beautiful young girl kicks f her dainty shoe as she swings in a luxuriant garden. We n almost hear the provocative rustle of petticoats as her ver gazes at her from his vantage-point in the undergrowth. thed in a shaft of glorious sunlight, the girl is the focus of e composition. Her porcelain perfection, pink dress and eeping upward movement all bring the viewer's eyes – and r lover's – to her. This type of painting, with its frivolity d lightness of touch, characterizes the Rococo period.

Fragonard is known for taking this style to its greatest heights. There were other artists at that time – Fragonard's own master, François Boucher, and the Venetian, Giovanni Battista Tiepolo – who were equally important painters. But it was Fragonard who so perfectly embodied the Rococo spirit – all powder, perfume and artifice, with a highly polished finish.

► Amigoni, Boucher, Greuze, Lancret, Tiepolo, Watteau

an-Honoré Fragonard. **b** Grasse, 1732. **d** Paris, 1806. **The Swing**. 1767. Oil on canvas. **h**81 × **w**64.5 cm. **h**31⅞ × **w**25⅜ in.
llace Collection, London

Francis Sam

Around the Blues

Blue splotches of paint have been dripped, flicked and splattered onto the canvas with controlled abandon. Large areas of bare white canvas have been left untouched. Originally painted in 1957, the canvas was reworked by the artist in 1962. The painting is an important and monumental example of Abstract Expressionism. While no reference to the real world can be seen, it captures a particular feeling, movement and atmosphere. It vibrates with an intensity of colour in which the edges of shapes are blurred with emotion.

This was the aim of the Abstract Expressionists: to allow movement without restraint, colour without outline, emotion without reality. Francis was a major figure in this group. He was also a master of watercolour. Some of his most famous works are from the 'Blue Ball' series which he created in the 1950s and 1960s.

► De Kooning, Pollock, Rothko, Still, Tobey

Sam Francis. b San Mateo, CA, 1923. **d** Santa Monica, CA, 1994. **Around the Blues**. 1957/62. Oil and magna on canvas. **h**274 × **w**487.5 cm. **h**108 × **w**192 in. Tate, London

against the backdrop of a brick-built apartment block flutters
an American flag. Behind the windows on either side stand
two women. Whilst this creates a degree of symmetry and
structure, the composition feels unbalanced – the top of the
flag is cropped, and the faces of the women are obscured.
The image suggests a contrast between the everyday realities
of those living inside the apartment and the public displays
of national identity symbolized by the flag and the passing
parade. Celebrated for his ability to capture the contradictions

and tensions that existed in America in the post-war period,
Frank selected this photograph as the opening image for his
influential book *The Americans*, a collection of eighty-three
photographs chosen from many thousands taken by him
whilst travelling across the country in the mid-1950s. The first
US edition of *The Americans* included an introduction written
by the Beat poet and novelist, Jack Kerouac.

► Cartier-Bresson, Evans, Hopper, Johns, Ruscha

bert Frank. b 1924, Zurich. **Parade – Hoboken, New Jersey**. 1955. Gelatin silver print. h21.3 × w32.4 cm. h8¼ × w12¾ in.
vate collection

Frankenthaler Helen

Mountains and Sea

Large splotches of blue, green and red decorate this impressive yet delicate and lyrical composition. The artist has used an unprimed canvas so that the colours seep into it like ink into blotting paper as soon as they are applied to the surface. Although Frankenthaler has decided where to place the colours, the staining is beyond her control as it depends on the absorbency of the canvas. *Mountains and Sea* is her first major stained painting. Its rich colours, fluid forms and ability physically to merge the foreground and background into the canvas had a substantial influence on Kenneth Noland and Morris Louis, who subsequently adopted this innovative technique. The abstracted quality of her landscap the spontaneity of her colours and the random quality of her staining are all elements that amount to an Abstract Expressionist painting. Her pictures are invariably large and evoke a unique sense of openness and delicacy.

► Gorky, Hodler, Louis, Noland, Pollock, Rothko

Helen Frankenthaler. b New York, NY, 1928. d Darien, CT, 2011. **Mountains and Sea.** 1952. Oil on canvas. **h**220 × **w**297.8 cm. **h**86⅝ × **w**117¼
On loan to the National Gallery of Art, Washington, DC

Freud Lucian

Benefits Supervisor Sleeping

A woman lies on a rather shabby sofa, her heavy, sagging physique appearing to pull her downwards. The artist has scrutinized every inch of her body, rendering each mark and blemish; the bold impasto of the paint mimics the textures and tones of her pale, fleshy skin. During his long career Freud became established as one of the most respected figurative painters working in Britain. With an increasing focus on the naked human form, Freud was committed to painting directly from life and refused to work from photographs. The model for the present painting, Sue Tilly, recalled that she sat for the painting two to three days each week over a period of nine months – with the artist insisting that she lay in position even when he was painting other areas of the composition, such as the floorboards. The artist was the grandson of the pioneering Austrian psychoanalyst Sigmund Freud.

► Auerbach, Bacon, Boucher, Kossoff

Lucian Freud. b Berlin, 1922. d London, 2011. **Benefits Supervisor Sleeping**. 1995. Oil on canvas. h151.3 × w219 cm. h59⅝ × w86¼ in. Private collection

Friedrich Caspar David

The Wreck of the Hope

The hard, jagged edges of a ruptured ice floe dominate this composition. They have been painted so precisely and crisply that they appear cold to the touch. The luminous light which bathes the scene causes the painting itself to glow. The wrecked ship, part of William Parry's expedition to the Arctic in 1819–20, seen on the right, is tiny in comparison to the ice – thus demonstrating the dominance of nature over man. Friedrich was a major figure in the Romantic movement, which sought to depict emotions such as loneliness and desolation. His paintings always drew out the spiritual nature of landscape, and often depicted nature at its most melancholy, lonely stretches of sea and mountains, or snowscapes bathed in strange and eerie luminosity. He was particularly interested in painting the effects of light and the seasons. His realistic yet symbolic landscapes embody the Romantic spirit, yet remain totally unique.

► Bierstadt, Church, Cozens, Nash, Turner

Caspar David Friedrich. b Greifswald, 1774. d Dresden, 1840. **The Wreck of the Hope**. 1824. Oil on canvas. **h**96.7 × **w**126.9 cm. **h**38½ × **w**50½ cm. Kunsthalle, Hamburg

Frink Dame Elisabeth

Goggle Head

Fascinating and frightening, this menacing head, its identity hidden by shiny goggles, suggests deliberate violence. It evokes images of sophisticated modern-day criminals, dictators' henchmen, or even Hell's Angels motorbike riders. Smooth in outline, it is executed in the shape of a Classical bust yet possesses a fearsome and disturbing quality. Random scratches, like those inflicted by an animal, cover its surface. Frink was one of the first British sculptors to create works in a Neo-Expressionist style, portraying her own feelings about the complex nature of humankind, its strengths and its vulnerabilities. She is equally well known for her sculptures of horses and dogs, which illustrate the sensitivity of her response to nature. Her last major commission was an impressive and dramatic figure of *The Risen Christ*, a bronze sculpture almost 4 metres (13 feet) high that is now fixed to the façade of Liverpool Cathedral.

▶ Algardi, Baselitz, Epstein, Giacometti, Houdon

Dame Elisabeth Frink. b Thurlow, 1930. d Woolland, 1993. **Goggle Head**. 1969. Bronze. h62.2 cm. h24½ in. Beaux Arts Gallery, London

Froment Nicolas

Virgin and Child

While tending his father-in-law's sheep, Moses is astounded by the vision of a burning bush. As a token of respect to this heavenly apparition, he removes his shoes. On the left an angel appears to witness the event with him. According to the Bible, God spoke to Moses through a burning bush, telling him that he was to deliver the Israelites from their oppressors and lead them to the land of milk and honey. Froment has chosen to include the image of the Virgin and Child because a burning but unconsumed bush was seen as a symbol of

Mary who bore a child but remained a virgin. Commissioned by King René of Anjou, this panel forms the central section of a triptych of the Burning Bush, which was painted for the church in which it still stands today. Little is known about this French artist who worked in and around Aix-en-Provence. His acute atttention to detail and great sensitivity to subtle effects of light and colour are elements which he possibly learned from Jan van Eyck.

► Van Eyck, Lochner, Schongauer, Van der Weyden, Witz

Nicolas Froment. Active in Uzès, 1450–90. **Virgin and Child**. 1476. Oil on panel. **h**410 × **w**304.2 cm. **h**161½ × **w**119¾ in.
Saint-Sauveur Cathedral, Aix-en-Provence

nylon string is wound around two intersecting sheets
curved perspex to create a complex three-dimensional
ttern of concave and convex folds. It was conceived as
rt of an unrealized 3-metre (15-foot) commission for the
so building in New York in 1949. With this extraordinarily
ereal sculpture Gabo has achieved an example of delicacy,
nsparency and weightlessness that was unprecedented. The
lpture seems to float as if suspended from an invisible cord
d, having no beginning or end, it conveys a sense of infinity.

Gabo was a Constructivist and this work is an example of the
movement in the way that it captures the indefinite expansion
of space. Gabo left his native Russia in 1922, and spent time
in Berlin and Paris before becoming an American citizen.
In 1952, he combined his artistic talents with architecture,
constructing an enormous monument for a department store
in Rotterdam.

► Hepworth, Lissitzky, Malevich, Rodchenko, Tobey

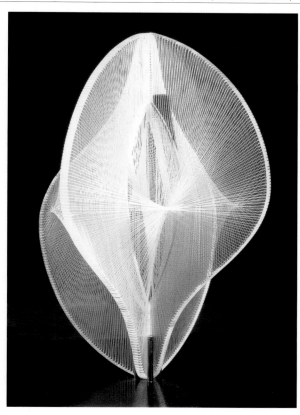

um Gabo. **b** Briansk, 1890. **d** Waterbury, CT, 1977. **Linear Construction in Space No. 2**. 1957-8.
ρex and nylon string on a wooden base. **h**38 cm. **h**15 in. Private collection

Gaddi Taddeo

Saint Eligius in the Goldsmith's Shop

In the Middle Ages artisans' shops often looked like the workshop in this painting. The large window opening onto the street would have allowed contact with customers. It would also have provided space to display wares. Gaddi was chosen among the best living painters of his time to produce a new high altarpiece for Pistoia Cathedral. This small scene, telling the story of St Eligius, would have formed part of the 'predella', a series of panels appearing under the main scene of an altarpiece. The saint was a goldsmith before becoming a priest, so he is shown here as the patron saint of goldsmiths. Gaddi was the godson of the painter Giotto, and was his disciple for 24 years. The use of vibrant colours and massive figures shows his master's influence. Gaddi was best known as a narrative painter. He was popular especially for his attention to detail and ability to tell a story.

► Giotto, Lorenzetti, Lorenzo Monaco, Orcagna

Taddeo Gaddi. b Florence, c1300. **d** Florence, 1366. **Saint Eligius in the Goldsmith's Shop.** c1365. Tempera on panel.
h35 × **w**39 cm. **h**13¾ × **w**15⅜ in. Museo del Prado, Madrid

Gainsborough Thomas

Mr and Mrs Andrews

Mr and Mrs Andrews are resting after an afternoon of shooting. To the right, their estate extends far into the distance. The sheaves of corn tell us it is autumn, and Mr Andrews' dog and shotgun imply that he has been hunting. Gainsborough possibly also intended to include a pheasant shot by this elegant English gentleman in the composition, but never completed the painting. His wife's beautifully executed blue satin dress is unfinished – the outline of a bird is visible on her lap. Robert Andrews and Frances Carter were married in November 1748 and it is thought that this portrait was painted as a celebration of this event. Unlike many of his contemporaries, Gainsborough was not an academic painter. His intuitive sense of style and colour, and superb handling of paint, make him one of the artistic geniuses of eighteenth-century Europe. Although he was a portrait painter by trade his true passion lay in painting the British countryside.

► Constable, Van Dyck, Van Eyck, Ramsay, Reynolds

Thomas Gainsborough. b Sudbury, 1727. d London, 1788. **Mr and Mrs Andrews**. c1750. Oil on canvas. h69.8 × w119.4 cm. h27¼ × w47 in. National Gallery, London

199

Gaudier-Brzeska Henri

Red Stone Dancer

Pulsating with all the power and vitality of an African tribal warrior, this statue ostensibly portrays a dancer. The geometrical rhythms of its surfaces are fragmented and distorted to reflect movement. Despite its vigour, the sculpture's gentle coils and the softness of its carving evokes the artist's appreciation of the human form. This piece was sculpted at a point when the artist was concerned with primitive forms and with abstraction. Born in France, he studied in England and settled in London in 1911. In

1914 he enlisted in the French army, and during this time he made wood carvings and continued to exhibit in London. Influenced by the work of Auguste Rodin and Constantin Brancusi who reduced figures to their most simplified form, Gaudier-Brzeska worked as a draughtsman and sculptor and was also closely linked to the Vorticist group. Potentially a great artist, he was killed in action in 1915 at the age of 23.

► Archipenko, Brancusi, Epstein, Lipchitz, Moore, Rodin

Henri Gaudier-Brzeska. b Saint-Jean de Braye, 1891. **d** Neuville-Saint-Vaast, 1915. **Red Stone Dancer**. c1913. Red Mansfield stone. **h**43.2 cm. **h**17 in. Tate, London

Gauguin Paul

Ia Orana Maria (Hail Mary)

yellow-winged angel alerts two young girls to the presence
Mary and the infant Jesus; the girls hold their hands
gether in a gesture of prayer. In the foreground are
eshly gathered bunches of bananas, perhaps placed as an
fering, and through the brightly coloured landscape of
owering trees we can see the huts of a small village. Whilst
e iconography is familiar, the figures and location are not
pically those of Western Christian art. *Ia Orana Maria* (Hail
ary) was one of the first paintings completed following

Gauguin's arrival in Tahiti, and his treatment of the subject is
illustrative of his romanticized view of the Polynesian island.
In his book *Noa Noa*, about his life there, he wrote, 'I have
escaped everything that is artificial and conventional. Here
I enter into Truth, become one with nature'. Gauguin based
the composition on a bas-relief in the Javanese temple of
Borobudur, of which he possessed a photograph.

► Van Gogh, Hiroshige, H Rousseau, Schongauer, Utamaro

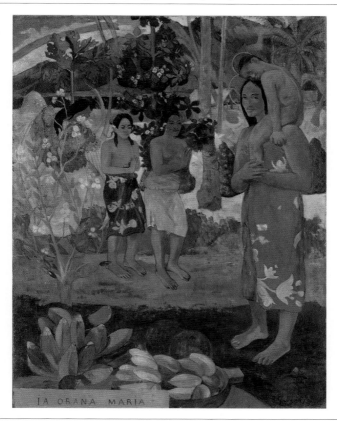

IA ORANA MARIA

ul Gauguin. **b** Paris, 1848. **d** Tahiti, 1903. **Ia Orana Maria (Hail Mary)**. 1891. Oil on canvas. **h**113.9 × **w**87.5 cm.
.4⅞ × **w**34½ in. Metropolitan Museum of Art, New York, NY

201

Gentile da Fabriano

The Adoration of the Magi

The three Magi are seen paying their respects to the newly born Christ. Each of the kings and the members of their group are elegantly dressed in gilded brocades. In fact, gold pervades this altarpiece, which was commissioned by the Strozzi family to adorn their chapel in the church of Santa Trinità. Only the wealthiest merchant family in Florence could choose such a subject, and encourage the free use of expensive blue pigment (lapis lazuli) and gold leaf. This practice was frequently employed to show off the patron's social position. Gentile came from the north of Italy but he painted in many different places. His work is typical of the International Gothic style, characterized by elegant refinement and an interest in secular and natural themes. Gentile reveals this in his realistic depiction of animals, birds and plants in many of his paintings.

► Gozzoli, Lorenzo Monaco, Mantegna, Overbeck, Pisanello

Gentile da Fabriano. b Fabriano, c1370. **d** Rome, 1427. **The Adoration of the Magi.** 1423. Tempera on panel. **h**300 × **w**282 cm. **h**118⅛ × **w**111 in. Galleria degli Uffizi, Florence

Gentileschi Artemisia

Judith and Holofernes

dith is shown at the gruesome moment when she separates olofernes' head from his body. Her determined look guides r steady hand, even though blood gushes out towards r and all over the bed. A strong light shining from the left minates the otherwise dark space, heightening the tension the moment. The drama, lighting and colouring of this ork are typical of a Baroque painting. The saturated colours the red velvet bedcover and the contrasting white sheets crease the picture's brutal goriness; it is difficult to imagine

this painting being made by a woman living in the seventeenth century. It was in fact created by the high-spirited daughter of Orazio, a well-respected painter. Once unrecognized because she followed in the footsteps of her father, Artemisia is now noted as an important and a fine artist in her own right.

► Caravaggio, Guercino, La Tour, Luini, Reni

temisia Gentileschi. b Rome, 1593. d Naples, 1652. **Judith and Holofernes**. c1620. Oil on canvas. **h**199 × **w**162.5 cm. **h**78⅜ × **w**64 in.
lleria degli Uffizi, Florence

Géricault Théodore

Officer of the Hussars

A decorated officer of the Hussars on a rearing mount charges into battle wielding his curved sword. The dynamism and expressiveness of this picture are created by the dramatic diagonal line flowing from top right to bottom left incorporating the horse's head with its flying mane, the dashing soldier as he stretches his arm across the horse's hindquarters, and the flowing tail and hind leg of the horse. The drama is heightened by a turbulent sky lit by fires. The composition is as cleverly balanced as the horse: the main body of the animal, and the rider with his curving sword, create a large circle which stabilizes the picture. Géricault was interested in horses and racing, and because of this developed a brilliantly rapid method of capturing a sense of movement. Painted with gusto in rich colours, this picture characterizes Géricault's style, which was to be such a great inspiration to later painters such as Eugène Delacroix.

► Böcklin, Delacroix, Van Dyck, Etty, Stubbs

Théodore Géricault. b Rouen, 1791. **d** Rouen, 1824. **Officer of the Hussars.** 1812. Oil on canvas. h349 × w266 cm. h137½ × w104¾ in. Musée du Louvre, Paris

Gérôme Jean-Léon

Bashi-Bazouk

The *bashi-bazouk* were irregular members of the Ottoman army – adventurers who were maintained by the Sultan but received no pay; they lived off loot. The word means 'corrupted head', or 'leaderless', and they were infamous for their lack of discipline and brutality. In this portrait, however, Gérôme depicts his sitter with characteristic interest and sympathy. Depicted in an off-profile view, this young African mercenary proudly displays his finery, from his pink silk coat and elaborate headwrap to the ivory-pommelled daggers and

decorated rifle. Trained in the Academic style of the French Académie des Beaux-Arts, and already known for his history paintings, Gérôme first visited Egypt in 1856, at the age of 32. For the next 40 years, in addition to mythological canvases and portraits, he would paint Orientalist works based on frequent visits to Egypt, Greece and Turkey, making available to an avid European audience supremely detailed pictures of daily life in the 'mysterious east'.

► Alma-Tadema, J-L David, Ingres, Leighton

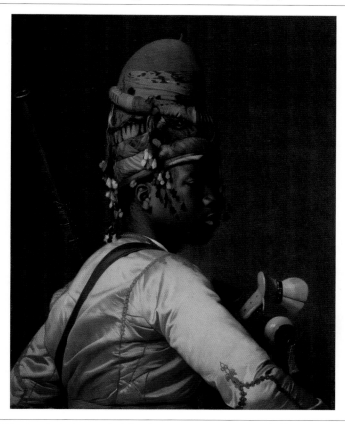

Jean-Léon Gérôme. b Vésoul, 1824. d Paris, 1904. **Bashi-Bazouk**. 1868–9. Oil on canvas. **h**80.6 × **w**66 cm. **h**31³⁄₄ × **w**26 in.
Metropolitan Museum of Art, New York, NY

Gertler Mark

The Merry-Go-Round

The open-mouthed figures on the roundabout become hardened into what look like brightly coloured mechanical toys. Whirling around, they have a simplistic yet sinister quality. As several are wearing uniforms, the painting is now viewed as a satire on the horror of war – it was at this time that the atrocities of the First World War were just beginning to dawn on the public. One of Gertler's best-known paintings, it was considered one of the most striking exhibits at the 1917 London Group Exhibition. Gertler was

also well-known for his still lifes and nudes, which he depicted in a quiet yet individual style. Gertler was born of Polish-Jewish parentage and brought up in a close Yiddish-speaking community. Renowned for being the life and soul of parties, he nevertheless suffered from serious depression. He committed suicide in his London studio at the age of 48.

► Bomberg, Van Dyck, Géricault, Lewis, Nash

Mark Gertler. b London, 1891. **d** London, 1939. **The Merry-Go-Round**. 1916. Oil on canvas. **h**189.2 × **w**142.2 cm. **h**74½ × **w**56 in. Tate, London

Ghiberti Lorenzo

David and Goliath

The artist has created a sense of remarkable depth in this shallow relief. Ghiberti achieved this effect by using the formal principles of perspective. For example, the three-dimensional figures of the foreground are set against a landscape that recedes into the distance. The scene is one of ten of the second set of large bronze doors to the Baptistry in Florence sculpted by Ghiberti. The doors are made up of ten large panels in which episodes from the Old Testament are shown. They are considered by many to express the height of Florentine art, particularly in their mastery of composition and perspective. The doors were a great inspiration to other Florentine Renaissance artists. Many years later Michelangelo praised Ghiberti's work, calling the doors the Gates of Paradise. In the last years of his life Ghiberti wrote his autobiography, which is the earliest by an artist to have survived.

► Castagno, Donatello, Pisano, Della Quercia

Lorenzo Ghiberti. b Florence, 1378. **d** Florence, 1455. **David and Goliath.** c1426-52. Gilt bronze. **h**79.5 × **w**79.5 cm. **h**31¼ × **w**31¼ in. Battistero di San Giovanni, Florence

Ghirlandaio Domenico

Portrait of Giovanna Tornabuoni

'Would that art could portray her character and virtue. No painting in the world would be more beautiful.' Despite this comment on the wall behind the sitter, the artist has successfully captured Giovanna's serenity, beauty and elegance. She is seated against a plain background, enabling the viewer to focus on her profile. This was a convention that was regularly used in Florentine Renaissance portraiture. The portrait is all the more poignant as the sitter died the year it was painted, only two years after her marriage. In addition

to producing portraits such as this, Ghirlandaio was an experienced fresco painter; indeed, the sitter's likeness also appears in a family chapel in Florence, which was the artist's largest undertaking. Ghirlandaio, at one point Michelangelo's teacher, was especially popular for his use of naturalistic detail and his ability to capture the life and style of his times.

► Botticelli, Filippino Lippi, Michelangelo, Pisanello

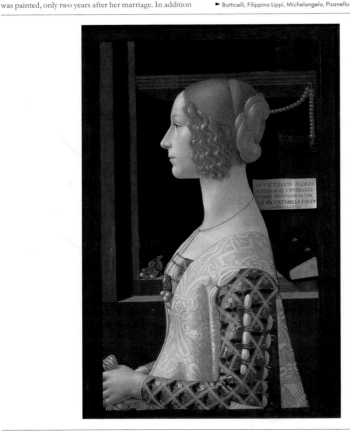

Domenico Ghirlandaio. b Florence, 1449. **d** Florence, 1494. **Portrait of Giovanna Tornabuoni**. 1488. Tempera on panel. **h**77 × **w**49 cm. **h**30¼ × **w**19¼ in. Fundación Colección Thyssen-Bornemisza, Madrid

Giacometti Alberto

Walking Man

his emaciated, monumental figure with a roughly pitted and textured surface is hauntingly powerful. Through its unnatural, elongated shape, the sculpture is intended to signify solitude and the absolute separation between ourself and our fellow man. It also underlines our fragility and the ephemeral nature of human existence. In contrast to other sculptors, Giacometti did not start with a large mass of material which he chipped and chiselled to find a form hidden within. His technique was to start with a metal skeleton and add clay to it, which he would then cast. Giacometti's singular style of expression kept him apart from the post-Second World War styles of painting and sculpture. Born in Switzerland, Giacometti settled in Paris in 1922. His paintings and drawings reflect the same restless, nervous quality as his sculptures. Made up of sharp, energetic strokes of paint they have a stark and haunting beauty.

► Archipenko, Auerbach, Dubuffet, Frink, Rodin, Smith

Alberto Giacometti. b Borgonovo, 1901. d Chur, 1966. **Walking Man**. 1960. Bronze. h183 cm. h72 in. Private collection

Giambologna

The Rape of a Sabine

Swirling with immense energy and furious movement, this tightly compacted composition, with its twisting outlines, creates a feeling of drama suitable for the subject. The illusion of writhing motion is initiated by the Sabine's outstretched arms, continued through the muscular, heroic figure of the Roman clasping the hips of his prey and resolved in the dominated man straddled below. The smoothly polished, sinuous form invites us to walk around the statue and to view it equally from all angles, rather than from a single viewpoint. Giambologna's use of the exaggerated gesture and his ability to convey a fervid sense of energy characterize the Mannerist style. Giambologna was strongly influenced by Michelangelo, and adapted his powerful forms to create a new kind of fluidity and elegance in sculpture. His numerous works include a number of fountains for the gardens of the Medici family.

► Bourdelle, Cellini, Michelangelo, Rosso Fiorentino

Giambologna (Jean de Boulogne). b Douai, 1529. d Florence, 1608. **The Rape of a Sabine**. 1581/3. Marble. **h**410 cm. **h**161½ in. Loggia dei Lanzi, Florence

Gilbert and George

Thumbing

Two figures in alternating blue, red and white clothing appear in what seems to be a window. A tall building in the distance dominates the background. With mock-serious expressions, the figures seem to be posing in a deliberately prankish manner. Perhaps they are 'thumbing' their noses at the conventions of traditional art. Gilbert and George have lived and worked together since 1967. As self-styled 'living sculptures', they portray themselves to the public in a variety of ways and media. Whatever they do or however they use themselves, it is usually with humour and deliberate bad taste. With their narcissistic pretensions they make themselves into objects of ridicule. Their work almost defies categorization, although with its gaudy colours and large scale, and in the way it debunks traditional art-historical values, it has affinities with the American Pop Art movement.

► Koons, Lichtenstein, Sherman, Warhol

Gilbert and George (Gilbert Proesch and George Pasmore). (Gilbert) **b** Dolomites, 1943; (George) **b** Devon, 1942. **Thumbing**. 1991. Photo-piece. **h**169 × **w**142 cm. **h**66½ × **w**56 in. Anthony d'Offay Gallery, London

Gilman Harold

An Eating House

This portrayal of working-class people in a humble interior has been painted with sensitivity and intensity. The artist has created a shallow space in which the bare walls and range of benches and tables appear as flat decorative colour planes of vermilion and emerald greens. The surface of the painting bears a grid mark which was imposed when the painting was still wet. Gilman probably used some kind of device to transfer the design from this painting to a smaller version, which bears the same title. With its clear, accurate portrayal of an ordinary scene and its intensity of colour, it is a fine example of work by an artist of the Camden Town Group. Sometimes called the 'English Post-Impressionists' because of their use of colour, this group of artists advocated the honest study of everyday life. The group often met in Walter Sickert's studio in Camden Town, an area of north London, hence its name.

► Modersohn-Becker, Orpen, Sickert, Vuillard

Harold Gilman. b Rode, 1878. d London, 1919. **An Eating House**. 1913/14. Oil on canvas. h57.2 × w74.9 cm. h22½ × w29½ in.
Sheffield City Art Galleries, Sheffield

Giordano Luca

The Dream of Solomon

Sleeping on his luxurious bed, the young king Solomon has a vision of God appearing amid a swirl of clouds and angels. God invests him with the heavenly light of Divine wisdom, for which Solomon is to become famous. Above him sits Minerva, the goddess of knowledge. The books and the lamb she holds are symbols of learning and patience. The building behind is a reference to the Temple of Jerusalem, built during Solomon's reign. The scene is painted with great vigour and expression. This, together with its decorative colour, characterizes Giordano's style and that of the late Baroque period. One of the most important decorative painters of the second half of the seventeenth century, Giordano was nicknamed 'Luca Fa Presto' because he worked so quickly. His airy compositions and delicate colours look forward to such eighteenth-century painters as Giovanni Battista Tiepolo.

► Bernini, Delacroix, Domenichino, Reni, Tiepolo

Luca Giordano. b Naples, 1634. d Naples, 1705. **The Dream of Solomon**. c1693. Oil on canvas. **h**245 × **w**361 cm. **h**96½ × **w**142 in. Museo del Prado, Madrid

Giorgione

The Tempest

Why is a naked woman feeding her child out in the open as a thunderstorm looms in the distance? Is this painting just an excuse to depict a poetic landscape, or does it have greater significance? No one has in fact been able to identify the subject of this picture, although many theories have been put forward. Indeed, much controversy surrounds this artist. There are no signed and dated works by him and matters are further confused by the fact that after his early death, many of Giorgione's pictures were completed by his pupils, including

Titian. Of all the Venetian painters Giorgione embodies the best of their painterly style. His loose, light brushstrokes and handling of colour and tone are all hallmarks of Venetian painting. Centuries after his death, Giorgione's pastoral landscapes were still much admired, and influenced great landscape painters such as Nicolas Poussin.

► Allston, Giovanni Bellini, Poussin, Titian

Giorgione. b Castelfranco, c1477. **d** Venice, 1510. **The Tempest.** c1508. Oil on canvas. **h**82 × **w**73 cm. **h**32$^{1}/_{4}$ × **w**28$^{3}/_{4}$ in. Galleria dell'Accademia, Venice

Giotto

The Lamentation

A group of men and women mourn the death of their Saviour as angels await his arrival in the heavenly realm. Emotional gestures, pained expressions and bright colours heighten the intensity of Mary's grief as she bends over Christ's dead body. Giotto caused a revolution in painting. He was one of the earliest artists to depict the illusions of real life, in terms of emotion and space, on a flat surface. This work, one of the many scenes depicting the life of the Virgin, is considered one of the most important works of the development of

Western art. With Cimabue, Giotto is often regarded as the founder of modern painting, as he broke away from the static, stereotyped conventions of his day. In 1334 he was appointed surveyor to Florence Cathedral and architect to the city. This was a tribute to his great fame as a painter rather than a consequence of any architectural knowledge.

► Cimabue, Duccio, Gaddi, Pisano, Van der Weyden

Giovanni di Paolo

The Creation and the Expulsion from Paradise

This sublime vision of the creation of the world may be based on Dante's description in *The Divine Comedy* – it certainly incorporates late medieval and Renaissance cosmological ideas. God the Creator, carried by seraphim and illuminated by heavenly light, presides over a global map of the world, a *mappa mundi*, encircled by concentric rings. These represent, from the centre, the four natural elements (earth, air, fire and water), the known planets (including the sun), and the twelve signs of the zodiac. To the right, Adam and Eve are being expelled from a richly floriated Garden of Eden by another angel, while the four rivers of Paradise issue from beneath their feet. Giovanni di Paolo was a master of the fifteenth-century Sienese school, but in his decorative style the influence can also be seen of the International Gothic, a sophisticated style current in the courts of France, Bohemia and northern Italy.

► Botticelli, Cranach, Van der Goes, Limbourg

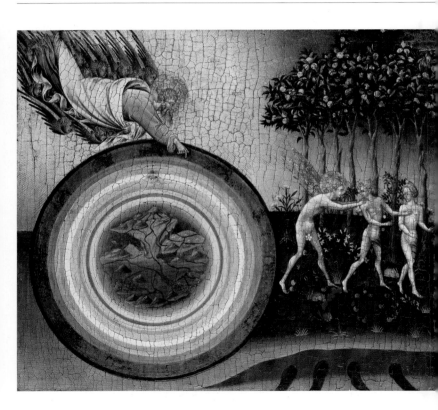

Giovanni di Paolo. b Siena, c1399. **d** Siena, 1482. **The Creation and the Expulsion from Paradise.** c1445. Tempera and gold on panel.
h46.4 × **w**52.1 cm. **h**18¹/₄ × **w**20½ in. Metropolitan Museum of Art, New York, NY

Giulio Romano

The artist has painted an entire room in fresco from floor to ceiling. Standing in the middle, the viewer feels surrounded by tumbling rocks and raging thunderbolts. With their bulging muscles, the Titans of Mount Olympus toss massive boulders as if they were as light as feathers, while the gods contemplate the chaos on Earth below. With its illusionistic perspectives and melodramatic emotion the fresco epitomizes the Mannerist style. Giulio Romano was both an architect and a painter. He began his career as one of Raphael's chief pupils, and his assistant. After his master's death he completed a number of Raphael's unfinished frescos in the Vatican. Later Giulio moved to Mantua, where he became Court painter to the Duke, a position once held by Andrea Mantegna. Here he excelled as an architect. He often designed buildings in order to shock and surprise the spectator, the most important of these being his own house in Mantua.

► Mantegna, Michelangelo, Raphael, Rosso Fiorentino

Giulio Romano (Giulio Pippi). b Rome, 1492. d Mantua, 1546. **Room of the Giants**. c1527. Fresco. Palazzo del Tè, Mantua

Van der Goes Hugo

The Fall of Man

Part lizard, part human, the serpent in this depiction of the fall of Adam and Eve is quite disturbing. Standing by the Tree of Knowledge, Eve, modestly covered by a strategically placed iris, stretches her arm to reach for a second apple, having already taken a bite of the first. The care with which each leaf, blade of grass and lock of hair is individually painted is astounding. (Notice the extraordinary plaits on top of the serpent's head.) This scene forms the left-hand panel of a diptych (an altarpiece made of two panels hinged together). The clear, luminous colours and straightforward description of the figures shown here are typical of painting in the Netherlands in the fifteenth century. The artist's fame spread as far as Italy, where one of his altarpieces caused a sensation in Florence. He is said to have been seized by madness while on a journey to Cologne in 1481; he died, still insane, the following year.

► Bouts, Campin, G David, Van Eyck, Memling, Van Scorel

Hugo van der Goes. b Ghent, 1440. d Brussels, 1482. **The Fall of Man**. c1470. Oil on panel. h32.3 × w21.9 cm. h12¾ × w8⅝ in. Kunsthistorisches Museum, Vienna

Van Gogh Vincent

Self-portrait

The artist stares with intense blue eyes that seem to ask questions he cannot answer. And yet this portrait, painted while Van Gogh was a voluntary patient in the asylum at Saint-Rémy, near Arles in the south of France, captures his psychological state of mind more by means of its colours and dynamic background textures than by any physical verisimilitude. The eddying waves of blue-grey pigment that turn greener in his jacket and waistcoat suggest a tumultuous mentality, and the contrasting colours of his face, neck and beard, immobile among the roiling brushstrokes, act as a spot-lit frame for those piercing eyes. He would be dead a year later. Van Gogh's influences ranged from Dutch Baroque genre scenes and the realistic depictions of peasants by Barbizon artists such as Jean-François Millet, to the Impressionists and Post-Impressionists whose work he saw in Paris. He combined them all into a uniquely expressive gestural style of painting in which emotional communication took precedence over naturalism.

► Auerbach, Derain, Van Dongen, Gauguin, Kokoschka, Signac

Vincent van Gogh. b Groot-Zundert, 1853. d Auvers-sur-Oise, 1890. **Self-portrait**. 1889. Oil on canvas. h65 × w54.2 cm. h25½ × w20½ in. Museé d'Orsay, Paris

Gontcharova Natalia

Street in Moscow

In a tranquil street, a woman dressed in elegant black walks out of the picture. Behind her a coachman calmly waits in his carriage. Apart from the woman's sad steps, there is no movement in this scene, which is a crystallization of a moment in time. All the forms have been reduced to simple, flat shapes – the squares and rectangles of the street and buildings, the circles of the wheels, and the shape of the woman's hat reflected in that of the cart. The forms have been painted in muted tones, adding to the atmosphere of

sadness. An air of forlorn hope blows through the painting. Gontcharova was profoundly interested in the popular folk art of Russia, and her own work for a time exuded a primitive quality that came from this interest. In 1915 she settled in Paris where she designed a number of stage sets for Sergei Diaghilev's *Ballets Russes*.

► Appel, Chagall, Jawlensky, Modersohn-Becker, Wallis

Natalia Gontcharova. b Russia, 1881. **d** Paris, 1962. **Street in Moscow**. 1909. Oil on canvas. **h**65 × **w**79 cm. **h**25½ × **w**31 in. Private collection

ese two identical, battery-powered clocks were initially
t to precisely the same time, but inevitably they fall out of
nc as the hours and days pass, one moving ahead as the
her falls behind. This inescapable loss of connection is the
etaphorical message of the work, which was created shortly
er the artist's partner was diagnosed with AIDS. The pale
ue paint of the wall behind was, according to Gonzalez-
orres, the colour of a beautiful memory. The piece reflects
ortality, human relationships and the passing of time, and

like much of the Cuban-born artist's work, it transforms
everyday objects into a meditation on love and loss. Gonzalez-
Torres combined elements of Conceptual art, Minimalism
and political activism to create a 'democratic' art – one that
required the interaction of the viewer to activate and complete
it. He was a master of allegory, using commonplace materials
such as newspapers or wrapped sweets to suggest personal
history and universal human emotion.

► Boetti, Broodthaers, Marclay, G Orozco

x Gonzalez-Torres. b Guáimaro, 1957. d Miami, FL, 1996. **Untitled (Perfect Lovers)**. 1991. Clocks and paint on wall.
.6 × w71.2 × d7 cm. h14 × w28 × d2³/₄ in. Museum of Modern Art, New York, NY

Gorky Arshile

The Waterfall

This apparently abstract painting is based on a small waterfall in a wood. It evokes a strong impression of a stream pouring through a rock, surrounded by overhanging trees and greenery. Vibrant colours evoke the serenity of bright sunlight and the sound of falling water. The beauty of the work lies in the artist's ability to express an almost spiritual peace through the images of forest and water. The painting shows the magical, dream-like elements typical of the Surrealist movement, towards which Gorky was moving at the time, and the spontaneity of Abstract Expressionism. Born in Armenia, Gorky emigrated to the USA in 1920. One critic has referred to him as an artist-in-exile, for whom art becam a homeland. Gorky would often use images from his native land in his paintings. After years of poverty, he achieved brief recognition but hanged himself after suffering severe psychological trauma.

► Ernst, Frankenthaler, De Kooning, Lam, Rothko

Arshile Gorky. b Khorkom Vari, 1904. **d** Sherman, CT, 1948. **The Waterfall**. 1943. Oil on canvas. **h**154 × **w**113 cm. **h**60½ × **w**44½ in. Tate, London

A tall, pensive figure stands in the half-light of the crypt beneath the eleventh-century cathedral of Winchester. He seems to have paused momentarily in thought, gazing quietly down at his hands, or perhaps at the reflection of ancient brick vaults in the water – for the crypt is often flooded, leaving the figure submerged as high as the knees. Of all Antony Gormley's sculptures, this one seems best placed to explore the artist's interest in the relationship of the human form to space and the spiritual. Like his cast-iron figures looking out to sea near Liverpool (*Another Place*, 1997), the sculpture evokes powerful emotions of which the surroundings are an integral part, simultaneously sublime and human, transcendent and haunting. The sense of solitary reflection recalls Gormley's statement that his works, moulded from his own body, attempt to treat the body not as a thing but as somewhere 'to materialize the place at the other side of appearance where we all live'.

► Archipenko, Donatello, Gaudier-Brzeska, Giacometti, Segal

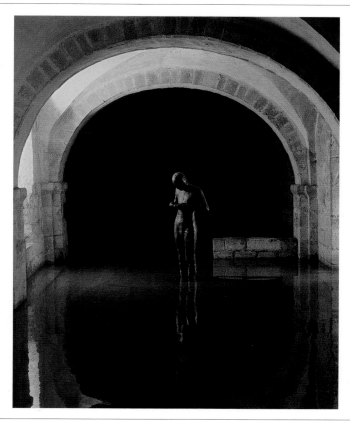

Antony Gormley. b London, 1950. **Sound II**. 1986. Lead, fibreglass, water. **h**188 × **w**60 × **d**45 cm. **h**76 × **w**23⅝ × **d**17¾ in.

Winchester Cathedral, Hampshire

223

Gossaert Jan

Saint Luke Painting the Virgin

St Luke sits at a lectern in a church, drawing the Virgin and Child, his hand guided by an angel. Gossaert (sometimes called Mabuse) was one of the first Flemish painters to visit Italy, and the influences of this trip can be seen clearly in the Renaissance-inspired architectural setting, in the way the light comes from one direction (that of the halo around the Virgin), and in the heavy, sculptural forms of the figures. However, the traditions of northern painting are also reflected in the lyrical folds of the draperies, which are entirely Flemish,

and in the uncomfortable pose of the kneeling saint. Gossae was one of a group of Netherlandish artists, nicknamed 'the Romanists', who wanted to follow the ideals of the Italian High Renaissance but were hampered by their Flemish realis and painstaking technique. Although he borrowed poses an details, the essence of Classicism escaped him. In 1527 he travelled in Flanders with Lucas van Leyden.

► Dürer, Van Eyck, Lucas van Leyden, Massys

Jan Gossaert (sometimes called Mabuse). b Maubeuge, c1478. **d** Middelburg, 1532. **Saint Luke Painting the Virgin.** c1520–5. Oil on panel. **h**109.2 × **w**81.9 cm. **h**43 × **w**32¼ in. Kunsthistorisches Museum, Vienna

Goya Francisco

Portrait of the Duchess of Alba

Dressed in the fashionable black costume of the elegant *majas* of Madrid, a veil cascading in folds around her head, the Duchess of Alba exudes an air of aristocratic beauty. Her monochrome but opulent clothing is described with marvellous energy. Set against a cloudless sky, she seems about to step into the viewer's presence. The Duchess was a prominent figure in Madrid society. It is likely that she was romantically involved with Goya at the time, suggested here by the words 'Solo Goya' to which she points, and the fact that 'Goya' and 'Alba' are inscribed on the rings of her hand. As he grew older Goya spent more time creating scenes of fantasy and terror. Although he remained a Court painter, many of his paintings were politically inspired by the French occupation of his country at that time. At the time of his death, Goya had completed some five hundred oil paintings and nearly three hundred etchings and lithographs.

► Gainsborough, Manet, Ramsay, Reynolds, Velázquez

Francisco Goya y Lucientes. **b** Fuendetodos, 1746. **d** Bordeaux, 1828. **Portrait of the Duchess of Alba**. 1797. Oil on canvas. 210 × w148 cm. **h**82½ × **w**58⅛ in. Hispanic Society of America, New York, NY

Van Goyen Jan

A Castle by a River with Shipping at a Quay

The warm, brown tones give a wonderful rustic air to the building on the right with its turrets and bay windows. Looking along the river into the distance, the colour gradually loses its strength. The low horizon evokes the flat plains of the Dutch landscape. This is emphasized by the vast, dominating, grey sky, a feature that was so important to seventeenth-century Dutch painters and which takes up almost three-quarters of the painting. Van Goyen was one of the first to capture a sense of light and atmospheric effects.

Most of his paintings were based on drawings that he made while travelling around the countryside, and it appears that he used these again and again, as the same scene appears in a number of his paintings. Van Goyen had many pupils and imitators. He produced countless works, and was certainly a great influence on landscape painting of the seventeenth and eighteenth centuries.

► Avercamp, Bonington, Boudin, Hobbema, Ruisdael

Jan van Goyen. b Leiden, 1596. d The Hague, 1656. **A Castle by a River with Shipping at a Quay**. 1642. Oil on canvas. h103 × w140 cm. h40½ × w55⅛ in. Private collection

Gozzoli Benozzo

The Journey of the Magi

Fur-trimmed capes, gold bridles, velvet robes and splendid horses – this is truly a magnificent procession. The subject of the Magi was often a favourite of affluent patrons because the use of opulent colours and gold leaf would highlight their own wealth and status. This example appears as a fresco on the walls of a chapel inside the palace of Cosimo de' Medici in Florence. It was unusual to have a chapel inside a private house, but Cosimo's magnificent palace broke with many traditions of the day. Gozzoli has included portraits of the family in the fresco, and the elegant young Magus in the gold robe is said to be Lorenzo de' Medici. The fresco is only a part of the chapel's decoration. A pupil of Fra Angelico and contemporary of the very different Andrea Mantegna, Gozzoli's rich sense of decorative pageantry provides a fine example of the International Gothic style.

► Fra Angelico, Gentile da Fabriano, Mantegna, Uccello

Graham Dan

Present Continuous Past(s)

A combination of Performance art and video installation, *Present Continuous Past(s)* produces a disorientating reconfiguration of the spatial and the temporal. Attached to the wall of a specially constructed room is a video camera; positioned directly below it is a monitor. The opposite wall and one adjacent wall are both mirrored. Events recorded by the camera are played back on the monitor with an eight-second delay. Whilst the viewer can see their live actions reflected in the mirrors, they simultaneously see their previous actions on the monitor. If the reflection of the monitor is not obscured, the camera will also record the action on the monitor that happened eight seconds previously; enabling the viewer simultaneously to see events that had occurred sixteen seconds ago. A pioneering figure of the Conceptual art movement in the 1960s, Graham has since employed a wide range of media including film, sculpture, performance and sound. He is also a respected writer and critic.

► Eliasson, Flavin, Kusama, A Piper

Dan Graham. b Urbana, IL, 1942. **Present Continuous Past(s)**. 1974. Mixed media including mirror, camera and monitor. **h**320 × **w**320 cm. **h**126 × **w**126 in. Musée National d'Art Moderne, Paris

El Greco

The Burial of Count Orgaz

irling forms and colours have been used here to create
ynamic, visionary image of Heaven. The subject of the
nting, Count Orgaz, was a Toledan dignitary who was
pious that the saints Augustine and Stephen appeared
raculously at his funeral to lower his body into the tomb.
ove, his soul ascends to the heavenly realm as members
the local nobility and clergy look on. Born in Crete, El
eco trained in Venice and Rome before moving to Toledo.
e fashionable style at that time was the Classical manner

of Michelangelo, Raphael and Titian. El Greco transformed
these powerful influences into his own distinctive, intensely
spiritual style with its elongated forms, sweeping movement
and bright, sometimes unearthly, colours. In this way, El
Greco's work can be seen to epitomize the Mannerist
movement at its height.

► Andrea del Sarto, Michelangelo, Raphael, Titian

Greco (Domenikos Theotocopoulos). **b** Crete, 1541. **d** Toledo, 1614. **The Burial of Count Orgaz**. 1586. Oil on canvas.
7.7 × **w**360.7 cm. **h**192 × **w**142 in. San Tomé, Toledo

Greuze Jean-Baptiste

The Guitarist

Dressed in theatrical clothes, a young man listens intently as he carefully tunes his guitar. His tired, wide-open eyes and bedraggled look hint at the struggles of his outwardly jovial life. This is a richly painted scene, complete with all the details of the seventeenth-century Flemish genre painters, whose manner Greuze has tried to emulate. Greuze's scenes of everyday life often had a moral tale to tell. These pictures became increasingly popular in eighteenth-century France and were widely praised by moral philosophers such as Denis Diderot. When the style of the day shifted towards Neo-Classical artists such as Jacques-Louis David, however, Greuze went out of fashion. Unfortunately, his desire to remain popular led him to use painting in an insincere and sentimentalized manner. For this reason many of his paintings have been overlooked for their important contribution to art until recently.

► Ter Brugghen, J-L David, Hogarth, Honthorst, Steen

Jean-Baptiste Greuze. b Tournus, 1725. **d** Paris, 1805. **The Guitarist.** c1760. Oil on canvas. **h**71 × **w**57 cm. **h**28 × **w**22½ in. Musée des Beaux-Arts, Nantes

Grimshaw Atkinson

Nightfall down the Thames

full moon dominates this riverscape, casting a green ght over the River Thames and the ships floating on it. he reflection of light on the water leads the viewer's eye the dome of St Paul's Cathedral in the distance. In such ysterious moonlight, however, the well-known London ndmark looks strangely different to the way it would look daylight. The composition of the painting is symmetrical d smooth. It is unbroken by any movement except e vertical pattern of the skeleton-like masts across the

skyline. Grimshaw is best known for this kind of night townscape, which was often lit by bright moonlight. Like his contemporary James Abbott McNeill Whistler, whose nocturnal scenes are well known, and who supposedly commented, 'I thought I had invented the Nocturne until I saw Grimmy's moonlights', Grimshaw had a great love for the River Thames.

► Friedrich, Spilliaert, Turner, Whistler

kinson Grimshaw. b Leeds, 1836. d Leeds, 1893. **Nightfall down the Thames**. 1880. Oil on board. **h**40.2 × **w**63.1 cm. 5⅞ × **w**24⅞ in. Leeds City Art Gallery, Leeds

Gris Juan

Glasses, Newspaper and a Bottle of Wine

The artist has used sliced sections of newspaper to create this unusual interpretation of a still life. The objects – glasses, newspaper and bottle of wine – have been taken whole and then fragmented, painted and glued back together again within the confines of parallel vertical planes in the Cubist technique. Gris has created a sense of perspective and different levels of space by positioning these planes in front of or behind each other. The importance of this work lies in its innovative method of portraying different sections of an object simultaneously, while rejecting the conventions of light and shade. The artist has thus created a new kind of reality. Although Gris was never a Cubist by intention, this work is seen as an example of the movement's style. Spanish by birth, Gris lived most of his working life in Paris and his work remained essentially Cubist in form until his death.

► Archipenko, Braque, Kupka, Léger, Picasso, Schwitters

Juan Gris. b Madrid, 1887. **d** Paris, 1927. **Glasses, Newspaper and a Bottle of Wine**. 1913. Collage, gouache, watercolour, coloured chalks and charcoal on paper. **h**45 × **w**29.5 cm. **h**17¾ × **w**11⅞ in. Private collection victorious Napoleon defeats the Italians at the battle of Arcole in 1796. The strong character of Bonaparte's face was obviously studied from life and gives the painting a very realistic feeling. This is not a generalized representation of victory but rather a depiction of a specific, contemporary event. Although trained by his close friend the Neo-Classical painter Jacques-Louis David, Gros became a leader in the move towards Realism and Romanticism in French painting the end of the eighteenth century. His sombre palette and naturalistic compositions were a reaction to the strong colours and theatrical set-pieces of the Neo-Classicists. Gros was made official war painter by Napoleon, and successfully captured the atmosphere of the moment. In the 1820s, however, Gros attempted to return to a more Neo-Classical style, and his popularity diminished. He slipped into obscurity, and committed suicide in 1835.

► J-L David, Delacroix, Géricault, Lawrence

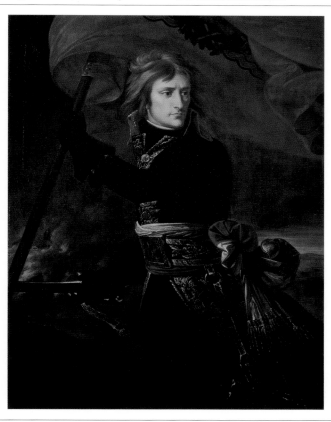

Baron Antoine-Jean Gros. **b** Paris, 1771. **d** Bas-Meudon, 1835. **Napoleon Bonaparte on the Bridge at Arcole**. 1796/7. Oil on canvas. 134 × w104 cm. **h**52¾ × **w**41 in. Hermitage Museum, St Petersburg

233

Grosz George

An elegant lady in heels and a fur collar haughtily curls her nose at a dapper gentleman who winks at her in a fashionable street. Only interested in their own flirtatious exchanges, they do not notice the old man in a threadbare suit begging for money. This watercolour scathingly caricatures the appalling social conditions of post-First World War Germany. A satire on the affected patriotism, selfish greed and depraved sensuality of the period, it is one of many which the artist produced that have a nightmarish quality. Grosz's disgust

at a decaying society of distorted morals, propaganda and self-indulgence led him to vent his anger through his biting satirical caricatures, and eventually to emigrate to the USA. His work gradually came to combine the satire of old with a new romanticism. He began his career as a caricaturist and became a leading member of the Dada group in Berlin after 1918.

► Daumier, Dix, Hausmann, Schwitters

George Grosz. b Berlin, 1893. **d** Berlin, 1959. **Berlin Streetscene**. 1930. Watercolour, ink and oil on paper. **h**60 × **w**46 cm. **h**23½× **w**18 in. Private collection book in one hand, John the Baptist points towards the dying figure of the crucified Christ. The Latin inscription behind his arm reads, *Illum oportet crescere, me autem minui* ('He must increase, but I must decrease'). Christ's elongated fingers are splayed by the force of the nails, blood trickles from the gash in his side, and his flesh is covered in festering wounds. Mary Magdalene kneels at the foot of the cross with her perfume pot beside her, and the Virgin Mary faints into the hands of John the Evangelist. Grünewald's aim was that the viewer should be moved with the same intensity of emotion as the figures in the painting. He was a contemporary of Albrecht Dürer and considered as popular. Ironically, however, he was known by the wrong name for three hundred years; his real name was in fact Mathis Gothardt Neithardt and he was misnamed Grünewald by a seventeenth-century biographer.

► Dürer, El Greco, Masaccio, JC Orozco, Rouault

atthias Grünewald (Mathis Gothardt Neithardt). **b** Würzburg, 1470/5. **d** Halle, 1528. **The Crucifixion.** c1515. Oil on panel.
h269 × **w**307 cm. **h**106 × **w**120⅞ in. Musée d'Unterlinden, Colmar

Guardi Francesco

An Architectural Caprice

Through an arcade a piazza opens out, and a wide staircase leads up to a monumental building. The scene is peppered with incidental detail, such as the sheets draped over the balcony and the elegantly dressed nobles giving coins to the beggar-boy. All of this animates and enlivens the picture. Although it is an invented cityscape, Guardi used elements of his native city to create a plausible Venetian view. Guardi owes much to the example of Canaletto, an artist with whom he has always

been closely associated and who was perhaps his master. Unlike Canaletto's precise technique, however, Guardi's style is characterized by the freedom and spontaneity of his brushwork, adding a great sense of gusto to the scene. Full of romantic, half-invented elements, Guardi interprets rather than reproduces Venice, capturing a sparkle of light and movement which is absent from Canaletto's interpretations of the same city.

► Bellotto, Bordone, Canaletto, Pannini, Siberechts

Francesco Guardi. b Venice, 1712. d Venice, 1793. An Architectural Caprice. c1770/80. Oil on canvas. h54 × w36 cm. h21⅓ × w14¼ in. National Gallery, London

Guercino

Jacob Receiving Joseph's Coat

The elderly Jacob is seen at the moment of being given the cloak of his favourite son Joseph, whom his jealous brothers have sold into slavery. The cloak is stained with the blood of a goat in order to fool Jacob into thinking Joseph has been killed by a wild animal. Jacob raises his right hand and rolls his eyes heavenward, as if pleading with God. The cloak rests on a marble balustrade, which takes on the appearance of a mortuary slab. Dramatically set against a sombre sky, the figure of Jacob dominates the canvas with its robust monumentality. The condensed, heightened emotion of the picture makes this a masterpiece of the Baroque spirit. Guercino was a pupil at the Carracci Academy, but was also influenced by the realism and intensity of Caravaggio's art. Although dramatic lighting similar to Caravaggio's has been used, in this painting it has been softened to enhance the richness of the colours.

► Caravaggio, Carracci, Jordaens, Reni, Ribera

Guercino (Francesco Barbieri). **b** Cento, 1591. **d** Bologna, 1666. **Jacob Receiving Joseph's Coat**. c1625. Oil on canvas.
h115.5 × w94 cm. **h**45½ × **w**37 in. Burghley House, Stamford

Gursky Andreas   99 Cent

Row after row of brightly coloured candy bars form an
intricate geometric pattern. Taken from a vantage point
looking down upon the floor of an American convenience
store, Gursky's photograph captures the systematic nature
of the modern retail experience. The anonymous shoppers
browsing the aisles appear consumed by the mass of products
on display; isolated figures overwhelmed by the modern
world. The son of successful commercial photographers,
Gursky's huge-format photographs monumentalize the

mundane and the familiar. From close-up images of industrial
carpets to densely populated panoramic views of factories
and stock exchanges, Gursky creates images in which the
subject matter can often appear subservient to the formal
qualities of the composition. In the early 1980s Gursky
attended the Staatliche Kunstakademie in Düsseldorf, where
he studied for six years with Bernd and Hilla Becher. He
found early inspiration in the work of Jeff Wall.
► Becher, Estes, Shore, Struth, Wall

Andreas Gursky. b Leipzig, 1955. **99 Cent**. 1999. Chromogenic colour print. **h**207 × **w**337 cm. **h**81½ × **w**132½ in. Private collection

Guston Philip

Sleeping

A tramp-like figure, possibly the artist himself, lies in a dark and gloomy place. The cartoon character has been portrayed with deliberate clumsiness, the paint applied in bold, forceful strokes with a limited palette of reds, pinks, black and white. Painted in the last phase of the artist's career, this work is an ironic comment on low-life urban society. Although Guston was closely associated with the Abstract Expressionists in his earlier period, in 1970 he publicly abandoned this style for a rather raucous form of figuration with the explanation, 'I got sick and tired of that purity, wanted to tell stories.' Using a comic-strip technique and harsh discordant colours, his paintings comment on such social topics as the homeless and the Ku Klux Klan. Guston taught painting until the late 1950s when he was awarded a Ford Foundation grant and his international reputation was swiftly established with a major retrospective at the Guggenheim Museum in 1962.

▶ Baselitz, Kline, De Kooning, Pollock, Rothko

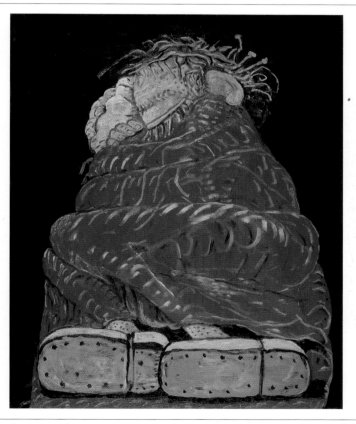

Philip Guston. b Montreal, 1913. d Woodstock, NY, 1980. **Sleeping**. 1977. Oil on canvas. h213.3 × w175.2 cm. h84 × w69 in. Private collection

Hals Frans

The young man has been painted with dazzling vigour and spontaneity. The artist's furious brushstrokes give the painting an almost impressionistic quality. This creates a strong sense of character and movement in the boisterous youth, whose real presence is suggested by his hand thrusting out of the canvas and into the viewer's space. The painting is probably not a true portrait but what was known as a 'vanitas' scene, dwelling on the inevitability of death and the shortness of life. The skull represents death, while the young man symbolizes

youth and vigour. Hals was a successful portrait painter who worked in Holland in the early seventeeth century. He is well known for his vivid style, using rapid brushwork to capture fleeting gestures and expressions. However, this quality is quite different from his contemporary Rembrandt's more introverted insight into the personality of the sitter.

► Ter Brugghen, Claesz, Honthorst, Rembrandt, Rubens

Frans Hals. b Antwerp, 1581. **d** Haarlem, 1666. **Portrait of a Young Man with a Skull**. c1626/8. Oil on canvas. **h**92 × **w**81 cm. **h**36 × **w**32 in. National Gallery, London

This collage of a stylized 1950s interior is a landmark in post-war art. The artist has combined cut-up photographs and cuttings from magazines to create a consumer paradise – albeit a wittily sardonic one. The 'POP' on the oversized lollipop is crucial as it is probably the first visual reference to the word which heralded a major new movement in art. The imagery Hamilton has used embodies the American Pop Art movement which used symbols from contemporary mass media, popular culture and advertising. Hamilton played

a seminal role in the development of the British strain of Pop Art. This collage was made for an exhibition called 'This is Tomorrow', in London's Whitechapel Art Gallery. For Hamilton in the 1950s, the indispensable categories for tomorrow's world were: 'Woman Food History Newspapers Cinema Domestic appliances Cars Space Comics TV Telephone Information'. Later in his career he used computer technology to create innovative works.

▶ P Blake, Hausmann, Höch, Jones, Schwitters

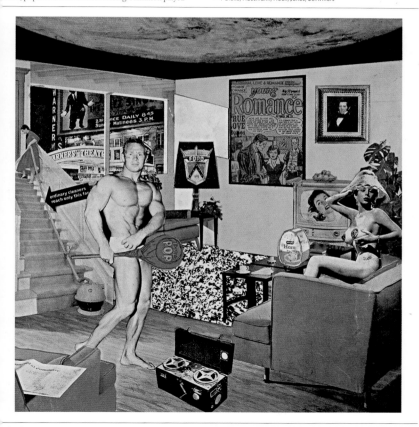

Hammershøi Vilhelm

Interior with a Girl at the Clavier

Cool, delicate pastel tones suggest a scene of peaceful serenity, with a girl seated at a clavier with her back to the viewer. A white tablecloth with crisp folds leads the eye into the shallow depth of the room, which is enclosed by a pale-coloured wall. The uncluttered composition recalls the spare, austere style of Japanese prints, yet the whole painting breathes a freshness and vitality, and is flooded with the clear, sharp Scandinavian light. Hammershøi was a Danish painter of quiet interiors in muted colours, chiefly grey, and his refined style has something mystical about it, suggesting the work of seventeenth-century Dutch artists such as Jan Vermeer and Pieter de Hooch. His art has a timeless quality, but it also offers a nostalgic escape into the past. Although he had to wait a long time for recognition of his work, he was much respected by his contemporaries.

► Bonnard, De Hooch, Metsu, Sickert, Vermeer

Vilhelm Hammershøi. b Copenhagen, 1864. **d** Copenhagen, 1916. **Interior with a Girl at the Clavier.** 1901. Oil on canvas. **h**56 × **w**44 cm. **h**22 × **w**17 in. Private collection

Harsh, dramatic lines of black paint dominate a pale, bland background. There is strength and energy in the heavy calligraphy of the bundled sheaves of lines, assembled in a criss-cross pattern. Hartung's forceful and expressive image is an example of the intuitive and spontaneous work known as Art Informel. The essence of Hartung's image is that when he started with his brush and blank canvas he had no preconceptions of the finished object. Born in Germany, Hartung settled in Paris in 1935 and subsequently assumed French citizenship. He became one of the most famous French abstract painters. His elegant and distinctive work usually incorporates calligraphy, not unlike that used in Chinese art, and the paintings are generally untitled and can only be distinguished by numbers. He joined the French Foreign Legion at the outbreak of the Second World War, and lost a leg in 1944.

► Dubuffet, Fautrier, Riopelle, Soulages, Tàpies

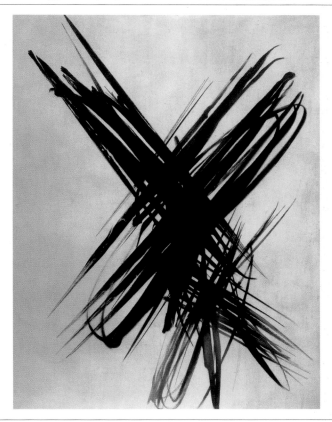

Hans Hartung. b Leipzig, 1904. d Antibes, 1989. T 1956/7. 1956/7. Oil on canvas. h161 × w122 cm. h63⅜ × w48 in. Private collection

Hassam Childe

The Room of Flowers

A woman in a pink dress lounges on a divan, lazily reading in a light-filled room crowded with books, paintings, tables, chairs, ornaments and flowers. The house is on the Maine-New Hampshire coast and belonged to Celia Thaxter who used it to entertain poets and artists (Hassam among them). Hassam worked as a wood engraver and illustrator before going to Boston and then to Paris to study art. He was converted to French Impressionism on seeing the work of Claude Monet, although his initial academic training hindered him from completely adopting its principles. Many of his early paintings, atmospheric scenes of city streets in rain, snow or twilight, stress fleeting impressions of movement. He chose times of day or weather conditions which presented technical challenges, such as reflections on wet pavements, and he also favoured studies of women. Hassam was popular in his own lifetime, and often won medals and awards.

► Cassatt, Chase, Hammershøi, Monet, Sargent, Whistler

Childe Hassam. b Boston, MA, 1859. d New York, NY, 1935. **The Room of Flowers.** 1894. Oil on canvas. h86.4 × w86.4 cm. h34 × w34 in. Private collection

Hausmann Raoul

The Art Critic

Holding a Venus pencil in his right hand, a heeled shoe glued to his brain, his eyes and mouth hidden by superimposed features and with a sharp segment of a 50 deutschmark bank note embedded in his neck, Hausmann's view of this art critic is both critical and controversial. Through whose eyes does he really see? Whose words does he really speak? And whose payroll is he on? One of the many self-proclaimed inventors of photomontage, Hausmann used cut-up photographs and pages from newspapers and magazines to construct his world of cynical imagery. This work is an example of the Dada movement, whose members would incorporate ordinary objects into their art, often employing an absurd sense of humour. In 1923, Hausmann abandoned painting and four years later invented the optophone, an apparatus which turned kaleidoscopic forms into music.

▶ P Blake, Ensor, Grosz, Hamilton, Höch, Schwitters

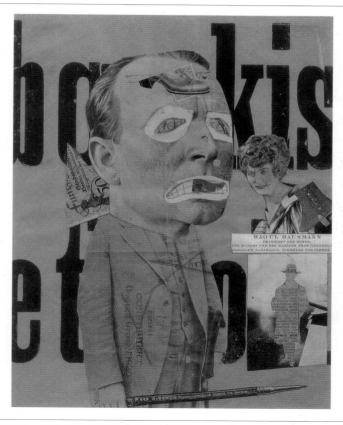

Raoul Hausmann. b Vienna, 1886. d Limoges, 1971. **The Art Critic.** 1919/20. Photomontage. **h**31.7 × **w**25.4 cm. **h**12½ × **w**10 in. Tate, London

Hayter Stanley William

Claduègne

Continuous wave-like patterns created by curving ribbon forms charge this hypnotic print with a swirling rhythm and a feeling almost of electricity. The sharp colours give this pattern, which has neither beginning nor end, an acidity that paradoxically also has the qualities of velvet. Although born of a long line of artists, Hayter began his career in the oil industry before becoming one of the foremost graphic artists of his time, ceaselessly experimenting with textures and colours in new techniques. He was one of the earliest members of the Surrealist movement, but made his greatest mark as a master innovator of printmaking and engraving. Most of his life was spent in Paris where, in 1926, he founded the famous studio, Atelier 17, an experimental workshop where artists of all nationalities, such as Pablo Picasso, Marc Chagall, Alberto Giacometti and Yves Tanguy, could work together. During the Second World War, it moved to New York, but returned to Paris in 1950.

► Chagall, Giacometti, Hartung, Picasso, Riley, Tanguy

Stanley William Hayter. **b** London, 1901. **d** Paris, 1988. **Claduègne**. 1972. Etching on paper. **h**49 × **w**60 cm. **h**19¼ × **w**23½ in. Private collection

Heckel Erich

Windmill, Dangast

Waves of bright, loosely applied colours sweep up the canvas in rhythms and encircle the windmill on the brow of a hill, the focal point of the painting. Red, yellow, blue, green and black clash vigorously with each other, creating a vibrating tension, yet this simple composition has a strange, lyrical quality. Heckel studied architecture before turning to painting and was a superb lithographer. He fled from his native Germany to Switzerland in 1944, after over seven hundred of his paintings were removed from German museums by the Nazis. His work was much influenced by Vincent van Gogh and the Fauves – a name given to several artists whose paintings were full of distortions, flat patterns and vivid colours. He eventually formed part of a small group who wished to free themselves from established artistic doctrines, developing an intensely Expressionistic style called 'Die Brücke', or the bridge, which suggests a connection of their art to that of the future.

► Derain, Van Gogh, Kirchner, Matisse, Vlaminck

Erich Heckel. b Döbeln, 1883. d Radolfzell, 1970. **Windmill, Dangast**. 1909. Oil on canvas. h69 × w80 cm. h27 × w31½ in. Wilhelm-Lehmbruck-Museum, Duisburg

De Heem **Jan Davidsz**

Still Life of Dessert

A profusion of fruits and exotic foods mingle with an array of ornate goblets, jars and wine bottles on a sumptuously laid table. This rich visual feast glows with lavish, sensual colour and, although appearing haphazard, was in fact composed with great care. In the Netherlands at the time, artists would display their skill by painting a wide range of objects, often with rich allusions and hidden symbolism of Christian, philosophical and metaphysical ideas. This work, however, is purely a celebration of the senses. De Heem is considered by many to be the greatest Dutch still-life painter, whose deep, brilliant colours and sure touch suggest that he may have studied the works of Jan Vermeer. He was the most gifted of a family of artists, and inspired still-life painters of the seventeenth and eighteenth centuries, as well as Henri Matisse, who admired this particular work so much that he made two copies of it.

► Arcimboldo, Claesz, Kalf, Ruysch, Snyders, Vermeer

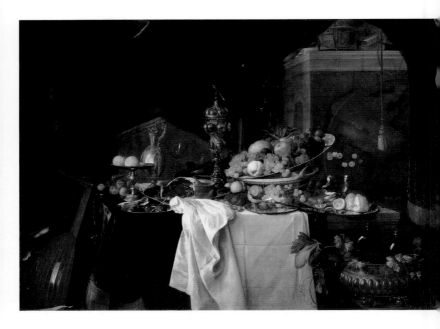

Jan Davidsz de Heem. b Utrecht, 1606. **d** Antwerp, 1683/4. **Still Life of Dessert**. 1640. Oil on canvas. **h**149 × **w**203 cm. **h**58½ × **w**80 in. Musée du Louvre, Paris

Heizer Michael

Dissipate 2

Five rectangular depressions scar the Nevada desert. Randomly placed, their arrangement was decided after Heizer dropped five matchsticks on to a piece of paper, in a Dada-like challenge to rational design. *Dissipate 2* formed part of *Nine Nevada Depressions*, a group of works created by digging into the earth along the California/Nevada border. The desert became a huge flat canvas on which Heizer drew, carving out negative sculptures defined by empty space, by absence that is nevertheless palpably present. The trenches were originally lined with wood, which was left to deteriorate. According to Heizer, 'As the physical deteriorates, the abstract proliferates, exchanging points of view.' *Nine Nevada Depressions* was one of the first 'earthworks' in the movement that came to be called Land art. Site-specific, responding directly to its surroundings, Land art is often created, as here, in remote or abandoned places, to which the journey is a kind of pilgrimage, an integral part of the experience of the work itself.

► Adams, Long, Matta-Clark, Smithson

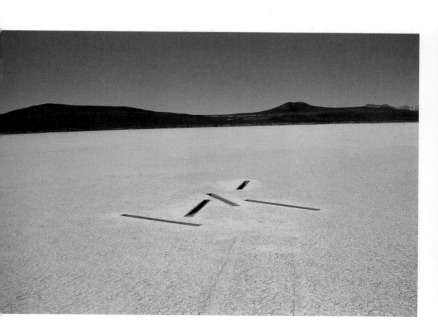

Michael Heizer. b Berkeley, CA, 1944. Dissipate 2. 1968. Five wood-lined excavations, each d30.5 × l365.8 × w30.5 m.
d2 × l144 × w12 in. Overall area, l1524 × w1372 cm. l600 × w540 in. Black Rock Desert, Gerlach, NV

249

Hepworth Barbara

Hollow Form with White Interior

Holes in the wood invite the viewer to peer through them. Made from the scented African hardwood guarea, the piece has been polished smooth, its gleaming surface contrasting sharply with the chiselled and painted hollows. Although abstract in style, the sculpture, the curves of which may reflect the artist's early memories of the undulating Yorkshire countryside, conveys a sense of harmony with the natural world. Hepworth began, like Henry Moore, by piercing holes in her works and went on to carve out the insides, as in caves

hollowed out by the sea, often using string or wire to suggest a musical instrument. Although Henry Moore was an influence, she developed her own spare and economic style largely of abstract sculpture, without allying herself to any particular movement. She married the painter Ben Nicholson and settled in St Ives, Cornwall, where she drew inspiration from its dramatic coastline and landscape.

► Archipenko, Arp, Gabo, Moore, B Nicholson

Barbara Hepworth. b Wakefield, 1903. **d** St Ives, 1975. **Hollow Form with White Interior**. 1963. Partially painted guarea wood. **h**99 cm. **h**39 in. Private collection

Heron Patrick

Fourteen Discs: July 20,1963

Blocks of pure tint are arranged with delicate precision in order to create harmony of form and colour. Either painted or inscribed on the canvas are a series of discs. With no subject matter to disturb the visual purity of the group of different forms and colours, this abstract has subtle lyrical qualities and could be seen as a refined sensual meditation. Heron, a painter, writer and textile designer, was a conscientious objector during the Second World War, and worked as a farm labourer. He was associated with the artist

Ben Nicholson and the sculptor Barbara Hepworth in St Ives in Cornwall, and all three, in their different ways, followed an abstract style. As well as teaching at the Central School of Art in London, he was also an art critic for some years. Many one-man exhibitions of his work have been held worldwide.

► Hepworth, Klee, Lanyon, Matisse, Miró, B Nicholson, Noland

Patrick Heron. b Leeds, 1920. d Zennor, Cornwall, 1999. **Fourteen Discs: July 20, 1963**. 1963. Oil on canvas. h152 × w213 cm. h59 × w83 in. Collection of the artist

Hesse Eva

Sequel

Ninety-one irregular cast-latex balls lie randomly on a thin latex mat, which serves as a platform and at the same time reveals, in its suppleness, every crevice and curve of the floor, mediating between the art and the space that contains it. Industrial latex is meant to be cast, but for this mat Hesse used the material like paint, brushing it on layer by layer to build up a smooth but ragged, irregular surface like handmade paper. The imperfection of the forms was essential to their artistry, and represented for her the creative process itself. During a

brief career lasting only a decade before her death aged 34, Hesse became a leading proponent of Process art (sometimes called Post-Minimalism), embracing organic forms in contrast to the machine-made perfection and objectivity of Minimalism, and insisting that the process of creation was as important as the work of art that resulted from it.

► Arp, Bourgeois, Hepworth, Kapoor, Noguchi

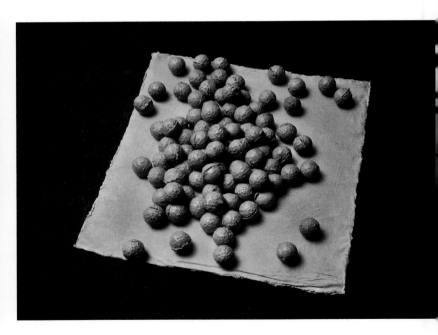

Eva Hesse. b Hamburg, 1936. **d** New York, NY, 1970. **Sequel.** 1967. 91 latex spheres, pigment and cheesecloth. Installation variable, sheet **w**76.2 × l81.3 cm. **w**30 × l32 in. Art Institute of Chicago, Chicago, IL

Hicks Edward

The Peaceable Kingdom

...ide-eyed animals, cherubic children and an idealized ...ndscape give this painting a sense of natural order. In the ...ckground, William Penn, the founder of the US state of ...nnsylvania, concludes a treaty with the Indians, further ...phasizing goodwill and harmony. The naïve style and ...sic colour scheme reinforce the work's simple message. ...r Hicks, the Peaceable Kingdom represented the eleventh ...apter of the book of Isaiah, which praises peace between ...en and animals. It was a subject that Hicks returned to

again and again, and scores of versions exist, each with minor variations. Hicks, an active Quaker preacher, began as an apprentice to a coachmaker, painting decorative panels for coaches, and went on to paint tavern signs. His landscapes reflected the Christian values he preached and he sold them to finance his missionary travels. His honest approach is typical of early American painting.

▶ Agasse, Bassano, J Bruegel, Catlin, H Rousseau

...ward Hicks. **b** Bucks County, PA, 1780. **d** Langhorne, PA, 1849. **The Peaceable Kingdom**. c1833/4. Oil on canvas. **h**44.5 × **w**59.3 cm.
.../₂ × **w**23¹/₂ in. Philadelphia Museum of Art, Philadelphia, PA

Hilliard Nicholas

Young Man Among Roses

The motto 'My praised faith causes my suffering', inscribed in Latin at the top of this portrait, echoes the themes of love found in contemporary sonnets by Shakespeare. This miniature, idealized portrait of a lovesick young dandy may have been a gift to a woman with the intention of showing his love was sincere. Hilliard, probably the most famous English painter of his time, believed that portraits should be painted without shadows so as to flatter the sitter, and according to his own account, Queen Elizabeth I agreed with him. He trained as a goldsmith in his father's shop and began painting miniatures at the age of 13. He later worked for the Queen as a goldsmith and portrait painter, selling miniatures of her to toadying courtiers for huge sums of money. He set a new tradition in portrait painting, but never achieved in his larger works in oils the quality and delicacy of his miniatures, many of which were actually worn as jewellery.

► Dobson, Holbein, Kneller, Moron

Nicholas Hilliard. b Exeter, c1547. **d** London, 1619. **Young Man Among Roses** (portrait miniature). c1590. Watercolour on vellum. **h**13.4 × **w**7 cm. **h**5¼ × **w**6¾ in. Victoria and Albert Museum, London

...rudging wearily across a wooden bridge over a river are ...ree figures and a donkey, silhouetted against the moon. ...contrast, a comical group of figures in the foreground is ...own as if in daylight. Firm, rigid outlines define the shapes, ...hich are filled in with solid blocks of colour. The Japanese ...tist Hiroshige was a younger contemporary of Hokusai, ...d was much impressed by the older master's more austere ...yle, although his own works are freer and more realistic in ...lour. His prints have come to epitomize Japanese art in their

unsophisticated, poetic simplicity. Seen in their own day as merely popular art, his landscapes had an electrifying effect on European artists at the end of the nineteenth century, when they began to be imported to the West. The Impressionists in particular were profoundly influenced by Hiroshige's fresh approach, and Claude Monet collected a large number of his prints.

► Araki, Degas, Hokusai, Monet, Utamaro, Whistler

...do Hiroshige. b Edo, 1797. d Edo, 1858. **Moonlight, Nagakubo**. 1840. Polychrome woodblock print on paper. **h**22 × **w**34 cm.

... × w13½ in. British Museum, London

255

Hirst Damien

A platinum cast of a human skull has been encrusted with 8,601 flawless diamonds. In the centre of the forehead sits a large pink diamond called the Skull Star Diamond. Costing a reputed £14 million to make, in 2007 the work was exhibited in the 'Beyond Belief' show at the White Cube gallery in London with a price tag of £50 million. Whilst clearly evoking the tradition of the *memento mori*, *For the Love of God* marked a continuation of Hirst's preoccupations with ideas of shock, fear and mortality – qualities with which he first became synonymous in the 1990s with his series of works in which dead animals were preserved in vitrines of formaldehyde. Hirst's oeuvre includes paintings as well as sculpture; much of it produced by his many assistants in multiple editions. It has been suggested that the title of the present work was inspired by his mother's remark, 'For the love of God, what are you going to do next?'

► Cattelan, Claesz, Judd, Koons

Damien Hirst. b Bristol, 1965. **For the Love of God**. 2006. Platinum, 8601 diamonds and human teeth. **h**17.1 × **w**12.7 cm. **h**6¾ × **w**5 in.
Private collection

Hobbema Meindert

Road on a Dyke

Warm brown tones dominate this peaceful, autumnal scene. Winding paths which lead the eye into the picture create an illusion of depth. Hobbema was meticulous in reproducing accurately the play of light on every leaf and blade of grass, and the ripples made by the ducks on the pond. Animals and humans are secondary here to the beauty of the landscape itself; only a close look reveals the houses, half-hidden by trees. Hobbema was a friend and pupil of Jacob van Ruisdael, and the two men even occasionally painted the same views,

but Ruisdael tended to give the scene drama, while Hobbema preferred to give the impression of a particular place. In the 1670s, at the height of his powers, he became, by marriage, collector of Amsterdam's wine tax, and from that moment his painting dwindled almost to nothing. For the last 40 years of his life, he devoted his energy not to art but to inspecting casks of wine.

► Bierstadt, Constable, Corot, Van Goyen, Ruisdael

Meindert Hobbema. b Amsterdam, 1638. d Amsterdam, 1709. **Road on a Dyke**. 1663. Oil on canvas. h108 × w128.3 cm. 42½ × w50½ in. Private collection

Höch bombards us with a disorientating and complex arrangement of images and words. Political and military leaders, artist and writers – some of them morphed into grotesque hybrid creatures – are scattered within a landscape of industrial components. In this politically loaded work, the artist successfully captures the chaos and fragmentation that affected German society in the years following the First World War. The only female member of the Berlin Dada group, Höch helped to pioneer photomontage as an avant-garde medium. The rather long title of the work not only implies a violent attack against the culture of greed that she saw in Germany at the time, but also the process of cutting involved in making the montage. The kitchen knife also has domestic connotations. The bottom left corner of the work includes a small portrait of the artist pasted over a map showing the European countries in which women had gained the right to vote.

► Dix, Grosz, Hausmann, Kruger, Schwitters

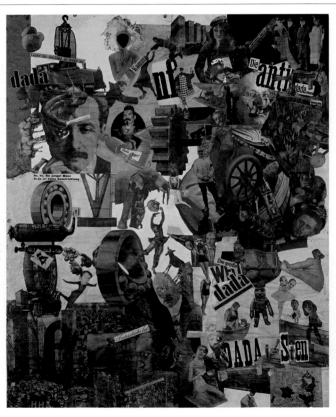

Hannah Höch. b Gotha, 1889. **d** Berlin, 1978. **Cut with the Kitchen Knife Through the Last Weimar Beer-Belly Cultural Epoch in Germany**, 1919. Photomontage and collage with watercolour. **h**114 × **w**90 cm. **h**44 ⅞ × **w**35¼ in. Nationalgalerie, Staatliche Museen zu Berlin

Under the intense, Californian sun, an unseen figure creates a splash in a pool. Hockney applied paint with rollers, using small brushes for the splash to suggest its sound exploding in the stillness. In one of his most consciously planned and provocative images, he contrasts the fleeting moment with the skilled technique that captured it. A conscientious objector who worked as a hospital orderly during his National Service, he was persuaded away from abstract art by fellow-student RB Kitaj, and from his earliest work was associated with the Pop Art movement. A visit to California (where he would live for many years) inspired the famous series of swimming pool and lawn and sprinkler paintings, which coolly observe this expensive, leisured world. A brilliant draughtsman, Hockney often embraces the latest technological developments. In the 1980s he exhibited drawings sent via fax machines, and more recently has created works using an iPad.

► P Blake, Hamilton, Hopper, Kitaj

David Hockney. b Bradford, 1937. **A Bigger Splash**. 1967. Acrylic on canvas. **h**243.8 × **w**243.8 cm. **h**96 × **w**96 in. Tate, London

Hodgkin Howard

Lovers

At first sight this painting seems abstract, but in fact it represents a memory of a real encounter. The ecstasy of the lovers is conveyed through the dramatic swirls of intense colour. As is his habit, Hodgkin uses wood as a base for the painting and carries the paint over onto the frame itself, incorporating it into the picture. He has said that painting must relate to relationships, and he usually shows people captured at a precise moment, reflecting some intense, personal memory. During time spent in India, Hodgkin was attracted by traditional Indian art. Its influence can be seen in his use of brilliant colour and his preference for small-scale works. His style, however, is entirely individual and personal. An inventive and prolific printmaker, he has also developed a strong reputation in this field. In 1985, Hodgkin won the UK Turner Prize for contemporary art.

► Chagall, Heron, Kossoff, Matisse, Rodin, Rothko

Howard Hodgkin. b London, 1932. **Lovers.** 1984-9. Oil on panel. **h**171.5 × **w**185.4 cm. **h**67½ × **w**73 in. Private collection

ghly ordered and symmetrical, the formal elements of
s painting have been carefully balanced to create a sense
calm. In the cool air of early morning the lake is pink,
lecting the glow of the rising sun. Our view of it has been
tricted, flattened and simplified as if to present us with
ly the essence of the scene, with all unnecessary detail
minated, and composed in a rhythmic pattern of layers of
rms and colour. Hodler evolved a highly decorative style
landscape with strong colours and outlines, using parallel

motifs for his effects. He was influenced by Camille Corot
and Gustave Courbet in the early part of his career but later
his paintings showed the artist's interest in Symbolism, with
its hidden meanings in objects, and in Art Nouveau, with
its curling tendrils and stylized leaves. The linear, flat style
which he eventually developed, using colour as an important
element, heralds the Expressionist movement.

► Böcklin, Corot, Courbet, Denis, Frankenthaler, Witz

dinand Hodler. b Bern, 1853. d Geneva, 1918. **Lake Thun**. 1905. Oil on canvas. **h**80.2 × **w**100 cm. **h**31½ × **w**39⅓ in.
ée d'Art et d'Histoire, Geneva

Swirling brushstrokes, applied with verve and panache, mingle together in a multitude of vibrant colours. Hofmann sought in this formless abstract to express the spirit or soul. He deliberately avoided both applying the paint with conscious care, and having a preconceived idea of how he wanted the painting to look, as if his artist's hand, left to itself, would create the image he wanted. In his drive to reproduce the visions in his mind's eye, Hofmann even eliminated the brush, pioneering the technique of pouring or dribbling the paint directly onto the canvas to create strong explosive patterns. This search for the ultimate expression of a mood or emotion, free from all artistic conventions, was known as Abstract Expressionism. Hofmann, as painter and teacher, was one of its most important advocates and his work greatly influenced Jackson Pollock. Born in Bavaria, Hofmann lived in both Munich and Paris for several years before emigrating to the USA in 1932.

► Frankenthaler, Gorky, De Kooning, Pollock

Hans Hofmann. b Weissenberg, 1880. **d** New York, NY, 1966. **Fairy Tale**. 1944. Oil on wood. **h**152 × **w**92 cm. **h**59½ × **w**36 in. Private collection

is afternoon, a chair lies overturned, cards are strewn on
e carpet and the debt collector rolls his eyes in exasperation.
te nights of drinking and gambling, overspending on
opulent house and the whims of an indolent wife are
tirized in this portrait. For Hogarth, criticism of taste was
so criticism of manners and he mocks the grotesque objets
art on the mantelpiece, the florid, fantastical clock and
e marble bust which looks more like a pig than a Roman
ble. Apprenticed to an engraver, he learned the trade and

eloped with the engraver's daughter. Tiring of conventional
art forms, he specialized in scathing, even savage, visual
commentaries on social conditions, made up of a series of
pictures which told a story. Engravings were made from the
original oils and their immense popularity made him famous.
Although his works parallel those of the Rococo painters in
France, his comic wit and style are utterly English.

► Boucher, Chardin, Fragonard, Steen, Watteau

lliam Hogarth. b London, 1697. d London, 1764. **The Tête à Tête, from *Marriage A-la-Mode*.** c1743. Oil on canvas.
9.9 × w90.8 cm. h27½ × w35¾ in. National Gallery, London

263

Hokusai Katsushika

Majestically simple and unsophisticated, this view of the much venerated Mount Fuji is direct and immediate. For many, this is the ultimate representation of Japan's most famous landmark. Rather than following the conventions of perspective, the Japanese artist Hokusai produced an image straight from his imagination, a view as fresh and pure as it appeared in his mind's eye. He was apprenticed to a wood engraver who taught him conventional painting and book illustration, but he later abandoned this for the coloured woodcut designs of the Ukiyo-e (or 'floating world') school, which concentrated on ordinary things in everyday life. He delighted in feats of artistic skill, dashing off in a few strokes of the brush the momentary landing of a sparrow on an ear of corn, for example. The bold simplicity of his designs and use of colour greatly influenced European artists, particularly Édouard Manet and his circle.

► Hiroshige, Hodler, Manet, Utamaro, Whistler

Katsushika Hokusai. b Edo, 1760. d Edo, 1849. **Mount Fuji in Clear Weather**. c1823-9. Polychrome woodblock print on paper. **h**27 × **w**38 cm. **h**10½ × **w**15 in. British Museum, London

Holbein Hans

The Ambassadors

The two sitters, so confident of their importance, are Jean [de] Dinteville, the French Ambassador to England, and his [fri]end, George de Selve, Bishop of Lavaur. An elaborate [co]llection of musical, astronomical and scientific instruments [sy]mbolizes their learning and power. The sundial sets the [sc]ene precisely at 10.30 am on 11 April. Holbein shows that [all] this magnificence and arrogance must end in the grave, [ho]wever, by contrasting their splendid richness with symbols [of] death: the broken string on the lute, and the distorted skull

yawning before them which can be seen only if standing to one side of the picture. Holbein was the greatest portrait painter of his time and was appointed official painter to the English Court. His portraits of Henry VIII, his queens and ministers illustrate Holbein's masterful technique and gift for revealing character. He died in London, a victim of plague.

► Claesz, Dürer, Van Eyck, Hals, Massys, Sittow

Holzer Jenny

Truisms

During a baseball game between the New York Mets and the San Francisco Giants, the scoreboard suddenly projects a pithy statement that seems at first arbitrary, then thoughtfully relevant. It is one of Jenny Holzer's 'truisms'. Holzer first began to explore the idea of language as art while studying literature and philosophy in New York. Simplifying complex and abstruse thoughts from her readings into short statements, she exhibited signs in Manhattan telephone booths and on buildings, eventually extending her oeuvre to include the electronic billboard in Times Square and the Guggenheim Museum ramp. Combining computer-controlled LED lights and axioms derived from classical philosophy, Holzer's aphorisms are deliberately challenging: 'Abuse of power comes as no surprise', 'There is a fine line between information and propaganda'. The anonymous, silent voice speaks in streaming light diodes, sending concise opinions in seamless cycles of light, thoughts inspiring thought.

► Baldessari, Kruger, Merz, Nauman, Wool

Jenny Holzer. b Gallipolis, OH, 1950. **Truisms**. 1977–9. Electronic sign. **h**732 × **w**976 cm. **h**288 × **w**384¼ in. As installed at Candlestick Park, San Francisco, CA, 1987

ree young boys and a fisherman weigh down the starboard e of a sailboat as it tacks against the breeze. Painted in the ne year that Mark Twain wrote *Huckleberry Finn*, *Breezing* ▸ evokes a sense of childhood, fresh air and summers tside that is typical of Homer's work of the mid-nineteenth ntury. His work is indeed considered the most authentic pression of American country life in the 1860s and 70s. The all boat is registered in Gloucester, Massachusetts, a small vn on the New England coast that was popular amongst

artists and where Homer spent many summers during the 1870s. Although Homer's choice of subject matter and his honest representation of the world around him is sometimes compared to the work of the contemporary French Impressionists, he was never directly influenced by them. With Thomas Eakins, Winslow Homer is considered the leading American representative of naturalism, the realistic depiction of the contemporary world.

▸ Bellows, Bingham, Eakins, Pissarro

nslow Homer. **b** Boston, MA, 1836. **d** Prout's Neck, ME, 1910. **Breezing Up**. 1876. Oil on canvas. **h**61.5 × **w**97 cm. **h**24⅛ × **w**38⅛ in. tional Gallery of Art, Washington, DC

Honthorst Gerrit van

Christ Before the High Priest

Christ stands before the high priest of Judea, brought there by Roman soldiers to be questioned about his teachings in light of the Jewish laws that are written in the book lying between them. The flickering candle flame forms the centre of the composition, its intense light harshly illuminating the face and pointing finger of the priest, and then more gently Christ's robe, face and crossed hands; the surrounding soldiers fade into the shadows. Honthorst was a master of the nocturnal scene, and the most famous member of the Dutch *caravaggisti*, followers of Caravaggio. These early seventeenth-century artists were fascinated by the Italian painter's vigorous manipulation of light and shadow which, combined with minimal settings and compositions of only a few figures, were used to create darkly atmospheric scenes. Carefully directing a single light source, Honthorst fills a potentially static scene with drama and suspense.

► Bernini, Ter Brugghen, Catena, Caravaggio, Jordaens

Gerrit van Honthorst. b Utrecht, 1592. **d** Utrecht, 1656. **Christ Before the High Priest**. c1617. Oil on canvas. **h**272 × **w**183 cm. **h**107 × **w**72 in. National Gallery, London

De Hooch Pieter

Woman and a Maid with a Pail in a Courtyard

This peaceful picture of a domestic event is carefully built up of tiny, meticulously observed details. The clear light gives the scene a sharp reality, in which the two figures would seem almost locked in a timeless, enclosed world were it not for the open door of the courtyard looking out onto a street. The doorway was a favourite device of De Hooch's: he would often paint a dark foreground, with an open door leading to a brightly lit inner room. There is an atmosphere of calm, of ordinary, everyday life, but there is also a sense that its

quiet and simplicity are in themselves beautiful. De Hooch's early paintings usually showed two or three people engaged in household tasks, in a room flooded with light. His later works abandoned these wonderfully lit, simple homes for rather forced scenes of high life. The people in them became richer, while the paintings themselves were poorer, and lost the quality of light.

► Ter Borch, Dou, Metsu, Steen, Vermeer

Pieter de Hooch. b Rotterdam, 1629. d Amsterdam, 1684. **Woman and a Maid with a Pail in a Courtyard**. 1660-5. Oil on canvas.
53 × w42 cm. h20¾ × w16 in. Hermitage Museum, St Petersburg

269

Hopper Edward

Cape Cod Evening

On the step of a house sits a man; to his right is a woman, her arms firmly folded across her body. The woman looks towards a dog that stands in the long grass, its attention drawn to some unknown event outside the picture. The scene has an eerie quality. The darkness of the locust tree grove and the opacity of the house's windows suggest that something may be hidden within. The various elements within the painting also appear somehow detached, as if the house or the people do not really belong there. Hopper's painting captures the long-lasting despair that followed the Great Depression in America. As nature imposes upon their land, there is a sense that progress has come to a halt for this couple, living in what was once, perhaps, a thriving rural community. The artist recalled that the painting was not of a specific place nor modelled on specific people, but was an accumulation of sketches and mental impressions.

► Estes, Hockney, Wood, Wyeth

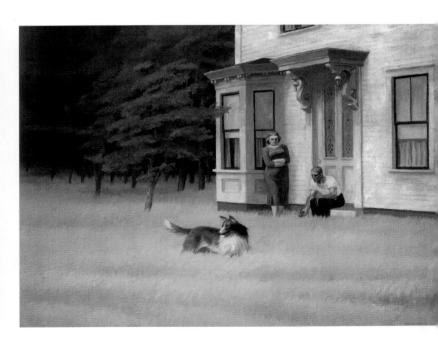

Edward Hopper. b Nyack, NY, 1882. **d** New York, NY, 1967. **Cape Cod Evening**. 1939. Oil on canvas. **h**76.2 × **w**101.6 cm. **h**30 × **w**40 in.
National Gallery of Art, Washington, DC

Houdon Jean-Antoine

Bust of Denis Diderot

This life-sized terracotta bust of the French philosopher still bears the marks of the sculptor's hands as he modelled the wet clay. Diderot's eyes look away from the viewer, separating his world from ours. Following the same style of the Roman busts of Antiquity, the sculpture for which this is a study is smooth and flawless, but this rougher working model gives insight into the mind of the artist as he developed his ideas into three dimensions. Houdon, the most celebrated French sculptor of the eighteenth century, narrowly escaped imprisonment during the Revolution. His most numerous works, however, are portraits, which include some of the greatest men of his time. His fame was such that the Americans commissioned from him a statue of their general, George Washington, to honour his victory in the American War of Independence; it stands in the Capitol at Richmond, Virginia.

► Algardi, Canova, Frink, Roubiliac

Hunt William Holman

The Awakening Conscience

Looking into this typical Victorian drawing room, we see a woman start up guiltily from her lover's knee, in mid-song, suddenly aware that what she is doing is wrong. Victorian values are reflected here, and the picture was intended to be a moral commentary. The patterned fabrics, grainy woods, busy wallpaper and garish colours are typical of Hunt's meticulous, almost obsessive, attention to detail. With Dante Gabriel Rossetti and John Everett Millais he founded the Pre-Raphaelite Brotherhood, dedicated to observing nature

accurately, but was the only one who remained faithful to its principles. Of all the Pre-Raphaelite painters he and Ford Madox Brown were most interested in representing moral and social values in contemporary Victorian life. Hunt tried to paint 'in direct application to Nature', using friends rather than professionals as models. He completed few pictures, spinning each one out as if he lacked the motivation to finish it and begin another.

► Fra Angelico, Botticelli, Brown, Millais, Rossetti

William Holman Hunt. b London, 1827. **d** London, 1910. **The Awakening Conscience.** 1853. Oil on canvas. **h**76.2 × **w**55.9 cm. **h**29¼ × **w**21¾ in. Tate, London

Named after the collector who first bought the picture, Ingres's *Bather of Valpinçon* is a calm representation of Classical beauty in the human nude. Softened by the delicate reflected light, the bather suggests a cold, languid eroticism, made ambiguous by her refusal to meet the viewer's gaze. The only sound or movement is that of a small spout of water, and the spartan interior seems to freeze the scene in time and space. Ingres was a superb draughtsman, but remained emotionally detached from his subjects and showed little interest in the expression of the human face. The polished perfection of his work was inspired by his Renaissance idol, Raphael. A leading figure in the Classical tradition of nineteenth-century France, Ingres painted many idealized and exotic oriental scenes with voluptuous nudes, although all the detail was second-hand, since he never travelled outside Europe.

► Boucher, Canova, J-L David, Leighton, Maillol, Prud'hon

Jean Auguste Dominique Ingres. **b** Montauban, 1780. **d** Paris, 1867. **The Bather of Valpinçon**. 1808. Oil on canvas. **h**146 × **w**97.5 cm. **h**57½ × **w**38⅓ in. Musée du Louvre, Paris

273

Ivanov Alexander

The Appearance of Christ to the People

St John the Baptist, wearing a cloak over his tunic of animal skins, raises his reed cross to the crowd that presses around him, and preaches the word of God to his followers. Ivanov illustrates the two things that mattered most to this rough visionary: his foretelling of the coming of Christ and the baptisms he carried out in the river Jordan. On the left, some of the newly baptized can be seen clambering up the bank. Ivanov used Classical postures and dress, and adopted the restrained style of the Renaissance, hoping to achieve the same noble grandeur and harmony as the great painters Raphael and Michelangelo. Most of his adult life was spent in Rome, where he came under the influence of the Nazarenes, a religious artistic group. Although many of his Biblical paintings never got beyond the drawing stage, they combined a sense of mysticism with historical accuracy and original visual imagery.

► Canova, J-L David, Ingres, Overbeck, Poussin, Prud'hon

Alexander Ivanov. b St Petersburg, 1806. **d** St Petersburg, 1858. **The Appearance of Christ to the People**. 1837–57. Oil on canvas.
h540 × **w**750 cm. **h**212½ × **w**295¼ in. Tretyakov Gallery, Moscow

Jawlensky Alexei von

Schokko

This strong, reflective portrait of a fashionable woman has been painted in bold outlines. The intense clashing colours evoke powerful emotions of sensuality, yet her mask-like face suggests a sexual remoteness. The importance of this painting lies in Jawlensky's complete reliance on colour to construct the image and to give it its emotional power. The title of the painting originates in the young model: she asked for a cup of hot chocolate (*schokko*) and thus adopted the nickname. Russian-born, Jawlensky spent most of his life in Germany but his style was rooted in the art of his native country. It combined Fauvist elements, such as hard outlines and strong colour, with those of peasant art or the mysticism of Russian religious icons. This can be seen in one of his best-known works, the abstract series 'Heads', where features are reduced to straight, thick lines. The human face was a favourite theme: in his last series of paintings, 'Meditations', it became a symbol of tragedy.

► Van Dongen, Gontcharova, Kandinsky, Marc

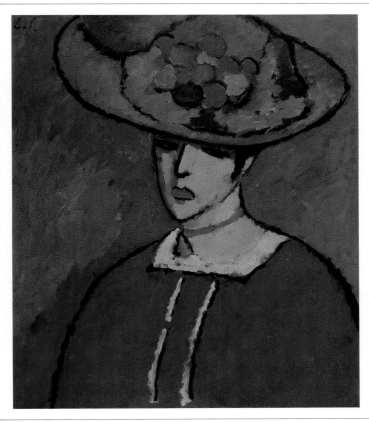

Alexei von Jawlensky. b Kuslovo, 1864. d Wiesbaden, 1941. Schokko. 1910. Oil on board mounted on canvas. h75 × w65 cm. h29½ × w24½ in. Private collection

John Gwen

The Precious Book

Cool tones dominate this simple portrait of a young girl reading. The white handkerchief in which she cradles the book, her absorption in it, and the picture's title itself imply that the book is special and deserves reverence. Born in Wales, Gwen John learned draughtsmanship at the Slade School in London, studied in Paris under James Abbott McNeill Whistler and developed an idiosyncratic personal style that was at once delicate and neurotic. Her portraits in particular (usually of women) had an obsessive quality. She modelled for the sculptor Auguste Rodin, became his mistress and moved to France to be near him, but this one-sided and disastrous liaison almost caused her to abandon her own work. During her lifetime, most of it spent in obscurity and self-neglect, she was overshadowed by her younger brother, Augustus, but is now recognized as the greater artist. She died unrecognized, a semi-religious recluse.

▶ Cassatt, Hammershøi, Morisot, Rodin, Sickert, Whistler

Gwen John. b Haverfordwest, 1876. d Dieppe, 1939. **The Precious Book**. c1920. Oil on canvas. h26.4 × w21 cm. h10⅜ × w8¼ in. Private collection

Johns Jasper

Three Flags

Johns chose to represent the American flag not because he was particularly nationalistic but because he was looking to paint the most banal, easily recognizable subject he could find. What better than the Star-Spangled Banner? Johns' flag does not fly from a mast in glory, it is not carried by a victorious soldier. It is flat, like a real flag would be if it were pinned on a wall. Johns has not represented a flag but presented us with a flag. He is not trying to fool us into believing that it is real, however. Encaustic, a medium used primarily by the

Greeks, gives the painting a thick, relief-like surface. Johns has superimposed three differently sized flags on top of one another, reinforcing the image, almost like a flashing light and creating a strange optical effect. With fellow American Robert Rauschenberg, Johns is regarded as one of the most important influences on American Pop Art.

► Duchamp, Oldenburg, Rauschenberg, Thiebaud

Jasper Johns. b Augusta, GA, 1930. **Three Flags**. 1958. Encaustic on canvas. **h**76.5 × **w**116 cm. **h**30⅛ × **w**45½ in.
Whitney Museum of American Art, New York, NY

277

Jones Allen

Man Woman

One of a series of paintings with the collective title 'Hermaphrodite', the headless male and female bodies melt into one another. The male figure in the brightly striped tie is in fact a self-portrait of the artist. In his preoccupation with sexuality, Jones wanted to show here the unity with another human being that can only be achieved by the sexual act. He was deeply influenced by Jungian psychology, and by the philosophy of Nietzsche who believed that the creation of art depends upon artists being able to integrate the male and female elements of their natures. *Man Woman*, an early example by Jones of a Pop Art work, is a visual representation of this theory. His paintings often tell a story. In the late 1960s and 1970s he was to explore further the erotic ideas in his work and consequently many of his images of women are seen as sexually provocative.

► Hamilton, De Kooning, Polke, Warhol, Wesselmann

Allen Jones. b Southampton, 1937. **Man Woman**. 1963. Oil on canvas. **h**213 × **w**188.5 cm. **h**84½ × **w**74½ in. Tate, London

Jordaens Jacob

The Four Evangelists

The four Evangelists contemplate the Scriptures, which in turn inspire their own writings. Jordaens gives us an insight into their personalities as they are absorbed in the study of the sacred text which rests on a table. The half-length figures dominate the space, almost obliterating the background of red velvety drapery and a glint of sky. A pupil of Peter Paul Rubens, Jordaens has captured his master's vivid colouring, brushwork and skill in portraying natural flesh tones. The vigorous realism of the composition owes far more to the influence of Caravaggio, however, whose style Jordaens would have seen reflected in works by the Italian painter's followers in Utrecht. Although his early paintings were technically weak, but robust, Jordaens developed as an artist, his style became more sombre and he was later patronized by the kings of Spain and Sweden.

► Ter Brugghen, Guercino, Honthorst, Rubens

Jacob Jordaens. b Antwerp, 1593. **d** Antwerp, 1678. **The Four Evangelists**. c1625. Oil on canvas. **h**134 × **w**118 cm. **h**53 × **w**46½ in. Musée du Louvre, Paris

Judd Donald

Untitled

This sculpture, from the series 'Stacks', consists of a vertical arrangement of identical rectangular boxes, attached to a wall at right-angles in a mathematical sequence. It demonstrates Judd's simplification of shape, volume, colour and surface, and reduces art to its basic essential: the cube. Minimalist in style, like all his other pieces, the work is deliberately intended not to represent, imitate or express anything, nor is it 'composed' in any traditional sense. To achieve minimal personal contact with his work, the metal or plexiglass boxes he used were put together in a factory, spray-painted and placed in position by other people. All his pieces were called 'Untitled' and were as plain as possible because he believed that a work of art should be looked at as a whole, not as a collection of parts. In addition to sculpture, Judd designed his own furniture and designed and built several houses.

► Andre, Flavin, Johns, LeWitt, Ryman

Donald Judd. b Excelsior Springs, MO, 1928. d New York, NY, 1994. **Untitled**. 1993. Brass and green plexiglass. h457.2 cm. h180 in. Private collection

Kabakov Ilya & Emilia

Treatment with Memories

Treatment with Memories begins at a shabby wooden door that leads into a gloomy corridor from which additional doors lead in to six curtained rooms. In each is a narrow hospital bed, three small stools, on which the viewer may sit, and a screen on to which images of the absent occupants imaginary past are projected. Ilya and Emilia Kabakov provide an accompanying narrative via headphones in each room. Combining fiction with biography, the artists create unsettling and often oppressive environments that recall the fears of life under a totalitarian regime, as well as more universal feelings of anxiety and despair. However in their allusions to the realms of fantasy and dreams they also celebrate the resilience of the human spirit. Before leaving the Soviet Union in the late 1980s, Ilya was an established figure within the 'unofficial' Conceptual art movement in Moscow. He first collaborated with his wife, Emilia, in 1989 – the extent of her involvement depending on the requirements of each project.

► Araki, Boltanski, Kienholz, Kippenberger

Ilya Kabakov. b Dnepropetrovsk, Ukraine, 1933. **Emilia Kabakov. b** Dnepropetrovsk, Ukraine, 1945. **Treatment with Memories.** 1997. Wood, board, hospital bed, slide projection. Dimensions variable. As installed at the Whitney Biennial, NY

Kahlo Frida

The artist's hallucinations and imaginings run riot in this painting. It shows a bathtime reverie, in which images of death, pain and sexuality float on the water's surface. As in many of her pictures, it is a kind of self-portrait, with Kahlo's own legs painted from the bather's viewpoint, showing her deformed foot with its cracked big toe. Her injuries, as the result of a serious road accident at the age of 15, destroyed her hopes of becoming a doctor. This painting, considered to be her most Surrealist, is also the most complex of all her works, with its multitude of minute and irrationally arranged detail. She was married to the painter Diego Rivera; they had a turbulent relationship, and at one time she became a lover of Leon Trotsky. Kahlo has become something of a cult figure partly because from the mid-1940s she suffered from spinal problems and, bedridden, continued to paint, often in terrible pain, until her death.

► Carrà, De Chirico, Dalí, Delvaux, O'Keeffe, Rivera

Frida Kahlo. b Mexico City, 1907. **d** Mexico City, 1954. **What the Water Gave Me**. 1938. Oil on canvas. **h**96.5 × **w**76.2 cm. **h**38 × **w**30 in. Private collection

Kalf Willem

Still Life with Lobster, Drinking Horn and Glasses

A collection of exotic and opulent objects laid out on the table is here painted with great brilliance and depth of colour. A lobster, a drinking horn with its glittering mount of silver filigree work, crystal goblets, a lemon and a Turkish carpet are painted with such fine attention to detail that Kalf creates the illusion that they are real and could be touched. Each object has been carefully placed so that the group forms a harmony of colour, shape and texture. The warm light enveloping the objects gives them a luxurious, jewel-like quality and their rarity, sumptuousness and extravagance reflect the refined tastes of Dutch seventeenth-century collectors, in a period when still lifes were immensely popular. Kalf lived and worked mainly in Amsterdam. The deep, rich colours of the paintings of this still-life painter may have been influenced by the work of his contemporary, Jan Vermeer.

▶ Claesz, De Heem, W Nicholson, Sánchez-Cotán, Vermeer

Kandinsky Wassily   Cossacks

Colours, lines and shapes, hills and Cossacks with lances blend together in this strangely captivating semi-abstract painting. There is great beauty in its simple composition and a sense of delight in the free brushstrokes. Kandinsky believed that the true artist seeks to express only inner, essential feelings. Having originally trained in Munich for a career in law, Kandinsky soon recognized that his true gifts were in the world of art and he became one of the first and greatest pioneers of 'pure' abstract painting. He returned to Russia to teach from 1914 to 1922, founding the Russian Academy. The Russian influence in his work can be seen in his references to icons and folk art. For a time, he taught at the famous Bauhaus school of modern design. Kandinsky became aware of the power of abstract art after he saw 'extraordinary beauty, glowing with an inner radiance' in an abstract painting, before realizing that it was one of his own, seen upside-down.

▶ Delaunay, Gontcharova, Kirchner, Klee, Kupka, Miró

Wassily Kandinsky. b Moscow, 1866. **d** Paris, 1944. **Cossacks**. 1910/11. Oil on canvas. **h**95 × **w**130 cm. **h**37½ × **w**51⅛ in. Tate, London like a standing stone from a prehistoric site, the sandstone beacon (*It is Man*) seems wrapped in a mysterious aura. In the foreground, randomly placed slabs (*Untitled 11 Parts*) have been transformed by the application of more than a dozen coats of blue pigment, lending them an ethereal, weightless quality. Kapoor has tried to combine the spiritual with the forces of nature in these works, and to show in a new dimension – that of sculpture – that there is poetry in natural things. His sculptures, often made from stone or

fibreglass, coated with layers of powdered pigment, often involve more than one of the senses, particularly touch. They show the traditions of both East and West, and reflect ideas from philosophy, mythology and everyday life gathered on visits to his native India. In keeping with a culture that expresses philosophical or spiritual theories in terms of sensual images, some of his pieces take on the character of a totem, with extravagant forms and loud colour.

► Friedrich, Gabo, Klein, Long, Moore, Noguchi

Katz Alex

Cropped at the shoulders like a classical bust, with the calm, inscrutable expression that has become famous among images of artists' muses, Alex Katz's wife and favourite model, Ada, stands against a background of shimmering water and curving foliage. The ripples in her bathing cap suggest those on the surface of the lake, and the flecked brown eyes echo the patterns of light on the water. Working alongside the Abstract Expressionists in 1950s New York, Katz appropriated their vast scales and dramatic colours but insisted on recording what he saw. Less interested in inner feelings than external surfaces, he painted hairstyles and hats rather than emotions and his works continue to present the appearance rather than the psychology of figures from contemporary life – musicians, artists, suburbanites, friends and family. The hard lines, dramatic cropping and uninflected colours of billboard and advertising in his paintings anticipated Pop art in the 1950s and 60s, and give his work a contemporary freshness.

► Lichtenstein, Richter, Tuymans, Warhol, Wood

Alex Katz. b New York, NY, 1927. **Ada with Bathing Cap**. 1965. Oil on Linen. **h**152.4 × **w**182.9 cm. **h**60 × **w**72 in. Private collection

Kauffmann Angelica

David Garrick

an unusual and disarming approach, Kauffmann has captured the private, sensitive side of the great actor David Garrick's personality. The way in which Garrick turns around his chair to look out at the viewer is touching and intimate; was more often shown in a highly dramatic pose, as if were standing on stage. Born in Switzerland, Kauffmann gan painting portraits of Italian notables at the age of 11, d was persuaded by Sir Joshua Reynolds to go to London. he soon became famous for her Classical and mythological

pictures, and for her portraits. In the 1770s she was commissioned to do murals for houses built by the designer Robert Adam and his brother, whose soft colours and Antique style were well suited to her work. Many engravings were made of these Classically inspired, idyllic scenes which were used in the manufacture of objets d'art; their popularity made her name famous.

▶ Gainsborough, Poussin, Rosa, Vigée-Lebrun

gelica Kauffmann. b Chur, 1741. d Rome, 1807. **David Garrick**. 1764. Oil on canvas. **h**84 × **w**69 cm. **h**33 × **w**27⅛ in.
ghley House, Stamford

On Kawara makes art out of time, history and memory. His magnum opus is the *Today* series, also called *Date Paintings*, comprising a simple painting of a date, housed in a cardboard box lined with a newspaper clipping from the same day. Beginning with *Jan. 4, 1966*, each painting is executed in white paint on a dark background, using the language and grammatical conventions of the country in which it was painted; the clipping comes from a local newspaper. Some days more than one painting is made, and on many days none;

if the work is incomplete at midnight, it is destroyed. Kawara recording of countless dates from over a hundred cities so far is a form of artistic meditation. Time is experienced both as a lived abstraction and as a personal history, seen in the occasional subtitles he gives to the paintings: 'USA bombs Vietnam again', 'a friend came to the studio'. The dates, too, created within a rigid standardization, nevertheless reveal the process of their making in slight imperfections.

► Becher, Calle, Gonzalez-Torres, Kelley, Wool

On Kawara. b Kariya, Aichi, 1933. **21 OCT. 68**. 1968. Liquitex on canvas, cardboard box, newspaper. **h**20.5 × **w**25.5 cm. **h**8 × **w**10 in.
Private collection

group of found, stuffed fabric dolls is arranged with taxonomic precision, based on size and type; photographs in black and white exhibit individual dolls alongside a ruler, in the way of archaeological finds. Kelley thus imposes an analytic order on once-loved, now discarded, childhood objects. Mixing tasteless pop culture with philosophical themes in paintings, sculpture, performances and installations, Kelley's conceptual works expose the grimy underside of society and private life, questioning the conventions that surround religion, family,

sexuality, and the modern cult of victimhood. His irreverent 'punk' art is raunchy, uncomfortable and sometimes deliberately humiliating in its attempts to make the viewer examine his own preconceptions. Though Kelley's questioning of cultural norms would continue until his death, this piece marks his abandonment of craft objects in his work, following the refusal of critics to see his found toys as anything but evidence of the artist's infantile recidivism.

► Baldessari, Duchamp, Hirst, Koons, Ray

ike Kelley. b Detroit, MI, 1954. d Los Angeles, CA, 2012. **Craft Morphology Flow Chart**. 1991. 32 tables, 114 dolls, 60 photographs, he drawing. Dimensions variable. As installed at the Carnegie Museum of Art, Pittsburgh, PA

Kelly Ellsworth

Red Blue Green Yellow

Paint has been applied, without any evidence of the artist's hand, in flat areas of defined pure colour. A yellow panel has been placed on the floor at right-angles to the main painting, as if to sever any connection it might have with the ground, and suggesting a three-dimensional quality. In its emphasis on pure colour, use of space and incorporation of two flat surfaces, this work reflects the theories of the Post-Painterly Abstractionist movement of the 1960s. It is one of a group known as 'Specific Objects', hovering between painting,

relief and sculpture, and attacks preconceived ideas of the differences between sculpture and painting. Kelly studied in Boston and at the Académie des Beaux-Arts in Paris. His work is extremely varied: he has introduced broadly curving edges to his paintings and sculptures, and sometimes has eliminated colour altogether in favour of black, white and grey.

► Albers, Louis, Newman, Ryman, Stella

Ellsworth Kelly. b Newburgh, NY, 1923. **Red Blue Green Yellow**. 1965. Oil on canvas (bottom panel mounted on masonite). **h**222.2 × **w**137.1 × **d**222.2 cm. **h**87½ × **w**56 × **d**87 in. Margo Leavin Gallery, Los Angeles, CA

Two pairs of glasses and a pipe, resting in a bowl, have been placed on the corner of a table. The simple impact of these objects, along with their elegant arrangement, is illustrative of Kertész's pioneering approach to photographic composition during the first half of the twentieth century. Although on the surface the objects appear to have been chosen for their formal qualities, they have a rich associative value when it is realized that they belonged to one of the period's greatest abstract painters, Piet Mondrian. Taken in Mondrian's Paris studio, the image evokes the purity and clarity of vision that informed the Dutch artist's iconic paintings. Kertész had emigrated from his native Hungary to the French capital in 1925, becoming associated with many of the more progressive artists living in the city, including Fernand Léger and the Dada poet Tristan Tzara. The current work was included in Kertész's first solo exhibition held at the avant-garde Au Sacre du Printemps Gallery.

► Cartier-Bresson, Léger, Mondrian, W Nicholson, Weston

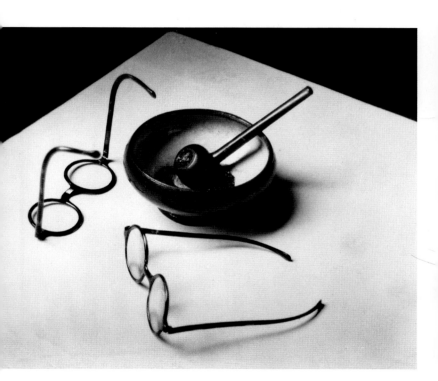

André Kertész. b Budapest, 1894. d New York, NY, 1985. **Mondrian's Pipe and Glasses**. 1926. Gelatin silver print, **h**8 × **w**9 cm. 3⅛ × **w**3½ in. Médiathèque de l'Architecture et du Patrimoine, Paris

Kiefer Anselm

Song of the Wayland

This monumental and awe-inspiring image of burned and ploughed fields under a raised horizon involved the use of a wide range of materials. The title refers to the myth of Wayland, the master blacksmith. Crippled by his king to prevent him leaving, Wayland raped the king's daughter and killed his two sons, then forged himself wings for his escape. Kiefer's association of this evil parable with the destruction so powerfully portrayed in the scorched landscape conjures up haunting memories, including the Holocaust. The theme of German culture, distorted during the Third Reich by Nazi doctrine, is central to his work. This painting could be seen as Neo-Expressionist in context (the revival of a style that emphasized the artist's reaction to an experience, rather than the facts of the experience itself). Kiefer's varied work includes large black-and-white woodcuts in bold outlines, and 'books' made from photographs or woodcuts.

► Baselitz, Beckmann, Boltanski, Hofmann, Kitaj

Anselm Kiefer. b Donaueschingen, 1945. **Song of the Wayland.** 1982. Oil, emulsion, straw, photograph and lead wing on canvas. **h**280 × **w**380 cm. **h**110⅓ × **w**149⅔ in. Private collection group of mannequins sit around a bar, each of their faces replaced with a clock set at ten minutes past ten. Infused with the sound of chattering customers and the smell of food and beer, this large tableau is a reconstruction of Barney's Beanery, a diner in West Hollywood famously frequented by actors, artists and musicians. Displayed on a newsstand outside is the headline 'Children Kill Children in Vietnam Riots'. According to the artist it was the shocking contrast between the escapism provided inside the Beanery and the

horrific realities of events elsewhere that had first inspired him to produce the work. Kienholz began to construct large-scale tableaux in the early 1960s. These were often uncompromising representations of the less palpable aspects of twentieth-century society. In 1981 he declared that all of his work produced after 1972 should be jointly attributed to himself and his wife, Nancy Reddin Kienholz.

► Gonzalez-Torres, Kabakov, Oldenburg, Segal

Kienholz. b Fairfield, WA, 1927. **d** Hope, ID, 1994. **The Beanery**. 1965. Mixed media. **h**213.3 × **w**182.9 × **d**670.5 cm. 4¼ × **w**72¼ × **d**264¼ in. Stedelijk Museum, Amsterdam

Kippenberger Martin

The Happy End of Franz Kafka's 'Amerika'

An eclectic assortment of desks, tables and chairs has been set out in a gallery to create a playful environment for conducting interviews. Alongside conventional office furniture, the artist has included beach chairs and raised lifeguard platforms. The large installation proposes a setting for a happy conclusion to Franz Kafka's unfinished, and posthumously published, novel *Amerika*, a book that the artist claimed he had never read. In Kafka's story the protagonist, Karl Rossman, applies for a job at the Nature Theatre of Oklahoma – an organization that promises to find work for everyone. It is the utopian idea of total employment that underlies Kippenberger's work. The different styles of furniture allude to the diverse range of people who would partake in the interview process. Kippenberger was one of the most prolific and respected German artists of his generation. Spanning a wide range of media, he avoided signs of stylistic consistency in his work.

► Demand, Kabakov, Kienholz, G Orozco

Martin Kippenberger. b Dortmund, 1953. **d** Vienna, 1997. **The Happy End of Franz Kafka's 'Amerika'.** 1994.
As installed at the Museum Boymans-van Beuningen, Rotterdam

rough brushstrokes and vitriolic colours which clash violently contribute to a feeling of desperate energy. The painting appears almost too small to contain the scene, suggesting a sense of expansion as if the colours were straining at the edges. This painting is characteristic of the sensual, vibrant colour, dramatic intensity and angular outlines of Expressionism. Kirchner was part of a group of Expressionists who called themselves 'Die Brücke', or the Bridge, implying that they connected the art of the past with

that of the future. There was some rivalry between himself and Erich Heckel, another member of the group: Kirchner would sometimes date his works too early, trying to prove that he was more innovative than the others. From 1917 Kirchner lived in Switzerland on health grounds as he was suffering from tuberculosis. In 1937, many of his works were confiscated by the Nazis as 'degenerate'; he committed suicide a year later.

► Van Gogh, Heckel, Kandinsky, Munch, Velázquez

rnst Ludwig Kirchner. b Aschaffenburg, 1880. d Davos, 1938. **Self-portrait with Model**. c1910. Oil on canvas. h149.9 × w100.3 cm.
₅9 × w39½ in. Kunsthalle, Hamburg

Kitaj R B

If Not, Not

The Gatehouse at Auschwitz dominates the scarred landscape, scattered with figures and fragments. The theme is clearly the genocide of the European Jews. Figures in the foreground contrast with the dream-like scenery, and include Kitaj's self-portrait as the grey man with the hearing-aid. This complex and seductive painting draws together a wide range of literary and artistic references, including T S Eliot's poem *The Waste Land*. In these strong references to visual culture and literature, Kitaj is interpreting the British

Pop Art movement. A painter of sharp intellect and literary allusion, he often portrayed panoramas of suffering people, in landscapes that are harsh and uncompromising. These heartfelt paintings, which he often felt were never finished, create a vision of a world that is cruel, in which only Nature herself is spared. He lived and worked mostly in England.

► Boyd, Burra, Hamilton, Kiefer, Lewis, Nash, Nolan

R B (Ronald Brooks) Kitaj. b Cleveland, OH, 1932. d Los Angeles, CA, 2007. If Not, Not. 1975-6. Oil on canvas. h152.4 × w152.4 cm. h60 × w60 in. Scottish National Gallery of Modern Art, Edinburgh

Senecio

his adaptation of the human face is divided by colour into ctangles. Flat geometric squares are held within a circle presenting a masked face and displaying the multi-coloured ostume of a harlequin. A portrait of the artist-performer enecio, it can be seen as a symbol of the shifting relationship tween art, illusion and the world of drama. This painting emonstrates Klee's principles of art, in which the graphic ements of line, colour planes and space are set in motion by energy from the artist's mind. In his imaginative doodlings,

he liked, in his own words, to 'take a line for a walk'. From 1921 to 1931 he was a brilliant teacher at the Bauhaus school of design, publishing many writings on his theory of art. Two years later, the Nazis exiled him from Germany, when over one hundred of his works were removed from German galleries as 'degenerate'.

► Albers, Braque, Delaunay, Dine, Feininger, Picasso

ul **Klee**. **b** Munchenbuchsee, 1879. **d** Muralto-Locarno, 1940. **Senecio**. 1922. Oil on canvas mounted on panel. **h**40.5 × **w**38 cm.
5 ⅞ × **w**15 in. Kunstmuseum, Basel

Klein Yves

IKB stands for International Klein Blue, a paint which Klein mixed personally and then patented. Its brilliant colour is maintained by the addition of synthetic resin to the blue pigment. Most of Klein's paintings are blue, as blue was an important colour to him, conveying a sensation of spirituality and freedom which is peculiar to his work. The power of the painting lies in its ability to invade the viewer's sensibility and exert a strong meditative influence. Klein is considered to be one of the most important post-war international artists

and was a leader of the European Neo-Dada movement, a style intended to shock and outrage. His work includes paintings that were deliberately burned, and the extraordinary 'Anthropométries' series, for which female models were smeared with the famous blue paint and dragged across the canvas under Klein's direction, to the accompaniment of his own symphony. Tragically, he died of a heart attack at the age of only 34.

► Christo, Fontana, Heron, Rothko

Yves Klein. b Nice, 1928. d Paris, 1962. **IKB 79**. c1959. Pigment and synthetic resin on canvas. h139.7 × w119.7 cm. h55 × w47⅛ in. Tate, London

Klimt Gustav

The Kiss

In a mass of patterns and shapes, the form of a kissing couple emerges from a field of flowers. Gold predominates the colour scheme, punctuated by the bright colours of the flowers and the rich decorative designs on the clothing. The eroticism of the image is conveyed through sensuous line, bold pattern and luscious colours which create a dream world that is also luxurious and decadent. Essentially a decorator, Klimt was a leader of the Vienna Secession, a group of artists and craftsmen who revolted against the conservative and moralizing works of the previous generation. Their new style is often called Art Nouveau. He produced a number of portraits, mainly of women, and some large allegorical and mythical paintings. Although he was most successful as a designer for the applied arts (such as mosaic), his murals for Vienna University were unpopular and widely considered pornographic.

► Burne-Jones, Moreau, Mucha, Schiele

Gustav Klimt. **b** Vienna, 1862. **d** Vienna, 1918. **The Kiss**. 1907/8. Oil on canvas. **h**180 × **w**180 cm. **h**70 ⅞ × **w**70 ⅞ in. Österreichische Galerie, Vienna

Kline Franz

Untitled

A total of five black, wide brushtrokes float on a thickly painted and richly textured white background, evoking sensations of vast spaces. Kline was inspired by the techniques of graphic illustration, and by the massive sections of partly constructed or demolished girders, railways, scaffolding and bridges of New York. The power of the painting lies in this expression of the violent tension between solid space represented by the dark paint, and vast, open space, represented by the white. Its connection to the American Abstract Expressionist movement (of which Kline was a leading representative) is demonstrated by the spontaneous gestures of the energetic yet simple brushstrokes. Kline was influenced by oriental calligraphy and normally limited his colour schemes to black, white and grey but by 1959 he began incorporating vivid colour into his paintings.

► Hartung, De Kooning, O'Keeffe, Pollock, Still, Tobey

Franz Kline. b Wilkes-Barre, PA, 1910. **d** New York, NY, 1962. **Untitled**. 1951. Oil on canvas. **h**182.9 × **w**198.2 cm. **h**72 × **w**78 in. Private collection

Everything about this portrait is luxurious: the gold braid, white silk, plush blue velvet, fluffy white feathers and curly wig all contribute to the magnificence of the sitter. He may be identified as a holder of the Order of the Garter by his gold chain, the blue band around his calf and the embroidery on his robe. Kneller's portraits of British nobility often repeated the pose and garments seen here. His practice was to paint the figure and the background first, then fill in the face when he was able to study the sitter in the flesh. On his arrival in

London, Kneller quickly became a leading portrait painter. He established a workshop with a large team of specialized assistants, which enabled the mass-production of portraits such as this one. He painted ten reigning monarchs including every English sovereign from Charles II to George II, and was massively conceited, believing that the world would have been a better place had God consulted him at the Creation.

► Dobson, Van Dyck, Hilliard, Lely, Moroni

Sir Godfrey Kneller. b Lübeck, c1646. d London, 1723. John, First Duke of Marlborough. c1705. Oil on canvas. h218.4 × w132 cm. 86 × w52 in. Blenheim Palace, Woodstock

301

Kokoschka Oskar

Portrait of a 'Degenerate Artist'

All the contours and peculiarities of the artist's face are outlined in a multitude of colour tones to suggest his anxiety and anger. This self-portrait shows Kokoschka as a self-proclaimed 'degenerate artist' whose innovative art was suppressed by the Nazis during the war. The violent brushwork appears both spontaneous and untidy, but behind it there is control, bringing together the jarring colours into a structured whole. Kokoschka's exaggeration and distortion of colour to convey deep emotions make this painting a prime example of Expressionism, a movement to which he was deeply committed. He taught at the Dresden Academy of Art, and also wrote Expressionist drama. Many of his works, with their vivid colour and restless energy, were politically symbolic. The tense situation in Germany forced him to leave Austria in 1934 for London, where he lived until finally settling in Switzerland in 1953.

► Beckmann, Dürer, Ensor, Munch, Nolde, Soutine

Oskar Kokoschka. b Pochlarn, 1886. d Montreux, 1980. **Portrait of a 'Degenerate Artist'**. 1937. Oil on canvas. h110 × w85 cm. h43¼ × w33½ in. Scottish National Gallery of Modern Art, Edinburgh

De Kooning Willem

Marilyn Monroe

The exhibitionist and slightly dizzy quality of the stunningly beautiful Hollywood star is captured here. Paint has been applied in swift forceful gestures to build up the image layer by layer. This painting, from a series entitled 'Women', belongs to one of De Kooning's non-abstract, or figurative, phases. He recognized that, like all female sex-symbols, Monroe is often viewed more as an object than as a whole person, and he portrayed her almost as a shop-window dummy, with no trace of eroticism. De Kooning was involved with the

New York-based Abstract Expressionists, who stressed the importance of spontaneity and of 'gestural' painting where colour is splashed or dribbled onto the canvas. Unlike many members of this group, however, De Kooning did not restrict himself to pure abstraction: his overriding subject had been the human (particularly female) figure. His artistic career encompassed many phases and in the 1970s he had turned to figurative sculpture.

► Appel, Baselitz, Frankenthaler, Guston, Warhol

Villem de Kooning. **b** Rotterdam, 1904. **d** East Hampton, NY, 1997. **Marilyn Monroe**. 1954. Oil on canvas. **h**127 × **w**76.2 cm.
50 × **w**30 in. Private collection

Koons Jeff

Puppy

Evocative of the softness and cuddliness of a small puppy, a huge sculpture stands like a war memorial in the forecourt of an eighteenth-century building. It consists entirely of living plants, whose exuberant flowers provide colour, while their withering away, which will lead to the work's self-destruction, is a metaphor for the impermanence of life. Koons's works are monuments of glitzy kitsch, or bad taste, in our age of throwaway culture, and the more shiny they appear, the more they appeal to his magpie eye. At one time Koons was a commodities trader, and he likes to include consumer goods of one sort or another in his sculptures. Floating in the centre of an aquarium or entombed in a slab of plexiglass may be a vacuum cleaner or a basketball. When he cannot achieve the effect he wants, he may even have a new material specially made for a piece, sometimes at enormous expense.

► Dine, Duchamp, Lichtenstein, Sherman

Jeff Koons. b York, PA, 1955. **Puppy**. 1992. Flowering plants, steel, wood and earth. **h**11.5 m. **h**38 ft. Originally at Schloss Arolsen, Germany; now at Museo Guggenheim, Bilbao

Kossoff Leon

This imposing church in London's Spitalfields dominates the scene in muted colours, thickly applied. Large brushfuls of paint, dragged or dripped onto the board, form a sort of churned-up, mud-like morass. The image of ordinary people in everyday life is unpretentious and deliberately avoids the picturesque. Although Kossoff was born and brought up in the East End of London, there is nothing English about his work. In fact he is more often associated with the Neo-Expressionists working in continental Europe. His pictures – usually portraits of family or friends and local scenes – always have great personal significance for him, and it is the vividness of his memory of this area of London which gives the painting such vitality and power. Working from charcoal drawings, Kossoff seeks out the universal quality in his subjects, while never becoming sentimental or overdramatic.

► Auerbach, Bomberg, Freud, Van Gogh, Lowry, Rembrandt

Leon Kossoff. b London, 1926. **Christchurch No. 1**. 1991. Oil on board. **h**146.7 × **w**100.4 cm. **h**57¾ × **w**39⅓ in.
Anthony d'Offay Gallery, London

Krøyer Peder Severn

Summer Evening on the Southern Beach

Immersed in their own private world, two elegantly dressed women walk on a deserted beach. The cool blue tones of the sea and sky, merging together on the horizon, and the almost grey sand, create an atmosphere of clarity and tranquillity. Scandinavian painters put a great deal of effort into capturing the effects of the clear northern light, often choosing simple subjects which took on fresh, pastel tones under the Arctic sun, and avoiding strong colours and deep shadows. Born in Norway, Krøyer was particularly interested in the effects of

light at different times of day, and how lamplight is affected by daylight. Initially influenced by the Spanish painter Diego Velázquez, he painted realistic scenes of Spanish and Italian workmen, which were noted for their moving pathos. He later became the leader of a seaside colony of artists at Skagen in Denmark, and his works became more cheerful. His last years, however, were dogged by mental illness.

▶ Boudin, Hammershøi, Spilliaert, Velázquez, Zorn

Peder Severn Krøyer. b Stavanger, 1851. **d** Skagen, 1909. **Summer Evening on the Southern Beach**. 1893. Oil on canvas. **h**100 × **w**150 cm. **h**39½ × **w**55 in. Skagens Museum, Skagen

A black-and-white image of a woman stares out at the viewer. Her face is split in half, one side positive, the other negative. Printed in bold type across the image is the statement 'Your Body is a Battleground'. During the 1980s Kruger produced a series of works in which provocative texts were juxtaposed with found images. Informed by her own experiences working as a graphic designer for magazines aimed at female readers, Kruger established a bold signature style – the works were always printed in red, white and black – through which she questioned the mechanisms of consumerism and gender politics. The polarized face of the model in the current work, when set against the text, implies a battle between opposing forces for which the prize is control of the female body. It was produced by the artist to signal her support of a protest march for women's rights that took place in Washington in 1989.

► Calle, Holzer, Lichtenstein, Rist, Wool

Barbara Kruger. b Newark, NJ, 1945. **Untitled (Your Body is a Battleground)**. 1989. Photographic silkscreen on vinyl. h284.5 × w284.5 cm. h112 × w112 in. Broad Art Foundation, Santa Monica, CA

Kupka Frantisek

Cathedral

Composed of a geometrical series of pure and dappled colours, arranged vertically and diagonally, this painting has an almost mesmeric quality. The rather dark tones seem to shimmer, and the broken colours appear constantly to merge and divide from each other. Kupka went beyond simply painting what the cathedral looked like, and tried instead to convey the light, sounds and impressions of the cathedral as they affected his imagination. Born in Czechoslovakia, he trained in Prague and Vienna before working as an illustrator in Paris where he pursued his interest in theosophy (a study of religion or philosophy based on an intuitive idea of God) and practised as a spiritualist medium. He and Wassily Kandinsky became pioneers of a new style of pure abstraction, derived from Cubism but more 'pure', which they called Orphism. Behind it was the idea that artists would paint new structures made of elements which they had created from their imaginations, and made real.

► Delaunay, Gris, Kandinsky, Mondrian, Pollock

Frantisek Kupka. b Opoczno, 1871. d Puteaux, 1957. **Cathedral**. 1913. Oil on canvas. **h**180 × **w**150 cm. **h**70 ⅞ × **w**59 in. Private collection

Kusama Yayoi

Peep Show/Endless Love Show

Installed as part of the exhibition 'Kusama's Peep Show/ Endless Love Show', this hexagonal space was lined with mirrors, while the floor was crowded with pulsing red, blue, white and green lights. Two small windows permitted viewers to peer inside. The installation exhibits the signature polka dots (in the form of round lightbulbs) and the sense of infinite, repetitive immersion and unbound space that have continued to characterize Kusama's art for over fifty years. From her early years in New York, where the now internationally renowned artist was part of the 1960s anti-art establishment, she has traded on her own neuroses and mental fragility (she has been a voluntary patient in a mental hospital in Japan since the early 1970s) to create works – paintings, sculptures, installations, performances – of cosmic infinity and obsessive excess. It has been suggested that rather than searching for meaning in her art, we should seek to discover the mental processes and ways of seeing that each work offers.

► Eliasson, Graham, Gursky, Riley, Vasarely

Yayoi Kusama. b Matsumoto, 1929. **Peep Show/Endless Love Show**. 1966. Hexagonal mirrored room, electric lights. Dimensions variable.
As installed at the Castellane Gallery, New York, NY

Lam Wifredo

The Jungle

Gathered at the edge of a jungle, into which their long, slender limbs seem to merge, is a group of strange creatures straight out of Lam's imagination. The mystery of the jungle is reflected in these extraordinary beasts which inhabit its unfathomable depths; greenish animals with vague, un-animal-like shapes and tribal heads, conjured up from hallucinatory dreams. In this, his best-known work, Lam brings together many elements – Latin-American, African and Oceanic – fusing them with the conventions of the European Modern Movement. He often made use of voodoo, folklore, totems, and jungle scenes – providing a brooding sense of forbidden fruits. Of Cuban origin, at one time he was involved with the Surrealists, who encouraged artists to follow the irrational promptings of their unconscious minds, producing dream-like and disturbing images. Both Lam and his friend Pablo Picasso were influenced by African and Oceanic sculpture.

► Bellmer, Brauner, Ernst, Giacometti, Matta, Picasso

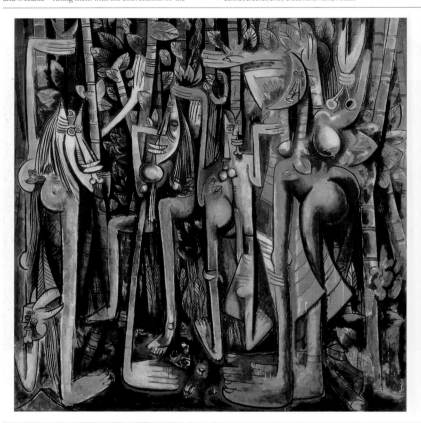

Wifredo Lam. b Sagua la Grande, 1902. **d** Paris, 1982. **The Jungle**. 1943. Gouache on paper mounted on canvas. **h**239 × **w**230 cm. **h**94¼ × **w**90½ in. Museum of Modern Art, New York, NY

Lancret Nicolas

A Lady in a Garden taking Coffee with some Children

Elegantly dressed figures sipping coffee from porcelain cups in a landscaped garden suggest a typically French setting. Although this is a refined, formal scene, it also shows an intimate family group. The youngest daughter has abandoned her doll in favour of a taste of the hot coffee which is tenderly offered by her mother, while the father watches over them all with an affectionate eye. The composition has been made more interesting by placing the figures to one side of the canvas, rather than in the centre. Lancret excelled at these pastoral evocations of aristocratic life, before the Revolution swept it away forever. Failing as a history painter, he spent the rest of his days painting *fêtes galantes*, pictures of figures in pastoral settings. He was famous for his portrayal of fairs, balls and village weddings in the style of his popular contemporary, Antoine Watteau.

► Boucher, Fragonard, Liotard, Prud'hon, Watteau

Nicolas Lancret. b Paris, 1690. d Paris, 1743. **A Lady in a Garden taking Coffee with some Children**. c1742. Oil on canvas.
h88.9 × **w**97.8 cm. **h**35 × **w**38½ in. National Gallery, London

Landseer Sir Edwin

Wild Cattle at Chillingham

As if showing their proud defiance in the face of adversity, the cows dominate this composition. In fact they have been disturbed by the presence of a frog. Destined for the Earl of Tankerville at Chillingham Castle, Northumberland, this fine painting demonstrates the qualities which made Landseer so popular: he appealed to Victorian taste by endowing animals with the semblance of human emotions. Inspired by the images of the Romantic novelist Sir Walter Scott, he travelled to Britain's remote places and painted animals and landscapes which he knew might one day be threatened. His father was an engraver who taught him to sketch animals from life and he was only 12 when he first exhibited at the Royal Academy. Queen Victoria's favourite artist, his most famous works are the bronze lions in Trafalgar Square. Despite his sentimentality, there is some evidence of a gratuitous cruelty which may have contributed to his mental breakdown. He died insane.

► Agasse, Cuyp, Marc, Stubbs

Sir Edwin Landseer. b London, 1802. **d** London, 1873. **Wild Cattle at Chillingham**. 1867. Oil on canvas. **h**228 × **w**156 cm. **h**89¾ × **w**61½ in. Laing Art Gallery, Newcastle upon Tyne

Lanyon Peter

Fly Away

The white mass, large yellow triangle, red bands and bold fluent brushstrokes of *Fly Away* form an apparently abstract composition. Lanyon embraced this heavily painted expressionistic style in the 1950s. In 1959 he took up glider flying and was able to obtain a totally new vision of the Cornish landscape. With this in mind, the blue-black rectangle on the right becomes the sea, the single white brushstroke and thin line of yellow become the quays of a harbour, and the red and yellow shapes assume the forms of elements of an aircraft floating in the atmosphere. Born in the English artists' colony of St Ives, Cornwall, Lanyon lived and worked there with associates Naum Gabo, Patrick Heron and Ben Nicholson for most of his life. He is acknowledged as an artist who reinvented the British landscape in the 1950s. Lanyon's career was unfortunately cut short by a fatal gliding accident in 1964 at the age of 46.

► Frankenthaler, Gabo, Heron, De Kooning, B Nicholson

Peter Lanyon. b St Ives, 1918. d Taunton, 1964. **Fly Away**. 1961. Oil on canvas. h122 × w183 cm. h48 × w72 in. Gimpel Fils Gallery, London

La Tour Georges de

The Cheat with the Ace of Diamonds

The card players' shifty eyes suggest that not one of them is honest. Only one cheat, however, obviously withholds two cards behind his back. The bright light, casting deep shadows, heightens the warm colours of their clothes. By contrast, the background is in total darkness, intensifying the areas of light. Although this is a Baroque painting, there is a geometric simplicity in the figures – for example in the oval face of the seated woman – that harks back to painters of the early Italian Renaissance such as Piero della Francesca. Many artists at this time travelled extensively, but La Tour spent his entire life in the French province of Lorraine. He specialized in candlelit scenes, achieving eerie effects with warm, glowing reds and browns, and their luminous quality is reminiscent of the works of Caravaggio. One of his paintings was accepted as a gift by the King of France, who liked it so much that he had all the works by other painters removed from his chambers.

► Caravaggio, Honthorst, Lucas, Piero della Francesca

Georges de La Tour. b Vic-sur-Seille, 1593. **d** Lunéville, 1652. **The Cheat with the Ace of Diamonds**. c1647. Oil on canvas. **h**106 × **w**146 cm. **h**41½ × **w**57½ in. Musée du Louvre, Paris

Laurencin Marie

The Dancers

Five beautiful dancers in diaphanous costumes practise their movements in this enchanting scene. The seductive pastel shades in which they are painted are typical of Laurencin's work, magnifying their almost ethereal quality. Her paintings convey her curious vision of a world peopled entirely by beautiful young girls, and perfectly embody the artistic mood of the 1920s in their lighthearted and decorative tone. She resisted the pressure of contemporary movements in art and retained her own individual style, demonstrated here in a straightforward portrayal of the dancers without any extraneous 'message'. Besides painting, she also illustrated books with watercolours. Laurencin had the advantage of being included in a social circle which included Pablo Picasso, Georges Braque, Henri Matisse, Juan Gris and Robert Delaunay and she held many artistic discussions in her Paris apartment.

► Degas, Dufy, Foujita, Toulouse-Lautrec, Utrillo

Marie Laurencin. b Paris, 1883. d Paris, 1956. **The Dancers**. 1937. Oil on canvas. h53.3 × w64.1 cm. h21 × w25¼ in. Private collection

Lawrence Sir Thomas

The Duke of Wellington

Although the inscription on this work states that this is how the Duke appeared at the battle of Waterloo, it is most unlikely that Wellington could have sustained such a staged pose with a fierce battle raging around him. Lawrence's approach is more staid and less realistic than that of Antoine-Jean Gros in the windswept portrait of his opponent, Napoleon, but like Gros, Lawrence wanted to achieve a romantic vision of a great leader – and furthermore, a victorious one. The son of an innkeeper, he was famed for

his portraits at the age of ten, painting Queen Charlotte at the age of only 20 and being appointed royal painter on the death of Sir Joshua Reynolds. With a reputation extending to Europe, he was commissioned by George IV to paint all the major figures in the struggle against Napoleon. His best work has great force; his worst was probably dashed off to pay debts: he had a huge income but was in constant difficulty.

▶ Clouet, Van Dyck, Géricault, Gros, Marini

Sir Thomas Lawrence. b Bristol, 1769. **d** London, 1830. **The Duke of Wellington**. 1818. Oil on canvas. **h**396.2 × **w**243.8 cm. **h**156 × **w**96 in. The Bathurst Collection, Sapperton

Brig on the Water

theatrical light is cast across the surface of the sea, the rk clouds above adding to the dramatic atmosphere. In e centre of the composition, just below the horizon, sits rig, dwarfed by the expanse of water. Whilst this was a e of sailing vessel known for its speed and agility, in this otograph it appears perfectly still. A trained artist, who hibited at the Paris Salon, Le Gray's beautifully crafted mposition owes obvious debts to the seascape tradition European painting. Making his first daguerreotypes in

1847, Le Gray was an important teacher and early technical innovator of photographic processes. At a time when it was not possible to capture sky and sea with clarity in a single image, Le Gray developed a combination technique that employed the incorporation of two separate negatives. *Brig on the Water* was his first exhibited seascape and sold over 800 prints during the first two months that it was available for sale.

► Adams, Church, Grimshaw, Steichen, Turner

ustave Le Gray. b Villiers-le-Bel, 1820. d Cairo, 1884. **Brig on the Water**. 1856. Albumen print from a collodion-on-glass negative.
2 × w41 cm. h12½ × w16¼ in. Victoria and Albert Museum, London

Léger Fernand

The Builders

The massive scale of the building is cleverly conveyed by cutting off the image at the top and bottom, so that it appears to stretch away endlessly in both directions. Strong horizontals and verticals etch its outline against the sky in intense primary colours. The massive robot-like workers, scrambling about on the girders, and the passing clouds contrast dramatically in shape and colour with the ironwork skeleton. Trained in an architect's office, Léger was fascinated by industrial technology, and by the dynamic shapes of

machinery and construction work. There is evidence in this painting of the Cubist movement in its harsh, angular lines and its focus on machinery. Léger worked in many areas: ceramics, stained glass, stage designs for the Swedish Ballet and even film – he made the first 'abstract' film, using objects as 'actors'. Among his last works were huge decorative murals for the UN building in New York.

► Boccioni, Brown, Delaunay, Gris, Picasso

Fernand Léger. b Argentan, 1881. **d** Gif-sur-Yvette, 1955. **The Builders**. 1950. Oil on canvas. **h**299.8 × **w**200 cm. **h**118 × **w**78¾ in. Musée National Fernand Léger, Biot

A sensuous, porcelain-skinned goddess gazes at her reflection as she prepares for her bath. The soft yellows, whites and flesh tones create a sense of calm while her elongated body is accentuated by the Ionic column behind her and the tall, thin shape of the canvas. The brushstrokes, invisible to the eye, are as smooth and polished as the still surface of the water. Lord Leighton, who studied art in Europe, was a leader of Classicism in Britain, his style and choice of subject being profoundly influenced by the statues and mythology of

Antiquity, which was in direct opposition to the Medievalism of the Pre-Raphaelites. He had an immediate success when his first picture was purchased by Queen Victoria. His paintings became hugely popular through mass-produced reproductions, and he was also an excellent sculptor. Lord Leighton was later elected President of London's Royal Academy.

► Alma-Tadema, Burne-Jones, Cranach, Ingres, Rossetti

Lord Frederic Leighton. b Scarborough, 1830. d London, 1896. **The Bath of Psyche**. 1890. Oil on canvas. h189.2 × w62.2 cm. 74¼ × 24¼ in. Tate, London

Lely Sir Peter

Charles I with James, Duke of York

Glancing nervously at his father's face, a son hands him a letter opener. The lack of intimacy between them may reflect the real relationship between father and son, as Charles I was a prisoner at Hampton Court when this portrait was painted. James, along with his brothers and sisters, lived at Syon House under the guardianship of the Duke of Northumberland. As few visits to the King were allowed, this is an important record of one such meeting. The subtle tones and rich modelling are hallmarks of Lely's style. The choice of Lely

for this commission demonstrates his increased status as portrait painter to royalty, succeeding Sir Anthony van Dyck. Ten years after he became a Master in the Haarlem Guild, Lely was in London and had painted the King as well as the royal children. A flood of portraits followed which made him one of the most influential portrait painters of the seventeenth century.

► Dobson, Van Dyck, Holbein, Kneller, Reynolds

Sir Peter Lely. b Soest, Westphalen, 1618. **d** London, 1680. **Charles I with James, Duke of York**. 1647. Oil on canvas. **h**126.4 × **w**146.7 cm. **h**49¾ × **w**57¾ in. Syon House, Isleworth

Leonardo da Vinci

Mona Lisa

The *Mona Lisa* is famous all over the world for her enigmatic smile and for being one of the few paintings by the most esteemed of the Renaissance masters, Leonardo da Vinci. The identity of the sitter remains unknown, and some debate still rages over whether the figure is indeed a man or a woman, but the painting, with its haunting landscape, rises above this controversy in the quality of its execution. A traditional Renaissance portrait in composition, its beauty lies in the oil painting technique (known as *sfumato*) created by Leonardo,

which allowed the artist to execute subtle, atmospheric shading that was impossible to produce with the egg-based tempera paint used by contemporary artists. Equally adept in anatomy, engineering and scientific and aeronautic pursuits, Leonardo completed a remarkably small number of paintings during his lifetime. Fortunately, numerous drawings and sketchbooks have survived to reflect the diverse talents of this genius.

► Dürer, Ghirlandaio, Massys, Ramsay, Sittow

Leonardo da Vinci. **b** Vinci, 1452. **d** Amboise, 1519. **Mona Lisa**. 1503/6. Oil on panel. **h**77 × **w**53 cm. **h**30¼ × **w**21 in.
Musée du Louvre, Paris

Lewis Wyndham

A Battery Shelled

The characteristically tortured landscape is painted in harsh, angular outlines. Billowing smoke from the shelled battery is shown as a series of segmented towers, and bomb craters appear as rigid waves, while the figures in the background are portrayed as mechanical robots. Lewis served on the Western Front during the First World War, first as bombardier, then as a war artist. This, his major work of that period, shows that he has toned down his pioneering abstract style in order to record the war, yet its brutality makes it clear that he thought war itself was absurd. Lewis, a novelist, art critic and superb portraitist, was during his own time one of the most influential experimentalist of British art. He was self-proclaimed leader of the Vorticist group established in London in 1914 and editor of the Vorticist magazine *BLAST* Tragically, illness left him blind for the last six years of his life

► Bomberg, Braque, Friedrich, Nash, Picasso

Wyndham Lewis. b At sea (off Nova Scotia), 1882. **d** London, 1957. **A Battery Shelled**. 1919. Oil on canvas. **h**152.5 × **w**317.5 cm. **h**72 × **w**125 in. Imperial War Museum, London

This white, open-cube structure is based on mathematical
uidelines. By showing projecting cubes which are defined
nly by their edges, LeWitt exploited the contradiction
etween what we know to be there and what we actually
ee, a characteristic that links this work to Conceptual Art.
he ideas of the Minimalist movement can be seen in
ne work's rigid adherence to geometric mathematical
alculations and its impersonal nature, with no fixed centre
f interest. LeWitt worked for an architect before becoming

an artist and made Minimalist sculptures which he called
'structures'. He had said that the idea behind a work is more
important than the work itself, and the planning is more
important than the construction. His wall drawings, a series
of lines, are sold like patterns, with a 'licence' to draw them in.
He then usually obliterated his own wall drawings once they
had been exhibited.

► Andre, Buren, Flavin, Judd, Vasarely

ol LeWitt. **b** Hartford, CT, 1928. **d** New York, NY, 2007. **Open Geometric Structure IV**. 1990. Painted wood. **h**98 × **w**438 cm.
88 ⅞ × **w**172½ in. Lisson Gallery, London

323

Leyster Judith

Self-portrait

The artist, dressed in her best and leaning back casually, one arm propped on the arm of her chair, is around nineteen or twenty years old. She looks directly at the viewer, smiling as if about to speak, holding the tools of her trade. On the easel is a laughing fiddler, but infrared examination reveals that Leyster originally painted the head and shoulders of a young woman here – whether this was a portrait or self-portrait is unknown. The reworking of this area with a fiddler may be a deliberate advertisement of her skills as a genre painter, a

popular and marketable speciality in the seventeenth century; others have suggested that it personifies the joy of artistic creation. Leyster was one of the very few professional female painters of the Dutch golden age. She was a member of the painters' guild, and was possibly a student of Frans Hals. Her compositions, usually comprising few figures and only minimal settings, dramatically lit, are intimate and assured.

► Anguissola, Cahun, Hals, Rembrandt, Vigée-Lebrun

Judith Leyster. b Haarlem, 1609. **d** Heemstede, 1660. **Self-portrait.** c1630. Oil on canvas. **h**74.4 × **w**65.3 cm. **h**29¼ in × **w**25¾ in. National Gallery of Art, Washington, DC

.ichtenstein's blown-up comic strip creates a powerful impact with its bold primary colours and direct style. The original artoon is faithfully reproduced but on a large scale, imitating he coarse screen technique (Ben Day dots) that is used for rinting cheap comics and newspapers. Lichtenstein used ass-produced imagery and the materials and products of he industrial environment, often extracting images from their riginal context and parodying them. By magnifying and over-mplifying these images he was not making a social comment on the content but trying to make people more aware of the aesthetics of 1960s USA. A prime exponent of American Pop Art, in which artefacts, mass media and products from modern life were used as art forms in themselves, Lichtenstein used popular imagery in his work. In 1993 a major retrospective exhibition of his work was held at the Museum of Modern Art in New York.

► Dine, Hamilton, Oldenburg, Rosenquist, Warhol

oy Lichtenstein. b New York, NY, 1923. d New York, NY, 1997. **In the Car**. 1963. Magna on canvas. h172 × w203.5 cm. h67¾ × w80⅛ in.   325
cottish National Gallery of Modern Art, Edinburgh

Limbourg Pol, Jean and Herman de

January

A fine example of miniature painting, this is a page from one of the greatest manuscripts of Northern European art. Illustrating January, identified by the stellar chart with the constellations of Capricorn and Aquarius, the festive banquet depicted in the main scene includes a portrait of the Duc de Berry who commissioned the manuscript. He is wearing a large fur hat and an elaborate blue and gold robe. Most of the paintings in this Book of Hours were executed by three brothers who joined the Duke's court in around 1410 and who all died in the same year as their patron, before the manuscript was complete. Their work is praised for its unprecedented attention to everyday detail and for its marvellous sense of narrative. A Book of Hours was used during the Middle Ages as a prayer book for private devotion. It recorded the daily cycle of monastic services throughout the year and this particularly sumptuous example devotes a single page to each month.

► Beauneveu, Del Cossa, Van Eyck, Fouquet

Pol, Jean and Herman de Limbourg. Active c1400. **d** place unknown, c1416. **January** (from the *Très Riches Heures*). c1413. Illumination on vellum. **h**24 × **w**15.2 cm. **h**9⅜ × **w**6 in. Musée Condé, Chantilly

Liotard Jean-Étienne

The Chocolate Pot

This charming portrayal of a maid carrying a tray with a cup of chocolate is striking for its direct and simple approach to an informal subject. The cool clarity of the picture's tones and the unbroken outline of the figure emphasize the pattern formed by the maid's colourful clothes against the plain background. This work has all the lightness and gaiety of Liotard's French Rococo contemporaries but without their artifice, and it looks forward to the figures of Jean Auguste Dominique Ingres and Édouard Manet. Liotard spent some years in Constantinople, where he was probably influenced by the tradition of Turkish miniature painting, whose characteristics can be seen here in the even lighting, clear tones and slightly formal expression of the maid. On his return to Europe he continued to wear the Turkish dress and beard he had adopted, enjoying the notoriety this gave him. In England, his portraits were successful, despite their being described by Walpole as 'too like to please'.

► Chardin, Fragonard, Greuze, Ingres, Manet, Watteau

Jean-Étienne Liotard. b Geneva, 1702. d Geneva, 1789. The Chocolate Pot. c1745. Pastel on parchment. h82 × w52 cm. h32¼ × w20½ in. Staatliche Kunstsammlungen, Dresden

Lipchitz Jacques

Half-standing Figure

The strict, mathematical composition of this work, with its layers of solid stone and intervening spaces, shows that the sculptor wanted to represent architectural, geometric forms, while creating a lyrical, harmonious whole. Lipchitz was one of the earliest sculptors to understand the principles of Cubism and to apply them to three dimensions, fragmenting forms to reconstruct them in terms of space and formal qualities of composition. Born in Lithuania, and training initially as an engineer, Lipchitz developed a very individual abstract style, making what he called 'transparent sculptures'. His later work of figures and animals in bronze was more dynamic and non-abstract. From 1941 he lived mainly in the USA and executed some important commissions there. In 1946 Lipchitz was commissioned to sculpt a Madonna for a modern church in France.

► Archipenko, Braque, Gaudier-Brzeska, Gris, Smith

Jacques Lipchitz. b Druskieniki, 1891. **d** Capri, 1973. **Half-standing Figure.** 1915. Stone. **h**98 cm. **h**38½ in. Tate, London

The plain blue background, unadorned pale tunic and
at highlight the wrinkled face and gentle eyes of this old
nan, whose portrayal is striking because it is so direct and
traightforward. He sits at an angle and although not looking
irectly at the viewer most of his face can still be seen. The
ld man's identity is unknown, yet much of his personality
hines through this portrait, which is painted in the graceful
nd simple style that characterized Filippino's work. Aged 12
hen his father, Fra Filippo Lippi, died, he set off alone for
Florence and a year later was working with Sandro Botticelli,
a former pupil of his father. His first major commission was
to complete a Florentine fresco left unfinished by Masaccio,
and it is his frescos that have made his name. Years spent in
Rome allowed him to study Roman remains, which became
so important to him that they would crop up repeatedly in his
paintings, whether they were appropriate to the subject or not.

► Botticelli, Ghirlandaio, Filippo Lippi, Masaccio

Iippino Lippi. b Prato, 1457. d Florence, 1504. **Portrait of an Old Man**. c1485. Fresco. **h**47 × **w**38 cm. **h**18½ × **w**15 in. Galleria degli
'fizi, Florence

329

Lippi Fra Filippo

The Coronation of the Virgin

An elaborate hierarchy defines the realms of the angels, saints, clerics and donors who look on at this coronation. Lippi's rotund figures and understanding of space ensure that the figures are not crushed together in an unrealistic manner. By employing the rules of perspective and subtle lighting techniques, the artist has depicted the crowd in a logical way. The viewer is drawn into the composition by means of the angel in the foreground and the bishop in the green robe on the left who looks directly out from the painting. The cleric looking out on the far left is a self-portrait of Lippi, who was sent as an orphan to a monastery at the age of eight to become a monk but found himself unsuited to the life. He eloped with a nun (who became the model for many of his Madonnas) but although he was later released from his vows in order to marry her, no wedding ever took place. Their son, Filippino, also became an important Renaissance artist.

► Fra Angelico, Filippino Lippi, Lorenzo Monaco, Martini

Fra Filippo Lippi. b Florence, c1406. **d** Spoleto, 1469. **The Coronation of the Virgin.** 1441/7. Tempera on panel. **h**200 × **w**287 cm. **h**78¾ × **w**113 in. Galleria degli Uffizi, Florence evolving geometric objects painted in delicate colours appear to be floating in the air, thus creating a sense of depth and an illusion of space. Some of the shapes are given three dimensions, and this suggestion of architectural forms was developed in Lissitzky's later works. In its concentration of pure form and colour, the drawing shows the influence of Suprematism, an abstract art form invented by Kasimir Malevich based on pure geometric figures. Lissitzky trained first as an engineer, then as an architect. Marc Chagall

appointed him professor of architecture and graphic art at the art school in Vitebsk, where he came under the influence of Malevich. His series of 'Prouns' is well-known – a number of abstract works of straight lines, dramatic architectural qualities and an overall flatness, with no suggestion of depth. Lissitzky's creative versatility extended to designs for costumes, exhibitions, posters and books.

► Chagall, Van Doesburg, Gabo, Malevich, Moholy-Nagy

Lissitzky (Eleazer Lissitzky). b Pochinok, 1890. d Moscow, 1941. **Composition**. c1920. Gouache, ink and pencil on paper.
41 × w33 cm. h16⅛ × w13 in. Private collection

Lochner Stefan

The Virgin and Child in a Rose Arbour

Doll-like angels serenade the Virgin and offer fruit to the Christ child while God the Father watches from above. The arboured rose garden in which the Virgin sits is a traditional symbol of her purity. With its grace and mysticism, its subtle technique, the sweetness of the Virgin's face and the pure colours of the robes, the work has a number of characteristics typical of Lochner. This is the earliest known work by this lyrical painter, who has been described as the last of the Gothic artists, and who was principal master at the Cologne school. The gentle modelling of his figures was given the name 'soft style'. Many images of the Virgin and Child painted by other fifteenth-century German artists in the Rhine valley bear similarities to this pretty and poetical painting, as do the images of the Virgin that can be found in some contemporary illuminated manuscripts.

► Botero, Campin, Van Eyck, Limbourg, Schongauer

Stefan Lochner. Active in Cologne, 1442. **d** Cologne, 1451. **The Virgin and Child in a Rose Arbour**. c1440. Oil on panel. **h**50.5 × **w**40 cm. **h**19 ⅞ × **w**15¾ in. Wallraf-Richartz Museum, Cologne

This linear sculpture has been created out of pieces of slate picked up on a walk through the Cornish countryside. Each one has been chosen at random, but is carefully placed in a straight line which can be moved to any place capable of accommodating its massive size. This work can be considered as Conceptual as the installation of the line represents the *idea* of the walk, which has already taken place. Long has extended the definition of sculpture to include a dimension of time; his sculptures are a record of the artist's journey through a landscape. This approach has taken him to all corners of the world. He marks his journey in different ways; he may leave a simple sculpture of stones, brushwood or seaweed, using basic shapes known to man for millions of years. Some of his sculptures are permanent, such as a line of rocks laid high in the Himalayan wilderness; the less permanent are exhibited in the form of photographs or maps.

► Andre, Buren, Christo, Heizer, Judd

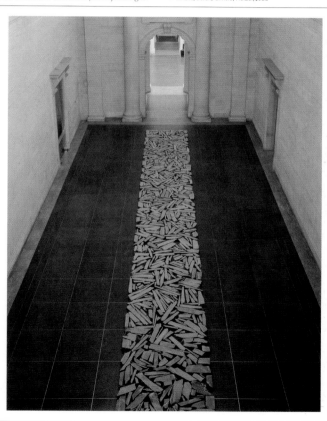

Richard Long. b Bristol, 1945. **Cornwall Slate Line**. 1990. Delabole slate. l2540 × w230 cm. l999 × w87 in. Previously installed at Tate, London; now installed at Lismore Castle, Ireland

Longhi Pietro

Exhibition of a Rhinoceros at Venice

Painted with a precise observation of detail born of an almost scientific curiosity, a rhinoceros stands in an enclosure, placidly munching hay, an exotic spectacle for a bemused audience dressed in costume for the Venetian carnival. This odd painting commemorates the rhinoceros which was toured around the European capitals by its captor, and brought to Venice in 1751. Longhi's small-scale pictures of middle-class Venetian life were theatrical and witty, but never satirical (unlike, for example, those by William Hogarth in England).

One of the most charming of all Venetian eighteenth-century painters, if somewhat innocent, Longhi dispassionately recorded the everyday events that captured his imagination. His many paintings were imitated by others or repeated by pupils, and although they show no great artistic genius, they form a valuable record of an eighteenth-century Venetian society, long past its peak and slipping into decadence.

► Agasse, Hicks, Hogarth, Teniers

Pietro Longhi. b Venice, 1702. **d** Venice, 1785. **Exhibition of a Rhinoceros at Venice.** c1751. Oil on canvas. h60 × w47 cm. h23½ × w18½ in. National Gallery, London

Lorenzetti Ambrogio

Allegory of Good Government

Dominating the composition from his magnificent throne sits the personification of Good Government. He is dressed as a judge in black and white – the colours of Siena. At his feet sit the twins Romulus and Remus, feeding greedily from a she-wolf – characters from Roman mythology used to symbolize the city's ancient origins. On the left is Peace, a Classically-inspired figure dressed in gauzy white robes and reclining on a suit of armour. Crowding round the platform are members of the Sienese community. This fresco is part of a cycle painted on the walls of the council chamber in Siena's town hall in order to inspire responsible government. The imagery is highly complex but Lorenzetti rose to the challenge and, by adding a wealth of incidental detail, proved himself to be one of the most brilliant and original artists of the fourteenth century. Together with his brother Pietro, Ambrogio was responsible for numerous civic and religious commissions in his native Siena.

► Duccio, Martini, Della Quercia, Raphael

Ambrogio Lorenzetti. Active in Siena, 1319. d Siena, c1348. **Allegory of Good Government** (detail). c1338/40. Fresco. Palazzo Pubblico, Siena

Lorenzo Monaco

The Coronation of the Virgin

The construction of this painting is typical of early Renaissance altarpieces. The principal scene is surrounded by smaller paintings set into the frame. The sequence of small panels along the lower edge combine to form a 'predella' depicting the Nativity. Above are scenes from the life of a saint; the gables show the Annunciation and Christ in Glory, while on each side, the frame is filled with individual saints. The way in which Lorenzo has crowded the saints around the Virgin and Christ, and his use of a dazzling range of colours, place him in the transitional period between the late Gothic and early Renaissance periods. Lorenzo was a monk and took his vows in a monastery famous for its illumination of manuscripts. He began as a miniaturist but progressed to altarpieces, painting this one for the high altar of Santa Maria degli Angeli in Florence.

► Duccio, Gaddi, Giotto, Filippo Lippi, Lorenzetti, Martini

Lorenzo Monaco. b Siena, c1370. **d** Florence, c1424. **The Coronation of the Virgin.** 1414. Tempera on panel. **h**450 × **w**350 cm. **h**177⅛ × **w**137¾ in. Galleria degli Uffizi, Florence

Lotto Lorenzo

Portrait of a Woman inspired by Lucretia

The Latin inscription praising Lucretia's exemplary life is clearly meant to associate the lady in this portrait with the Roman Lucretia who, after being defiled by the son of Tarquin, stabbed herself rather than live as a spoiled woman. Virtuous women from Antiquity were much admired during the Renaissance. Lotto's early works show the strong influence of Venetian painters such as Giovanni Bellini, but he was impressionable, reflecting a multitude of his contemporaries before developing his own idiosyncratic style based on the

Venetian interest in colour and light. His account book has survived (a rare occurrence), and shows that he was a difficult individual who achieved little financial success. A skilful portrait painter, able to bring his subjects vividly to life, his career took him from his native Venice to many parts of northern Italy. A few years before his death he became a lay brother in a monastery.

► Giovanni Bellini, Dossi, Luini, Palma Vecchio

Lorenzo Lotto. b Venice, c1480. **d** Loreto, c1556. **Portrait of a Woman inspired by Lucretia**. c1530–2. Oil on canvas. **h**96.5 × **w**110.6 cm. **h**38 × **w**43½ in. National Gallery, London

337

Louis Morris

Alpha-Phi

Thinned acrylic paint is poured in wing-like diagonal parallel lines, staining the bare canvas. As the rivulets of bright colour cover so small a proportion of the massive expanse, its dazzling near-emptiness irresistibly suggests a Zen-like spirit of meditation. Louis had developed in this work a new way of painting by rejecting shape and light in favour of pure colour, as the fabric of the canvas is literally soaked in paint. This concern with colour by saturation without visible brushstrokes, which magnifies the flatness of the picture plane, demonstrates the painting's connection with the Post-Painterly Abstraction movement in the USA. Louis usually worked on series of paintings at one time. These include the group 'Veils', in which the paint was poured vertically down the canvas, covering most of its area, and the 'Unfurleds' series, to which *Alpha-Phi* belongs.

► Frankenthaler, Hodler, Kelly, Noland, Rothko

Morris Louis. b Baltimore, MD, 1912. **d** Washington, DC, 1962. **Alpha-Phi**. 1961. Acrylic on canvas. **h**259.1 × **w**495.7 cm. **h**102 × **w**195 in. Tate, London

Lowry L S

Coming from the Mill

Factory workers pour in a stream from the mill at Salford. Observed with great affection and captured in muted colours, the scene has been painted straight onto the canvas with no preliminary sketch. Lowry portrays William Blake's 'dark satanic mills' with great sympathy and charm. Although often referred to as 'matchstick people', his figures are full of movement, vital and alive. This work provides a fascinating pictorial record of the industrial north of England, with its cotton mills and rows of back-to-back houses, scenes which often exist only as memory today. Lowry's raw style of painting is idiosyncratic and entirely individual, uninfluenced by the French Post-Impressionists. A clerk all his working life who kept away from the public eye, he studied art in his spare time and was not discovered until 1939, when he was 52, and then almost by accident. His first one-man exhibition followed immediately.

► W Blake, Burra, Gontcharova, H Rousseau

L S (Lawrence Stephen) Lowry. b Manchester, 1887. **d** Glossop, 1976. **Coming from the Mill**. 1930. Oil on canvas. **h**42 × **w**52 cm. **h**16½ × **w**20½ in. The Lowry Collection, Salford

Lucas van Leyden

The Card Players

Fashionably dressed in felt hats and colourful cloaks, a group of men and women sit round a table playing cards. Others look passively on, or take a more active interest in the proceedings. This charming picture, with its profusion of bright colours and careful composition, is fresh and appealing. A superb draughtsman, Lucas van Leyden liked to portray amusing scenes from everyday life. At the age of nine he learned to paint on glass and only a year later was a competent engraver. He was said to be a pupil of his father, although all his father's works have been lost. Lucas van Leyden and Gossaert travelled to Flanders, giving banquets for local painters, and he also spent time in Italy. The influence of Albrecht Dürer can be seen in his numerous woodcuts and engravings: Lucas van Leyden is believed to have been the first engraver to etch onto copper instead of iron.

► Ter Brugghen, Dürer, Gossaert, Honthorst, La Tour

Lucas van Leyden. b Leiden, 1494. d Leiden, 1533. **The Card Players**. c1520. Oil on panel. h34 × w48 cm. h14 × w18 in. Wilton House, Salisbury

Luini Bernardino

The Executioner Presents John the Baptist's Head to Herod

The Baptist's head is placed on a dish for Salome to take in to Herod, but instead of presenting a scene of horror, Luini tackles the subject with calm decorum. Salome's only gesture is to gently avert her eyes from the gory spectacle before her, with no indication of the revulsion or shock which we might expect in the circumstances. Luini was more interested in harmoniously balancing the elements of his picture than in illustrating a real life event. In fact, drama and tension were beyond his range of pictorial expression; he was better suited to painting tender Madonnas and saints in rich colours, using his subtle skill to create soft, smoky contours. Luini's style was entirely dominated by Leonardo da Vinci, who had come to Milan by 1483. Although he could not match Leonardo's profound analysis of character and feeling, Luini's imitations of Leonardo's work made him one of the most popular Milanese painters of his time.

► Gentileschi, Ghirlandaio, Leonardo, Lotto

Magritte René

The Treachery of Images

Magritte appears to contradict reality by nonsensically naming something that does not need to be named, at the same time as denying that it is what it obviously is. By writing 'This is not a pipe' beneath the picture of one, he illustrates that the image of an object must not be confused with something tangible and real. One of Magritte's most famous images, the painting questions the concepts of definition and representation. All is not as it appears to be, Magritte is saying; the picture thus presents a challenge to ordered society and an assault on the accepted way in which people see and think. Initially inspired by Giorgio de Chirico, Magritte's Surrealist paintings often use fantastic, disturbing and dream-like images, such as a steam train emerging from the centre of a fireplace, or a sky in which the clouds have turned into French loaves. Born in Belgium, Magritte began his career as a commercial artist, and this may be reflected in the sharpness and clarity of his work.

► Bellmer, Brauner, De Chirico, Dalí, Delvaux, Tanguy

Ceci n'est pas une pipe.

René Magritte. b Lessines, 1898. d Brussels, 1967. **The Treachery of Images**. 1928–9. Oil on canvas. h60 × w81 cm. h23⅝ × w31⅞ in. Los Angeles County Museum of Art, Los Angeles, CA

Maillol Aristide

The Three Nymphs

Originally conceived as a classic representation of the mythic Three Graces, this bronze statue has great solidity and weightiness in its smooth, rounded curves and restrained movements. Although Maillol's concept changed while he was working on the preparatory plaster casts, the mirroring effect of the three nudes, which gives the impression of three views of the same girl, is also typical of Classical representations of the Three Graces. Maillol did not adopt the rough surfaces, fluid shapes and intense energy of his contemporary, Auguste Rodin. He was more interested in calm than in drama, in timeless serenity than in fleeting expressions and emotions, seeking the eternal rather than the momentary. After spending several years designing tapestries, in the second half of his life he concentrated almost exclusively on sculpting the female nude, and revived the Classical ideas of Greece in the fifth century BC, in which figures had a fixed and monumental quality.

▶ Botticelli, Canova, Ingres, Powers, Rodin, Rubens

Aristide Maillol. b Banyuls-sur-Mer, 1861. **d** near Banyuls-sur-Mer, 1944. **The Three Nymphs**. 1930–37. Bronze. **h**160 × **w**144 cm. **h**63 × **w**56¾ in. Private collection

Malevich Kasimir

Suprematism

Geometric elements painted in basic colours appear to float as if suspended on the canvas. Malevich has created a complex composition by overlapping the forms to convey a sense of perspective and depth. A Suprematist work, it banishes every trace of subject, relying solely on the interaction between form and colour. Malevich was the founder of Suprematism, a system which strove to achieve absolute purity of form and colour. For him, this method constituted an expression of pure artistic feeling, or what he called 'non-objective sensation'. In 1918, he took the development of non-objective art to its logical conclusion in a series of works entitled 'White on White', consisting of a white square on a white background, the abstract to end all abstracts. Realizing at this point that he could take the concept no further, he reverted to figurative paintings.

► Gabo, Lissitzky, Moholy-Nagy, Popova, Rodchenko

Kasimir Malevich. b Kiev, 1878. **d** Leningrad, 1935. **Suprematism**. 1915. Oil on canvas. **h**101.5 × **w**62 cm. **h**40 × **w**24 in. Stedelijk Museum, Amsterdam

Man Ray

Displayed on a curved surface and ambiguous in its distorted triple exposure, this photograph suggests movement and sexual tension, dramatically emphasizing the female form. Man Ray was one of the most inventive photographers of his time, experimenting with and pioneering new techniques in what was then an exciting new medium. His rich, fertile imagination and irrational techniques as an artist fitted in well with the principles of Dada, an anti-art movement intended to shock and outrage. After studying art in New York, Man Ray founded a Dadaist group there and became a leading figure in the development of the Modern Movement. In the 1920s he moved to Paris, where he made several Surrealist films. Solarized images and the famous rayograph, a photographic image made without a camera, were his invention. Always at the forefront of the avant-garde, he influenced several generations of artists.

► Brauner, Dalí, Leighton, Sheeler, Sherman

Manet Édouard

Le déjeuner sur l'herbe

A nude woman sits in a glade, nonchalantly picnicking with two young gallants in contemporary clothes. The large canvas is treated with broad applications of colour, and the stark, direct lighting reduces the modelling of the figures to the bare minimum. Basing his figures on a composition by Raphael, and evoking the pastoral atmosphere of Giorgione, Manet has consciously tried to evoke the high ideals of Renaissance art. This daring mixture of ancient and modern – contemporary bohemian life given the context and scale of Classical art –

led to this painting being widely condemned by the critics when first shown. Manet's aim was to liberate artists from the doctrines of academicism and literary subjects. An artistic rebel, he developed a brilliant technique with much use of black. Later he was influenced by the Impressionists' lighter colours. It is ironic that he scandalized both art critics and public, yet revered conventional artists like Diego Velázquez and Titian.

► Courbet, Degas, Giorgione, Tissot, Titian, Velázquez

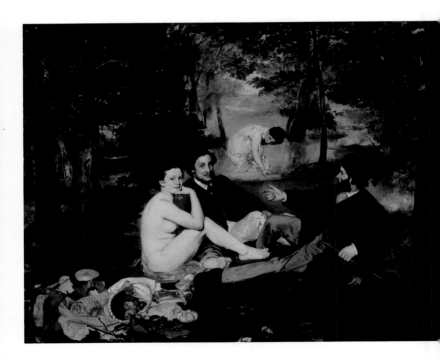

Édouard Manet. b Paris, 1832. d Paris, 1883. **Le déjeuner sur l'herbe**. 1863. Oil on canvas. **h**208 × **w**264.5 cm. **h**81¾ × **w**104⅛ in. Musée d'Orsay, Paris

Mangold Robert

This irregularly shaped canvas, whose bottom edge is parallel with the floor, has been painted with a roller. One of a series of 28 and named after the Greek pots in the Metropolitan Museum in New York, this Minimalist work has no image, suggests no emotion and is without movement. Mangold deliberately distorts a precise geometric form to question the way in which we perceive things. Often more interested in the preparation of an idea than in turning it into a work of art, Mangold is fascinated by works made up of sections put together to make a whole, and he likes an element of visual illusion. Through the years Mangold's painting has been highly varied and has included spray-painted wood panels and works on canvas which explore geometric proportions in canvas shape and content. In the 1980s he took on a more lyrical palette reminiscent of Henri Matisse.

► Andre, LeWitt, Lissitzky, Matisse, B Nicholson, Ryman

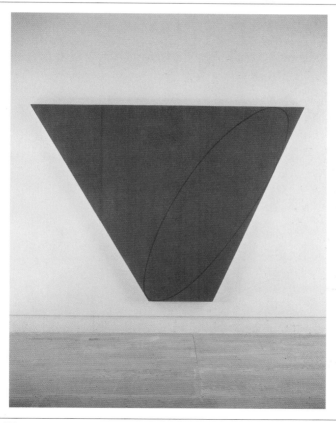

Robert Mangold. b North Tonawanda, NY, 1937. **Attic Series III**. 1990. Acrylic and coloured pencil on canvas. **h**229 × **w**310 cm. 90⅛ × **w**122 in. Private collection

Mantegna Andrea

The Agony in the Garden

Five angels appear to Christ as he prays, while three of his apostles sleep in the foreground, unaware that Judas and a crowd of soldiers are on their way to arrest Christ. Every aspect of the scene – the bizarre rock formations, the imaginary town, the rigid folds of drapery – is painted in stony, precise detail. Mantegna was of humble birth, but was adopted and taught by a minor painter, becoming one of the most important artists of his time. His style, as that of other Renaissance artists, was inspired by ancient Roman sculpture. Many of his works are in fact executed in *grisaille*, a painted imitation of marble or bronze relief. For much of his life Mantegna was Court painter to the Duke of Mantua, for whom he formed a major collection of Classical works of art. He was also a pioneer in the art of engraving and his engravings on classical subjects were later to influence Albrecht Dürer and others.

► Carpaccio, Dürer, Giulio Romano, Uccello

Andrea Mantegna. b Isola di Carturo, c1430/31. **d** Mantua, 1506. **The Agony in the Garden**. c1460. Tempera on panel. **h**63 × **w**80 cm. **h**24¾ × **w**31½ in. National Gallery, London

Manzù Giacomo

The Cardinal

With only a hand appearing to disturb the geometric unity of his voluminous robes, a cardinal reflects in priestly solemnity on the authority of his office. His conical shape is at once severe and lyrical, with no suggestion of the body beneath. A feeling for continuous, undisturbed outlines has contributed to the statue's lyrical qualities. Manzù's work represents a thread of harmony and figurative order running through the fragmented schisms of twentieth-century art. The first Italian artist for whom a museum was created during his lifetime,

Manzù was born the son of a shoemaker, and was apprenticed to a plasterer and a woodcarver before he began to study art. He was commissioned to make religious reliefs and statues of saints for many churches including St Peter's, Rome and also for the University of Milan. He later taught sculpture, reviving the Classical techniques of working in bronze.

▶ Algardi, Bacon, Brancusi, Maillol, Marini

Giacomo Manzù. b Bergamo, 1908. d Bergamo, 1991. **The Cardinal**. 1955. Bronze. h208 cm. h81⅞ in. Galleria Internazionale d'Arte Moderna di Ca' Pesaro, Venice

Marc Franz

Little Yellow Horses

Three yellow, curvaceous horses dominate the foreground of a detached hilly landscape. The main theme is colour, yellow signifying the passive female element, while the sensual red of the horses' flanks contrasts with the spiritual blue of the background. It is this use of luminous colour, coupled with the representation of the animals as symbols of a life-force and as projections of the artist's imagination, that make this one of Marc's most memorable images. In the way it uses colour and symbols to express the artist's inner feelings it is

a good example of the work of the group of Expressionist artists called Der Blaue Reiter ('the blue rider'). The two most important members, Wassily Kandinsky and Marc, invented the name because Marc liked horses, Kandinsky liked riders and they both liked blue. Most of Marc's paintings were of horses in strong colours, but from 1912 his work became more abstract. Tragically, he was killed at Verdun in 1916.

► Delaunay, Jawlensky, Kandinsky, Marini, Stubbs

Franz Marc. **b** Munich, 1880. **d** Verdun, 1916. **Little Yellow Horses**. 1912. Oil on canvas. **h**66 × **w**104.5 cm. **h**26 × **w**41⅛ in. Staatsgalerie, Stuttgart

The Clock, Marclay's magnum opus, is a 24-hour long video montage of thousands of clips taken from television and cinema. Each clip refers to the passage of time, either in the dialogue or through scenes in which a clock, watch (or, on occasion, a sundial) is visible. The film unfolds in real time – each reference synchronized with that of the audience. When an alarm clock in a scene from *American Gigolo* displays 2.05, that is the exact time at which it is seen in the theatre or gallery. Whilst the film jumps between genres and across cinematic history, Marclay's meticulous editing creates a seamless flow – at times leading to thought-provoking or amusing sequences. Born in California and raised in Geneva, Marclay's work has been shaped by an interest in performance and punk rock. Celebrated for his pioneering use of turntables and re-assembled records, his early pieces brought together cutting-edge music with the assemblage aesthetics of Dada and Surrealism.

► Alÿs, Gonzalez-Torres, Rauschenberg, Viola

Christian Marclay. b San Rafael, CA, 1955. **The Clock**. 2010. Single-channel video with sound. **dur** 24 hrs. Paula Cooper Gallery, NY

Marden Brice

Event

Serpentine lines move rhythmically across the surface of the canvas. Pushing up against the edges of the rectangular panels, their uncoiling ribbon-like forms are suspended in carefully balanced tension. Although the colours overlap, they never intertwine. Each occupies a defined plane within the shallow pictorial space. One of the most respected abstract painters of his generation, Marden first came to prominence in the 1960s with his minimalist monochrome paintings. In part inspired by Chinese and Japanese calligraphy, in the mid-1980s the artist started to introduce linear motifs into his work. Using a long brush, which enabled him to paint at some distance from the canvas, Marden imposed a set of compositional and formal rules, or systems, for each of the series of works that followed – each painting becoming a subtle variation of a theme. The slow, meditated-upon processes that underlie Marden's paintings encourage an equally contemplative approach on the part of the viewer.

► Albers, Diebenkorn, A Martin, Noland, Pollock

Brice Marden. b New York, NY, 1938. Event. 2004–07. Oil on linen. Each panel h180 × w120 cm. h72 × w48 in. Private collection

Marin John

Maine Islands

Painted as if seen through a window, this watercolour plays with the ambiguities of space. Marin has taken a favourite subject, a traditional seascape, and simplified it into its most basic forms and bright colours. Standing in a room overlooking an expanse of sea dotted with islands, he has enclosed the scene within a window frame, making the view itself look like a flat painting hung on a wall. By doing this he is playing a visual game with perceptions of flatness and depth. Marin originally trained and worked as an architect, and

his early works show the influence of James Abbott McNeill Whistler. He went on to develop a unique and individual style, filtered through Fauvism (with its distortions, flat patterns and violent colour) and Cubism (with its fragmentation of forms and play on perceptions), but seen from an American perspective. Although he sometimes painted in oils, he is best known for his watercolours, usually of landscapes or studies of architecture.

► Davis, Diebenkorn, Hodler, Turner, Whistler

John Marin. b Rutherford, NJ, 1870. d Cape Split, ME, 1953. **Maine Islands**. 1922. Watercolour on paper. **h**42.8 × **w**50.1 cm. 16 ⅞ × **w**19¾ in. Phillips Collection, Washington, DC

Marini Marino

Horseman

Solid and enigmatic, this statue with its simple outlines conveys a primitive sense of vitality and power. It is formal and sober, but rich in pathos and poetical feeling. Marini produced a series of horsemen which were inspired by seeing peasants fleeing from their villages in wartime. Like Giacomo Manzù, Marini was an individualist, never part of any artistic group or movement, and remaining faithful only to his own vision. The only influence upon him was that of the statues of Classical Greece. His best-known theme was that of the horse and rider, and he explored many versions of it over a long period of years. A leading Italian sculptor, he often combined different techniques to obtain the effect he wanted, but he was also a painter, whose portraits included such major figures as the composer Igor Stravinsky, the author Henry Miller and the artist Marc Chagall.

► Chagall, Clouet, Epstein, Lawrence, Manzù

Marino Marini. b Pistoia, 1901. **d** Viareggio, 1980. **Horseman**. 1947. Bronze. **h**101.6 cm. **h**40 in. Museum of Modern Art, New York, NY

Martin Agnes

Untitled

This early abstract work is one of the first to exhibit the delicate grid lines, restrained colour and mysterious intimacy that would characterize Martin's paintings for the rest of her life. While living in New York between 1957 and 1967, Martin began to experiment with symmetrical compositions comprising circles and squares, under the influence of such artists as Ad Reinhardt and Ellsworth Kelly. Her grid paintings, which some critics initially linked to the machine-edged Minimalist movement, are actually examples of

Abstract Expressionism, dense with gestural markings and unmistakable traces of the artist's hand. In their purity and meditative quality, the canvases suggest a spiritualism that reflects Martin's interest in nature (particularly the desert landscapes of New Mexico) and Eastern religions, notably Daoism. The paintings created after her return to Taos in 1967 became increasingly ethereal, the grids sometimes so faint that they seemed to be fading into a shimmering mist.

► Klein, Mangold, Marden, Mondrian, Newman

Agnes Martin. b Macklin, Saskatchewan, 1912. d Taos, NM, 2004. **Untitled**. 1960. Oil and ink on linen. h30.5 × w30.5 cm. h12 × w12 in. Private collection

Martin John

The Great Day of His Wrath

Concentrated into this huge landscape, under an ominously dark sky, are all the intensely dramatic effects that Martin could muster to show the awesome power of nature. It is nothing less than the end of the world. Mountains crumble, fires rage and bolts of lightning fall as God exacts his final revenge on mankind. In the centre, tiny figures, naked in their shame and disgrace, are sucked into the primeval void from whence they came. Nicknamed 'Mad Martin', this visionary began as a struggling heraldic and enamel painter, before his

fertile imagination produced the grandiose and lurid visionary paintings that created a sensation in England and Europe, and influenced J M W Turner and others. Inspired by the works of John Milton, his huge canvases showed Biblical subjects on a vast scale, peopled with tiny figures, exotic architecture and lurid, menacing skies. Paralysis from a stroke brought his career to an abrupt end.

► Bosch, Church, Cole, Cozens, Friedrich, Turner

John Martin. b Haydon Bridge, 1789. **d** Douglas, 1854. **The Great Day of His Wrath**. c1851–3. Oil on canvas. **h**196.5 × **w**303 cm.
h77³⁄₈ × **w**119³⁄₈ in. Tate, London

is painting depicts the moment in the Annunciation when
briel first appears to the Virgin to announce that she is to
the mother of Christ. His billowing cape and extended
ngs suggest that he has only just arrived. The words of his
eting are engraved on the gold background, as if issuing
m his mouth at that very moment. Mary recoils in horror
Gabriel's message, turning away from him and pulling her
ak around her for protection. The white lilies and Mary's
ok, traditional attributes of Annunciation scenes, are

depicted with unusual realism. With its elegant figures and
richly patterned surface this work is one of the most perfect
examples of the fourteenth-century Gothic style. Martini
worked for some of the most important and enlightened
patrons of his day, including the Sienese government,
the poet Petrarch and King Robert of Anjou.

▶ Fra Angelico, Duccio, Lorenzo Monaco, Tintoretto

Masaccio

The Holy Trinity

The vaulted arch in this painting is a perfect illustration of the linear perspective which fascinated contemporary Florentine artists. Masaccio painted this scene so that all the sightlines converge on a single point, just as we would see the lines painted on a straight road getting smaller as they stretch into the distance. The vaulting, columns and pilasters reflect the renewed interest in Classical architecture at the time. The figures have an impression of real, physical presence, of a solidity unknown before Masaccio. In his short life,

this pioneer became one of the greatest fifteenth-century Florentine painters, and an influence on those who followed Original and authoritative, he had the ability to convey the drama of a situation through a telling glance or gesture, and his economical techniques suggest a real sense of light and space. His major surviving works are frescos. Tragically, this brilliant painter died before he was 30.

► Grünewald, Masolino, Piero della Francesca, Rouault

Masaccio (Tommaso di Giovanni). b San Giovanni Valdarno, 1401. **d** Rome, c1428. **The Holy Trinity.** c1420. Fresco. **h**667 × **w**317 cm. **h**262½ × **w**124 ⅞ in. Santa Maria Novella, Florence

Masolino

The two saints may be identified by the objects in their hands. Paul holds a sword, from his days as a soldier, whereas Peter holds the keys of Heaven, given to him by Christ. Originally part of an altarpiece for the church of Santa Maria Maggiore in Rome, this panel was a collaboration between Masolino and Masaccio; the figures have Masaccio's characteristic solidity. Masolino is the more delicate artist of the two, as seen here in the soft features of Peter's face, and the relationship of colours in the robes. Masolino and Masaccio frequently worked together; Masolino, although the elder of the two, was profoundly influenced by Masaccio's style – so much so that experts often have difficulty in working out who painted what in their collaborations. The names Masolino and Masaccio, meaning 'Little Tom' and 'Big Tom', may have come from an attempt to tell them apart. After Masaccio's early death, Masolino reverted to the International Gothic style of his youth.

► Giotto, Lorenzo Monaco, Masaccio, Sluter, Uccello

Masolino da Panicale. b Panicale, c1383. d Florence, c1433. **Saint Peter and Saint Paul**. c1428. Oil on panel. h114.5 × w54.4 cm. h45 × w21⅜ in. Philadelphia Museum of Art, Philadelphia, PA

Massys Quentin

Portrait of a Man

The cross, feather, rose, paper and writing instruments indicate that this man is a notary, someone who certifies documents for the public, but his actual identity is not known. There is a directness in the way he looks out at the viewer, and a precision in the whole painting, from the accurate likeness of the sitter to the landscape beyond the arcade. Massys was profoundly influenced by Leonardo da Vinci and Albrecht Dürer, and his sitters are usually seen against a wooded or mountainous landscape (similar to that in the *Mona Lisa*).

There are other indications of Leonardo's influence: some of his original and ironical drawings are similar to Leonardo caricature heads of old men and women, called 'grotesques'. According to legend, Massys was a blacksmith who transformed himself into a musician and man of culture. A distinguished and realistic portrait painter, he developed a highly polished technique.

► Dürer, Holbein, Leonardo, Memling, Sittow

Quentin Massys. b Louvain, 1465/6. **d** Antwerp, 1530. **Portrait of a Man.** c1510. Oil on panel. **h**80 × **w**64.5 cm. **h**31½ × **w**25¼ in.
National Gallery of Scotland, Edinburgh

Matisse Henri

The Dinner Table (Harmony in Red)

flurry of primary colours dominates this dazzling painting
the interior of a room with a woman laying a table. The
tire surface is harmonized into a vibrant, unified pattern
pure colour which has been skilfully integrated into the
ructural composition, saturating the room. The tablecloth
erges with the wall, and the forms have been completely
attened, distorted and simplified. This enhances the lyrical
w of the ornamental forms and iridescent colours.
atisse has used colour as a means of expression rather than

description and has deliberately flouted the conventional rules
of drawing and perspective. He and his followers were called
'Fauves', or wild beasts, due to the primitive savagery of their
style. Matisse's Fauvist manner spanned the years 1905–8 and
his style continued to develop throughout his long career.
Colour always played a central role in his work, however, as
can be seen in the vibrant paper collages he produced in his
last years.

► Bonnard, Derain, Gauguin, Van Gogh, Heron, Kirchner

enri Matisse. b Le Cateau-Cambrésis, 1869. d Nice, 1954. **The Dinner Table (Harmony in Red)**. 1908. Oil on canvas. **h**180 × **w**246 cm.
1 × **w**97 in. Hermitage Museum, St Petersburg

Matta

Untitled

Strange shapes inhabit this fantastical, amorphous landscape. Visions from a dark imagination dart spontaneously across the picture surface and beyond, like electrical currents. They seem to resist any polar attraction to direct them into a semblance of compositional unity or rhythm. An unnatural blue-ish colour suffuses the scene with an aura of mystery and other-worldliness, while the pictorial forms seem to be the result of a bizarre symbiosis of organic limbs and mechanical components extending into infinite space. Matta first trained as an architect, but turned to painting in 1937. He spent the war years in New York and came into contact with many members of the Surrealist movement. His style of painting, using the 'automatic' technique of entirely free brushstrokes without rational control, is typical of Surrealism, and was to inspire Jackson Pollock and Arshile Gorky among others.

► Bellmer, Brauner, Gorky, Lam, Pollock

Roberto Sebastián Antonio Matta Echaurren. **b** Santiago de Chile, 1911. **d** Civitavecchia, Italy, 2002. **Untitled**. 1950. Oil on canvas. **h**130 × **w**195 cm. **h**51⅛ × **w**76¾ in. Latin American Masters, Beverly Hills, CA series of circular and droplet-shaped holes have been cut rough the floors of a five-story office building. Looking wn to the ground below, the effect is both vertiginous d amusing – the architectural structure appears to have en cut open like a tin can. After training as an architect, atta-Clark was inspired by the work of Land artists and the ropean Situationist movement to engage with buildings a less conventional way. Producing what he referred to as narchitecture', he modified a number of disused buildings

through the insertion of 'cuts'; a process that linked together spaces that had previously been defined as private and public. In one notable example, *Splitting*, a house was sliced completely in half. Central to Matta-Clark's art was an investigation into the transformation of found objects. The cuts in *Office Baroque, Antwerp* were inspired by overlapping shapes created by teacup stains that had been left on a drawing. Matta-Clark's father was the Surrealist painter Matta Echaurren.

► Fontana, Graham, Heizer, Matta, Whiteread

ordon Matta-Clark. b New York, NY, 1943. d New York, NY, 1978. **Office Baroque, Antwerp**. 1977. Destroyed.

363

Mehretu Julie

Dispersion

A densely layered kaleidoscopic mass of colour explodes across the canvas surface. Behind the calligraphic swooshes and monochromatic geometric forms – that appear to swirl around as if caught in some mysterious vortex – lies an elaborate linear structure. It is as if a painting by Kandinsky has collided head-on with an abstract design by Moholy-Nagy or Malevich. Incorporating and combining pre-existing architectural plans and designs, Mehretu's paintings suggest fantastical new maps that appear to represent both space and time. For the artist, the colourful abstract marks and shapes exist as a type of personal signifier, or language, belonging to the characters that occupy these complex Post-Modern landscapes. Born in Ethiopia, Mehretu later studied in Senegal and the USA. Her paintings bring together formal investigations into colour and line, with social issues pertaining to power, history and the formation of personal and cultural identity in the globalized world.

► Kiefer, Lissitsky, Malevich, Matta, Moholy-Nagy

Julie Mehretu. b Addis Ababa, 1970. Dispersion. 2002. Ink and acrylic on canvas. h230 × w370 cm. h90 × w144 in. Private collection

Memling Hans

One of the most famous triptychs painted by Memling, this work was commissioned for the high altar of the church at the hospital of Saint John (Sint Jan) in Bruges. Once known as the *Mystic Marriage of Saint Catherine*, it is dedicated to the Virgin and the two Saint Johns. The central panel shows the Virgin and Child enthroned, flanked by the two Johns, patron saints of the hospital, and saints Catherine and Barbara. The left wing depicts the beheading of Saint John the Baptist, and the right wing shows Saint John the Evangelist on Patmos,

with his vision of the Apocalypse. Episodes from the lives of the two saints were also painted in the landscapes between the columns behind the Virgin, and even in the column capitals. Probably a student of Rogier van der Weyden, Memling developed a theatrical yet analytical style, the elements of his paintings carefully ordered to create a unified visual spectacle. His bright colours, which replace the gold and silver of medieval paintings, add to the sense of space.

► Bouts, Campin, Duccio, Lochner, Van der Weyden

Hans Memling. b Seligenstadt, 1433. **d** Bruges, 1494. **Saint John Altarpiece**. 1474-9. Oil on oak panel. **h**173 × **w**173.7 cm **h**68 × **w**68 in (central). **h**173 × **w**78.9 cm. **h**68 × **w**31 in. (wings). Memlingmuseum, Bruges

365

Mengs Anton Raphael

Self-portrait

Dressed in a simple brown cloak with a red underjacket, Mengs presents us with a completely informal, unpretentious image of himself. His rather shabby clothing, unkempt hair and drained features with tired, swollen eyes are an honest depiction of an exhausted man, worn out with hard work and inner struggle. Many painters have made self-portraits, the best known being those of Vincent van Gogh and Rembrandt. These searching introspections, plumbed into the inner psyche, give a penetrating insight into the character of the artist. Often, as in this painting, all concrete details apart from a brush and a folder of sketches are excluded. A German by birth who worked mostly in Rome and Spain, Mengs was a painter of religious and historical subjects in the restrained emotions and heroic style of the Neo-Classical era, yet here he has let us have a glimpse of his real personality.

▶ Kauffmann, Raeburn, Rembrandt, Vigée-Lebrun

Anton Raphael Mengs. b Aussig, 1728. **d** Rome, 1779. **Self-portrait.** c1774. Oil on canvas. **h**102 × **w**77 cm. **h**40¼ × **w**30¼ in.
Hermitage Museum, St Petersburg

Merz Mario

Unreal City

The words *città irreale* ('the unreal city') are inscribed in neon light within a triangular framework. It is a brash, succinct statement on the artificial and transitory nature of contemporary urban life – but also an enigmatic and puzzling work. Its very elusiveness can be interpreted as the source of infinite ambiguities of meaning, demonstrating Merz's interest in exploring the fleeting, subtly changing processes of thought as a comment on the bland standardization of modern technological culture. Merz was an exponent of Arte Povera, a new form of Conceptual Art developed in Italy in the 1960s which aimed at disassociating artistic creation from the notion of high culture. As the name suggests, the defining criteria for Arte Povera were poverty and lack of refinement, whether of means, materials or effect; banality was raised to the level of art and commonplace objects were invested with metaphysical significance.

► Beuys, Flavin, Nauman, Oldenburg, Viola

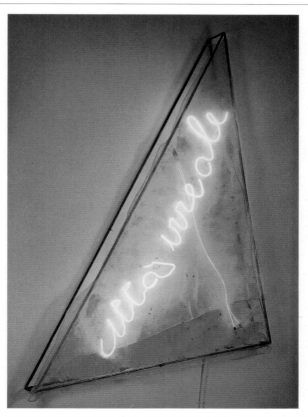

Mario Merz. b Milan, 1925. **d** Milan, 2003. **Unreal City**. 1968. Iron, wire mesh, wax and neon light. **h**200 × **w**164 cm. **h**78¾ × **w**64½ in.
Stedelijk Museum, Amsterdam

367

Metsu Gabriel

The Music Lesson

A delicate air of mystery enshrouds this little interior, in which a man and a woman are seated at a virginal. Ostensibly a music lesson, the picture probably also depicts a scene of courtship, where music acts as the accompaniment of love. The calm, balanced mood of this painting is achieved by its cool luminosity, as in the pale tones of the wall. Brilliant areas of pure colour, such as in the woman's red bodice and the man's blue hose, create delicate spatial harmonies. The carefully structured composition is based on the stable horizontals and verticals of the spinet, picture-frames and chair, with few diagonals intruding. Metsu was a pupil of Gerrit Dou, who specialized in domestic interior scenes. His paintings are rich in subtle poetical allusions, providing revealing insights into the lives of the Dutch middle classes in the seventeenth century.

► Ter Borch, Dou, Hammershøi, De Hooch, Vermeer

Gabriel Metsu. b Leiden, 1629. **d** Amsterdam, 1667. **The Music Lesson.** c1658. Oil on canvas. **h**38.4 × **w**32.2 cm. **h**15⅛ × **w**12¾ in. National Gallery, London

Michelangelo

Pietà

This most supremely elegant and graceful sculpture was begun by the young Michelangelo at the age of only twenty-three. The pyramidal composition, with the Virgin's startlingly youthful face at the apex, displays the sculptor's early mastery of form and contour, seen most clearly in the drapery. The tightly drawn, flat folds of Christ's loincloth contrast eloquently with the plump, complicated ruching of his mother's robes, and the generous sweep of the funeral shroud seems to cradle him as much as she does. Michelangelo is said to have been criticized for his unrealistically youthful depiction of Mary, whose face radiates serenity and acceptance rather than distraught grief. It was deliberate, he replied, for time could not mar the features of this most blessed of Virgins. Sculptor, painter, architect, engineer and poet, Michelangelo occupied the pinnacle of Renaissance art during his lifetime, and remains there today. This is the only work he ever signed – on the sash across the Virgin's chest.

► Bernini, Canova, Donatello, Giotto, Memling

Michelangelo Buonarroti. b Caprese, 1475. **d** Rome, 1564. **Pietà.** 1497–1500. Marble. **h**175 × **w**200 cm. **h**68½ × **w**78¾ in.
Papal Basilica of Saint Peter, Rome

Millais Sir John Everett

Ophelia

In an event taken from Shakespeare's *Hamlet*, the tragic figure of Ophelia is shown partially submerged in a stream into which she has fallen whilst out picking flowers. Ophelia is driven mad with grief following her father's murder by her lover Hamlet – Millais depicts the haunting image of Ophelia calmly singing as she allows herself to drown. To capture accurately the rich selection of flowers and foliage that surround Ophelia, Millais spent four months painting in the open air, an uncommon practice among artists at the time.

He subsequently painted the figure of Ophelia in his London studio, employing the model Elizabeth Siddal, who posed whilst lying in a bath. A talented artist from a very young age, Millais was a founding member of the Pre-Raphaelite Brotherhood. He became one of the most celebrated painter working in Victorian England, and was elected President of the Royal Academy in 1896.

► Burne-Jones, Hunt, Raphael, Rossetti, Waterhouse

Sir John Everett Millais. b Southampton, 1829. d London, 1896. Ophelia. 1851–2. Oil on canvas. h74 × w112 cm. h29⅛ × w44 in. Tate, London

Millet Jean-François

The Gleaners

Three peasant women collect the scanty remains of the harvest after it has been reaped. In the distance, the harvesters are loading up the plentiful crop. The cool, golden light gives a noble dignity to the figures, but this painting is more than a mere depiction of rural life. It is also a harsh social comment on the poor, peasant classes, reduced to labouring over the slim pickings left by the rich, who are far away on the horizon. Millet transformed scenes of heart-breaking poverty into images of epic heroism, depicting the noble toil of peasants and their intimacy with the land with flagrant realism. Although this provoked much criticism among his contemporaries, this painting is now regarded as one of the masterpieces of the nineteenth century. Millet's drawings are also notable for their sculptural simplification of form and their monumental qualities.

► Corot, Courbet, Daubigny, Pissarro, T Rousseau

Jean-François Millet. b Gruchy, 1814. d Barbizon, 1875. **The Gleaners**. 1857. Oil on canvas. **h**85.5 × **w**111 cm. **h**33⅝ × **w**43¾ in.
Musée d'Orsay, Paris

371

Miró Joan

Women and Bird in the Moonlight

Playing and mingling acrobatically with one another, these imaginary, frolicking figures project themselves vivaciously into the foreground. The background paint has been rubbed away to show the canvas underneath, lending it a raw, earthy quality. Evoking imagery from a primitive world, the magical figures conjure up thoughts of prehistoric cave-paintings, restored to us with all their freshness. The painting forms part of a series entitled 'Women and Birds' and is considered to be one of the most important of all this Spanish artist's

works. In its portrayal of weird, hallucinatory beings, which seem to spring from a subconscious dream-world, the picture is typical of the Surrealist movement, of which Miró became a prominent member. He worked with Max Ernst on the creation of the decor for Diaghilev's ballet *Romeo and Juliet*, and also executed a wide range of lithographs, etchings and ceramics throughout his life.

► Arp, Baumeister, Brauner, Dali, Ernst

Joan Miró. b Barcelona, 1893. **d** Palma, 1983. **Women and Bird in the Moonlight**. 1949. Oil on canvas. **h**81.5 × **w**66 cm. **h**32 × **w**26 in.
Tate, London

Modersohn-Becker Paula

Old Poorhouse Woman with a Glass Bottle

Gazing out in a deep reverie, an old woman firmly holds a foxglove in her hand. She sits at the very edge of the picture-plane in front of a field of poppies and an inverted bottle. The flowers, bottle and woman are all painted with great solidity; their massive shapes easily fill the canvas. Modersohn-Becker's sensitivity to colour is equally important to the composition. The sky, for example, glows with a luminous yellow-green light. Although she was born in Germany and worked there most of her life, the artist's frequent trips to

Paris gave her contact with the thick, textural technique of Vincent van Gogh and the solid, simple forms and colours of Paul Gauguin. This work was painted in the last year of Modersohn-Becker's life; she died tragically early at the age of 31. In its simplification of colour and form, and emphasis on line, her work anticipates German Expressionism.

▶ Gauguin, Van Gogh, Gontcharova, Jawlensky, Nolde

Paula Modersohn-Becker. b Dresden, 1876. **d** Worpswede, 1907. **Old Poorhouse Woman with a Glass Bottle**. 1907. Oil on canvas. **h**96 × **w**80.2 cm. **h**37¾ × **w**31½ in. Ludwig Roselius Sammlung, Bremen

Modigliani Amedeo

Female Nude

The female model leans against a chair in a plain interior which provides no distractions, allowing us to gaze at her beauty. The nude was Modigliani's main pictorial subject and this is considered to be one of his most beautiful portrayals. It is also one of his earliest works. The girl's submissive and serene expression gives the painting an erotic charge. The elongated, angular lines, and the almost sculptural quality of the sitter's face, are typical of the artist's work. Modigliani developed his own individual, restrained style of painting and was not closely affiliated to any movement although he was profoundly influenced by Cubism, African sculpture and the work of Paul Cézanne. A painter and sculptor, Modigliani lived at an exhausting pace. Born in Italy, he went to Paris in 1906 and spent the rest of his short life there. When he died, aged 35, of tuberculosis, his beloved girlfriend Jeanne Hébuterne committed suicide.

► Boucher, Brancusi, Cézanne, Foujita, Munch, Picasso

Amedeo Modigliani. b Livorno, 1884. **d** Paris, 1920. **Female Nude**. c1916. Oil on canvas. **h**92.4 × **w**60 cm. **h**36½ × **w**23 ⅝ in.
Courtauld Institute of Art Gallery, London

Moholy-Nagy László

CHX

A perfect illusion of objects suspended in space is created by this painting. The artist has placed geometric forms within the confines of a narrowing grid pattern to create an impression of three-dimensionality and perspective. The importance of this painting lies in the way it explores the ability of light and colour to move objects in a seemingly infinite environment. Influenced by the ideas of the Russian Constructivist movement, the artist has stripped the geometric forms of all ornamentation, using them to demonstrate the relationship between space and volume. Moholy-Nagy was active in industrial design, photography, sculpture, cinematography, writing and stage design. One of his notable commercial achievements was the creation of the special effects for Alexander Korda's movie *More Things to Come*. Hungarian by birth, Moholy-Nagy lived in Germany from 1920 to 1937 when he settled in Chicago and founded The Institute of Design.

► Gabo, Lissitzky, Malevich, Rodchenko

László Moholy-Nagy. **b** Borsod, 1895. **d** Chicago, IL, 1946. **CHX**. 1939. Oil on canvas. **h**76 × **w**96.5 cm. **h**29 ⅞ × **w**38 in. Private collection

Mondrian Piet

Composition

A simple black grid pattern interspersed with vivid sections of primary colour is boldly displayed in this geometrical composition. Mondrian developed a style that banished the conventions of three-dimensional space and the curved line. He wished to build his pictures from the simplest elements – straight lines and primary colours – which he moved around the canvas until he found the perfect composition balance. His aim was to create an objective art of discipline whose laws would somehow reflect the order of the universe. The use of pure line and colour highlights the painting's connection to the De Stijl movement, of which Mondrian was a leading member. For over twenty years he was based in Paris, before moving to London in 1938. After a bomb exploded close to his studio he travelled to New York where his compositions became slightly more colourful, reflecting the more restless rhythms of life in the land of Broadway and boogie-woogie.

► Albers, Van Doesburg, Judd, Malevich, Rodchenko

Piet Mondrian. b Amersfoort, 1872. **d** New York, NY, 1944. **Composition**. 1929. Oil on canvas. **h**45 × **w**45 cm. **h**17¾ × **w**17¾ in.
Solomon R Guggenheim Museum, New York, NY

Monet Claude

Impression, Sunrise

This painting of Le Havre, on the English Channel in northwest France where Monet grew up, gave the Impressionist movement its name. It was displayed in April 1874 at an exhibition by a group of artists calling themselves the Société anonyme des artistes peintres, sculpteurs, graveurs etc., who wanted to avoid the restrictions of the French Academy's annual juried Salon. Monet later explained the title as having been improvised for the show's catalogue. Since the painting was clearly not a typical seascape, he called it

Impression. The critic Louis Leroy appropriated the word in the title of his antagonistic review, 'The Exhibition of the Impressionists', thus unintentionally giving the new movement a name. A classic Impressionist landscape, the canvas exhibits none of the detail and finish that until that time were considered non-negotiable elements of a painting. Instead, the unblended colours, gestural brushwork and muddy details are just as Monet described them – an impression.

► Derain, Grimshaw, Pissarro, Signac, Turner

Claude Monet. b Paris, 1840. **d** Giverny, 1926. **Impression, Sunrise.** 1872. Oil on canvas. **h**48 × **w**62.5 cm. **h**19 × **w**24¾ in. Musée Marmottan Monet, Paris

Moore Henry

Recumbent Figure

Monumental and almost primeval, this carved statue seems to have been created more by the forces of nature than by man. Semi-abstract in form, its smooth and rounded outlines suggest the work of the elements, while at the same time evoking the soft curves and flowing outlines of a female body. Inspired by the vitality of ancient and primitive sculpture, Moore revived the tradition of direct carving into stone or wood. In so doing he emphasized the natural textures of his material, and in his massive works he consciously reflected the contours and qualities of landscape and rock. As a result, the simple, solid shapes of his sculptures have a powerfully brooding presence. One of the distinguishing hallmarks of his figures or groups was that they were often pierced. Moore's works are frequently displayed in the open air, and several of his commissions stand outside major buildings in North America and Europe.

► Bourdelle, Hepworth, Maillol, Manzù, Rodin

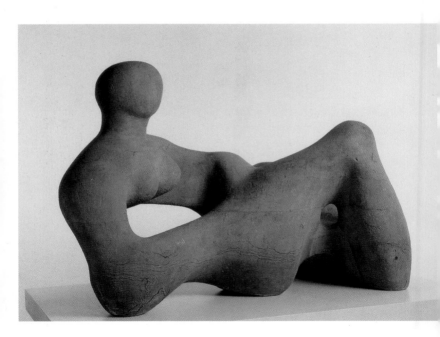

Henry Moore. b Castleford, 1898. **d** Much Hadham, 1986. **Recumbent Figure.** 1938. Green Hornton stone. **h**88.9 × **w**132.7 cm. **h**35 × **w**52¼ in. Tate, London

Morandi Giorgio

Still Life

Remote and imprisoned in their austere, cool tones, a collection of jugs, cups and containers is enveloped in a neutral background; they appear to exist in a complete vacuum. A sense of mystery pervades this simple, intimate scene. With its harmonious composition and subtle colour variations it conveys an air of meditative serenity. Morandi almost exclusively painted still lifes of bottles and jugs throughout his long career. He sought to express the pure, poetic beauty of these objects in his powerfully simple,

contemplative compositions. While he was influenced briefly by Giorgio de Chirico's idea of Metaphysical Painting, Morandi's withdrawn, sensitive personality led him to stand aloof from the intellectual turmoil and experiments of many contemporary artists. The sense of calm meditation that pervades his paintings invites comparison with the work of Jean-Baptiste-Siméon Chardin and Paul Cézanne rather than that of his contemporaries. He is also known for his etchings.

► Cézanne, Chardin, De Chirico, B Nicholson, De Staël

Giorgio Morandi. b Bologna, 1890. **d** Bologna, 1964. **Still Life**. 1960. Oil on canvas. **h**38 × **w**33.5 cm. **h**14 ⅞ × **w**13¼ in. Private collection   379

Moreau Gustave

Galatea

A sensual, naked nymph sits languidly in an exotic grotto, which is fantastically decorated with a profusion of colourful anemones, corals and other mineral flora. She is watched by an eerie, three-eyed monster. This picture is based on a story from Greek mythology, telling of the unrequited love of the Cyclops, Polyphemus, for the Nereid, Galatea. The technicolour myriads of underwater blooms, and the softness of the execution, give the painting a magical, dream-like quality. Moreau was associated with the Symbolist movement, whose painters moved away from the objective naturalism of the Impressionists. They preferred to derive their inspiration from an imaginative synthesis of often literary or mythological sources. As in this painting, they used colour and form to imbue their work with expressive rather than descriptive meaning. Moreau also painted a large number of watercolours, which were highly acclaimed by his contemporaries.

► Bonnard, Klimt, Modigliani, Mucha, Redon, Vuillard

Gustave Moreau. b Paris, 1826. d Paris, 1898. **Galatea**. 1880. Oil on panel. **h**85 × **w**67 cm. **h**33⅜ × **w**26⅜ in. Private collection

Morisot Berthe

The Cradle

young mother is watching devotedly over her sleeping
by in a cradle. The tenderness and love implicit in this
inting are achieved not only by the careful disposition of
e two figures but also in the subtle harmonies of colours
d delicate brushwork. The sensitive handling of textures,
ch as the diaphanous veil draped over the crib and the satin
rtain behind the woman (the artist's sister), enhance the
timacy of the scene. Morisot was the great-granddaughter
the eighteenth-century painter Jean-Honoré Fragonard.

She was taught by Édouard Manet (who became her brother-
in-law) and the even light and directness of this work owe
much to his influence. Later, she was to be heavily influenced
by Pierre Auguste Renoir. Although she often exhibited her
paintings alongside those of the Impressionists, Morisot's
work retained a feminine delicacy all of its own.

► Cassatt, Corot, John, Manet, Renoir, Reynolds

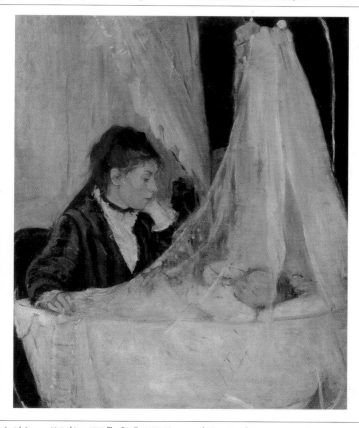

Moroni Giovanni Battista

Portrait of the Duke of Albuquerque

Splendidly regal, this man has been captured by Moroni in all his pompous dignity and luxurious clothing. He is carrying a sword, which probably refers to his readiness to defend the honour of his family and city in times of conflict. This chivalrous attitude is further reflected in his restrained and proud bearing, and also in the inscription on the wall: 'Here I am with no fear, and of death I have no terror'. It is an intimate and confident portrait, blending a striking realism with the artist's love of rich colours and sumptuous effects which he derived from the Venetian masters Giorgione and Titian. Free from unnecessary background detail, the simplicity of the composition lends distinction to the sitter. Moroni's grandiose treatment of the full-length portrait (especially those depicting ordinary people) made him one of the leading exponents of this type of picture in the sixteenth century.

► Dossi, Giorgione, Kneller, Lotto, Titian

Giovanni Battista Moroni. b Albino, 1520/5. **d** Bergamo, 1578. **Portrait of the Duke of Albuquerque.** 1560. Oil on canvas. **h**116 × **w**86 cm. **h**45⅝ × **w**33⅞ in. Private collection road, massive forms are dramatically applied in black paint n the white canvas. These heavy, slow-moving shapes have ngendered numerous and varied interpretations – from nallic symbols to musical notes – but none, in themselves, e totally convincing. The painting's quality lies in its power o suggest so many rich and varied analogies, however diverse ey may be. As the title suggests it is one of the numerous orks in the artist's 'Elegy' series, inspired by the Spanish vil War. It has become one of Motherwell's most renowned

images. Married to fellow artist Helen Frankenthaler, Motherwell was one of the principal members of the Abstract Expressionist movement. His spontaneity of technique and attention to formal rather than narrative qualities epitomize their approach. Apart from his paintings, Motherwell also made numerous drawings, prints and inspired collages of ripped paper which incorporate paint.

► Flavin, Frankenthaler, Kline, Louis, Ryman, Soulages

bert Motherwell. **b** Aberdeen, WA, 1915. **d** Provincetown, MA, 1991. **Elegy to the Spanish Republic No. 134**. 1974. Acrylic on vas. **h**237.5 × **w**300 cm. **h**93½ × **w**118⅛ in. Graham Gund Collection, Cambridge, MA

Moulins Master of

Coronation of the Virgin

Elegantly dressed in rich red and blue velvet brocades, the Virgin and Child are portrayed surrounded by angels and bathed in a mystical light. Behind them is a fantastical visionary background, and a crescent moon lies at their feet. The Master's refined technique brings out the luminous opulence of the jewels in the crown, and the elongated features of the Virgin have a marvellous lyrical quality. This highly accomplished artist was influenced by Hugo van der Goes and adopted the restrained elegance of his Flemish

contemporaries. One of the great French fifteenth-century painters, he was named after his principal work, a triptych in Moulins Cathedral. Little is known about him, including his real name, which has produced several theories about his identity. Some experts believe that he may have been the Court painter to the French King, Charles VIII.

► Van Eyck, Van der Goes, Filippo Lippi, Van der Weyden

Master of Moulins. Active 1480-1500. **Coronation of the Virgin.** c1500. Oil on panel. **h**157 × **w**142 cm. **h**61¾ × **w**55⅞ in.
Notre-Dame Cathedral, Moulins

As noble and spiritual as Joan of Arc, yet sensually provocative and appealing, a dream-like seductress stands resting her hand on a bottle of liqueur. The round decoration surrounding her head like a halo gives this temptress an almost divine appearance of rare beauty. Delineated in elongated, curvilinear strokes and coloured in pale, watery tones, this advertising poster is an example of the stylish elegance of Art Nouveau, of which Mucha was one of the chief exponents. The artists of the Art Nouveau style attempted to blend all categories of art into a decorative unity based on graceful, elegant linear forms. Mucha was largely responsible for popularizing many of the style's key motifs, such as undulations of flowing hair and flowers on slender twining stems. A prolific graphic artist, Mucha also designed jewellery, stained glass, furniture, stage sets and costumes. He spent much of his career in Paris, but returned to his native Czechoslovakia in 1910.

► Klimt, Moreau, Munch, Toulouse-Lautrec

Munch Edvard

The Madonna

A mysterious sensuality draws us into this vibrant painting of the Madonna, daringly depicted in a pose of naked abandon. Uneasily provocative, she exudes a challenging sexuality, but there is also an underlying sense of tragedy in her deep black hair and dark eyes. The swirling, tempestuous background seems to evoke a troubled soul. Munch's own life was tinged with death, illness and nervous crises. Born in Norway, he began his career painting in a more conventional manner but soon became interested in the work of Vincent van Gogh and Paul Gauguin. Instead of painting the world around him he began to seek to express his innermost feelings and desires through his art. The frenetic energy and simmering passions of his intense paintings made him a founder of the style known as Expressionism, in which emotive distortions and exaggerated colours are used to achieve maximum expressiveness.

► Bernini, Gauguin, Van Gogh, Kokoschka, Modigliani

Edvard Munch. b Løte, 1863. **d** Oslo, 1944. **The Madonna**. 1894/5. Oil on canvas. **h**91 × **w**71 cm. **h**35¾ × **w**28 in. Nasjonalgalleriet, Oslo

Murillo Bartolomé Esteban

The Immaculate Conception of the Escorial

A visionary painting of deep piety and religious sentiment, this depiction of the Madonna in the heavenly realm was commissioned for the Hospital de los Venerables Sacerdotes in Seville. The softness of the brushwork and the delicate yet rich colouring, bathed in a gentle light, imbue the composition with tenderness. Swirling, playful *putti* surround the Madonna like an aureole. The composition follows the form prescribed by seventeenth-century Spanish art theorists, but the painting is fired with Murillo's own brand of spiritual devotion. Compared with the harsh, almost brutal realism and heightened emotions of his Spanish contemporaries, Jusepe Ribera and Francisco de Zurbarán, Murillo's style is more tender and sentimental, reminiscent of the sixteenth-century Italian artist Correggio. His works were much in demand throughout Europe and were widely copied and imitated well into the nineteenth century.

► Andrea del Sarto, Correggio, Ribera, Velázquez, Zurbarán

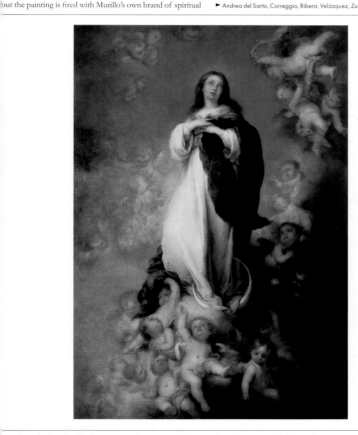

Bartolomé Esteban Murillo. **b** Seville, 1618. **d** Seville, 1682. **The Immaculate Conception of the Escorial**. c1678. Oil on canvas. h274 × w190 cm. h108 × w74¾ in. Museo del Prado, Madrid

Nash Paul

Dead Sea

This nightmarish image of a vast, static sea of wrecked metal is an imaginative and visionary transformation of a set of photographs taken by the artist at a dump for wrecked German aircraft near Oxford. Wings, wheels and fuselage are discernible in this mass of metal carnage. A bleak moonlight permeates the whole scene and evokes an eerie atmosphere of death and destruction. It is one of Nash's most compelling statements as an official war artist to the Air Ministry in the Second World War, capturing the tragedy and triumph of those bitterly glorious years. Although influenced by Surrealism, Nash remained essentially an artist of visionary landscapes. The dramatic content of his work is sometimes associated with the Neo-Romantics, who practised a strongly theatrical, romantic style of painting in the 1930s and 40s. His artistic range included engravings, book illustrations, industrial design and photography.

► Bomberg, Burra, Friedrich, Lewis, Wadsworth

Paul Nash. b London, 1889. **d** Boscombe, 1946. **Dead Sea**. 1940-1. Oil on canvas. **h**101.6 × **w**152.4 cm. **h**40 × **w**60 in. Tate, London ckering neon lights flash words which are boldly written in loured capital letters. A sense of wonder and enchantment generated both by the medium, through which the messages ysteriously appear like judgements from on high, and the words themselves, which flash on and off in arbitrary quences. The overlapping phrases contradict each other d can be taken to represent the ambiguities inherent in man communication and the multi-layered meanings of orldly experience. The use of signs and symbols to convey 'hidden' meanings and messages has been a popular feature of art (especially in northern Europe) since the Middle Ages. Nauman takes this idea to its ultimate expression by means of representation and association: the work of art has itself become the message, presented in a pure and distilled form.

► Beuys, Flavin, Merz, Oldenburg, Viola

uce Nauman. b Fort Wayne, IA, 1941. **Life Death, Knows Doesn't Know**. 1983. Neon tubing with clear glass suspension frames. am.203.2 cm. **diam**.80 in. Anthony d'Offay Gallery, London

Neel Alice

Andy Warhol

The pale, fragile figure of Andy Warhol sits in apparent contemplation, his eyes closed. His hands, held firmly together, rest upon his lap. Warhol is wearing a surgical corset. Across his abdomen stretch large scars, the result of gunshot wounds from an assassination attempt two years earlier. Neel was seventy when she painted this portrait; Warhol was in his early forties. The psychological intensity of the portrait, as well as the apparent vulnerability of the sitter, is intensified by the lack of attention that Neel has awarded to the surroundings, which appear unfinished. In the 1930s Neel had been closely associated with the left-wing cultural scene in New York, painting portraits of some of its leading figures. Eschewing artistic trends, she retained an unwavering commitment to her own distinct figurative style throughout her life. During the 1970s she became a celebrated figure among supporters of the feminist movement.

▶ Clemente, Kokoschka, Schiele, Sutherland

Alice Neel. **b** Merion Square, PA, 1900. **d** New York, NY, 1984. **Andy Warhol**. 1970. Oil on canvas. **h**152.5 × **w**101.5 cm. **h**60 × **w**40 in. Whitney Museum of American Art, New York, NY.

Newman Barnett

Covenant

Austere in its restraint and direct in its simplicity, a flat field of red is divided and ordered by two thin, vertical stripes of brown and cream-white. Traditional artistic techniques have been discarded in favour of creating a pure tension between the asymmetrical blocks of smooth colour. The arrangement of the stripes encourages the viewer to concentrate on the spatial experience of pure colour; they make the picture plane almost open out before us. These stripes, which came to be known as 'zips', were to become a trademark of Newman's style, making him one of the most minimalistic of the American Abstract Expressionist painters. Rather than beauty, Newman sought to suggest a sort of mystical abstraction; he intended that we should not only look at his paintings but also sense the refined spirituality and mysticism suggested by their colours and sheer size. He was deeply influential on younger painters of the 1960s.

▶ Flavin, Judd, Reinhardt, Rothko, Ryman, Serra

Barnett Newman. b New York, NY, 1905. d New York, NY, 1970. Covenant. 1949. Oil on canvas. h121.9 × w152.4 cm. h48 × w60 in.
Hirshhorn Museum and Sculpture Garden, Washington, DC

Nicholson Ben

August 1956 (Val d'Orcia)

A series of lyrical, arabesque lines, typical of Nicholson's work in the 1950s, weave between some apparently abstract forms that on closer inspection turn out to be everyday objects such as bottles, glasses, plates and jugs. Only the essence of the flat, coloured outlines has been captured, each reduced to a fragmented geometrical shape that is arranged on a white table set against a half-grey, half-brown background. Nicholson was interested in the innovations of Cubism, where forms are split and viewed simultaneously from different angles, as well as in the pure structural compositions of Piet Mondrian. Both of these influences are synthesized in his painting. A pioneer of abstract art, Nicholson played a significant role in the European avant-garde while maintaining attachment to the landscape and still-life forms. His career spanned over 60 years, embracing his revolutionary carved reliefs, paintings, drawings and prints.

► Braque, Hepworth, Mondrian, Morandi, W Nicholson, De Staël

Ben Nicholson. b Denham, 1894. **d** London, 1982. **August 1956 (Val d'Orcia)**. 1956. Oil and pencil on board. **h**122 × **w**214 cm. **h**48 × **w**84 in. Tate, London

Nicholson Sir William

The Lustre Bowl with Green Peas

On a white tablecloth is placed a simple lustre bowl, its gentle luminosity beautifully set against the dark velvety background. To the foreground is a pile of green peas, their reflection captured in the surface of the bowl. An accomplished and respected painter of portraits and landscapes, as well as a successful graphic artist, it was in his still life compositions that Nicholson revealed his unquestionable technical prowess. Whilst his still lifes are often formally very simple, by juxtaposing objects and materials of contrasting tones

and textures, Nicholson created arrangements that convey a rich sensuality. Although some of the objects selected by the artist may have had some personal significance, they were predominantly chosen for their aesthetic, rather than symbolic value. Nicholson was closely associated with many cultural figures of his day – including Whistler, who encouraged him to paint – yet he chose not to align himself with artistic movements. His eldest son was the artist Ben Nicholson.

► Chardin, Morandi, B Nicholson, Orpen, Whistler

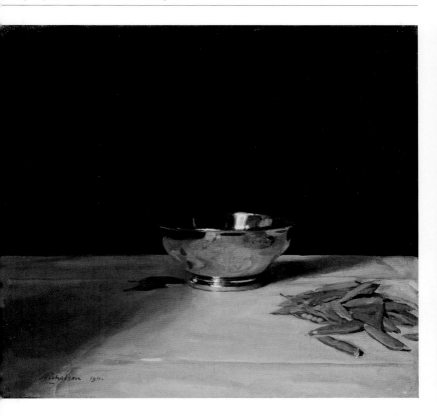

ir William Nicholson. **b** Newark-on-Trent, 1872. **d** Blewbury, 1949. **The Lustre Bowl with Green Peas**. 1911. Oil on canvas.
.55 × w60 cm. **h**21½ × **w**23½ in. Scottish National Gallery of Modern Art, Edinburgh

Noguchi Isamu

Stone of Spiritual Understanding

Suspended in mid-air like a gravity-defying, magical object, a solid bronze stone exudes the vitality and palpable presence of the forces of nature. Its sheer rawness is presented unashamedly, as if to assert that the stone's inner qualities are more significant than anything it could be carved, or cast, to represent. Buddhist philosophy (which strongly influenced Noguchi) ascribes such principles to natural objects. Noguchi believed sculpture to be 'the perception of space, the continuum of our existence'. Working briefly with Constantin Brancusi (from 1927 to 1928), he derived much of his inspiration from the older sculptor's work. His own sculptures, however, are invested with a new elemental and primordial dynamism, of which the material itself is the essence. In addition to sculpture Noguchi concerned himself with theatre and costume designs, garden plans and even playground facilities.

► Bourgeois, Brancusi, Calder, Kapoor, Moore, Smith

Isamu Noguchi. b Los Angeles, CA, 1904. d New York, NY, 1988. **Stone of Spiritual Understanding**. 1962. Bronze, wood and metal. h133 cm. h52¼ in. Museum of Modern Art, New York, NY

Nolan Sir Sidney

Gray Sick

, bearded man, with his hands clenched and an intense expression on his face, is secured to the back of a camel with ope. The relentless heat and scorching desert are evoked y the cloudless, oppressive blue sky and the ridges of roded earth underfoot. In August 1860 a group of 18 men eft Melbourne on the first expedition to cross Australia. Although the expedition completed its objective it was badly rganized and ended in disaster. Charles Gray, one of the xplorers, suffered from severe headaches and dysentery and had to be lashed to the saddle of his camel; he died at sunrise on 17 April 1861. In 1949 Nolan travelled from his native Melbourne to paint in the outback of Queensland, describing the lives of explorers and the toll of the forces of nature upon them. He also painted a series of paintings of the notorious bushranger Ned Kelly. Nolan is widely recognized as the leader of the modern Australian school of painting.

► Boyd, Cole, Kitaj, Marini

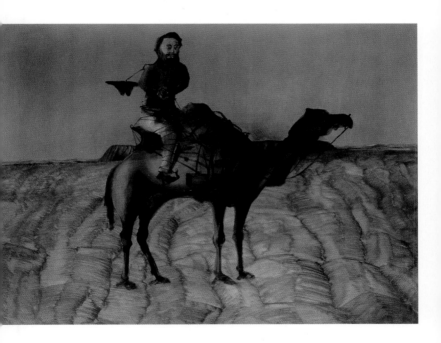

Noland Kenneth

Gift

Concentric circles of paint surrounded by bare canvas create the image of an apparently spinning target. This illusion of movement is produced by the irregular staining caused by the paint as it is absorbed into the unprimed canvas. Concentrating the effect of colour by using a thinned acrylic paint for this staining, Noland leaves a large area unpainted in order to achieve maximum visual intensity. He was one of the first artists to exploit the possibilities of bare canvas in this way. The technique of staining adds a visual ambiguity:

the paint actually becomes part of the weave of the canvas. This painting is connected to the Post-Painterly Abstractioni movement in its exploitation of the flat canvas surface and in the precisely centred image, which generates no physical o emotional reverberation beyond itself. Noland often painted in series, using the same motif recurrently. These included th target, chevron and lozenge shapes.

► Albers, Frankenthaler, Louis, Ryman, Stella

Kenneth Noland. b Asheville, NC, 1924. d Port Clyde, ME, 2010. Gift. 1962. Acrylic on canvas. h182 × w182 cm. h72 × w72 in. Tate, London

Nolde Emil

Red Poppies

Watery splotches of colour seem to float across the paper. The shapes of the poppies and their vivid red colour are the most important elements of the composition. Nolde trained as a furniture-maker, turning to painting later in his career. Most of his works are imbued with the deep emotions characteristic of the German Expressionist artists of whom he was perhaps the most powerful. His goal was to 'grasp what lies at the very heart' and 'transform nature by infusing it with one's own mind and spirit'. Common subjects for

Nolde included Biblical scenes and landscapes, many of which were based on the expression of his own beliefs. He was initially swept up by the nationalism of the Nazis, only to be condemned by Hitler as a menace to society and officially prohibited to paint, draw or produce any kind of art whatsoever. He nevertheless continued to do so and lived and worked in Germany for the rest of his life.

▶ Ensor, Modersohn-Becker, Pechstein, Vlaminck

Emil Nolde. b Nolde, 1867. **d** Seebüll, 1956. **Red Poppies**. c1920. Watercolour on paper. **h**34.3 × **w**48.3 cm. **h**13½ × **w**19 in.
Leonard Hutton Galleries, New York, NY

O'Keeffe Georgia

Radiator Building

Rising above the dusky street-lights of a New York night and topped by a gleaming, decorative pinnacle, a tall skyscraper towers over the surrounding buildings. Its slender form is punctuated by the bright lights of the windows, giving it the appearance of a glittering jewel in the night sky. A strange light projects upwards from behind, illuminating the misty, wintery sky and the vaporous emanation on the right. Balancing this on the left is a glowing red horizontal band with neon light. O'Keeffe's work is sometimes termed 'Precisionist' because of its machine-like clarity. As well as simplified renditions of urban architecture she is known for her paintings of mountains, bones and flowers – the latter often on a giant scale. Her clear, simple forms, bordering on naïvety, and unconventional choice of subject matter, made her a pioneer of a new modernism in the USA.

► Davis, Estes, Hopper, Sheeler, Stieglitz

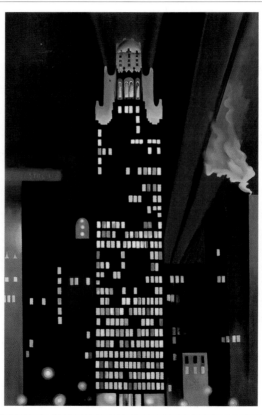

Georgia O'Keeffe. b Sun Prairie, WI, 1887. **d** Santa Fe, NM, 1986. **Radiator Building.** 1927. Oil on canvas. **h**121.9 × **w**76.2 cm. **h**48 × **w**30 in. Fisk University, Nashville, TN

Oldenburg Claes

Giant Hamburger

Absurd and kitsch, this massively over-sized version of a twentieth-century icon evokes a sense of incredulity. The artist's desire to imitate and displace one of the most potent symbols of American culture enhances its power and impact. Not only in its unconventional subject matter but also in its soft form it crushes all preconceived notions of traditional sculpture being solid and hard. Oldenburg was an American Pop artist concerned with making art from materials and products from the commercial environment. He wanted his

art to reflect contemporary, everyday life in all its complexity and change. This work clearly takes its cue from the American 'fast-food' empire that was developing, at meteoric speed, in the 1960s. In 1964 Oldenburg established a shop in Green Street, New York, from which he sold painted plaster replicas of food and other commodities.

► Dine, Duchamp, Hamilton, Lichtenstein, Segal, Warhol

Claes Oldenburg. b Stockholm, 1929. **Giant Hamburger**. 1962. Printed sailcloth stuffed with foam. **h**132 × **w**213 cm. **h**52 × **w**82⅞ in.
Art Gallery of Ontario, Toronto

Orcagna

Saint Matthew and Stories from his Life

Both the central figure in this painting – Matthew, the patron saint of Florentine bankers – and the use of gold leaf, allude to the Bankers' Guild who commissioned this work to adorn the church of Orsanmichele. This style of painting, called 'gold ground' because of its background, is typical of fourteenth-century Florence. The figures are idealized, colourful and highly patterned, but they do not have the realism and depth evident in the work of Giotto (Orcagna's artistic predecessor in Florence) or in later works. As was customary, this painting was a collaboration between the master and his assistants, working in a single workshop. In this case, Orcagna (local slang for 'archangel' – his real name was Andrea di Cione) was the main master, but he died before the work was finished. It was completed, in his style, by his younger brother Jacopo, who was a member of the workshop.

► Duccio, Giotto, Masolino, Lorenzo Monaco

Orcagna (Andrea di Cione). b Florence, c1320. d Florence, 1368. **Saint Matthew and Stories from his Life.** c1367. Tempera on panel. **h**291 × **w**265⅜ cm. **h**114⅝ × **w**104⅜ in. Galleria degli Uffizi, Florence

Organ Bryan

Prince Charles

The Prince of Wales sits in a relaxed pose, dressed in casual clothes in front of a green fence. Painted almost entirely of blue and green, only a few elements in the painting are not in these two colours – the Union Jack, the Prince's face, and his boots and shirt collar. Organ revolutionized the traditional approach to portraits of the monarchy. He has not chosen to depict his sitter with the pomp and ceremony associated with his position, but as an intelligent, aware and sensitive man who has just finished a friendly game of polo. In the

1970s Organ was commissioned to paint the portraits of four members of the British royal family, three of which now hang in London's National Portrait Gallery. A consummate draughtsman and insightful portrayer of character, Organ was also the first non-French citizen to be commissioned to paint a French President (François Mitterrand).

► Hockney, Kauffmann, Richter, Sutherland

Orozco Gabriel

La DS

A car has been cut lengthways into three sections; the middle part removed, and the remaining sections seamlessly reassembled. Through this modification the artist encourages us to look anew at a familiar object. Whilst the physical alterations to the vehicle are substantial, the classic design is still instantly recognizable; its appearance accelerated. Made by the artist for inclusion in his first solo show in Paris, Orozco selected the DS with an awareness of the iconic status awarded to this model of Citroën in France. During the exhibition – contrary to art gallery conventions – visitors were encouraged to touch, or even sit inside the car (one seat remains in the front, and one in the back). Conspicuously international in his outlook, Mexican-born Orozco's eclectic approach to making art resists a straightforward categorization. Often displaying a perceptive employment of humour, he works across a range of media including drawing, sculpture, painting, photography, video and installation.

► Broodthaers, Cattelan, Dalí, Duchamp, Oldenburg

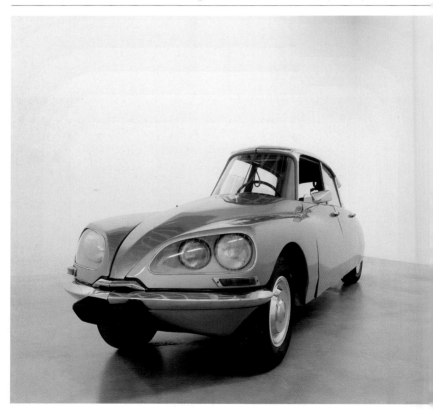

Gabriel Orozco. b Veracruz, 1962. **La DS.** 1993. Modified Citroën DS. **h**140 × **l**482.5 × **w**115 cm. **h**55¼ × **l**189⅞ × **w**45¼ in.
Centre National des Arts Plastiques, Paris

Orozco José Clemente

Modern Migration of the Spirit

This sensational image is a scene from Orozco's large fresco portraying Christ as a militant revolutionary destroying his cross. A mountainous junk heap of various remnants of modern civilization rises up behind him. While creating this work, the artist developed a technique which evolved from his meticulous study of ancient Mexican mural paintings and masonry. The evocative message seems to be that the all-powerful Creator-Destroyer figure of Christ is calling for the total destruction of the prevailing forms of modern politics,

religion and society. The Expressionist nature of this fresco is implicit in its principal theme of dramatic upheaval and change, subjects which Orozco had been passionate about since the Mexican Revolution of 1910. He was a politically committed artist and promoted the cause of peasants and workers by painting large murals depicting scenes from the life and history of the Mexican people.

► Botero, Grünewald, Rivera, Rouault, Siqueiros, Tamayo

José Clemente Orozco. b Zapotlán el Grande, 1883. d Mexico City, 1949. **Modern Migration of the Spirit**. 1933. Fresco. Dartmouth College, Hanover, NH

Orpen Sir William

The Café Royal in London

Under the glittering ceiling of a fashionable meeting-point for well-to-do Edwardians, a congregation of successful artists gathers together. The stiff demeanour and elegant dress-code give a sense of formal bohemianism to this group portrait of Orpen and his friends, which includes the artists Augustus John, William Nicholson, James Pryde and Alfred Rich. Orpen has diluted this stiffness by depicting two of the figures chatting between tables. A highly acclaimed society portraitist in his day, Orpen owed his success to his confident style and precise, angular technique which captured the often haughty, 'upper-crust' Edwardian character of his sitters. Orpen specialized in 'conversation pieces', which was a type of group portrait where the sitters are engaged in some everyday occupation. One of the most famous of these is his *Homage to Manet*, with Walter Sickert and other artists grouped in front of Édouard Manet's *Portrait of Eva Gonzalès*.

► Bazille, Manet, W Nicholson, Renoir, Sargent, Sickert

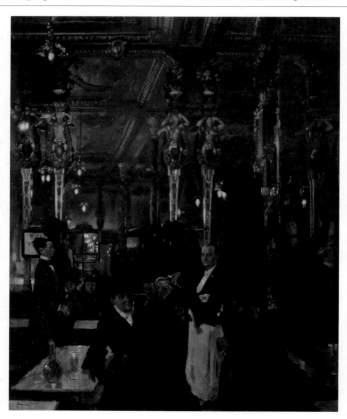

Sir William Orpen. b Stillorgen, 1878. **d** London, 1931. **The Café Royal in London**. 1912. Oil on canvas. **h**138 × **w**114 cm. **h**54⅓ × **w**44⅞ in. Musée d'Orsay, Paris

Van Ostade Adriaen

Interior with Peasants

In a cluttered interior, a mother and child sit by a window as three boorish men carouse noisily in the background. The household is clearly one of great poverty, emphasized by the mussel- and egg-shells strewn around the untidy floor. Other objects in the scene, such as the spinning-wheel and wool-winding frame, represent not the pastimes of the idle rich but the instruments of hard labour for the poor. The baby's refusal of its mother's food may refer to a moral message ('Poverty comes to those who refuse what is offered to them') although the overall tone of the painting is more decorative than moralizing. Ostade was a prolific artist who specialized in painting scenes from daily life (called 'genre' paintings), many of which featured peasants in interiors. In his later works, his palette became more colourful and his peasants better behaved and their rooms tidier. One of his pupils was Jan Steen, who also depicted this type of popular subject matter.

► P Bruegel, De Hooch, Rembrandt, Steen, Vermeer

Adriaen van Ostade. b Haarlem, 1610. **d** Haarlem, 1685. **Interior with Peasants.** 1663. Oil on panel. **h**34 × **w**40 cm. **h**13⅓ × **w**15¾ in.
Wallace Collection, London

Overbeck Johann Friedrich

The Adoration of the Magi

Figures based on simple geometric forms; a landscape which recedes into a hazy distance; colours dominated by the blue and gold robe of the Virgin and the subject of the Adoration: all are elements more appropriate to a fifteenth-century Italian altarpiece than a nineteenth-century German painting. Overbeck idolized the artists of the Italian Renaissance and sought to recreate their style. This work is even painted on a wood panel, in the manner of a Renaissance altarpiece. After 1810, Overbeck left Germany for Rome where he was better able to study the masters he so admired. There he converted to Roman Catholicism and co-founded an artistic group which became known as the 'Nazarenes'. The Nazarenes aimed to revive the spirit of early Medieval religious brotherhoods, and set up their workshop in an abandoned cloister. Their work was influential on the Pre-Raphaelite Brotherhood in England.

► Fra Angelico, Brown, Gentile da Fabriano, Gozzoli

Johann Friedrich Overbeck. b Lübeck, 1789. **d** Rome, 1869. **The Adoration of the Magi.** 1813. Oil on panel. **h**49.7 × **w**66 cm. **h**19½ × **w**26 in. Kunsthalle, Hamburg

Palma Vecchio

The Holy Family with Mary Magdalene and the Infant Saint John

Colour and light effects are as important to this painting as its subject. The tones in the Virgin's robe, for example, fluctuate from dark to light red as the garment drapes over her knees. In contrast to this realistic depiction, the Virgin's face is idealized into a cherubic image. These characteristics are deeply rooted in Venetian painting and follow the painterly tradition of Giorgione. Like the older artist, Palma Vecchio specialized in the placement of a religious subject in an idyllic, pastoral setting. These often featured plump,

sweet-faced blonde women, who became a hallmark of the artist's style. He was an accomplished portrait painter and also received a large number of ecclesiastical commissions. These included several large altarpieces depicting the Virgin and Child surrounded by saints (a composition called a *sacra conversazione*). His most famous is the Santa Barbara altar in Santa Maria Formosa, Venice.

► Giorgione, Michelangelo, Sebastiano del Piombo, Titian

Palma Vecchio. b Serina, c1480. **d** Venice, 1528. **The Holy Family with Mary Magdalene and the Infant Saint John.** c1520.
Oil on panel. **h**87 × **w**117 cm. **h**34¼ × **w**46 in. Galleria degli Uffizi, Florence

407

Pannini Giovanni Paolo

Roman Capriccio

Pannini has combined a selection of Rome's ancient monuments in one image, creating a celebration of its glorious past. The circular building to the left is the Colosseum, with Trajan's column standing in front; at its base is the figure of the Dying Gaul. On the right stand the Arch of Constantine in the background and a set of three free-standing Corinthian columns in the foreground. Born in Piacenza, Pannini moved to Rome where the city's impressive ruins inspired him to paint views of historical events, scenes of contemporary life,

and imaginary combinations of actual buildings, but in the wrong context (such as the work shown here). He was the first painter to specialize in views of this kind and his enormous output of work became very popular among tourists, equal in some ways to the views of Venice by Canaletto, whose style was at first similar to his own.

► Canaletto, Guardi, Poussin, Siberechts

Giovanni Paolo Pannini. b Piacenza, c1692. **d** Rome, 1765. **Roman Capriccio**. 1734. Oil on canvas. **h**97.2 × **w**134.6 cm. **h**38¼ × **w**53 in. Maidstone Museum and Art Gallery, Maidstone

Parmigianino

The Madonna with the Long Neck

The elongated, languid features of the Virgin, Child and attendant angels were purposefully exaggerated by the artist – hence this painting's popular title. Parmigianino has taken the static harmony associated with fifteenth-century paintings, such as those by Raphael and Perugino, and infused the composition with a new vibrancy and movement. This tendency is often called Mannerism, because of its conscious stylization and attempt to rework the balanced proportions of the Renaissance. Parmigianino's elegant and intimate

paintings exemplify the early Mannerist style. He usually used compositions with a few figures, rather than crowd scenes, so as to lay emphasis on the grace and languor of his figures. A native of Parma – from where he took his name – Parmigianino spent most of his life working there. This painting, however, was made after he had spent some time in Rome, where he studied the work of artists such as Raphael.

► Correggio, El Greco, Pontormo, Raphael, Signorelli

Patinir Joachim

Saint Jerome in a Rocky Landscape

Fantastic geological structures dominate this visionary landscape, which has been conjured up from Patinir's fertile imagination. The grand, sweeping vista is punctuated by tiny figures and architectural confections. Carefully observed and sensitively depicted, the detailed topography of the scene makes it a convincing setting for the diminutive figure of the hermit saint to inhabit. Patinir has unified light, atmosphere and physical elements to create what must be one of the earliest real landscape paintings – a genre whose popularity

has never dimmed. The smooth finish and technical perfection of the painting are typical of Patinir's style. His naïvely imaginative landscapes had a great and lasting influence on Flemish painting; with their extraordinary blend of fantasy and naturalistic detail they anticipate the works of Jan Bruegel in particular.

▶ Altdorfer, Antonello, J Bruegel, Van Eyck, Leonardo, Reni

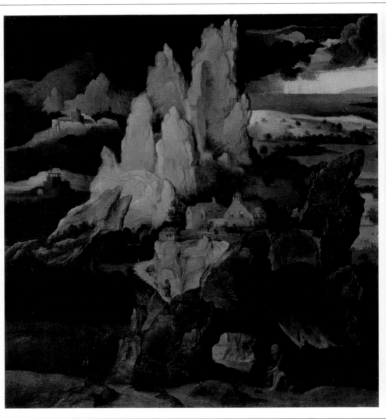

Joachim Patinir. b Place unknown, c1485. **d** Antwerp, 1524. **Saint Jerome in a Rocky Landscape.** c1515-24. Oil on panel. **h**36 × **w**34 cm. **h**14¼ × **w**13½ in. National Gallery, London

Pechstein Max Hermann

Meadow at Moritzburg

All elements of this townscape are exaggerated. The perspective is distorted, the buildings and figures are reduced to basic shapes while the vivid pinks, blues, greens and yellows heighten the emotion of the scene. The paint has been applied to the canvas in varying degrees of thickness. At times it is so thin that the white canvas shows through the paint. The artist has deliberately ignored the realities of the natural world in search of a more expressive type of art. Pechstein was part of a group of artists with similar, Expressionist, goals who linked themselves in a movement called 'Die Brücke' ('the bridge'). Pechstein was one of the first artists of this group to achieve popularity. Perhaps this is because his paintings tended to be more decorative and less profound than those from other artists in the group, such as Ernst Ludwig Kirchner. His vibrant sense of colour was greatly influenced by the work of Henri Matisse and other Fauvist painters.

► Heckel, Kirchner, Matisse, Nolde, Schmidt-Rottluff

Max Hermann Pechstein. b Zwickau, 1881. **d** Berlin, 1955. **Meadow at Moritzburg.** 1910. Oil on canvas. **h**70.2 × **w**80.3 cm.
h27⅝ × **w**31⅝ in. Leonard Hutton Galleries, New York, NY

Perry Grayson

The Rosetta Vase

The surface of a yellow vase has been decorated with a rich arrangement of words and images. From the branches of a tree – which has been titled 'The Institution' - we can read the statements 'MUSEUM AS CATHEDRAL', 'THE CULT FOR MODERN ART' and 'COLONIALISM'. On the opposite side of the vessel appears an image of a small child, titled 'THE ARTIST'; its various body parts carrying phrases such as 'fantasy world', 'Career Enhancement' and 'Vanity'. Although the vases produced by Perry are at first glance very charming, the provocative, witty and, at times, crude captions and images that adorn them challenge any initial presumptions that these are solely decorative objects. Straddling the boundary between art and craft, Perry's works present a twenty-first-century reworking of the ancient Egyptian Rosetta Stone, an object that was key to the modern translation of hieroglyphs. The title of the present work alludes to the ancient Egyptian Rosetta Stone, an object that was key to the modern translation of hieroglyphs.

► Cragg, Gilbert and George, Hiroshige, Walker

Grayson Perry. b Chelmsford, 1960. **The Rosetta Vase.** 2011. Glazed ceramic. **h**78.5 × **w**40.7 cm. **h**31 × **w**26 in. Private collection

Perugino

Altarpieces with a Virgin and Child surrounded by the patron saints of a family often adorned family chapels. Here the saints Michael the Archangel, Catherine of Alexandria, Apollonia and John the Evangelist are included, each identifiable by his or her attributes, representative of the saint's life. Apollonia, for example, holds the forceps that were used to pull out all her teeth in an attempt to get her to renounce the Christian faith. The gracefully elongated, rather sentimentalized figures, with drooping postures and tilted heads, are typical of Perugino's style. As was customary at the time he generally employed simple compositions, such as the arrangement used here with the Virgin and Christ above and four saints below. Perugino worked throughout Italy, especially in Umbria, but is perhaps best known as the teacher of Raphael whose early works are very close to his master's style.

▶ Andrea del Sarto, Della Quercia, Raphael, Signorelli

Perugino (Pietro Vannucci). b Città della Pieve, 1445/50. d Fontignano, 1523. **The Virgin and Child with Saints.** c1500. Oil on panel. h273 × w211 cm. h107½ × w83 in. Pinacoteca Nazionale, Bologna

Picabia Francis

Amorous Parade

There is nothing inherently erotic about this machine, but its title triggers our imagination. Within moments, the gangling apparatus has become charged with sexual connotations of a hilarious, yet unsettling, nature. This fantastic, complex contraption is primarily intended as a comment on man's activities and experiences. It could be interpreted as a parody of the noisy thrashing of love-making. In its playful ambiguity it displays Picabia's innovative and unusual imagination, which has invested an inanimate, un-erotic object with sexual undertones. This irrational and absurd humour connects the painting with the non-conformist Dada movement. Picabia was a leading figure in this anti-art, anti-reason movement, and together with Marcel Duchamp helped create a Dadaist group in the USA. He later turned to Surrealism, and in the 1920s and 30s produced a remarkable series of collages.

► Davis, Duchamp, Grosz, Hausmann, Léger

Francis Picabia. b Paris, 1879. d Paris, 1953. **Amorous Parade**. 1917. Oil on canvas. h96.5 × w73.7 cm. h38 × w29 in. Private collection

Picasso Pablo

Weeping Woman

The searing emotion of grief experienced by this distraught woman is reflected with great intensity in the harsh colours and rigid paint-strokes. The viewer's attention is immediately focused on the cold blue and white area around her mouth and teeth; her eyes and forehead are dislocated – literally broken up with sorrow. The figure echoes those of Picasso's monumental painting *Guernica*, executed in the same year, which portrays the massacre of women and children in the Spanish Civil War. The work shown here is one of the most expressive examples from a series by Picasso entitled 'Weeping Women'. The way the woman's face has been distorted and fragmented is a development of Cubist ideas. Picasso, who with Georges Braque was the inventor of Cubism, executed an immense body of work through his long and much publicized life. Born in Spain, Picasso moved to Paris in 1901 and spent the rest of his life in France. He is considered the greatest artist of the twentieth century.

► Boccioni, Braque, Gris, Jawlensky, Kupka, Léger

Piero della Francesca

The Procession of the Queen of Sheba

This quiet detail of a larger fresco shows the Queen of Sheba, accompanied by her handmaids and courtiers, kneeling in veneration at the rough wooden bridge across the river Siloe, which she has miraculously recognized as being made from the tree that grew on Adam's grave. The figures of the ladies-in-waiting are among the most graceful in all fifteenth-century painting, their calm, beauty and rich clothing evoking a scene of serene adoration. Piero was one of the most rigorously mathematical artists of the Renaissance, and his fascination with geometry and perspective is shown here in the harmonious grouping of geometric forms against a landscape of sublimely tranquil colours, and in the masterful foreshortening of the body of the white horse. The story of the Queen of Sheba's meeting with Solomon was thought during the Middle Ages to allegorize the marriage of the Church and Christ, and to be proof of the triumph of Christianity over paganism.

► Fra Angelico, Filippo Lippi, Massaccio, Uccello

Piero della Francesca. b Borgo Santo Sepulchro, c1415. **d** Borgo Santo Sepulchro, 1492. **The Procession of the Queen of Sheba**. c1450s. Fresco. **h**336 × **w**747 cm. **h**130 × **w**294 in. Basilica di San Francesco, Arezzo

Piero di Cosimo

Perseus Freeing Andromeda

Fantastic, curly crests of waves echo the horror of the monster attacking Andromeda who is chained to a rock. Racing to the rescue of his true love, Perseus is first depicted flying into the scene from the right, and later standing on the monster's back, poised to slay the beast. Subjects from Classical mythology were popular in Renaissance painting because they implied that the owner was acquainted with Ancient texts, which were enjoying a fashionable revival at this time. This work is one of a series which once hung in the palace of the Strozzi family in Florence. Piero di Cosimo often depicted his subjects in a bizarre fashion, which led to rumours of his own eccentric behaviour. He lived for many years as a recluse and is reputed to have eaten nothing but hard-boiled eggs – which is an unlikely tale. He also worked on designs for masques, festivals and processions.

► Botticelli, Perugino, Pollaiuolo, Raphael, Signorelli

Piero di Cosimo. b Florence, 1461/2. d Florence, 1521. **Perseus Freeing Andromeda**. c1513. Oil on panel. h70 × w123 cm. 27½ × w48⅜ in. Galleria degli Uffizi, Florence

417

Pietro da Cortona

Glorification of the Rule of Urban VIII

Painted on the ceiling of one of Rome's most sumptuous palaces, this ambitious fresco is a celebration of the powerful and noble Barberini family. It also represents an allegory of Divine Providence. The daunting grandeur of this composition is based around an illusionistic architectural structure, which is seen from below, with the sky appearing to open out above. This type of perspective, known as *sotto in sù* (Italian for 'up from under') is typical of Baroque ceiling decoration. The spectator's attention is quickly channelled by the swirling fluidity of the design to its focal point, where angels carry the papal tiara and St Peter's keys – representing the Papacy of Urban VIII, himself a member of the Barberini family. All sense of mass and gravity is dissolved in the sparkling colours and brilliant light, making this one of the great masterpieces of Baroque art.

► Bernini, Domenichino, Giordano, Guercino

Pietro da Cortona (Pietro Berrettini). b Cortona, 1596. **d** Rome, 1669. **Glorification of the Rule of Urban VIII.** 1633–9. Fresco. Palazzo Barberini, Rome

Piper Adrian

Cornered

This video installation, comprising a television screen on which is played a recording of Piper's performance, first literally entraps the artist and then figuratively corners the audience. Piper sits behind a desk backed into a corner. She is seemingly confined by the desk, the upturned table in front of it and the chairs in front of that. She calmly declares, 'I am black'. She then argues that most Americans, as a result of widespread miscegenation, are part black, and demands to know what we, the viewers, intend to make of that knowledge.

Will we continue to accept the status quo, or begin to live differently? Like much of her work, the piece is blunt, uncompromising and didactic – for Piper has been a professor of philosophy as well as an artist. Her intimate and unsettling performances are about raising consciousness – of racism and, peripherally, sexism and class – and her interrogatory (some might say hectoring) method is intended to make the viewer confront his or her own hidden prejudices.

► Holzer, Kruger, Rist, Sherman, Walker

Adrian Piper. b New York City, 1948. **Cornered**. 1988. Table, chairs, monitor, two framed birth certificates of Adrian Piper's father, lighting. Museum of Contemporary Art Chicago, IL

Piper John

Holkham, Norfolk

Solid architectural forms are highlighted in bright yellow, white and pink, beneath a dramatically stormy sky. The water in the foreground reflects the sketchy buildings and a fountain. Sombre tones evoke a brooding feeling, with the charged emotional content of the English Romantic landscape tradition. The composition has been reduced and distilled into an almost abstract form. Piper experimented with abstract art in the 1930s but, disillusioned with the limitations of non-representational painting, had returned to a more naturalistic approach by the time this picture was painted. His deeply personal style is characterized by a synthesis of Romanticism and topographical accuracy. During the Second World War he was an official British war artist and in that capacity produced a number of watercolours depicting the bombed areas of Bath and Coventry. A versatile artist, Piper worked in fields as varied as book illustration, stained glass, textiles and theatre design.

► Bonington, Cozens, Nash, Siberechts, Turner

John Piper. b Epsom, 1903. **d** Fawley, 1992. **Holkham, Norfolk**. 1939. Oil on canvas mounted on panel. **h**51 × **w**76 cm. **h**20 × **w**30 in. Private collection

Ginepro d'Este

er hair pulled back to reveal a high forehead, and dressed
an elaborately embroidered gown, this elegant woman is
ortrayed as being at the height of fashion. She is identifiable
a member of the noble Este family of Ferrara from the
attern on her sleeve. The sprig of juniper (*ginepro* in Italian)
nned to her shoulder, alludes to the sitter's first name. She
shown in profile, a pose which recalls the artist's skills as
portrait medallist. The profiles in his medals were as crisply
ndered as in this painting. Such natural details as the flowers

and butterflies are typical of the International Gothic style,
of which Pisanello was the main Italian exponent after
Gentile da Fabriano. His numerous drawings of animals,
although conforming to the decorative conventions of the
time, demonstrate a lively interest in the realistic depiction
of nature.

► Gentile da Fabriano, Ghirlandaio, Mantegna

anello (Antonio Pisano). b Pisa, c1395. d Place unknown, c1455. **Ginepro d'Este**. c1436–8. Tempera on panel. **h**43 × **w**30 cm.
7 × **w**12 in. Musée du Louvre, Paris

Pisano Andrea

Saint John the Baptist

Sculpted with a delicacy of line and lyrical fluency, this bronze relief shows St John baptizing a group of people in the River Jordan. Behind him is a mountain with trees, completely out of scale but conveying the setting successfully within the limited space. Pisano probably trained as a goldsmith. Such a skill would have enabled him to apply refinement and meticulous detail to the figures, which have been executed with elegant, curving swathes of drapery. This panel comes from the first of three sets of doors made for the Baptistry at Florence,

for which Pisano sculpted 28 scenes from the life of the Baptist, the city's patron saint. (The other two sets of doors were made in the fifteenth century by Lorenzo Ghiberti.) Each scene is set within a quatrefoil frame, a fashionable form imported from Gothic France. He influenced Donatello, Ghiberti and Luca della Robbia.

► Ghiberti, Giotto, Piero della Francesca, Della Quercia

Andrea Pisano. b Pontedera, c1290. **d** Orvieto, 1348. **Saint John the Baptist**. 1330/3. Gilt bronze. **h**50 × **w**43 cm. **h**19⅔⅞ × **w**16⅞ in. Battistero di San Giovanni, Florence

Pissarro Camille

Landscape at Chaponval

This tranquil landscape embodies the bucolic peacefulness of the countryside. Vibrant hatching strokes have been used to enliven the painting's surface. With a very simple subject and a restricted palette of colours, Pissarro has achieved a range of subtle effects. A feeling of intimacy and direct personal contact with the scene, reminiscent of the paintings of Camille Corot, is enhanced by the skyline landscape, which is depicted in a series of horizontal bands with very little sky showing. These bands, made up of field, houses and sky, seem almost to sit on top of one another. His reduction of the landscape to a spontaneous, intricate web of rapidly applied pure tones is typical of the experiments of the Impressionists. Born in the West Indies, Pissarro arrived in Paris in 1855 where he became a prolific artist and a key figure in the Impressionist circle. He was the only artist to exhibit at all the Impressionist exhibitions.

► Boudin, Cézanne, Corot, Daubigny, Monet, Sisley

Camille Pissarro. b St Thomas, 1830. d Paris, 1903. **Landscape at Chaponval**. 1880. Oil on canvas. **h**54 × **w**65 cm. **h**21¼ × **w**25½ in. Musée d'Orsay, Paris

Poliakoff Serge

Abstract Composition

A series of flat, two-dimensional planes of colour interpenetrate in a lyrical formation. The geometric composition is defined by the shape of the canvas; this is apparent in the artist's quartering of the dominant forms of colour. Poliakoff's mastery of the brush is demonstrated by the multiplicity of hues that have been incorporated within each colour section. This controlled, expert handling of the paint (ground by the artist himself), combined with the positioning of the intersecting abstract forms of colour, make this picture an important example of the post-war Art Informel movement. A Russian emigré who came to Paris in 1923 with his aunt, the singer Nadia Poliakoff, he began his first abstract compositions in 1937. He achieved fame when he was awarded the Kandinsky Prize for painting in 1947, from which time he progressed steadily towards his foremost position among the abstract painters of the École de Paris in the 1950s.

► Delaunay, Riopelle, Soulages, De Staël, Vieira da Silva

Serge Poliakoff. b Moscow, 1906. **d** Paris, 1969. **Abstract Composition**. 1952. Oil on canvas. **h**89 × **w**130 cm. **h**35 × **w**51⅛ in.
Archives Serge Poliakoff, Paris

The female nude is represented by a chorus line of strippers, their fetishistic stilettos crushing a male underfoot. His impotence is symbolized by a flightless bird. Conventional fine art images – the supine nude, and the knight triumphant over the serpent – are transposed into soft porn. Polke left East Germany for Düsseldorf in the 1960s. Together with Gerhard Richter and others he formed a German branch of the Pop Art movement then emerging in Britain and the USA. He boldly combined the atmospheric colour experiments of Abstract Expressionism with photography, and graphics appropriated from comic books and pulp fiction. His work demolishes the barriers between 'high' art and 'low' popular culture. Polke's subject matter is often provocative: his paintings of the 1970s and 1980s, with their images of concentration camps and traces of bodily fluids, confront the taboo of Germany's wartime history.

► Baselitz, Jones, De Kooning, Sherman, Wesselmann

Sigmar Polke. b Oelsnitz, 1941. d Cologne, 2010. **Three Girls**. 1979. Mixed media on paper. h99.8 × w69.9 cm. h39⅜ × w27½ in. Anthony d'Offay Gallery, London

Pollaiuolo Antonio

Apollo and Daphne

Daphne is seen in the process of transforming herself into a laurel tree in order to escape from Apollo. (Smitten with her, he subsequently wore a laurel wreath in deference to her memory.) This small scene is painted in a delicate, jewel-like manner. Mythological paintings of this size often adorned chests or cupboards in Renaissance Florence, but it is not clear if this painting was ever set into a piece of furniture. Antonio and his brother Piero were important Florentine goldsmiths, sculptors and painters who executed commissions for the city of Florence and its cathedral, and for prominent Florentine families such as the Medici. Antonio is also famous for his engravings, especially the *Battle of the Nudes* in which he explored the human form in a variety of positions. Fascinated by anatomy, he was one of the first artists to dissect the human body in order to understand its inner workings and structures.

► Botticelli, Raphael, Van Scorel, Verrocchio

Antonio Pollaiuolo. b Florence, c1432. **d** Florence, 1498. **Apollo and Daphne.** c1470. Oil on panel. **h**29.5 × **w**20 cm. **h**11⅝ × **w**7⅞ in. National Gallery, London

Pollock Jackson

Number 1a, 1948

Pollock's violent method of dripping and smearing paint onto the canvas in dramatic, sweeping gestures is strikingly apparent in this painting. He would pour and fling the paint, using sticks and knives, onto an unstretched canvas which had been tacked to a hard wall or floor. This enabled him to walk round it and allowed him almost to *become* the gesture of the painting. Pollock's highly innovative technique became known as Action Painting. Such radical elements as the abandonment of easel painting and the lack of traditional perspective make

this work an important landmark in post-war international art. Its connection with Abstract Expressionism lies in its energetic technique and freedom of expression. Pollock's paintings are not as random as they may seem; the artist said, 'I want to express my feelings rather than illustrate them ... I *can* control the flow of paint: there is no accident, just as there is no beginning and no end.' Pollock died in a car crash in 1956.

► Frankenthaler, Hofmann, Kline, De Kooning, Motherwell

Jackson Pollock. b Cody, WY, 1912. d Springs, Long Island, NY, 1956. **Number 1a, 1948**. 1948. Oil and enamel on canvas. 172.7 × w264.2 cm. h68 × w104 in. Museum of Modern Art, New York, NY

Pontormo Jacopo

The Visitation

This painting depicts the biblical episode of the Virgin, pregnant with Christ, meeting her cousin Elizabeth, who is pregnant with John the Baptist. Pontormo has subordinated the story as a whole to the embrace of these two women. Any superfluous detail has been eliminated. The emotion of the meeting has been heightened by the use of bright, almost fluorescent, colours and elongated figures with dark, sunken eyes. Distorted shapes and intensely brilliant hues are characteristic of Pontormo's style, which provides a fine example of Mannerism at its height. He trained in the Florentine school but as his painting style suggests, he was something of an eccentric. His neurotic and withdrawn character is revealed in his diary, which chronicles the details of his daily life sometimes to the point of obsession. Agnolo Bronzino was a pupil and follower.

► Beccafumi, Bronzino, Parmigianino, Rosso Fiorentino

Jacopo Pontormo. b Pontormo, 1494. **d** Florence, 1556. **The Visitation**. 1530/2. Oil on panel. **h**202 × **w**156 cm. **h**79½ × **w**61½ in. Pieve di San Michele, Carmignano

Popova Ljubov

Space-Force Construction

Overlapping geometric shapes, painted in muted colours, appear to be floating on the unpainted plywood background. The interplay of these various circles, curves and diagonal lines is enhanced by multicoloured shadows which contribute to the effective play of light. A further sense of depth is created by the diagonal lines, which appear to extend beyond the picture. In its emphasis on colour and form and the use of added shadow to increase perspective, the painting demonstrates the influence of Constructivism. From 1921

Popova turned her talents towards textile, costume and set design. In tune with the spirit of Constructivism, she believed that art should serve a useful purpose, claiming that 'no artistic success has given me such satisfaction as the sight of a peasant or a worker buying a length of material designed by me'. One of the most important members of the Russian avant-garde, she died prematurely of scarlet fever, at the height of her career.

► Lissitzky, Malevich, Moholy-Nagy, Rodchenko, Tatlin

Ljubov Popova. b Moscow, 1889. **d** Moscow, 1924. **Space-Force Construction**. c1920–1. Oil on panel. **h**77.7 × **w**77.7 cm. **h**30⅝× **w**30⅝ in. Private collection

Poussin Nicolas

The Arcadian Shepherds

An elegiac inscription – *Et in Arcadia Ego* ('Even in Arcadia I [ie Death] am present') – on an ancient Roman sarcophagus arouses the curiosity of a group of shepherds. This melancholy phrase sets the tone for the bucolic, enigmatic painting. Its warm, autumnal colours and carefully staged figures give a resigned, tragic air to the picture, as the shepherds' pastoral idyll is broken by the reminder that death occurs even in the most perfect of worlds. Reminiscent of the mysterious paintings of Giorgione,

this work also represents Poussin's more serene strain of the Baroque spirit, which was based on the Classicism of Raphael and the Antique. In sharp contrast to the theatrical emotionalism of such contemporaries as Peter Paul Rubens and Gianlorenzo Bernini, Poussin's paintings emphasize form and moral content. They were highly praised by the intellectuals in Rome.

► Bernini, Claude, J-L David, Giorgione, Raphael, Rubens

Nicolas Poussin. b Les Andelys, 1594. **d** Rome, 1665. **The Arcadian Shepherds**. 1638-9. Oil on canvas. **h**85 × **w**121 cm. **h**33½ × **w**47½ in. Musée du Louvre, Paris

Powers Hiram

The Greek Slave

Gracefully and smoothly carved, a statuesque young woman stands, apparently peacefully, looking to her left. On closer inspection, we notice that her hands, held tenderly by her side, are in fact tied to chains. At first glance she appears to be a Greek goddess, at second she is a Greek Christian, sold to the Turks as a slave. (Poignantly coinciding with the Greek War of Independence, the statue was well received.) The soft surface and grace of her form give a calm and subtle lyricism to the figure. Powers was one of the leading American sculptors of the nineteenth century. He achieved great fame with *The Greek Slave*, one of his best-loved works, which was cast in many copies. His preciseness of handling, emotional restraint and choice of subject matter – reminiscent of the work of the Greeks and Romans – are all ingredients that link him to the high ideals of Neo-Classicism, the style which then dominated European and American sculpture.

► Canova, Donatello, Leighton, Maillol, Moore

Hiram Powers. **b** Woodstock, VT, 1805. **d** Florence, 1873. **The Greek Slave**. c1843. Marble. **h**166.4 cm. **h**65½ in.
Yale University Art Gallery, New Haven, CT

Primaticcio Francesco

Danaë

Danaë is depicted naked, seated on her bed in a sumptuously coloured room, with her maid and *putti* in attendance; above her falls a shower of gold. In Greek mythology, Danaë was locked in a bronze tower by her father Acrisius, King of Argos, when an oracle predicted his murder by a son of hers. Zeus appeared in the form of a shower of gold to seduce her. In 1532 Primaticcio was summoned by Francis I to France, to work with Rosso Fiorentino on the decoration of the King's palace at Fontainebleau. There he devised elaborate

decorative schemes, specializing in a combination of painting and stucco in high relief such as that shown here. Primaticcio was a painter, sculptor and architect; his combined skills gave the interior decoration of the palace its full, opulent expression. He greatly influenced the formation of the French Renaissance style, but sadly many of his decorative schemes have now been destroyed.

► Cellini, El Greco, Pontormo, Rosso Fiorentino

Francesco Primaticcio. b Bologna, 1504. **d** Paris, 1570. **Danaë**. c1533–40. Oil on panel with stucco reliefs. **h**105 × **w**254 cm. **h**41⅓ × **w**100 in. Château de Fontainebleau, Fontainebleau

Prud'hon Pierre-Paul

The Empress Josephine

A beautiful and thoughtful young woman rests on a red shawl in a rocky glade. The delicate sleeve of her Empire-style dress has slipped from her shoulder as she gazes, deep in thought, across the picture. Once married to a viscount who was guillotined during the French revolution, Josephine married Napoleon I in 1796. Riddled with infidelity, their relationship was passionate and unpredictable. Josephine was unable to bear her husband a son, and the marriage was declared null and void in 1810. Napoleon commissioned this portrait shortly after his consecration as Emperor. A Frenchman by birth, Prud'hon travelled to Italy in 1784 where he was deeply impressed by the work of Antonio Canova, Correggio and Leonardo da Vinci. Supported by both of Napoleon's wives, he became a rival of Jacques-Louis David and is known for his depictions of romantic and mysterious women.

► Canova, Correggio, J-L David, Leonardo

Pierre-Paul Prud'hon. b Cluny, 1758. d Paris, 1823. **The Empress Josephine**. 1805. Oil on canvas. **h**244 × **w**179 cm. **h**96 × **w**70½ in.
Musée du Louvre, Paris

Della Quercia Jacopo

Virgin and Child with Saints

This free-standing group of statues of the Madonna and Child with Saints decorates an altar in a Sienese church. The Madonna's solid pose and the heavy folds of her gown lend her an air of great monumentality, yet she also expresses human tenderness and charm. A graceful 'S' curve is apparent in her stance, which gives a lyrical movement from her inclined head through to her left foot, emphasized by the flow of drapery. This pose (known as *contrapposto*) is reflected in the figures of the saints. Such a delicate swaying movement

is a typical feature of Gothic art, although Della Quercia has also given the forms a solidity characteristic of the new ideas of the Renaissance. A contemporary of Donatello and Lorenzo Ghiberti, Della Quercia's work became very well known – even Michelangelo copied one of his works when he painted the Sistine ceiling.

► Cimabue, Donatello, Duccio, Ghiberti, Michelangelo

Jacopo della Quercia. b Siena, 1374/5. d Siena, 1438. **Virgin and Child with Saints** (detail). c1423–5. Gilt wood. **h**140 cm. **h**55.1 in. San Martino, Siena

Raeburn Sir Henry

Revelling in the winter weather on the frozen lake of an Edinburgh suburb, a sprightly Church minister is depicted nonchalantly ice-skating in an exaggerated, semi-theatrical pose. His conservative, black attire stands out sharply against the blurred grey of the background. The depiction of a member of the Church establishment in such a manner not only reveals the humour of the painter, but also his intimacy with the sitter. As one of Scotland's most popular artists, Raeburn captured the personalities of Edinburgh's

Golden Age during the Enlightenment. He is said to have produced over 1,000 portraits. These included poets, scholars, philosophers and local dignitaries, as well as the colourful Highland lairds, who were freely painted with humour and joviality. Raeburn was knighted by King George IV in 1822 and the following year, only a few months before his death, was appointed His Majesty's Limner for Scotland.

► Goya, Mengs, Ramsay, Vigée-Lebrun

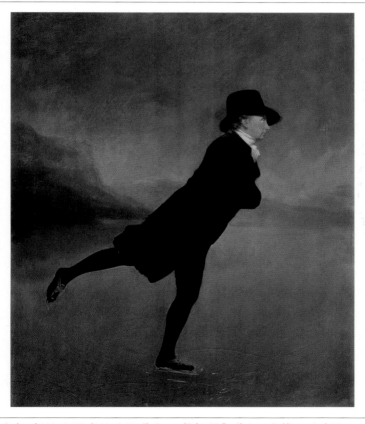

Sir Henry Raeburn. b Edinburgh, 1756. d Edinburgh, 1823. **The Reverend Robert Walker Skating on Duddingston Loch**. 1784.
Oil on canvas. h76 × w64 cm. h30 × w25⅛ in. National Gallery of Scotland, Edinburgh

Ramsay Allan

Lady Robert Manners

Softly modelled, this exquisite oval portrait exudes a sense of tenderness and a sympathetic grasp of character. Painted with a feathery sense of touch and executed in muted, pastel colours, the form and demeanour of the noble lady are conveyed with flattering delicacy. The son of a poet, Ramsay was one of the foremost portraitists of his day – the Scottish counterpart to Sir Joshua Reynolds and Thomas Gainsborough. Although he worked mainly in London, becoming the Court Painter to George III in 1760, he first trained in Edinburgh before continuing his studies in Italy. Here he was impressed by the elegance of the contemporary Italian painters, especially Pompeo Batoni who produced many portraits of aristocratic English visitors to Rome. Ramsay went on to develop his own style of captivating charm and sensitivity. He was also much influenced by the refined finesse of contemporary French art.

► Batoni, Gainsborough, Mengs, Raeburn, Reynolds

Allan Ramsay. b Edinburgh, 1713. **d** Dover, 1784. **Lady Robert Manners.** c1756. Oil on canvas. **h**74.3 × **w**61.6 cm. **h**29¼ × **w**24¼ in. National Gallery of Scotland, Edinburgh

Raphael

The School of Athens

A group of animated men, young and old, gather in a vast hallway. Five figures crouch over a compass and slate to discuss geometry, while others (holding a globe and a starry sphere) discuss astronomy. In turn these bustling groups debate the seven liberal arts. The two figures at the centre of the composition, walking towards us with assurance and appearing to exude an unreal sense of calm, are Plato and Aristotle, the two greatest philosophers of the Ancient world. In October 1508 Pope Julius II commissioned a group of artists to redecorate his private apartments. *The School of Athens* and other frescos in the Stanza della Segnatura took Raphael about three years to complete. Younger than either Leonardo or Michelangelo, Raphael is seen with them to epitomize the high point of Renaissance art. A prolific and ambitious man, an architect, painter and designer of sculpture, Raphael is considered one of the greatest draughtsmen of Western art.

► Leonardo, Michelangelo, Perugino, Pollaiuolo, Poussin

Raphael (Raffaello Sanzio). b Urbino, 1483. **d** Rome, 1520. **The School of Athens**. 1508–11. Fresco. **w**770 cm. **w**303 in.
Palazzo del Vaticano, Rome

Rauschenberg Robert

Reservoir

An assortment of commonplace objects is boldly displayed against a bespattered background. The clock at the upper left was set when the artist began to work on the painting; the other clock was set to record the time of completion. This 'combine' painting illustrates Rauschenberg's method of selecting and combining groups of disparate images and objects. He did not do this in order to make social comment but rather to break away from the traditional idea of picture space. He wanted, in his own words, 'to act in the gap between' art and life. Rauschenberg incorporated mundane objects into his work as naturally as many artists had traditionally used paint. This provided much of the inspiration for the Pop Art movement in the USA. One of the most notorious gestures of this self-consciously avant-garde figure was his cabled reply to a request by Parisian gallery-owner Iris Clert for a portrait: 'This is a portrait of Iris Clert if I say so – Robert Rauschenberg.'

► Broodthaers, Duchamp, Hamilton, Johns, Schwitters

Robert Rauschenberg. b Port Arthur, TX, 1925. **d** Captiva, FL, 2008. *Reservoir*. 1961. Oil, pencil, fabric, wood and metal. **h**217.2 × **w**158.7 cm. **h**85½ × **w**62¼ in. National Museum of American Art, Washington, DC

Ray Charles

Family Romance

Hand in hand stand a father and mother, along with their two children, a boy and a girl – the archetypal nuclear family. Bold in their nakedness, the artist has crafted each figure with a high degree of realism down to each individual hair. However, in contrast to this anatomical accuracy we are instantly aware of a strangeness of scale. In choosing to standardize the height of each figure to just less than 135 cm (4ft 5in), the adults have been necessarily reduced in size, while the two children are noticeably enlarged. The result is unnerving. The children have

taken on a menacing presence, their physical frames more imposing than those of their parents. Based in Los Angeles, Ray has produced works across a wide range of media including photography, film, sculpture and installations. He was inspired early in his career by the work of Anthony Caro.

▶ Caro, Hirst, Kelley, Koons, Oldenburg

Charles Ray. b Chigaco, IL 1953. **Family Romance**. 1993. Painted fibreglass and synthetic hair. **h**134.5 × **w**215.9 × **d**27.9 cm. **h**53 × **w**85 × **d**11 in. Museum of Modern Art, New York, NY

Redon Odilon

The Cyclops

In this scene from Greek mythology, Polyphemus, the giant Cyclops, spies upon the naked nymph Galatea, with whom he is hopelessly in love. The giant's huge eye casts a longing gaze over the object of his devotion. More horrifying than Gustave Moreau's rather more romantic treatment of the same theme, Redon's interpretation has a terrifyingly nightmarish quality. In accordance with Symbolist theories, Redon was more interested in exploring the inner psyche than in depicting reality in a straightforward manner. His aim was to find a

form of artistic expression that would inspire introspection and thought on the part of the viewer. His belief in an enchanted inner vision led to the creation of highly imaginative paintings and lithographs, with fantastical subjects representing fragments of dreams. Redon also produced vibrantly colourful landscapes and flower paintings. His work was very influential on the work of a group of younger Symbolists who called themselves the Nabis.

► Bonnard, Denis, Matisse, Moreau, Rouault, Vallotton

Odilon Redon. b Bordeaux, 1840. **d** Paris, 1916. **The Cyclops.** 1898/1900. Oil on panel. **h**64 × **w**51 cm. **h**25¼ × **w**20⅛ in.
Rijksmuseum Kröller-Müller, Otterlo

Rego Paula

The Family

An apparently innocent family scene is undermined by disturbing, sexually-charged undercurrents. The main action takes place between the furious youth and his determined sister who conveys an incestuous sexual thrill as she presses her body close, helping her kind, trusting mother to undress him. This theme of rebellion and domination, with all its erotic undertones, provides the twist and ambiguity of the scene. The painting is representative of the style for which Rego has become internationally renowned. Simple yet sinister, her paintings are characterized by their monumentality and psychological drama. They often deal with ambiguous relationships between men, women and children. Rego has also executed etchings based on her own interpretation of nursery rhymes and J M Barrie's *Peter Pan*, providing us with disturbing scenes from the traditional stories.

▶ Balthus, Modersohn-Becker, Spencer, Weight

Paula Rego. b Lisbon, 1935. **The Family.** 1988. Acrylic on paper mounted on canvas. **h**213.4 × **w**213.4 cm. **h**84 × **w**84 in. Saatchi Collection, London

Reinhardt Ad

Abstract Painting, 1959

A glowing suffusion of grey envelops this canvas. Distilled and immaculate, its pure surface is violated only by a very faint cross, barely visible to the naked eye. A shrouded atmospheric aura emanates from the painting's depths. The iconic image of the cross has been treated in an abstract way, taking the expressive qualities of colour to their fullest extreme. Nothing is allowed to intrude upon the stark intensity of the work. Reinhardt reduced art to its ultimate essence. Associated with the Abstract Expressionists in the USA, he entirely eschewed all literal and painterly overtones in his search to refine the purest of statements. Also a theoretician and teacher, he was adamant that art should be completely separate from life, and life from art, saying, 'Art is art-as-art and everything else is everything else. Art-as-art is nothing but art.' Only abstract art, he believed, could express this pure standard.

► Kelly, Newman, Rothko, Ryman

Ad Reinhardt. b Buffalo, NY, 1913. **d** New York, NY, 1967. **Abstract Painting, 1959**. 1959. Oil on canvas. **h**274.3 × **w**101.6 cm. **h**108 × **w**40 in. Private collection

Rembrandt

Self Portrait at the Age of Sixty-Three

Painted the year he died, this portrait shows the artist as an old man in a velvet cap and a doublet with fur collar. Rembrandt successively darkened the painting with layers of overpainted details until only the face – with its bulbous nose, weary eyes and worried brow – remains highlighted, circled by a hazy aura. Thick impasto in the beard and collar make them stand out from the background, and the hands are only just illuminated. A master of light and shadow, Rembrandt used his technique to enhance the drama of scenes such as his famous *Night Watch*. His numerous self-portraits, painted over some forty years, contain narrative alongside representation, not only documenting his appearance but telling the story of his life, from humble beginnings to happy marriage and professional success, then personal tragedy and poverty. Some canvases appear to have been painted not as portraits per se, but as *tronie*, a type of Dutch genre painting that showed a stock character in exotic or historical costume.

► Caravaggio, Leyster, Rosa, Rubens, Titian

Rembrandt van Rijn. b Leiden, 1606. **d** Amsterdam, 1669. **Self-portrait at the Age of Sixty-Three.** 1669. Oil on canvas. **h**86 × **w**70.5 cm. **h**33¾ × **w**27¾ in. National Gallery, London

Reni Guido

Aurora

In Reni's masterpiece, frescoed on the ceiling of the central hall in a Roman garden palazzo, the young Apollo drives the chariot of the sun, bringing light to another day. Before his four rearing horses is Aurora, or Dawn, driving away the darkness of night from the idyllic landscape below in a daring chromatic contrast of orange and blue-violet. Surrounding the god's chariot, dancing in his light, are the Hours. Guido Reni was one of the most successful and influential of seventeenth-century Italian painters, whose classicising art was influenced by the work of Raphael and Parmigianino. He was a member of the Bolognese school fostered by the Carracci brothers, but his *Aurora* has none of the lasciviousness of Annibale Carracci's fresco *The Triumph of Bacchus and Ariadne* in the Galleria Farnese. Instead, *Aurora* is characterized by Classical restraint, however bold the colouring, with several of the figures copied from Roman sarcophagi.

► Carracci, Domenichino, Raphael, Parmigianino

Guido Reni. b Bologna, 1575. **d** Bologna, 1642. **Aurora**. 1614. Fresco. **h**280 × **w**700 cm. **h**110 × **w**275½ in. Casino dell'Aurora, Palazzo Rospigliosi-Pallavicini, Rome

Renoir Pierre Auguste

Ball at the Moulin de la Galette

en in top hats and boaters and women in pretty dresses
atter, drink and dance under the glowing lights of this
mous Parisian dance hall. Renoir loved this subject and
ainted it a number of times, reproducing the patterns made
y the light as it catches the figures moving around the floor.
any of Renoir's friends acted as models for the dancers.
he couple in the middle distance are his favourite model
arguerite Legrand and the Spanish painter Don Pedro de
olares y Cárdenas. Like all Impressionists, Renoir painted

from life as he sat in the dance hall; his friends assisted him
each day in moving his canvases back and forth to his studio.
At the time the *Moulin de la Galette* was painted, Renoir was
working very closely with Claude Monet. They spent much
time painting outdoors, capturing the fleeting effects of
sunlight as it scatters across a landscape. With his 'rainbow
palette', Renoir painted over 6,000 canvases of women,
children, flowers and fields.

► Bazille, Cassatt, Monet, Morisot, Sisley, Toulouse-Lautrec

erre Auguste Renoir. b Limoges, 1841. d Cagnes, 1919. **Ball at the Moulin de la Galette**. 1876. Oil on canvas. h131 × w175 cm.
13⅜ × w68⅞ in. Musée d'Orsay, Paris

445

Reynolds Sir Joshua

The Countess Spencer with her Daughter Georgiana

The tenderness of this charming portrait is emphasized by the delicate way in which the mother clasps her arms around her young daughter. The lace and silk of the countess's dress are skilfully painted with a minimum number of brushstrokes. This rather loose manner of painting is continued in the shaggy hair of the dog, and the cloudy sky in the background. Reynolds is best known for the manner in which he married the Grand Style of the great Italian masters with portraits of the English aristocracy. Although grandeur and formality

are minimized in this picture, they are alluded to in the background elements of the column, drapery and brooding clouds. Reynolds is credited with having elevated portrait-painting in Britain to a height equalling that of the great Italian masters. His status during the reign of George III was such that when the King formed the Royal Academy in 1768, Reynolds was appointed its first President.

► Dobson, Gainsborough, Lely, Morisot, Rigaud, Ramsay

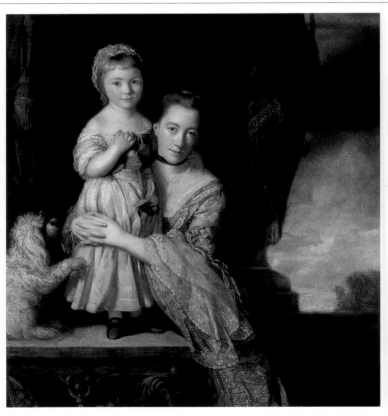

Sir Joshua Reynolds. b Plympton, 1723. **d** London, 1792. **The Countess Spencer with her Daughter Georgiana.** 1760/1.
Oil on canvas. **h**122 × **w**115 cm. **h**48 × **w**45¼ in. Collection of The Earl Spencer, Althorp

Ribera Jusepe

Saint Paul the Hermit

Paul the Hermit was the first Christian saint to seek a life of solitude, meditation and asceticism. Here he is depicted an old man, worn out by the frugal austerity of a life spent the Egyptian desert. Yet he is still fired by religious ardour he contemplates the skull before him, a symbol of man's ortality. The harsh, theatrical lighting emphasizes the saint's gging muscles, furrowed brow and expressive hands, giving e painting a startling sense of realism. Ribera's art invokes e fervent spirituality of seventeenth-century Spain, which

is expressed with a strong and dramatic use of light and shade (*chiaroscuro*) derived from the Italian artist Caravaggio. Ribera settled in Naples in 1616, and his style laid the foundation for the great tradition of Neapolitan painting with its emphasis on what one critic has called 'the poetry of the repulsive'.

► Caravaggio, El Greco, Guercino, Reni, Zurbarán

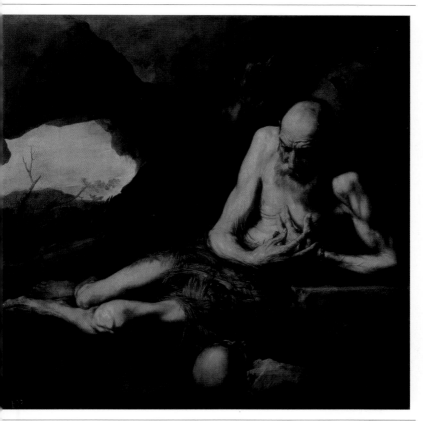

sepe Ribera. b Játiva, 1591. d Naples, 1652. **Saint Paul the Hermit**. 1640. Oil on canvas. h143 × w143 cm. h56¼ × w56¼ in.
useo del Prado, Madrid

Richter Gerhard

Betty

The artist's daughter Betty is painted with photographic detail. She sits very near to the surface of the picture, as in a close-up camera shot. The painting could not really be called a portrait of Betty, however, as it teaches us very little about her. Richter has chosen to paint his daughter as she turns away; her face is invisible. Instead he has concentrated on the red, white and pink patterns of her jacket and dress, and her hair gathered at the back of her head. Richter has undermined accepted notions of painting and representation, giving us a painting that looks like a photograph, a portrait that literally turns its back on convention. Continually discovering new ways of expression, Richter's work is extremely diverse. The wall in the background of this painting resembles some of the very different abstract works that Richter creates. These monochrome, thickly painted canvases evoke sadness and despair and were executed in response to the Vietnam war.

► Dix, Estes, Organ, Schad

Gerhard Richter. b Dresden, 1932. **Betty**. 1988. Oil on canvas. **h**102 × **w**72 cm. **h**40$\frac{1}{8}$ × **w**28$\frac{3}{4}$ in. Collection of the artist

Rigaud Hyacinthe

Louis XIV

Louis XIV, the Sun King, stands in a pose of elegant superiority amid a display of crimson curtains and royal accoutrements. The *fleur-de-lis* in his ermine-lined coronation robes is echoed in the upholstery of the throne and the stool on which rests his crown. Rigaud trained in his father's tailoring workshop, which may explain his lovingly detailed depiction of costume – down to the jewelled shoe buckles – and textiles. Louis was sixty-three when this canvas was painted as a gift for his grandson, Philip V of Spain. It was

a sensation at court and was reproduced in several copies; it never left France. This portrait, and Rigaud's painting of Louis XV, established the prototype for portrayals of European monarchs that remained influential throughout the eighteenth century. Although the likeness is realistic, the painting functioned less to represent the king's character than to express the absolute power of the monarchy.

► Drouais, Van Dyck, Kneller, Lely, Reynolds

Hyacinthe Rigaud. b Perpignan, 1659. d Paris, 1743. Louis XIV. 1701. Oil on canvas. h277 × w194 cm. h109 × w76½ in.
Musée du Louvre, Paris

Riley Bridget

Cataract 3

Red, turquoise and grey curves undulate across the canvas in a uniform sequence, evoking an illusionary sense of movement. The canvas seems distorted by the almost hallucinatory image, as its colours appear to vibrate with a dazzling intensity. This technique of exploring and exploiting the fallibility of the eye provokes a powerful sensation on the spectator. The painting's connection with the Op Art movement is apparent in the interplay of colour and lines which produces a stunning, shimmering optical illusion.

Riley's aims go beyond the merely scientific, however. She sees the elements she uses as being as much a part of nature as are trees, clouds and hills. More than a sum of their formal and colouristic parts, her paintings vibrate with a magical lyricism. Riley's first paintings, in the early 1960s, were almost all in black and white. Her work has developed dramatically over the years and she has recently tended to paint straight parallel lines in intense colours.

▶ Albers, Louis, Vasarely, Vieira da Silva

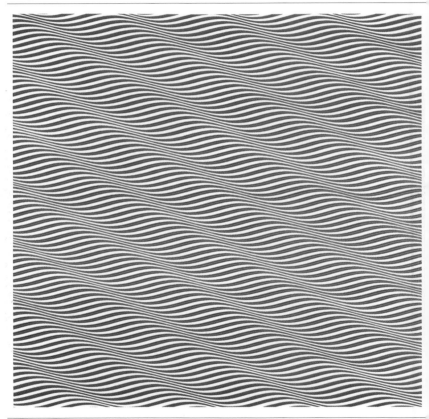

Bridget Riley. b London, 1931. **Cataract 3**. 1967. Emulsion on canvas. **h**221.9 × **w**222.9 cm. **h**87⅜ × **w**87¾ in. British Council, London

Riopelle Jean-Paul

Large Composition

Irregular patches of vivid colour create a lyrical image, like a mosaic of flickering light. The densely layered paint is applied directly from the tube with a palette knife, creating intense areas of pure colour which are interwoven with threads of pigment. The structure of this painting is based on the ink and watercolour works Riopelle had developed a couple of years earlier, combining free calligraphic gestures and coloured *taches* or stains. This is one of the first paintings to exploit this technique, and demonstrates Riopelle's controlled use of thick areas of flaming colour. The heavily textured surface and free application of paint connect this work to the Art Informel movement. Born in Montreal, Riopelle lived in Paris from 1948. Although he moved away from Surrealism, he continued to work in an abstract format while developing a looser paint application.

► Fautrier, Hartung, Pollock, Tobey, Vieira da Silva

Jean-Paul Riopelle. b Montreal, 1923. **d** Ile aux Grues, 2002. **Large Composition**. 1949–51. Oil on board. **h**170.2 × **w**260.5 cm. **h**67 × **w**102½ in. Private collection

Rist Pipilotti

Ever is Over All

Enveloped in a gentle melody, we see projected on one wall a slow-motion, roving view of green meadows full of red flowers. On the adjacent wall is another colour-saturated projection, also in slow motion, in which a woman in a blue dress and red shoes walks down a car-lined street. She smiles, the picture of innocence, as she smashes a car window with the long-stemmed red flower she carries. A passing policewoman salutes cheerfully as she skips to the next car and attacks again. Rist delights in provocative art that juxtaposes feminism and female sensuality with fairy tales and modern culture (even her nickname comes from the children's story *Pippi Longstocking*). Her sophisticated, imaginative works combine humour and irony with an earthiness that refuses to take itself too seriously while challenging the viewer's assumptions. Here, fiction (the ruby slippers, the magic wand) is combined with contemporary reality (urban aggression and wanton vandalism) to produce a whimsical yet anarchic scene.

▶ Abramović, Cahun, Kruger, Sherman

Pipilotti Rist. b Grabs, St Gallen, Switzerland, 1962. **Ever is Over All**. 1997. Video/sound installation. Dimensions variable. **dur** 1hr 45 min. Museum of Modern Art, New York, NY

The Tortilla Maker

he peace and tranquillity of this kitchen, where peasant
omen are preparing tortilla, are conveyed by the painting's
mplicity of colour and form. Executed at a time when
ivera was beginning to paint frescos, the influence of this
pecialized technique can clearly be seen in the sensitive
andling of the warm, glowing colours, which express a sense
f nostalgia and intimacy. The importance of the painting
es in its representation of Mexican culture, and the way in
hich it reflects Rivera's firm convictions about the essential

human dignity of people. Although he was earlier influenced
by Cubism, this painting demonstrates Rivera's ability to work
in the Classical style, using the Mexican subjects that were so
close to his heart. He was also deeply inspired by the ancient
Mayan and Aztec cultures. Rivera was active in the Mexican
revolution and throughout his career remained a politically
committed artist. He is renowned for his large-scale murals.

► Botero, Gauguin, Kahlo, Rego, Spencer, Tamayo

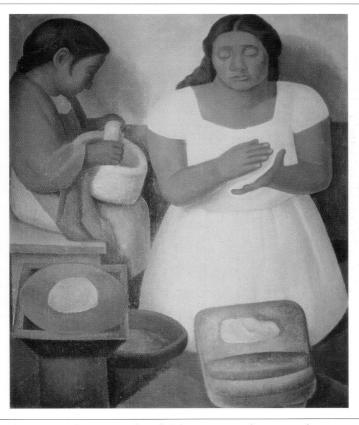

iego Rivera. b Guanajuato, 1886. d Mexico City, 1957. **The Tortilla Maker**. 1926. Oil on canvas. h107.3 × w89.5 cm. h42½ × w35¼ in.
niversity of California, San Francisco, CA

Della Robbia Luca

Madonna and Child between Two Angels

'Della Robbia blue' has become a standard term for the glaze pioneered by the Della Robbia family. The depth of the blue is heightened by the juxtaposition with a pure white glaze. Reliefs such as this are categorized neither as painting nor sculpture; they fall between the two media. Like his contemporary Lorenzo Ghiberti, Luca della Robbia was concerned with the depiction of three-dimensional space in a shallow plane. His introduction of colour, however, enabled him also to reproduce the colouristic effects of a painter.

The subtle modelling and crisp lines of this sculpture could not have been achieved without a strong understanding of drawing – the basis for both painting and sculpture. Luca was ranked by contemporaries as one of the great artistic innovators of the fifteenth century. His flourishing workshop was inherited by his nephew, Andrea, who continued to produce terracotta sculptures.

► Ghiberti, Filippo Lippi, Pisano, Della Quercia

Luca della Robbia. b Florence, 1400. **d** Florence, 1482. **Madonna and Child between Two Angels.** 1475/80. Glazed terracotta. **diam.** 100 cm. **diam.** 39⅓ in. Museo Nazionale del Bargello, Florence

Rodchenko Alexander

Composition (Overcoming Red)

Triangular shapes balanced in front of circles create a three-dimensional illusion, which is enhanced by the dark shading on the left diagonals of the triangles. The flat forms are divided by colour and appear to rotate. Composed of strictly geometric designs traced with a compass and ruler, the painting reflects the artist's search to create elementary shapes in pure, primary colours. In the same year as this painting Rodchenko exhibited his famous *Black on Black* painting, a response to Kasimir Malevich's 'White on White'

series. Rodchenko's desire to reduce painting to its abstract, geometric essentials led to his incorporation into the Constructivist movement. In common with other members of this group he later gave up easel painting in favour of design and the applied arts. He was particularly active in industrial design, typography and photography, the latter often exploiting unusual perspectives and angles of vision.

► Van Doesburg, Gabo, Lissitzky, Malevich, Tatlin

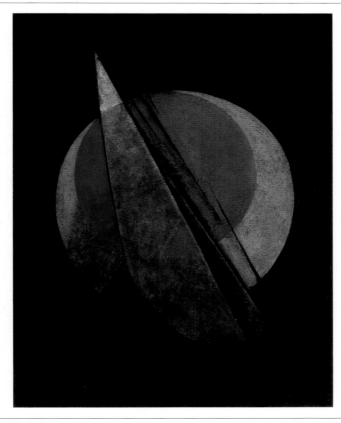

Alexander Rodchenko. b St Petersburg, 1891. d Moscow, 1956. **Composition (Overcoming Red)**. 1918. Oil on canvas. h78.5 × w62 cm. h30⅞ × w24⅜ in. Annely Juda Fine Art, London

Rodin Auguste

The Kiss

Two lovers are locked in an infinite embrace. The emotional force and vitality of this monumental sculpture have made it into one of the world's best-known works of art. The softly flowing forms of the lovers contrast starkly with the block of roughly hewn marble to which they are attached – symbolic of their earth-bound union. Both passion and despair are evoked by the paradox of the sensuality of flesh rendered so believably in cold inanimate stone, emphasizing as one critic put it 'the impossible union of souls by their bodies'. Rodin's interest in the idea of liberating the human figure from stone reflects his admiration for Michelangelo. He belongs to a universal tradition of sculpture and is both a product of late Romanticism and a herald of modern art. The pulsating energy and form of his statues, such as this, have had an enormous impact on twentieth-century artists.

► Bourgeois, Brancusi, Canova, Giambologna, Michelangelo

Auguste Rodin. b Paris, 1840. d Meudon, 1917. The Kiss. 1888–9. Marble. h183.6 cm. h72⅓ in. Musée National Auguste Rodin, Paris

Romney George

Mrs Mary Robinson, 'Perdita'

Confidently attired in a fashionable black silk cape and grey muff, her powdered hair folded behind a white cap, an elegant lady looks towards us with a coy demeanour. Her pretty features are sharply delineated in a soft, formal style. Mrs Mary Robinson was an actress, and was nicknamed 'Perdita' after playing that role in Shakespeare's *A Winter's Tale* at the Drury Lane Theatre in London. An attractive and charming woman, she enjoyed a brief liaison with the Prince of Wales around the time that this portrait was made. Thomas Gainsborough and Sir Joshua Reynolds also painted her. Romney was a fashionable portraitist, and at one time was considered the equal of Reynolds and Gainsborough. After a visit to Rome he dreamed of painting ambitious historical works in the 'Grand Style', but despite numerous preparatory drawings this dream was never realized. His popularity declined in the 1790s and he left London to return to his native Kendal, where he died.

► Gainsborough, Lawrence, Raeburn, Ramsay, Reynolds

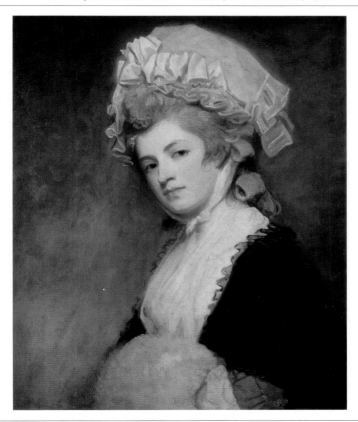

George Romney. b Dalton-le-Furness, 1734. d Kendal, 1802. **Mrs Mary Robinson, 'Perdita'**. 1781. Oil on canvas. h76 × w63 cm. 30 × w24¾ in. Wallace Collection, London

457

Rosa Salvator

Self-portrait

Regarding us over his shoulder with a rueful, disdainful expression, the artist appears to be admonishing us with disapproval. Indeed, inscribed on the tablet he holds are the words, 'Be silent, unless what you have to say is better than silence.' The stern message of this sombre self-portrait is made even more real by Rosa's dark cloak and hat, giving him an almost sinister quality; the strange, horizonless sky appears to make him loom threateningly above us. Rosa was greatly influenced by the almost cruel realism of Jusepe Ribera, who had settled in Naples by 1616, and his own much-admired 'savagery' was evident even in his poetic landscapes. This particular quality was to be important for the Romantic landscapists of the later eighteenth and nineteenth centuries. Rosa was not only a painter but turned his hand to engraving, poetry, music and acting.

▶ Dürer, Kauffmann, Mengs, Ribera, Vigée-Lebrun

Salvator Rosa. b Naples, 1615. **d** Rome, 1673. **Self-portrait.** c1645. Oil on canvas. **h**116 × **w**94 cm. **h**45¾ × **w**37 in. National Gallery, London

This striking image seduces the viewer with its brash colours and erotic overtones. The visual devices Rosenquist has used are those of commercial advertising: the half-open lips, perfectly manicured nails and provocatively placed stick give off suggestive signals, while the bold cropping of the image and the flat, commercial colours used have an immediate impact. These facile images are undermined, however, by the baffling composition of the canvas – why is one-half of the woman's face (supposedly that of Marilyn Monroe) obscured by a large glass tumbler? The painting demonstrates the power of advertising, which has become one of the foundations of urban society. Its use of popular imagery links it with the Pop Art movement in America. Rosenquist had impeccable credentials as a Pop artist: his early years were spent painting billboards and gasoline signs around the USA. He turned to painting as an art form in 1960.

► De Kooning, Lichtenstein, Oldenburg, Warhol, Wesselmann

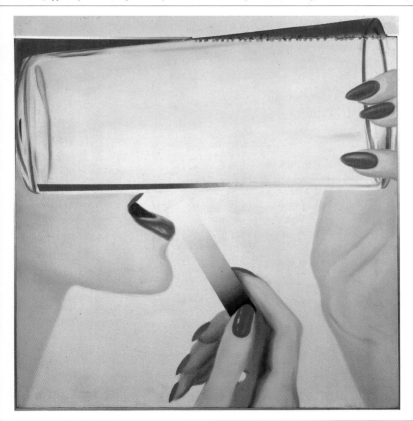

James Rosenquist. b Grand Forks, ND, 1933. **Study for Marilyn**. 1962. Oil on canvas. h95.2 × w91.5 cm. h37½ × w36 in. Private collection   459

Rosselli Cosimo

The simple harmony of this composition is typical of fifteenth-century Florentine altarpiece design. The presence of saints John the Baptist and Zenobius (patron saints of Florence) indicates that this altarpiece once stood in a Florentine church. The desires of Renaissance clients often dictated more than just the subject of an altarpiece; in this case, St Andrew and St Bartholomew were probably included because they were the patron saints of the commissioning client. Blue paint, made of ground lapis lazuli (a semi-precious stone), was the most expensive of all tempera pigments, so the more blue included in a painting, the more expensive it became. Blue was therefore reserved for the most important passages in a painting, such as the robes of the Virgin. The use of perspective in painting was an issue of great artistic debate in Renaissance Florence. Here Rosselli's use of one-point perspective is visible in the marble floor tiles. Rosselli's pupils included Piero di Cosimo.

► Masaccio, Piero della Francesca, Piero di Cosimo

Cosimo Rosselli. b Florence, 1439. **d** Florence, 1507. **The Virgin and Child Enthroned with Saints**. c1478. Tempera on panel. **h**190.5 × **w**175.2 cm. **h**75 × **w**69 in. The Fitzwilliam Museum, Cambridge

Rossetti Dante Gabriel

The Day-dream

The painting itself gives no indication as to the nature or subject matter of the absorbing day-dream of this beautiful woman, yet her reverie is so consuming that both her book and her flower lie forgotten in her lap. The many hues of green which surround her in the folds of her dress, and the leaves on the branches which enshrine her, add to the overall sensuality of this painting. As with many of Rossetti's works it presents us with an idealized vision of womanhood. Rossetti was a co-founder of the Pre-Raphaelite Brotherhood, whose artistic aim was to return to the simplicity of paintings before the time of the Italian High Renaissance artist Raphael, as a reaction against contemporary Victorian artists. This work illustrates certain characteristic Pre-Raphaelite techniques, such as the use of luminous expanses of bright colour, meticulous attention to detail and the study of outdoor subjects. Rossetti also wrote poetry which echoed the themes in his paintings.

▶ Fra Angelico, Botticelli, Burne-Jones, Hunt, Millais, Moreau

Dante Gabriel Rossetti. b London, 1828. **d** Birchington-on-Sea, 1882. **The Day-dream**. 1880. Oil on canvas. **h**159 × **w**93 cm. **h**62½ × **w**36½ in. Victoria and Albert Museum, London

ROSSO Fiorentino

Moses Defends the Daughters of Jethro

Jethro's seven daughters were prevented from watering their father's flock by a group of obstinate shepherds whom Moses fought off single-handedly. Moses' twisted and muscular body is seen in the centre of the composition fiercely beating a figure on the floor. The static, stunned daughter top right, the billowing pink cloak top left, and the intertwined forms, contorted poses and oddly perverse scattering of truncated limbs in the foreground, show Rosso Fiorentino at the height of Mannerism. This style was a development from the stability and order associated with Renaissance artists such as Perugino. Towards the end of his career, Rosso left his native Italy to work on the palace of François I of France at Fontainebleau. Rosso, who earned his name because of his shock of red hair, was rumoured to have committed suicide; it is more likely that he died from natural causes.

► Bourdelle, Bronzino, Giulio Romano, Pontormo, Primaticcio

Rosso Fiorentino (Giovanni Battista di Jacopo). b Florence, 1494. **d** Fontainebleau, 1540. **Moses Defends the Daughters of Jethro.** c1523.
Oil on canvas. **h**160 × **w**117 cm. **h**63 × **w**46 in. Galleria degli Uffizi, Florence

Rothko Mark

Untitled

Rectangular expanses of intense colour float upon the canvas. Their blurred edges make the colour masses appear to vibrate with a misty, magical quality. An ethereal luminosity suffuses the painting, dissolving all tension of form and contrasts of tones into an inner glow. Restrained yet deeply evocative, Rothko's works give the feeling of containing some burning truth, as if they represent the embodiment of long and arduous meditation. Born in Russia, Rothko emigrated to the USA with his parents in 1913. Largely a self-taught painter, he usually worked on a huge scale. He wanted to immerse the viewer in a total colour experience, saying, 'I paint large pictures because I want to create a state of intimacy. A large picture is an immediate transaction; it takes you into it.' Rothko was a leading figure in Abstract Expressionism, and his formless canvases evoke the true spirit of the movement – an ultimate response to the unattainable mysteries of the human psyche.

► Heron, Kelly, Newman, Pollock, Ryman, Serra, Still

Rouault Georges

Christ on the Cross

Christ, the cross and the surrounding figures are depicted in simple, outlined areas of colour. The cross dominates the composition and fills the entire canvas. Rich colours and crudely drawn forms add to the power of this image of salvation. The whole effect, especially the heavy black lines which delineate the coloured areas, is reminiscent of stained glass. Rouault was indeed apprenticed in stained glass before entering the studio of Gustave Moreau to train as a painter. In this print Rouault has used luminous streaks of colour to express his profound religious devotion. He has used the medium of aquatint, a form of etching that gives fluid, paint-like effects. The expressive, emotional content of his work recalls contemporary German Expressionist painting. Nevertheless, Rouault's style was completely his own, characterized by bright, emotive colours and harsh black outlines.

► Grünewald, Kirchner, Masaccio, Pechstein, Vlaminck

Georges Rouault. b Paris, 1871. **d** Paris, 1958. **Christ on the Cross**. 1936. Aquatint on paper. **h**64.8 × **w**48.7 cm. **h**25½ × **w**19⅛ in. Private collection

Roubiliac Louis-François

Sir Isaac Newton

This statue of Sir Isaac Newton – mathematician, physicist, astronomer and philosopher – proudly proclaims its subject's status as a man of unique talent. The grandiose marble is imposing and monumental, as if Roubiliac wished to convey Newton's supreme genius through his towering presence. The features are vividly sculpted with a superbly confident technique, and brought to a smooth, highly polished finish. The resulting statue breathes an air of vitality and restrained exuberance. As befits the eighteenth-century Age of Reason,

Roubiliac's work exudes the calm grandeur of greatness. As a young man, he left his native France and settled in England, where he made his name with a statue of Handel carved for London's Vauxhall Gardens. He became a highly acclaimed sculptor, gaining numerous commissions. His wide range of work includes statues of men of the Enlightenment and nobles, and numerous portrait busts and monuments.

► Canova, Houdon, Moroni, Powers

Rousseau Henri

The Monkeys

Three monkeys peer out from behind the thick foliage of the jungle, while an unusual bird perches on a delicate branch laden with heavy leaves. The uninhibited imaginativeness of the scene is typical of Rousseau's view of the world. The intense colours, crisply painted shapes and meticulous attention to detail demonstrate his naïve style. This imaginary jungle derives its inspiration from Rousseau's numerous visits to the Parisian botanical garden, the Jardin des Plantes. Rousseau was an amateur painter who attracted the attention of the Parisian avant-garde when he exhibited at the Salon des Indépendants in 1885. He became widely admired by Pablo Picasso and his circle for his fresh, direct vision, so obviously untrammelled by academic training. Rousseau's nickname Le Douanier ('the customs agent') stems from his profession in the French Customs service.

► Ernst, Gauguin, Hicks, Lam, Picasso, Vlaminck

Henri Rousseau (Le Douanier). b Laval, 1844. **d** Paris, 1910. **The Monkeys.** 1906. Oil on canvas. **h**145.5 × **w**113 cm. **h**57⅓ × **w**44½ in. Philadelphia Museum of Art, Philadelphia, PA

Rousseau Théodore

The Forest of Fontainebleau, Morning

A simple forest scene is painted in shimmering, pearly tones. Composed within an encircling arch of trees, the painting is marvellously fresh and intimate. The cows, enveloped by the misty, early morning air, are delicately reflected in the silvery puddle in which they stand. Rousseau has given careful attention to the depiction of the damp forest with its pale, subtly changing dawn light. Inspired by the work of Jacob van Ruisdael and other Dutch landscapists of the seventeenth century, as well as by the Englishman John Constable, he wished to introduce a freer, un-academic style of landscape to French painting. In the 1840s he settled in the village of Barbizon, in the forest of Fontainebleau, where he began to paint the surrounding countryside with intimacy and realism. Rousseau became one of the founders of the Barbizon School, who aimed to paint the scenery and peasant life of their adopted locale in an unprettified, direct manner.

➤ Constable, Corot, Daubigny, Hobbema, Millet, Ruisdael

Théodore Rousseau. b Paris, 1812. d Barbizon, 1867. **The Forest of Fontainebleau, Morning**. 1850. Oil on canvas. **h**98 × **w**134 cm. **h**38½ × **w**52¾ in. Wallace Collection, London

Rubens Sir Peter Paul

The Judgement of Paris

Mercury, with his billowing cloak, has led three goddesses to Paris. They are Juno, with a peacock, Venus, with Cupid, and Minerva, with her helmet and shield bearing a Gorgon's head. Adorned with jewels and very little else, the women stand before Paris who holds the golden apple he will award to the most beautiful of the three. Rubens has displayed this most popular of mythological subjects with the verve and grandeur so typical of the Baroque style that he pioneered. Sumptuous colour and sinuous brushstrokes have been used to evoke

the rich sensual female figures. In 1630 Rubens married the 16-year-old Hélène Fourment. After this date his style became imbued with a lyrical tenderness. To achieve this, Rubens used rich colours inspired by the Venetian masters, Titian and Veronese. Rubens' fluid brushwork and luscious colouring, and the rich emotion of his compositions, contributed to his reputation as the greatest Baroque painter north of the Alps.

► Van Dyck, Jordaens, Maillol, Titian, Veronese

Sir Peter Paul Rubens. b Siegen, 1577. **d** Antwerp, 1640. **The Judgement of Paris**. 1632–5. Oil on panel. **h**144.8 × **w**193.7 cm. **h**57 × **w**76¼ in. National Gallery, London

Ruisdael Jacob van

A Mountainous Wooded Landscape with a Torrent

Warmly spacious, with a wealth of closely observed naturalistic detail, this landscape's rich, autumnal tones celebrate the beauty of the countryside. It is not a static scene of chocolate-box prettiness, however; the restless, moving sky suggests that the weather is about to change, while the gushing river reminds us of the potentially destructive power of natural forces. Ruisdael instilled a sense of grandeur and drama into his works, which depict both the flat plains of his native Holland and the more rugged and dramatic areas of northern Germany. This painting demonstrates how the expressive possibilities of the sky became increasingly important to Dutch painters, not only serving to balance the composition but also breathing air and space into the scene. The appeal of Ruisdael's work lies in its naturalistic approach. He is acclaimed by many as the greatest and most versatile of all seventeenth-century Dutch landscape painters.

► Claude, Constable, Van Goyen, Hobbema

Jacob van Ruisdael. b Haarlem, 1628. **d** Amsterdam, 1682. **A Mountainous Wooded Landscape with a Torrent**. c1655. Oil on canvas. **h**77.5 × **w**95 cm. **h**31 × **w**38 in. Private collection

Against a pristine blue sky, the stark gleaming forms of a gasoline station stretch across the surface of a huge canvas. The bold lettering and the dynamic diagonal composition signal the optimism and ambitions of the modern motoring era. In the top right corner is a half-torn western magazine, perhaps representing a changed landscape. The presence of the magazine also adds to the stillness of the scene – it appears static – fixed in place, rather than blowing in the wind. Encouraged by his experiences as a commercial artist,

Ruscha rejected the popular gestural painting of the Abstract Expressionists in favour of a more premeditated, deadpan style. His graphic, brilliantly coloured compositions, many of which incorporate text, were aligned with the burgeoning American Pop art movement. First appearing in his 1963 book *Twentysix Gasoline Stations* (a photographic record of a section of Route 66), images of gasoline stations have been a recurring motif in his work.

► Estes, Frank, Hamilton, Hockney, Wesselmann

Ed Ruscha. b Omaha, NE, 1937. **Standard Station, Ten-Cent Western Being Torn in Half**. 1964. Oil on canvas. **h**165 × **w**308.5 cm.
h65 × **w**121½ in. Private collection

Ruysch Rachel

Still Life of Flowers

Resplendent against a backdrop of Classical buildings and a distant statue, a crystal vase glows with the luminous textures of colourful flowers. The scrupulous rendering of detail and the artist's brilliant technique give an added sense of depth and clarity to the surface of this painting. A veil of rich, creamy light descends gently onto the softly depicted floral arrangement. A further demonstration of Ruysch's technical skill is the inclusion of insects on the flowers, a commonly used device at the time. Floral still lifes were a popular subject in Dutch seventeenth-century painting. They were regarded not only as a celebration of nature but as a symbol of the transience of life on earth: even natural beauty will eventually decay. Ruysch was one of the most successful Dutch painters of floral still lifes, excelling at naturalistic depictions of beautiful bouquets. Her paintings continue to be as highly prized as the jewel-like arrangements they imitated.

► Fantin-Latour, De Heem, Kalf, Vermeer

Rachel Ruysch. **b** Amsterdam, 1664. **d** Amsterdam, 1750. **Still Life of Flowers**. 1689. Oil on canvas. **h**67.2 × **w**55.2 cm. **h**26½ × **w**21¾ in.
Private collection

Ryman Robert

Courier II

White enamel paint has been applied to a thin, unframed aluminium sheet screwed to the wall with metal bolts. These fasteners form an integral part of the blank composition, which aims to rid the painting of any trace of painterly illusion. The work provides the spectator with an ecstatic tranquillity that is constant in its intensity; it also demonstrates the unique interaction between the flatness of the picture's surface and the wall-plane behind. The work's connection with Minimalism is demonstrated by the lack of emotion and illusionism in the painting's construction. Ryman's work concentrates on emphasizing the qualities of the materials used – both the paint itself and its support (canvas, plastic, aluminium and so on). From the mid-1960s he has used exclusively white paint, so as not to distract attention from these concerns. He continues to experiment with a wide range of media and brushstrokes.

► Andre, Kelly, Mangold, Rothko, Serra, Tobey

Robert Ryman. b Nashville, TN, 1930. **Courier II**. 1985. Impervo on aluminium. **h**40.6 × **w**40.6 cm. **h**16 × **w**16 in. Private collection

Salviati Francesco

Charity

Salviati was a great admirer of Michelangelo and has adapted the intertwined figures of the *Doni Tondo* for this painting of Charity. Not only is the composition similar, but the obsession with muscular form and the play of light over the surface of the skin are also derived from Michelangelo. While Salviati achieves a strikingly three-dimensional, sculptural quality, this painting is too studied and self-conscious to merit the same status as Michelangelo's masterpiece. Nevertheless, this work is characteristic of the Florentine art of the time, which had become somewhat encumbered by the genius of the previous generation. Also influenced by the graceful fluidity of the work of Parmigianino, Salviati was the earliest and most convinced of the converts to a Roman ideal of Mannerism. He took his surname from one of his early patrons, Cardinal Salviati.

► Bronzino, Michelangelo, Parmigianino, Signorelli

Francesco Salviati. **b** Florence, 1510. **d** Rome, 1563. **Charity**. 1543/5. Tempera on panel. **h**156 × **w**122 cm. **h**61½ × **w**48 in. Galleria degli Uffizi, Florence

Sánchez-Cotán Juan

Still Life

Painted with astonishing immediacy and presence, this simple still life is startlingly illusionistic. The fruit and vegetables assume a monumental quality as a result of their meticulous depiction and dramatic lighting by the artist. The way they have been positioned – either hanging from strings or placed on an ambiguous window-like structure – is highly unconventional since it goes against the tradition of northern still lifes. These were generally set table-pieces depicting lavishly prepared food and its trappings. Here,

by contrast, the vegetables are humble and unadorned and have been taken out of the context of eating. The message, if any, is ambiguous, but the austerity and sense of order of the painting seem to imply some higher purpose. Sánchez-Cotán's still lifes contributed to the elevation of the genre to a status that was more than merely decorative. He became a Carthusian monk in 1603 and also painted religious pictures in Granada and Seville.

► De Heem, Kalf, Ruysch, Snyders, Zurbarán

Juan Sánchez-Cotán. b Orgaz, 1561. d Granada, 1627. **Still Life**. c1600–10. Oil on canvas. **h**69.5 × **w**96.5 cm. **h**27⅓ × **w**38 in. Private collection

Sander August

Pastry Chef

This photograph of a chef is a study in spheres, from the bald head and round face to the massive fist, bulging belly and even the bowl that he stirs. Light streaking across the floor from the left separates subject from background, and the small depth of field further blurs the surroundings, isolating the figure. The portrait was taken as part of series called 'People of the Twentieth Century', with which Sander intended to document German society. Adamant that photography and painting were completely different, his photographs are sharp and unambiguous, free from manipulation and non-judgemental. His purpose was investigative, and his sitters were meant to represent types, not to be explored as individuals – and yet personal character is unmistakable in the way Sander allowed each person to present themselves, asserting their place in society. A selection of portraits was published as *Face of Our Time* (1929) but was banned in 1936 as the subjects did not conform to the Nazis' ideal Aryan type.

► Cartier-Bresson, Evans, Soutine

August Sander. b Herford, Rhine Province, 1876. **d** Cologne, 1964. **Pastry Chef**. 1928. Gelatin silver print. **h**27.3 × **w**21 cm. **h**10¾⅓ × **w**8¼ in.   475
Private collection

Sargent John Singer

Carnation, Lily, Lily, Rose

At dusk in a summer garden in the village of Broadway, in the English Cotswolds, two little girls light Japanese lanterns. Dolly and Polly, were the daughters of the illustrator Frederick Barnard, with whom Sargent stayed in the summer of 1885. Painted over many evenings during the ten minutes or so when the light was just right, the composition shows the garden from a child's viewpoint, the lilies outsize and the lanterns casting a fairy-tale glow over the scene. Sargent's career spanned the years of Impressionism, then Fauvism and Cubism, but though he sometimes used Impressionistic techniques, he remained devoted to his own form of realism; he was particularly admired for his ability to draw with the brush. His main influences were Velázquez, van Dyck and Gainsborough – and his representations of contemporary socialites and power brokers in a highly distinctive Grand Manner style brought him both commercial success and social acclaim, along with some critical disdain.

► Chase, Degas, Orpen, Reynolds, Velázquez

John Singer Sargent. **b** Florence, 1856. **d** London, 1925. **Carnation, Lily, Lily, Rose**. 1885-6. Oil on canvas. **h**174 × **w**153.7 cm. **h**68½ × **w**60½ in. Tate, London

Sassetta

This scene depicts the moment when St Francis renounces his family in favour of life in the Church. Francis had given to the Church money belonging to his father, who then appealed to the civil courts. Francis tore off his clothes, saying that they were his father's and he no longer recognized any father but God. In this scene he has abandoned his clothes at the feet of his enraged father and runs to the Bishop, who offers both real and symbolic protection. This panel was once part of a large double-sided altarpiece which told the story of the life of St Francis and originally stood in the church of San Francesco in the town of Borgo Sansepolcro. Sienese painters of the early fifteenth century were less interested in perspective and proportion than their Florentine counterparts; this scene is therefore not as realistic as a Florentine work of the same period would be. What it lacks in realism, however, it makes up for in its graceful sophistication and subtle use of colour.

► Duccio, Giotto, Piero della Francesca

Sassetta (Stefano di Giovanni). b Siena, c1392. d Siena, 1450. **Saint Francis of Assisi Renouncing his Earthly Father**. 1444. Tempera on panel. h87.5 × w52.5 cm. h34½ × w20¾ in. National Gallery, London

Savery Roelandt

Orpheus

Surrounded by a motley collection of the animals and birds of the forest, who are drawn by the irresistible charm of his music, Orpheus reclines in a rocky, wooded glade near a river. He is seen playing a violin, the honeyed tones of which mesmerize the colourful array of exotic creatures. Savery delighted in richly detailed, lush, decorative landscapes with an assortment of flora and fauna. Although highly fantastic and idealized, and very much in the Mannerist tradition, the topography of these landscapes is in fact based on the

Alpine scenery Savery saw while travelling in Switzerland in the early 1600s. He made several dozen paintings of Orpheus and the Garden of Eden which gave him the opportunity of depicting his favourite subjects in magical worlds. His lively, detailed paintings, which are crammed with incident, show the influence of Jan Bruegel.

► J Bruegel, Hicks, Patinir, Piero di Cosimo

Schad Christian

Portrait of Doctor Haustein

With a catheter in his breast pocket, Doctor Haustein stares candidly out of the painting at us. Behind him looms the menacing shadow of his lover, a model called Sonja. The macabre tension created by this painting was almost prophetic: three years after it was completed Haustein's wife committed suicide because of her failed marriage, and in 1933 the doctor poisoned himself when he learnt that the Gestapo were about to arrest him. Schad himself was uninterested in politics and concentrated on subjects that had psychological rather than social implications. Isolated and introspective, his subjects often take on a hallucinatory degree of reality. Schad has been described as the coldest of the New Objectivity painters, a group of German artists who aimed to achieve a new kind of unidealized, objective realism. His work has all the precision and exactitude of a surgical operation, and this painting is typical of his style.

► Beckmann, Dix, Grosz, Richter, Sheeler

Christian Schad. b Miesbach, 1894. d Keilberg, 1982. **Portrait of Doctor Haustein**. 1928. Oil on canvas. h80.5 × w55 cm. h4¾ × w21⅔in. Fundación Colección Thyssen-Bornemisza, Madrid

Schiele Egon

Seated Woman with Bent Knee

Charged with a nervous energy, Schiele's model is portrayed seated on the ground in an informal pose. She looks directly at the viewer; her gaze and pose are erotic, yet the painting is less threatening than many of Schiele's portraits of women. Her sinewy features, anguished hands and contorted neck make this powerfully compact picture all the more disturbing. Schiele's intense and distorted images are uncompromising in their expression of human feeling. Deeply affected by Sigmund Freud's explorations of the unconscious, Schiele's work gave form to his own anxieties and insecurities. His career was brief but prolific, and many of his works are sexually explicit. Indeed, this led to the artist's brief imprisonment for 'making immoral drawings'. The acute nervous intensity of his style has made him one of the most important Expressionist painters, although he never formally identified himself with the movement. He died prematurely of influenza, just as his work was recognized.

► Balthus, Baselitz, Klimt, Kokoschka, Munch

Egon Schiele. b Tulln, 1890. d Vienna, 1918. **Seated Woman with Bent Knee.** 1917. Gouache, watercolour and black crayon on paper. h46 × w30 cm. h18½ × w12 in. Národní Galerie, Prague

Schmidt-Rottluff Karl

Flowering Trees

The dark rich colours and harsh treatment of forms, such as the violently delineated tree that dominates the landscape, have been painted in a forceful and dynamic style which quivers with vitality. Like Vincent van Gogh 20 years earlier, the artist has used heavily laden brushstrokes, applied in layered planes of contrasting, saturated hues. These are not the true colours of nature, but reflect the artist's own sensitivities and state of mind. The surging vibrancy and impassioned style of this painting, and the freedom of its

execution, are characteristic of German Expressionism of which Schmidt-Rottluff was a leading exponent. During the Second World War Schmidt-Rottluff was severely persecuted by the Nazis who removed all of his paintings from German galleries and forbade him to paint. His work was reinstated in 1945, from which time the artist lived in East Germany.

► Van Gogh, Heckel, Kirchner, Nolde, Pechstein

Karl Schmidt-Rottluff. b Rottluff, 1884. d Berlin, 1976. **Flowering Trees**. 1909. Oil on canvas. **h**69 × **w**81 cm. **h**27¼ × **w**31¾ in. Private collection

Schnabel Julian

Mele

The surface of this unusual and expressive portrait is made from bits of broken china, onto which the image has been painted. Schnabel was inspired by some walls in the Park Güell in Barcelona, designed by the Catalan architect Antoni Gaudí, which had been surfaced with a mosaic of ceramic fragments. He was also influenced by the Surrealists' experiments with 'automatic' drawing, a form of art which was supposed to come directly from the unconscious. Schnabel's 'plate paintings' such as this enabled him to

paint on a surface without seeing the immediate effect. The fragmented surface causes the image to recede in places, the china acting as a screen rather than a medium to project the image. Schnabel painted on other unconventional surfaces, including velvet and tarpaulin. In the 1980s he was considered the *enfant terrible* of American art.

► Motherwell, Rauschenberg, Schwitters, Twombly

Julian Schnabel. **b** New York, NY, 1951. **Mele**. 1987. Oil and china plates on wood. **h**152 × **w**122 cm. **h**60 × **w**48 in. Private collection

Schongauer Martin

It is surprising that this Madonna and Child look away from each other. Each seems absorbed in a different world, even though the Virgin tenderly cradles the Christ child and he has his arms around her neck. Schongauer was a pioneer in printmaking and was much admired by Albrecht Dürer. He concentrated on images of the Virgin that were very similar to the altarpiece shown here. This is Schongauer's only documented painting, yet his talents as a printmaker are evident even in paint. For example, the sharp folds

of Mary's robe which are divided into planes of light and shadow parallel the manner in which an engraver would represent tones. Prints were cheap and easy to transport. This would have facilitated the rapid dispersion of Schongauer's compositions, thereby making his reputation over a large area of Europe. Schongauer was much influenced by Flemish art, especially apparent in the exquisite details of the flowers and birds in this painting.

► Bouts, Campin, Dürer, Lochner, Van der Weyden

Martin Schongauer. b Colmar, c1435. **d** Breisach, 1491. **The Madonna of the Rose Garden**. 1473. Oil on panel. **h**200 × **w**115 cm. **h**78¾ × **w**45¼ in. Saint Martin, Colmar

An assortment of items – including a used envelope, a postcard, discarded packaging and bus tickets – have been attached to a piece of board. Combined with words picked at random from newspapers, and daubed with paint, they have been arranged without meaning to form a collage. The result is a balanced, abstract composition made from meaningless fragments: Schwitters has created art out of non-art. His random collection of objects undermines the traditional notion of art as something expressive, or

meaningful. A talented poet as well as an artist, Schwitters was associated with the Dadaists, a group of writers and artists active from 1915 to 1922, who wanted to disrupt the public's complacency and acceptance of traditional values. Schwitters was refused membership to the Berlin Dada group and established his own branch in Hanover which he named 'Merz', a word derived from the proper noun Com*merz*bank.

► Duchamp, Ernst, Gris, Hamilton, Man Ray, Schnabel

Kurt Schwitters. b Hanover, 1887. **d** Ambleside, 1948. **Picture of Spatial Growths – Picture with Two Small Dogs.** 1939. Collage on board. **h**96.5 × **w**68 cm. **h**38 × **w**26¾ in. Tate, London

Adam and Eve

The robust, statuesque figures of Adam and Eve, framed by lush trees and with a river landscape winding its way into the distance, dominate this scene from the Garden of Eden. Scorel was much travelled and his style of painting synthesizes the delicacy of his Netherlandish predecessors with the substantiality of form of Italian art. The bold nudity and the solid forms of the figures, contained within a firm, confident outline, are typical of Scorel's style of religious painting and reveal the influence of the Italian Renaissance

artists Michelangelo and Raphael whom the artist knew when he lived in Rome. His northern roots enabled him to depict the landscape with great sensitivity and fill it with delightful details such as the small animals in the foreground. Scorel was so famous by the mid-sixteenth century that he was asked to restore the great Ghent altarpiece by Jan van Eyck.

► Dürer, Van Eyck, Van der Goes, Massys, Michelangelo

Sebastiano del Piombo

The Death of Adonis

Venus learns of the death of her lover Adonis who, having been slain by a boar, lies dead in the background. The asymmetrical composition with a concentration of figures on the right of the canvas, and the pointing fingers, outstretched arms and moving heads which create movement within the painting, are typical of Sebastiano's style which is free from the rigidity of earlier Renaissance paintings. The nudes and surrounding landscape are bathed in a delicate light characteristic of the art of Sebastiano's native Venice,

in particular the work of Giorgione who was his friend and teacher. Sebastiano also worked in Rome where he came into contact with Raphael but he was more strongly influenced by Michelangelo who gave him sketches and cartoons to develop. The solid, muscular bodies in this painting reflect the artist's deep understanding of Michelangelo's nudes.

► Giorgione, Michelangelo, Palma Vecchio, Raphael, Titian

Sebastiano del Piombo. b Venice, c1485. **d** Rome, 1547. **The Death of Adonis**. c1511. Oil on canvas. **h**189 × **w**285 cm. **h**74½ × **w**112¼ in. Galleria degli Uffizi, Florence

Segal George

Bus Riders

Four ghost-like figures appear to have been frozen in time in the everyday activity of riding on a bus. Segal created plaster-casts of his friends and family and placed them in familiar settings to highlight the banal but necessary activities that are routinely performed by all of us. Although rough on the outside, inside each cast bears the imprint of every detail of the sitter's clothes and skin. Like real people on a bus these figures keep themselves to themselves. Segal's intention was to portray the anonymity of the mundane, daily actions that are imposed on us by the society in which we live, and to capture mankind's sense of alienation in the modern world. His plaster men and women sit in chairs, eat in diners and shave their legs. The portrayal of familiar activities which the spectator could relate to was typical of Pop Art, a movement which developed in America in the 1960s.

▶ Dine, Hamilton, Oldenburg, Rosenquist, Wesselmann

George Segal. b New York, NY, 1924. **d** North Brunswick, NJ, 2000. **Bus Riders**. 1964. Mixed media. **h**175.2 × **w**193 cm. **h**69 × **w**76 in.
Hirshhorn Museum and Sculpture Garden, Washington, DC

Serra Richard

Clara, Clara

Two immense plates of steel curve towards each other as if drawn by an irresistible, resonating force. The sculpture dominates rather than decorates the public square in which it stands, its uncompromising presence aggressively stating the power of its structural might. Serra, who lives in New York, works in a variety of commonplace materials, including metal squares, firebricks, logs and rusted nails, and demonstrates in a Conceptual way a material's ability to express energy and develop tensions with the structures surrounding its newly created form. *Clara, Clara* is Minimalism taken to its paradoxical extreme – the most simple, unadorned message of purity of form amplified into a new dimension. Serra's work has kindled awe, despair and also much controversy. To some it offers a forlorn glimpse of a world free from mundane function. Richard Serra insists that his works are illustrated in black and white.

► Andre, LeWitt, Noguchi, Smith

Richard Serra. b San Francisco, CA, 1939. **Clara, Clara.** 1983. Cor-Ten steel. **h**3.6 × **w**36.6 m. **h**12 × **w**120 ft. Originally in the Jardin des Tuileries, Place de la Concorde, Paris. Now in the Square de Choisy, Paris

Seurat Georges

Sunday Afternoon on the Island of the Grande Jatte

Seurat has painted a typical Sunday afternoon at the Grande Jatte, a popular site on an island in the River Seine to the north-west of Paris. He visited the Grande Jatte every day for six months to make preparatory drawings of the landscape and to sketch numerous figures, such as the woman with her fashionable bustle and the mother and child, before creating this carefully planned composition in his studio. When the painting was first shown it was received with great indignation by the majority of artists and critics. They strongly disapproved of Seurat's revolutionary new painting technique, known as 'Pointillisme'. The surface of the painting is broken up and the colour painted onto the canvas as dots of pure colour. When viewed at a distance the dots appear to fuse together, creating a mesmerizing haze of brilliant colour. Seurat died of a severe infection at the age of 32.

► Dufy, Monet, Pissarro, Signac, Vlaminck, Vuillard

Georges Seurat. b Paris, 1859. d Paris, 1891. **Sunday Afternoon on the Island of the Grande Jatte**. 1884-6. Oil on canvas. h207.5 × w308 cm. h81¾ × w121⅓ in. Art Institute of Chicago, Chicago, IL

Severini Gino

Pierrot the Musician

Pierrot the musician, dressed in an immaculate white costume which contrasts with his black mask of the *commedia dell'arte*, sits in a room with brightly patterned walls. In 1910 Severini joined the Futurist movement, a group of artists and writers who expressed the dynamism of the modern world by representing machines and figures in motion, and went on to create some masterpieces of Futurist art. He was much influenced by Georges Seurat, evident in his use of pure colour, and became friends with a number of Cubist artists,

including Pablo Picasso. The calm composition of this painting and the precision and care with which Severini has executed the stiff folds of Pierrot's outfit, his rubbery hands and the guitar, marks the artist's movement away from the influence of Futurism and Cubism and towards a rekindling of the Neo-Classical spirit which dominated Severini's work until his death.

► Balla, Boccioni, Ter Brugghen, Greuze, Picasso, Seurat

Gino Severini. b Cortona, 1883. **d** Paris, 1966. **Pierrot the Musician**. 1924. Oil on canvas. **h**130 × **w**89 cm. **h**51⅛ × **w**35 in.
Museum Boymans-van Beuningen, Rotterdam

Sheeler Charles

Windows

Skyscrapers soar up into the Manhattan sky. The windows of these 36-storey buildings are not intended to give the spectator an insight into the people who live and work inside but to create an abstract pattern across the surface of the precisely painted picture. In 1920 Sheeler took a series of photographs of New York's skyscrapers which he used to make a film called *Mannahatta*. These images of a complex arrangement of buildings, shadows and windows inspired him to make his first 'Precisionist' paintings. Along with Stuart

Davis, Georgia O'Keeffe and others, Sheeler reveals in his work a pristine, static, unpopulated approach to the North American environment, executed in styles ranging from photographic realism to pure abstraction. The reflections suggested in this painting have been influenced by Sheeler's use of superimposed images in his photography.

► Davis, Estes, O'Keeffe, Richter, Schad, Stieglitz

Charles Sheeler. b Philadelphia, PA, 1883. d Dobbs Ferry, NY, 1965. **Windows**. 1951. Oil on canvas. h81.3 × w51.1 cm. h32 × w20⅛ in. Hirschl and Adler Galleries Inc., New York, NY

Sherman Cindy

Untitled No. 96

This photograph is reminiscent of Victorian art in its romantic portrayal of a meditative young woman. The symbolic motifs of the Pre-Raphaelites, however, are replaced with the brash surfaces of modernity; the young woman becomes a teenager; the 'letter' she holds is a section of the lonely hearts column; and the framing is cinematic. *Untitled No. 96* is one of an ongoing series of photographic tableaux which Sherman stages, acts in and directs. Sherman is the 'star' of all her works where, heavily disguised, she acts out a series of narratives often drawn from cinema or the history of great art. Her increasingly baroque works of the late 1980s have moved into *grand guignol*. The female body is dismembered or replaced with pornographic prosthetics in a violent evocation of the image as a corpse and woman as victim. But Sherman's disrespect for traditional values combines with grim humour to form a powerful and original artistic approach.

► Cahun, Dine, Estes, Gilbert and George, Man Ray, Millais

Cindy Sherman. b Glen Ridge, NJ, 1954. **Untitled No. 96**. 1981. Colour photograph. **h**61 × **w**122 cm. **h**24 × **w**48 in. Museum of Modern Art, New York, NY

Shore Stephen

This image of a vast landscape obstructed by a banal man-made image of nature is Shore's ironic comment on both. Published in *Uncommon Places* (1982), a series of photographs taken on road trips across the USA between 1973 and 1979, it exemplifies not only Shore's fascination with everyday intersections between the American people and their landscape, but also his brilliant colour sense. Shore was a leading representative of the so-called New Topographic school of photography, which arose in the mid-1970s.

'Stylistic anonymity' was the aim of these photographers, who were inspired by Conceptual art; pictures were 'stripped of any artistic frills… eschewing entirely the aspects of beauty, emotion and opinion'. Shore, who had photographed Andy Warhol in The Factory, was also influenced by Warhol's fascination with the banal and the popular – making art out of the things, or the scenes, that other people regarded as non-art.

► Adams, Eggleston, Frank, Gursky, Ruscha

Stephen Shore. b New York, NY, 1947. **US 97, South of Klamath Falls, Oregon, July 21, 1973**. 1973. Chromogenic print.
h51 × **w**61 cm. **h**20 × **w**24 in. Metropolitan Museum of Art, New York, NY

Siberechts Jan

A View of Longleat

Longleat is one of the largest and most impressive monuments of Elizabethan architecture. Siberechts, a Flemish landscape painter who lived in England from 1672, specialized in the depiction of noble country houses and was commissioned to record this masterpiece of the English Renaissance just as a photographer might record the erection of a modern building today. Siberechts has chosen a bird's-eye view of Longleat, but the strict symmetry and dispassionate style of the painting has made it rather stiff and, it could be said,

more of a topographical record of the building than a work of high art. The few figures lingering in the grounds of the house give little indication of courtly life, but Siberechts has managed to imbue the scene with a certain restrained formality which would have appealed to the taste of the seventeenth-century English nobility.

► Canaletto, Guardi, Pannini, Piper

Jan Siberechts. b Antwerp, 1627. d London, 1703. **A View of Longleat**. 1675. Oil on canvas. h111.8 × w172.7 cm. h44 × w68 in. Private collection

Sickert Walter

Ennui

Time seems to stand still in this languid setting. A man puffs on his cigar and stares into the distance, while a young woman head in hand and stifled by boredom, gazes up at a painting on the wall which she must have looked at a hundred times before. Born in Germany of Danish and Irish descent, Sickert was trained in Paris, where he became friends with Edgar Degas and the French Impressionists. He was also the pupil of James Abbott McNeill Whistler in London. He specialized in painting landscapes, townscapes and portrayals of daily life. These reflected the same interests as his friends in Paris although he differs from them in his use of sombre colours and rough dark tones. Sickert was the most important British Impressionist although his work is not typical of Impressionist painting. His studio in Camden Town, London, became a meeting-place for the avant-garde artists and writers of his day.

► Degas, Gilman, Hammershøi, Orpen, Whistler

Walter Sickert. b Munich, 1860. **d** Bathampton, 1942. **Ennui.** c1914. Oil on canvas. **h**152.4 × **w**112.4 cm. **h**60 × **w**44 in. Tate, London

Signac Paul

The Papal Palace, Avignon

Small patches of pure colour are fused together optically to create an image of the Papal Palace at Avignon. On the left, picked out in hues of green, stands Avignon's famous bridge. A devotee of Georges Seurat's 'Pointillist' technique, Signac placed complementary colours next to each other without blending them together. The result is a series of dots that merge together when viewed from a distance. Signac exploited the Impressionists' discoveries about how colour changes under different light conditions. The purples and pinks which dominate this painting, for instance, are similar to the colouring of Claude Monet's famous visions of the cathedral at Rouen. Seurat himself was opposed to his ideas being over-verbalized, but his early death enabled Signac to expound theories on Neo-Impressionism and the use of colour. From around 1900 he abandoned the round dots of Pointillism and began to use square spots of primary colours.

► Boccioni, Monet, Pissarro, Seurat

Paul Signac. b Paris, 1863. **d** Paris, 1935. **The Papal Palace, Avignon**. 1900. Oil on canvas. **h**73.5 × **w**92.5 cm. **h**29 × **w**36¼ in. Musée d'Orsay, Paris

Signorelli Luca

The Flagellation of Christ

Christ, tied to the column at the centre of the composition, is being beaten at the behest of Pontius Pilate who does not believe that he is the Son of God. The sculptural reliefs in the background, the Corinthian capital of the column and the decorative frieze at the bottom of the painting reflect the Renaissance interest in motifs from classical Antiquity. Strong, oblique lighting, including the shadows cast on the ground, helps to define the three-dimensional space of the scene. The muscular calves of the figures and strong symmetrical

composition are characteristic of Signorelli's style of painting which was greatly influenced by Piero della Francesca, his teacher, and the brothers Antonio and Piero Pollaiuolo. His beautiful black-chalk drawings of the body in motion were the most rigorous studies of the nude before Michelangelo.

▶ Perugino, Piero della Francesca, Pollaiuolo, Sassetta

Luca Signorelli. b Cortona, c1450. **d** Cortona, 1523. **The Flagellation of Christ.** c1490. Oil on panel. **h**85.5 × **w**62 cm. **h**33¼ × **w**24⅜ in. 497
Pinacoteca di Brera, Milan

Siqueiros David Alfaro

Death and Funeral of Cain

Crowds of people have congregated as if in anticipation of experiencing a miraculous religious vision – but instead a grotesque dead chicken lies slumped across the cliff-top in front of them. The crowd's inability to recognize the inanity of the object they are venerating emphasizes the futility of their mission. Siqueiros was one of the founders (with Diego Rivera and José Clemente Orozco) of the school of mural painting which developed in Mexico after the Revolution. The bold composition of this painting, its striking use of

colour and free mixture of reality and fantasy, influenced by the Surrealists and Mexican folk art, is reminiscent of the artist's work in murals. A political activist and revolutionary, Siqueiros was imprisoned and exiled many times throughout his life. His impassioned style of painting has immense power and vitality and is ripe with dynamic and provocative suggestions and ideological meaning.

► JC Orozco, Rivera, Snyders, Tamayo

David Alfaro Siqueiros. b Santa Rosalia, 1896. **d** Cuernavaca, 1974. **Death and Funeral of Cain**. 1947. Acrylic on panel. **h**76 × **w**96 cm. **h**29⅞ × **w**37¾ in. Museo de Arte Carrillo Gil, Mexico City

Sisley Alfred

Subtle tones of white and grey form the colour-base of this almost monochromatic winter scene. The thickly and distinctly applied paint gives depth and heaviness to the snow as if it is accumulating on the ground, walls and trees. The sketchily painted small figure fixes the centre of the picture and our attention, and gives a sense of purpose and scale to the landscape. Sisley's quest to capture colour and light led him to experiment in varying atmospheric conditions. He was greatly influenced by Claude Monet with whom he evolved an impressionistic style. Their search to translate visual perceptions into pure effects of luminosity and tones is the basis of Impressionism, of which Sisley became a leading exponent. Sisley was almost exclusively a landscape painter. His predilection for roads and pathways leading into the painting, which opens fan-like in this snow-scene, reveals the influence of Camille Corot.

► Avercamp, Corot, Monet, Pissarro

Alfred Sisley. b Paris, 1839. d Moret-sur-Loing, 1899. **Snow at Louveciennes**. 1878. Oil on canvas. h61 × w50 cm. h24 × w19¾ in. Musée d'Orsay, Paris

Sittow Michiel

Downcast eyes, hair parted in the middle, a close-fitting headdress and a halo heighten the mood of this demure, tranquil and pensive portrait. It is believed that the subject has been depicted as a saint in deference to her pious character. The alternating Ks and roses of her elaborate gold necklace and the shells which ring the bodice of her dress have led to the suggestion that the sitter is Katherine of Aragon. Sittow was an Estonian artist who trained in Bruges under Hans Memling and continued the Netherlandish tradition of detailed portraiture while living in Italy and Spain. His style is very smooth and realistic and it is unlikely that a photograph of this woman would be any more exact than the artist's precise likeness. Besides a few exquisite religious works painted in brilliant but subtle colours, only a small number of Sittow's beautiful and highly perceptive portraits have survived – including this fine example.

► Anguissola, Clouet, Holbein, Memling

Michiel Sittow. b Reval, 1468. **d** Reval, 1525/6. **Katherine of Aragon**. c1503/4. Oil on panel. **h**29 × **w**20.5 cm. **h**11½ × **w**8⅛ in.
Kunsthistorisches Museum, Vienna

Sluter Claus

The Prophets Daniel and Isaiah

The realistic facial expressions, the detail of Isaiah's two-pronged beard, the decorative brocade on the edge of his garment and the intricacy of his loosely tied belt, are all elements hitherto unseen in north European sculpture. Rather than an archetypal image of a prophet, Sluter has created a thoughtful, intelligent man with an individual personality. In 1383 Philip the Bold, Duke of Burgundy, founded a Carthusian monastery at Champmol near Dijon in France. In the 1390s he commissioned the greatest

craftsmen available to create a group of buildings and monuments for this site. One of these artisans was Sluter, who produced a large well to stand by the entrance to the ducal chapel. Known as *The Well of Moses*, it comprised six life-size prophets carved in stone, surmounted by a wooden crucifix and five statues. These figures, which include the prophets Daniel and Isaiah, are seen as one of the most important influences on northern sculpture.

▶ Donatello, Ghiberti, Della Quercia, Van der Weyden

Claus Sluter. Active in Haarlem, c1380. **d** Dijon, 1405. **The Prophets Daniel and Isaiah**. 1404–5. Stone. **h**169 cm. **h**66½ in. Hôpital la Chartreuse, Dijon

Smith David

Australia

Steel plates and rods have been welded together to create a large abstract form. In defiance of the weight of its material the sculpture appears light and full of energy, as if poised to spring free from its heavy base. Smith rejected traditional modes of sculptural production, based on the monolithic block of stone or bronze, instead choosing to work in a way that was akin to drawing in space. The strength and flexibility of the steel rods enabled Smith to create open expansive forms in which negative space becomes an integral part of the work. Originally a painter, Smith was inspired to work with welded metal in the 1930s after seeing photographs of sculptures produced by Picasso and Julio Gonzalez. Partly because of its title, it has been suggested that the present work could be interpreted as the abstracted form of a kangaroo.

► Caro, Chamberlain, Picasso, Tatlin

David Smith. b Decatur, IN, 1906. **d** South Shaftsbury, VT, 1965. **Australia**. 1951. Painted steel on cinder block base. **h**202 × **w**274 × **d**41 cm. **h**79½ × **w**107⅞ × **d**16⅛ in. Museum of Modern Art, New York, NY

Smithson Robert

Asphalt Rundown

A truck tips a load of asphalt down a gravelly hillside. The sticky black substance creates a dark shadowy stain. With relatively little control over the form that the finished work takes, the artist's role is that of an instigator. Although earlier in the decade he had produced Minimalist-type sculpture, with *Asphalt Rundown* Smithson signalled his position as an innovator of Land art. Unlike gallery exhibited art objects (which could be readily moved) these large-scale works were site specific. Since Land artists tended to work with natural materials in locations far from the urban centres of the contemporary art world, most viewers experience these often-temporary works though the non-site medium of photography. In the same year that *Asphalt Rundown* was completed, the artist started construction of his most iconic 'earthwork', *Spiral Jetty*. Smithson was tragically killed in a plane crash whilst inspecting one of his works in 1973.

► Adams, Heizer, Long, Matta-Clark, Soulages

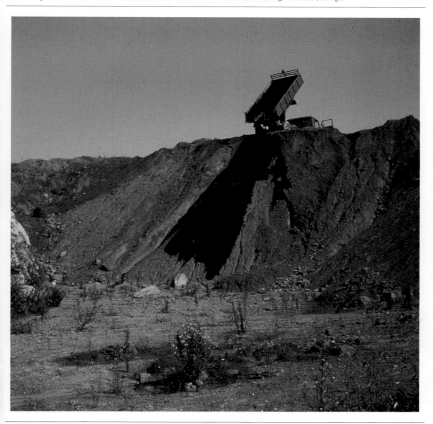

Snyders Frans

A Game Stall

A man in a dandified costume holds a dead peacock amidst a panoply of plumed poultry and game in this richly stocked market stall. His two dogs look on inquisitively, tempted by the tasty morsels on display. Snyders was concerned with the whole effect of colour, texture and feeling. No part of this canvas is left free of meticulous detail, creating a visual gourmet drama that is marvellously rendered in sumptuous colouring and with great craftsmanship. Snyders painted many vigorous hunting scenes and was the first painter to specialize in animal still lifes (large compositions featuring fruit, flowers, dead game and so on). His talent and luscious painting style were highly praised by his contemporaries, including Jacob Jordaens and his close friend Peter Paul Rubens with whom he collaborated to paint the still-life and animal parts of his exuberant hunting scenes.

► Fabritius, De Heem, Kalf, Rubens, De Troy

Frans Snyders. b Antwerp, 1579. **d** Antwerp, 1657. **A Game Stall.** 1620s. Oil on canvas. **h**170 × **w**254 cm. **h**67 × **w**100 in. York City Art Gallery, York

Sodoma

The Descent from the Cross

Billowing draperies of oranges, reds, greens and blues add vibrancy to this scene of Christ's body being taken down from the cross. Sodoma's work is characterized by beautiful colours, subtle effects of light and a poetic feel for landscape. The background in this painting is believed to have been inspired by Flemish painters such as Jan van Eyck, although many Italian artists, including Leonardo da Vinci, also used landscape as a background feature. Renaissance paintings such as this were often made by a group of artists, or workshop, working under one master. The master was responsible for the composition and for painting key elements of the work, while his assistants would complete the background and secondary figures. Despite this team effort, the painting would still have been considered a product of the master's hand. Born in Lombardy, he worked in both Siena and Rome where he received many important commissions.

► Van Eyck, Leonardo, Memling, Signorelli, Van der Weyden

Sodoma (Giovanni Antonio Bazzi). b Vercelli, 1477. **d** Siena, 1549. **The Descent from the Cross.** c1505/10. Oil on panel.
h414 × **w**264 cm. **h**163 × **w**104 in. Pinacoteca Nazionale, Siena

Soulages Pierre

Painting 16

Strong broad strokes of black paint sweep down the canvas in a heavy, bold formation. The large black mass, intensified by the contrasting small white gleams of light, gives the painting a monumental and serene aspect. It is this skilful illumination, combined with the sculptural quality of the distinctive forms, which makes the picture so unique. The work's connection to the Art Informel movement is demonstrated by the constrained freedom of the brushstrokes which have been articulated to create a powerful abstract composition. Born in south-west France, Soulages settled in Paris in 1946 and started to work in an abstract style that is reminiscent of the prehistoric dolmens and Romanesque sculpture of his native Auvergne. Soulages' paintings often consisted of broad bands, usually as black and shiny as patent leather, intersecting one another to form latticed structures against bright colours.

► Hartung, Kline, Riopelle, Da Silva, De Staël

Pierre Soulages. b Rodez, 1919. **Painting 16**. 1965. Oil on canvas. **h**162 × **w**130 cm. **h**64 × **w**51 in. Private collection

Soutine Chaim

The Little Pastry Cook

Thick smears of paint animate the surface of this picture. The distorted forms and excited colouring give an air of disjointed vivacity to the cook. Soutine's turbulent style was influenced by the expressive and dynamic work of Vincent van Gogh, although he protested not to like the Dutchman's work. Indeed, Soutine claimed to despise the work of his contemporaries and was indifferent to the experiments of the Fauves and the Cubists. He preferred to paint in his own unique style and declared a close affinity with Old Masters such as Rembrandt. Born in Lithuania, Soutine moved to Paris in 1913. His usual subjects were still lifes, tempestuous landscapes – with dark clouds and moving trees – and psychologically revealing portraits of valets and bakers. The highly charged movement and impulsive brushstrokes in his paintings anticipate the free style of Willem de Kooning and embody the spirit known as Expressionism.

► Bacon, Van Gogh, De Kooning, Rembrandt, Schiele

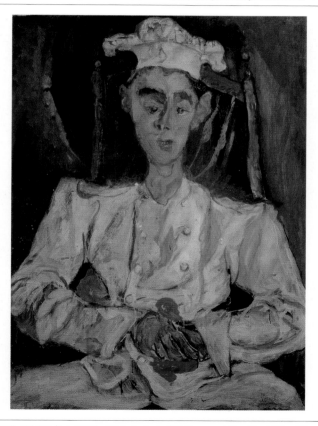

Chaim Soutine. b Smilovitchi, 1893. d Paris, 1943. The Little Pastry Cook. c1922. Oil on canvas. h72 × w54 cm. h28⅓ × w21¼ in. Musée de l'Orangerie, Paris

Spencer Sir Stanley

Saint Francis and the Birds

A naïve and enlarged figure of St Francis, his back towards us, gesticulates wildly with his arms outstretched as he looks up to the sky. Ducks, hens and birds on the roof gaze upon him as if in adoration. The large figure dominates the canvas; strangely, his hands have been reversed. The paint has been applied in broad, flat swathes giving the surface a tapestry-like pattern, while the figures are solid, almost cylindrical in form. This imaginative and lively painting was rejected by the Royal Academy, probably because its outrageous humour offended the arbiters of good taste. Spencer depicted Christianity as a living, everyday experience and drew most of his inspiration from the small village of Cookham in Berkshire. Francis is clad in green rather than his usual brown habit because Spencer used his father, who wore his dressing-gown and bedroom slippers, as the model for the saint.

► Botero, Gauguin, Rego, Rivera, H Rousseau, Sassetta

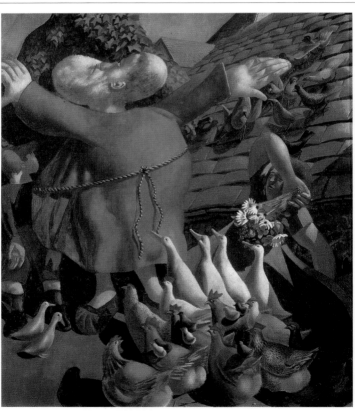

Sir Stanley Spencer. b Cookham, 1891. **d** Taplow, 1959. **Saint Francis and the Birds.** 1935. Oil on canvas. **h**71 × **w**61 cm. **h**28 × **w**24 in. Tate, London

Spilliaert Léon

Moonlit Beach

At first glance the strong lines and broad bands of tone in this picture make it look like an abstract work of art. As the viewer's eye becomes accustomed to the painting, however, a beach scene becomes apparent; the sweeping, pale light of the moon highlights waves coming into the shore and dark breakwaters stretching into the sea. Similarly, the colours – which at first seem limited – become richer as the eye begins to appreciate the subtle differences in tones and the searing white of the rising moon. The artist has concentrated on the effect of moonlight on a beach at night rather than a realistic depiction of the scene, and has thus captured effectively the mood of this solitary place. Spilliaert is known for his economy of form in haunting landscapes that are devoid of human life. Most of these paintings were executed in and around his native Ostend.

► Grimshaw, Krøyer, Le Gray, Marin, Mucha

Léon Spilliaert. b Ostend, 1881. d Brussels, 1946. **Moonlit Beach**. 1908. Ink, watercolour and pencil on paper. h50 × w65 cm. 19⅔ × w25½ in. Private collection

De Staël Nicolas

Red Bottles

The vibrant luxuriousness of the paint in this still life is used by De Staël to convey a calm beauty. The space around the bottles is almost as rich as the objects themselves which float in the creamy texture of the paint's surface, evoking a sense of timelessness. The painting's importance lies in its delicate balance of abstract and representational imagery, and its interplay between and control of powerful hues of exquisite colour and form. De Staël has eliminated background, ornament and outline, a feature which characterizes his lyrical style. He began his career as an abstract painter, and was much influenced by Georges Braque, but as he began to paint more freely his paintings became more figurative. His favourite themes from this period were musicians, athletes, nudes and still lifes. De Staël committed suicide shortly after this picture was painted.

► Braque, Morandi, B Nicholson, Vieira da Silva

Nicolas de Staël. b St Petersburg, 1914. **d** Antibes, 1955. **Red Bottles**. 1955. Oil on canvas. **h**73 × **w**100 cm. **h**28¾ × **w**39⅜ in. Private collection

Steen Jan

The Christening Feast

A proud father holds his new-born child while friends
and relations gather round to gossip, admire the baby and
to partake of the christening feast being prepared by the
three women on the right of the painting. This happy, bustling
tableau accurately depicts a typical scene in a seventeenth-
century Dutch household. In the foreground, however,
the artist has painted broken eggs, a well-known symbol of
mortality. This is to remind us of the death that waits for
everyone, even at the celebration of a birth. Steen was one

of the most popular of all Dutch genre painters. A pupil of
Jan van Goyen, he initially painted landscapes but went on
to depict scenes of middle-class life. The son of a brewer,
he supplemented his artist's income from 1654 by becoming
an inn-keeper. It is certain that this and many other paintings
were influenced by the merrymaking he saw at that time.

► Dou, Van Goyen, Van Ostade, De Troy, Watteau

Jan Steen. b Leiden, c1626. d Leiden, 1679. **The Christening Feast**. 1664. Oil on canvas. **h**89 × **w**109 cm. **h**35 × **w**42¾ in.
Wallace Collection, London

Steichen Edward

The Pond – Moonlight

A row of shadowy trees, back-lit by the rising moon, is reflected in the soft, dreamy, still surface of a pond. Representative of Steichen's preference for capturing scenes in partial darkness or twilight, *The Pond – Moonlight* is a masterpiece of early pictorial photography. Committed to showing that the camera could be used for more than documentation, in his photography Steichen experimented with a variety of novel techniques, including pouring liquids on camera lenses and shaking the camera during exposure.

His expressive, painterly images were central in establishing the status of photography as a fine art medium. Predating the widespread introduction of colour photography, the current example was reworked by hand using light-sensitive gums. Only three prints of *The Pond – Moonlight* are known to exist. Each version – printed using different photographic techniques, and under the supervision of Steichen – is unique.

► Eliasson, Grimshaw, Le Gray, Monet, Stieglitz

Edward Steichen. b Bivange, 1879. **d** West Redding, CT, 1973. **The Pond – Moonlight**. 1904. Platinum, cyanotype, and ferroprussiate print. **h**38.7 × **w**48.2 cm. **h**15¼ × **w**19 in. Museum of Modern Art, New York, NY

Stella Frank

Kastura

This massive wall-relief is constructed from sections of brightly painted aluminium which have been fixed to a rectangular base. Stella has skilfully balanced the monumental quality of the work with the apparent freedom of its support, offered by a discreet curved grille structure which permits the spectator to see through to the wall behind. The three-dimensional abstract cut-outs challenge the traditional confines of the picture plane as their freedom of construction permits no defined edges. The work shows a number of influences. One of these is Minimalism, demonstrated in the use of mass-made material and the industrial method of enlarging a maquette which was hand-made by the artist. Another is Abstract Expressionism, evident in the freely applied paint. Stella's wide range of work includes highly innovative prints, some of which are monumental in size.

► Caro, Hofmann, Johns, Kelly, Pollock, Ryman

Frank Stella. b Malden, MA, 1936. **Kastura**. 1979. Oil and epoxy on aluminium and wire mesh with metal tubing. h292.1 × w233.7 cm. h115 × w92 in. Museum of Modern Art, New York, NY

Stieglitz Alfred

The Flatiron Building

The recently completed Fuller Building towers high above the trees of a snow-covered Manhattan park. Nicknamed the Flatiron because of its distinctive shape, the narrow verticality of the office block (at the time the tallest in New York) is carefully framed by the tree in the foreground. It forms a stark contrast between nature and the man-made. In his photography of this period, Stieglitz was influenced by the designs of Japanese woodcut prints – evident in the current image in the silhouetted tree and the tiny figures passing through the park. As well as helping to establish photography as a fine art medium, Stieglitz actively promoted the work of avant-garde painters and sculptors. As founder and manager of the 291 gallery in New York, he organized some of the earliest exhibitions in America of numerous contemporary European artists, including Picasso, Matisse and Brancusi. Stieglitz was married to the American painter Georgia O'Keefe.

► Frank, Hiroshige, O'Keefe, Sheeler, Steichen

Alfred Stieglitz. b Hoboken, NJ, 1864. d New York, NY, 1946. **The Flatiron Building**. 1903. Gravure on vellum. **h**32.8 × **w**16.8 cm. **h**12⅞ × **w**6⅝ in. Museum of Modern Art, New York, NY

Still Clyfford

Painting, 1944

The black expanse of paint, applied with a palette knife, is interrupted by a jagged red line which cuts through it like lightning and is in turn sliced through with yellow and white streaks of fire. Typical of Still's style, this work was painted at a formative period when most of his contemporaries were working with archaic themes, literary subjects and mythical creatures. Still broke new ground with his thickly applied abstract areas of colour which appear like slabs of earth, and his diverse textural surfaces. His paintings were an early example of Abstract Expressionism which, reminiscent of the Surrealists and their 'automatic' painting, sought to release the creativity of the unconscious mind by emphasizing spontaneity. Like his fellow Abstract Expressionists Jackson Pollock, Barnett Newman and Mark Rothko, Still tended to work on a massive scale. From 1961 he lived in rural Maryland in virtual isolation from the New York art world which he scorned.

► Burri, Motherwell, Newman, Pollock, Rothko

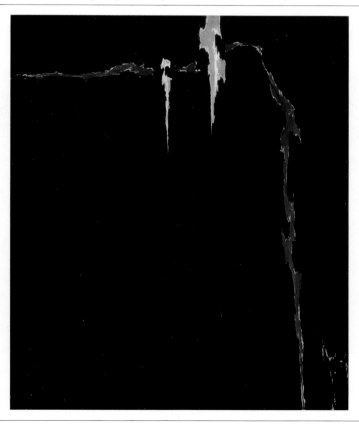

Clyfford Still. b Grandin, ND, 1904. **d** Baltimore, MD, 1980. **Painting, 1944.** 1944. Oil on canvas. **h**264.5 × **w**221.4 cm. **h**104⅛ × **w**87¼ in. 515
Museum of Modern Art, New York, NY

Struth Thomas

Pantheon, Rome

Thomas Struth began as a painter, studying under Gerhard Richter in the early 1970s, before coming under the influence of photographers Bernd and Hilla Becher and their precise black-and-white studies of industrial structures. Many of his photographs communicate a sensibility to art history and the fine arts. Unusually for Struth, this image was staged and artificially lit, but it echoes the theme of his 'Museum' series, in which he photographed the tourist-filled museums and churches – pictures of people looking at pictures,

underlining the relationship between the viewer and the work. The Pantheon was first a temple to all the gods, then a Catholic church, and is now a tourist attraction. Struth's interest in history and in the presence of 'the sublime in the mundane' are clearly exhibited here, as is what critics have called the 'double subject' of his photographs – not merely the place and the people shown, but also the 'mental spaces', the events and ideas that shaped them.

► Becher, Gursky, Richter, Wall

Thomas Struth. b Geldern, 1954. **Pantheon, Rome**. 1990. Chromogenic colour print. **h**183.5 × **w**238 cm. **h**72¼ × **w**93¾ in. Private collection

Reflecting the ideals of the country over which he presided, his portrait of the first President of the United States is an honest representation executed without pomp. The muted colours sublimate the background in favour of the face, which is painted with great realism to reflect Washington's trustworthy and capable character. At the beginning of the eighteenth century Stuart was the most celebrated American portraitist. He lived to paint all of the first five Presidents. During the American War of Independence he lived in London and studied with the history painter Benjamin West, a fellow countryman. He returned to North America with an understanding of the portraiture of the British artists Thomas Gainsborough and Sir Joshua Reynolds, which he infused with a characteristically frank American approach. His portrait of Washington is used as the basis for the President's image on dollar bills.

► Gainsborough, Houdon, Lawrence, Reynolds, West

Gilbert Stuart. b North Kingstown, RI, 1755. d Boston, MA, 1828. **George Washington**. 1795. Oil on canvas. **h**76.8 × **w**64.1 cm. 30¼ × 25¼ in. Metropolitan Museum of Art, New York, NY

Stubbs George

Mares and Foals in a Landscape

With a deft and steady hand, Stubbs has faithfully and delicately reproduced the horses and the foliage above them. The minutely observed details, such as the tail hairs and hooves, the individual colouring of each horse and the delicately painted leaves of the oak tree, have been captured with remarkable accuracy. Stubbs earned an unrivalled reputation as a painter of horses, dogs and wild animals for noble patrons. Primarily an anatomist, his depictions of horses came from hours of observation and scientific study.

To assist him in his work Stubbs drew detailed anatomical studies from every conceivable angle, thoroughly examining the bone and muscle structure of horses in order truly to understand how to portray the mechanics of movement. His paintings are more than mere scientific studies, however, and show a masterful understanding of design and composition.

► Agasse, Audubon, Bassano, Marc, Marini

George Stubbs. b Liverpool, 1724. **d** London, 1806. **Mares and Foals in a Landscape**. 1763-8. Oil on canvas. **h**99.1 × **w**158.8 cm. **h**39 × **w**62½ in. Tate, London

Sutherland Graham

Portrait of Somerset Maugham

William Somerset Maugham, the English novelist and playwright, sits against a vibrant yellow wall looking quietly dignified. His features are almost caricature-like, especially his jowls and jutting chin, which appears to push his head out of the picture, towards the viewer. Sutherland was one of the leading British artists of the twentieth century. He painted many landscapes and religious paintings and in his later years became a successful portrait painter of the famous. His semi-abstract style, balanced by a superb draughtsmanship, always followed the laws of realism but his use of amorphous-like forms and agonized imagery, which had a strong influence on the young Francis Bacon, created much controversy. When this painting first appeared it was criticized for making Maugham look like 'an old Chinese madam in a brothel in Shanghai' and his famous portrait of Winston Churchill was so loathed by Lady Churchill that she destroyed it following her husband's death.

► Auerbach, Bacon, Freud, Organ

Graham Sutherland. b London, 1903. **d** London, 1980. **Portrait of Somerset Maugham**. 1949. Oil on canvas. **h**137 × **w**64 cm. **h**54 × **w**25⅛ in. Tate, London

Tamayo Rufino

Woman with Red Mask

Painted in glowing sensuous colours, a woman – wearing a red mask and with a mandolin on her knees – sits upright on a chair. The sense of mystery surrounding the figure is enhanced by the intentionally limited yet vibrant colour-range of the artist's palette. Tamayo was deeply influenced by Pablo Picasso and the Cubists. This is one of the first works executed by the artist incorporating angular outlines. It is very likely that it was painted straight onto the canvas without the use of a preparatory sketch. Like his fellow Mexican

Diego Rivera, Tamayo combined Mexican folk themes with a diversity of European styles, chiefly Cubism, Surrealism and Expressionism, and consistently demonstrated the pictorial values of the Mexican people and their folklore. This was painted before Tamayo's first visit to Europe in 1950. He also worked for a long time in the USA.

► Jawlensky, JC Orozco, Picasso, Rivera, Severini

Rufino Tamayo. b Oaxaca, 1899. **d** Mexico City, 1991. **Woman with Red Mask**. 1940. Oil on canvas. **h**121 × **w**85 cm. **h**54⅞ × **w**33¾ in.
Private collection

Tanguy Yves

The Invisibles

Abstract, biomorphic shapes climb rapier-shaped objects and appear to float upwards against a menacing, clouded sky. Tanguy was much influenced by de Chirico and joined the Surrealist movement after meeting the Surrealist writer and guru André Breton in 1925. The title and theme of this painting refer to Breton's idea of the existence of invisible animals who have escaped man's sensory frame of reference by means of camouflage. The painting's visionary quality is a clear illustration of Surrealist imagery: Tanguy has allowed

his subconscious to 'create' these beings, whose existence is uncertain yet impossible to disprove. This is a common theme in much of his Surrealist art, where amorphous creatures tend to inhabit barren, hallucinatory landscapes of the mind. Neatness and precision were deeply ingrained in his personality, and these qualities are also evident in his paintings.

► Bellmer, Brauner, De Chirico, Matta, Miró

ves Tanguy. b Paris, 1900. d Woodbury, CT, 1955. **The Invisibles**. 1951. Oil on canvas. h98.5 × w81 cm. h38⅞ × w31⅞ in. Tate, London

Tàpies Antoni

Grey Ochre

The thick surface of this painting has been incised and lacerated by the artist to evoke feelings of desolation and anger, and a sense of the ravages of time. It represents a physical, forbidding obstacle yet also conveys a certain beauty and elegance through its partial destruction. Tàpies experimented with different materials, combining oil paint with crushed marble, powdered pigment or latex, for example, to create huge desolate surfaces which he covered with creases, incisions and fossil-like imprints. A sense of elapsed time, intimated by the ravaged surface of the paint, apparently worn by a duration greater than that of the artist's hand, is one of the key elements that gives Tàpies' work its enduring power. Tàpies is widely considered the most important post-war Spanish artist and his work has achieved international acclaim. Later in his career he produced heavy clay sculptures of everyday objects such as baths and chairs.

► Burri, Dubuffet, Fautrier, Hartung, Riopelle

Antoni Tàpies. **b** Barcelona, 1923. **d** Barcelona, 2012. **Grey Ochre**. 1958. Oil and marble dust on canvas. **h**259.7 × **w**194.3 cm. **h**102¼ × **w**76½ in. Tate, London

Created in a moment of political enthusiasm, this leaning spiral was designed to be twice the height of the Empire State Building in New York and to have alternately rotating central sections. Space is ordered into fragmented compartments that are formally related to each other as in a mathematic equation. Tatlin was the founder of Constructivism, a Russian art movement that grew out of artistic experiments with abstraction but later turned to more utilitarian concerns. He advocated the idea of the 'artist engineer' and saw the primary role of Constructivism as fulfilling social needs. Tatlin also created a series of hanging relief constructions using a variety of materials such as wood, metal, glass and wire and employing exclusively geometric forms. This masterpiece, a symbol of Constructivist ideals combining the disciplines of sculpture and architecture, was never constructed. The piece illustrated is a modern replica of the original model.

▶ Gabo, Lipchitz, Malevich, Popova, Rodchenko, Sheeler

Vladimir Tatlin. **b** Kharkov, 1885. **d** Novodevichye, 1953. **Monument to the Third International.** 1919. Wood, iron and glass. 420 cm. **h**165⅓ in. Musée National d'Art Moderne, Paris

Teniers David

The Archduke Leopold's Gallery

A patchwork of paintings is on display in this gallery belonging to the Regent of the Spanish Netherlands, Leopold Wilhelm of Austria. There was a widespread growth in art collecting during the seventeenth century when aristocrats, noblemen and rich bankers accumulated vast numbers of works by contemporary artists and Renaissance masters. This room is crammed with recognizable paintings by Titian, Peter Paul Rubens, Raphael, Giorgione and Annibale Carracci, among others, many of which are now in the

Kunsthistorisches Museum in Vienna. The large, bearded figure of the Archduke is being shown the paintings by Teniers himself who was appointed Court Painter to the Archduke and Keeper of his paintings. He made many copies of the pictures in the collection and produced over 2,000 paintings, of every kind of subject, during his long and prolific career.

► Bazille, Dou, Metsu, Vermeer, Zoffany

David Teniers (The Younger). b Antwerp, 1610. **d** Brussels, 1690. **The Archduke Leopold's Gallery.** 1651. Oil on canvas. **h**127 × **w**162.6 cm. **h**50 × **w**64 in. Petworth House, Petworth

Thiebaud Wayne

Various Cakes

A display of delicious cakes has been painted in bright, lurid colours – making them appear even more false and synthetic than they are in reality. Thiebaud's early work was devoted to the depiction of all-American foods, especially pies, which he executed in an impassive, realist style using thick, juicy pigment. He often repeated variations of a single object as though they were on display in a cafeteria, presenting them almost as ritualistic offerings to the spectator. The blatant rendition of the unmistakable consumer items, concentrating on their texture, colour and shape, makes the painting an important example of American Pop Art. Thiebaud worked as a freelance cartoonist and illustrator in New York before deciding to become an artist at the age of 29. He now lives and works in Sacramento and San Francisco and concentrates more on the landscapes and cityscapes of his immediate environment.

► Dine, Morandi, Oldenburg, Rosenquist, Wesselmann

Wayne Thiebaud. b Mesa, AZ, 1920. **Various Cakes**. 1981. Oil on canvas. **h**63.5 × **w**58.4 cm. **h**25 × **w**23 in. Private collection

Tiepolo Giovanni Battista

The Meeting of Antony and Cleopatra

The Egyptian queen Cleopatra, dressed and coiffed in eighteenth-century finery, is greeted by the Roman general Marc Antony, while her barge floats behind her on a pretty sea. The story of the star-crossed lovers was a popular one in the eighteenth century; this depiction, one of a pair of vast frescos on an operatic scale, decorates the ballroom of the Palazzo Labia, once the home of wealthy Venetian textile merchants. The work magnificently illustrates the skills for which Tiepolo, arguably the greatest painter of his day, was

fêted: his theatrical celebration of ancient history and myth, in paintings full of brilliant colour, full of artistic caprice (*capriccio*) and imaginative fantasy (*fantasia*). For large frescos such as this, Tiepolo collaborated with Girolamo Mengozzi Colonna, a specialist in architectural illusions who also designed operatic stage sets. Together they created works of art that fulfilled the eighteenth-century view of painting as theatre – a story acted out in pictures.

► Amigoni, Boucher, Fragonard

Giovanni Battista Tiepolo. b Venice, 1696. **d** Madrid, 1770. **The Meeting of Antony and Cleopatra.** c1750. Fresco. **h**650 × **w**300 cm. **h**256 × **w**118 in. Palazzo Labia, Venice

Tinguely Jean

Trophy of Chasse-Le-Golem

This ramshackle sculpture is created from a variety of incongruous objects that have been welded together. The addition of an electric motor enables the static object to be transformed into a living work of art. When the electric current is turned on the wheel slowly begins to revolve, clanking and groaning the assemblage into action. The motile quality of the sculpture connects it to the Kinetic Art movement, based on the idea that light and movement can create a work of art, while its use of manufactured items together with its exhibitionist nature make it a late example of New Realism. Throughout the late 1950s and 1960s Tinguely created self-propelling, edible and musical machines. He is renowned for organizing a number of public events which involved the construction and rapid deterioration of machines, the most famous of which occurred at the Museum of Modern Art in New York in March 1960.

▶ Calder, Klein, Nauman, Viola

Jean Tinguely. b Fribourg, 1925. d Bern, 1991. **Trophy of Chasse-Le-Golem**. 1990. Iron, steel, rubber band, electric motor and hippopotamus jaw-bone. h177.8 cm. h70 in. Gimpel Fils Gallery, London

527

Tintoretto Jacopo

The Annunciation

The Archangel Gabriel, accompanied by numerous cherubs, violently bursts in upon a startled Virgin. In contrast to contemporary scenes of the Annunciation, the Virgin is represented living in a house of decayed splendour and she is dressed in simple clothes. Outside, Joseph works on his carpentry, unaware of the dramatic events occurring within. Little is known of Tintoretto's early years but he claimed to be a pupil of Titian. He is representative of the Italian Mannerist style and his work is marked by its outstanding sense of drama, achieved by the use of unexpected viewpoints and striking perspective, extreme contrasts of scale and brilliant effects of light and colour. Tintoretto became the embodiment of Venice's cultural energies; during his long and prolific career he left the city just once, for a brief visit to the city of Mantua.

► Fra Angelico, Bordone, Martini, Palma Vecchio, Titian

Jacopo Tintoretto. b Venice, 1518. **d** Venice, 1594. **The Annunciation**. 1583/7. Oil on canvas. **h**421.6 × **w**544.8 cm. **h**166 × **w**214½ in.
Scuola Grande di San Rocco, Venice

Tissot James

Holiday (The Picnic)

Yellowing leaves of the chestnut tree shade a group of well-dressed men and women who are enjoying a picnic beside a pond. The canvas, painted in the backyard of Tissot's London house, which was near Lord's Cricket Ground, sparkles with colour and exquisite detail. In his depiction of daily life in an outdoor setting, Tissot shares the realism of French artists such as Édouard Manet. His style is also akin to that of the Impressionists, who were working at exactly the same time as Tissot, but his paintings differ in their crystal-clear vision and

elegant society subjects. Tissot often focused on finely dressed women, adorned in the latest fashions and casting a spell over their men. His paintings have recently enjoyed a well-deserved revival in popularity; for many years they were regarded as the epitome of late Victorian vacuous and decadent society.

► Dufy, Fragonard, Manet, Renoir, Sargent

James Tissot. b Nantes, 1836. **d** Buillon, 1902. **Holiday (The Picnic).** c1876. Oil on canvas. **h**76.2 × **w**99.4 cm. **h**30 × **w**39⅛ in. Tate, London

Titian

Diana and Actaeon

Sumptuous colour, captivating movement and harmonious composition mark this as a masterpiece of Titian's work. The young prince Actaeon has stumbled upon Diana, the virgin huntress and symbol of chastity (identified by her crescent moon), who is bathing with her nymphs in a remote grotto in the forest. Diana is so incensed at Actaeon for having glimpsed her divine nudity that she transforms him into a stag, to be hunted to death by his own hounds. Titian's imaginative powers reached their zenith in the interpretations of ancient legends and Classical myths which he created during the 1550s at the instigation of Philip II of Spain, his principal patron. Titian was the greatest of Venetian painters. During his last years his style developed a very free handling which almost anticipated the work of the Impressionists in its rendering of colour and light and ease of form.

► Guercino, Lotto, Rubens, Veronese, Vouet

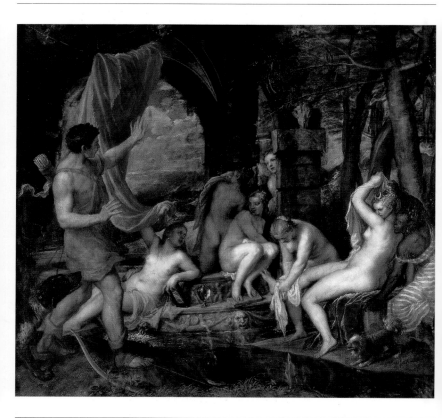

Titian (Tiziano Vecellio). b Pieve di Cadore, c1488/9. d Venice, 1576. **Diana and Actaeon**. 1556-9. Oil on canvas. h184 × w202 cm. h72½ × w79½ in. National Gallery of Scotland, Edinburgh

Tobey Mark

White Journey

The surface of the paper swarms with minute abstract signs and scratches of paint creating an apparently chaotic pattern. The frenetic rhythm created by these intricate and delicate lines is typical of Tobey's style; it is this sophistication and dynamism that has made his work so popular with collectors. Although the composition is similar to paintings created by members of the Abstract Expressionist movement, notably Jackson Pollock, Tobey pursued a unique parallel development partly through the influence exerted on him by the Far East. He was deeply influenced by Chinese calligraphy and was one of the first American intellectuals to become interested in Zen Buddhism. Tobey achieved international recognition in the 1950s as one of America's foremost painters and enjoyed a strong reputation in Europe which was developed by his highly successful and influential Swiss dealer Ernst Beyeler.

► Kline, Marden, Pollock, Riopelle, Ryman

Mark Tobey. b Centerville, WI, 1890. **d** Basel, 1976. **White Journey.** 1956. Distemper on paper. **h**113.5 × **w**89.5 cm. **h**44⅜ × **w**35¼ in. Beyeler Collection, Basel

Toulouse-Lautrec Henri de

Dance at the Moulin Rouge

The Moulin Rouge, a dance hall in Montmartre, Paris, still exists today. At the end of the nineteenth century it was a popular venue for middle-class gentlemen who, accompanied by women of dubious character, were entertained by lively spectacles and dancing. Toulouse-Lautrec, now one of the best known of all nineteenth-century French artists, frequently spent whole nights at the Moulin Rouge, drinking and sketching music-hall stars and members of royalty who wandered into this dark, somewhat seedy world. The

rapid style and visible brushstrokes of this work show that Toulouse-Lautrec painted it as he sat in the dance hall. An aristocrat by birth who was severely disabled in childhood, Toulouse-Lautrec always felt isolated from society by his deformity. He preferred the company of the marginal classes and surrounded himself with the actresses, clowns, dancers and prostitutes who became the subjects of his paintings.

▶ Degas, Laurencin, Renoir, Seurat, Severini

Henri de Toulouse-Lautrec. b Albi, 1864. **d** Gironde, 1901. **Dance at the Moulin Rouge.** 1890. Oil on canvas. **h**115 × **w**150 cm. **h**45¼ × **w**59 in. Philadelphia Museum of Art, Philadelphia, PA

De Troy Jean-François

The Oyster Lunch

Inside a sumptuously decorated Rococo palace, a group of wealthy nobles, dignitaries and aristocrats are enjoying a lavish feast of oysters and champagne. De Troy's rich use of colour, influenced by the work of Titian and Peter Paul Rubens, and the meticulous attention paid to details, such as the crusty bread on the table, the baskets of oysters in the foreground and the bottles left to cool in the ice-cabinet, give a sense of the extravagance of this event. The painting was commissioned by Louis XV for his private apartments at Versailles. De Troy enjoyed a great reputation in his day as a skilful decorator, portraitist and genre painter. He spent much time in Italy enjoying social as well as artistic activities and in 1738 he was appointed director of the Académie de France in Rome. There he is alleged to have died of grief upon receiving the terrible news that he was to return to France and leave behind the woman he loved.

► De Heem, Kalf, Lucas van Leyden, Rubens, Titian

Jean-François de Troy. b Paris, 1679. **d** Rome, 1752. **The Oyster Lunch.** 1735. Oil on canvas. **h**186 × **w**120 cm. **h**73¼ × **w**47¼ in.
Musée Condé, Chantilly

Turner J M W

Snowstorm: Steamboat off a Harbour's Mouth

A small ship is caught in the heart of a storm and struggles to keep afloat. The sea, snow and smoke from the ship's engine have been sucked together in a swirling mass of lashing wind and spray which Turner has captured with all the unhesitating spontaneity of a modern abstract artist. Well ahead of his time, few people understood Turner's work during his lifetime but today he is regarded as the most masterly of British painters. His work in watercolours and oils captures the magical effects of light, colour and movement in pale glowing colours. Towards the end of his life Turner showed particular interest in the conflict between the elements. In order to paint this picture and capture the true atmospheric effects of a storm, he is said to have had himself tied for four hours (at the age of 67) to the bridge of a steamboat, sailing from Harwich in bad weather.

► Church, Cozens, Friedrich, Martin, Monet, Pollock

J M W (Joseph Mallord William) Turner. b London, 1775. d London, 1851. **Snowstorm: Steamboat off a Harbour's Mouth**. 1842.
Oil on canvas. **h**91 × **w**122 cm. **h**36 × **w**48 in. Tate, London

Tuymans Luc

Lumumba

Patrice Lumumba looks thoughtfully towards us, yet his focus appears to be elsewhere. An independence leader and the first legally elected prime minister of the former Belgian Congo (now the Democratic Republic of the Congo), Lumumba was assassinated following a coup in 1961. Belgium-born Tuymans was inspired to paint the portrait following investigations into his own country's involvement in the overthrow of Lumumba's government. Considering the contentious nature of its subject, it is difficult to extract any clear meaning or comment from the work – perhaps itself a reflection on the hidden events of the country's colonial past. Like many of Tuymans' works, *Lumumba* is based on a photograph, yet rather than working directly from the image the artist painted it from memory. By creating a subtle distance between his painting and the perceived objective accuracy of photographs, the artist questions the role of images in shaping histories and our formation of memories.

► Close, Dumas, Katz, Neel, Richter

Twombly Cy

Bolsena

Random scrawls and scribbles animate the surface of this painting, recalling the freedom of expression of a child's drawing. The loose, unordered style allows forms and images to emerge and melt in the imagination. The system of lines has its own meaning, although to the observer this meaning may be unclear. The artist's paintings are deliberately meant to represent something unintelligible or inexplicable. Twombly was totally unhindered by traditional formulae and ideas of composition. Like the Abstract Expressionists, he favoured a formless, prosaic response to the creative impulse. Lines, scribbles and lettering form the substance of his pictures, usually on a white or partially white background. Twombly showed some affinity with Jackson Pollock, although his works are more disjointed and deliberately provocative and lack Pollock's innate lyricism and harmony.

► Basquiat, Dubuffet, De Kooning, Pollock, Schwitters

Cy Twombly. b Lexington, VA, 1928. **d** Rome, 2011. **Bolsena.** 1969. Oil, coloured chalk and pencil on canvas. **h**200 × **w**240 cm. **h**78¾ × **w**94½ in. Private collection

Uccello Paolo

The Battle of San Romano

This is one of three panels illustrating the Florentine victory over the Sienese at the Battle of San Romano in 1432 which was commissioned by the wealthy banker Leonardo Bartolini Salimbeni in Florence. This image shows the leader of the Florentine troops, Niccolò da Tolentino, mounted on a white horse during battle. Uccello was fascinated with how to depict space and became absorbed in the art of perspective and foreshortening. This is particularly evident in the corpse dressed in battle armour and the broken lances which lie on the ground as if they have fallen on the receding lines of the picture's perspective. Uccello's genius, however, expresses itself here above all in the profusion of detail and curious forms and in the marvellously fanciful background. A painter, mosaicist, decorator and master of marquetry, Uccello was one of the most skilled and conscientious craftsmen of his time.

► Castagno, Gozzoli, Masaccio, Piero della Francesca

Paolo Uccello. b Florence, 1397. d Florence, 1475. **The Battle of San Romano**. c1438–40. Tempera on panel. h182 × w320 cm. h71½ × w126 in. National Gallery, London

Utamaro Kitagawa

Lovers

Two lovers, their faces almost hidden, embrace in a room that opens out onto a garden terrace. Their naked bodies can be glimpsed through the delicate swathes of the patterned silk kimonos. The print is composed of flowing lyrical lines which gracefully delineate the forms and there is no shading or suggestion of depth. A master of the woodblock print, Utamaro was the first Japanese artist to become well known in the West. In contrast to the Western tradition, he was not concerned with creating natural poses and depth but flat shapes and patterns. His approach greatly influenced artists such as Edgar Degas in the nineteenth century, who were seeking a new mode of expression and a fresh way of viewing the world. This print comes from *The Poem of the Pillow*, probably the finest of Utamaro's erotic albums. Sumptuously produced with an astonishing collection of colour prints these books also depicted amusing scenes from Japanese legends.

► Cellini, Degas, Gauguin, Hokusai, Rodin, Whistler

Kitagawa Utamaro. b Tokyo, 1753. **d** Tokyo, 1806. **Lovers** (from *The Poem of the Pillow*). 1788. Woodblock print on paper. **h**24.8 × **w**37.4 cm. **h**9¾ × **w**14¾ in. Victoria and Albert Museum, London

Utrillo Maurice

Flag Over the Town Hall

An air of tranquillity dominates this simple view of a small town where a group of people are gathered outside the white wall of a garden. Only the French flag flying above the town hall is painted in bright colours, punctuating the otherwise earthy tones of the canvas. Utrillo was the illegitimate son of Suzanne Valadon, an artist and model of Auguste Renoir, Edgar Degas and Henri de Toulouse-Lautrec. She persuaded her son to start painting in 1902, following one of the many bouts of alcoholism and drug abuse which afflicted him throughout his life, and he revealed a remarkable talent. An intense feeling of atmosphere dominates many of Utrillo's paintings, enhanced by his unerring use of colour and tone. Utrillo produced mostly townscapes, including many street scenes of the area around Montmartre. These became so popular that they have spawned countless imitations and forgeries.

▶ Degas, Dufy, Foujita, Laurencin, Renoir

Maurice Utrillo. b Paris, 1883. **d** Dax, 1955. **Flag Over the Town Hall.** 1924. Oil on canvas. **h**98 × **w**130 cm. **h**38½ × **w**51⅛ in.
Musée de l'Orangerie, Paris

Vallotton Félix

Landscape with Trees

The sinuous curves of the trunks and the clumped masses of leaves are the focal point of this study. The trees have been reduced to their simplest shapes and the pattern created by the trunks is silhouetted against the evening sky. Vallotton was a member of the Nabis, a group of late nineteenth-century French painters, including Pierre Bonnard, Édouard Vuillard and Maurice Denis, who were deeply influenced by Paul Gauguin's use of Symbolism and flat, pure colour. Like the Impressionists, Vallotton was interested in painting nature from life. He did not share their wish to capture the fleeting moment, however, preferring to focus on the tangible shapes and colours before him. The result is a meticulous and sometimes cruelly realistic style through which his landscapes often achieve great depth of feeling. After visiting an exhibition of Japanese prints in 1890, Vallotton became a prolific wood-engraver.

► Bonnard, Denis, Gauguin, Hiroshige, Pissarro, Vuillard

Félix Vallotton. b Lausanne, 1865. **d** Paris, 1925. **Landscape with Trees.** 1911. Oil on canvas. **h**100 × **w**73 cm. **h**39½ × **w**28¾ in.
Musée des Beaux-Arts, Quimper

Vasarely Victor

Pal-Ket

Purple, blue and green geometric shapes, arranged in a chessboard pattern, appear to float on and distort the canvas. Through using opposing systems of perspective and violently contrasting colours, Vasarely deliberately created an optical illusion, giving an impression of movement to the painting. The shapes appear to shift under the eye. Vasarely was one of the pioneers of Optical art, known by the nickname Op Art, which developed alongside Pop Art in the 1960s. Op Art is based on the idea that the artist, whether painter or sculptor, can persuade the spectator to see visual illusions by creating optical effects. Vasarely was fascinated with the concept of perception and how real or ambiguous images can be created by using exact geometric principles. Hungarian by birth, Vasarely moved to Paris in 1930. His work in painting, sculpture, prints and drawings is always abstract in nature and relies on the manipulation of visual sensations for its effect.

► Albers, Flavin, Hayter, Riley, Vieira da Silva

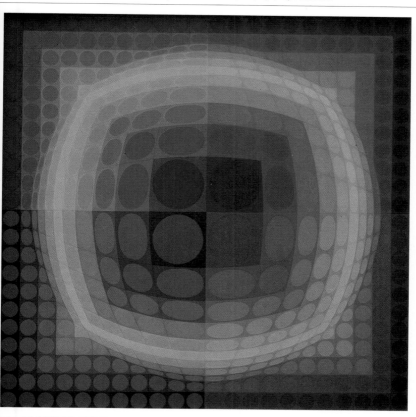

Victor Vasarely. b Pécs, 1906. d Paris, 1997. Pal-Ket. 1973–4. Acrylic on canvas. h151.2 × w150.8 cm. h59½ × w59⅜ in.
useo de Bellas Artes, Bilbao

Velázquez Diego de Silva y

Las Meninas

The five-year-old daughter of King Philip IV of Spain, the Infanta Margareta-Teresa, stands in the centre of the canvas surrounded by her retinue of maids and dwarfs. Velázquez has depicted himself on the left of the canvas, painting a huge portrait of the King and Queen who can be seen reflected in the mirror directly behind the Infanta's head. Velázquez is one of the greatest portraitists of all time and this work is considered the masterpiece of his final years. He was little influenced by other artists although in 1623 he was appointed Court Painter in Madrid and became aware of Titian's work in the Spanish Royal Collection. He also met Peter Paul Rubens, who shared his studio for a short while and is believed to have inspired Velázquez to visit Italy. Velázquez had a deeply sensitive appreciation of character. His painting is characterized by freely painted harmonies of colour and tone and a unique blend of realism with atmosphere.

► Goya, El Greco, Kirchner, Rubens, Titian, Zurbarán

Diego de Silva y Velázquez. b Seville, 1599. **d** Madrid, 1660. **Las Meninas.** 1656. Oil on canvas. **h**318 × **w**276 cm. **h**127 × **w**108½ in. Museo del Prado, Madrid

Vermeer Jan

Woman in Blue Reading a Letter

A solitary young woman stands in her blue morning jacket, reading a letter – surely a love letter. The quiet intensity of the scene is emphasized by her tight, drawn-in pose, and subliminally by the high-backed chairs that seem to stand as protective barricades. The negative space of the pale walls is carefully designed to embrace the figure, creating both physical and emotional depth. The wall-map acts as foil to the severity of the composition, its swirling patterns suggesting the turmoil of the reader's thoughts. This work is one of the most spartan of all Vermeer's paintings, but it is also one of his most sumptuous, for the expensive ultramarine pigment used for the figure's jacket was also incorporated into the chairs, the bar and ball holding the map, and even into the blue-grey walls. Vermeer was influenced by the domestic genre scenes of his contemporary Pieter de Hooch, but Vermeer's paintings, such as this one, suggest a deeper self-reflection and atmospheric mood.

► Dou, Van Eyck, Hammershøi, De Hooch, Metsu

Veronese

The Finding of Moses

The silk brocade of the dress worn by the principal figure is so crisp and delicately portrayed it is tempting to touch its luxurious folds. Venetian artists are often said to have been great colourists, but Veronese was arguably the greatest of them all. The deep blues, ochres and transparent greys of the dresses display his fondness for rich hues and bright tones. In this painting, a late work, his finesse with loose brushwork can also be admired. Veronese specialized in vast narrative paintings of biblical, allegorical or historical subjects in which he included crowds of elegantly dressed figures, accompanied by courtiers, musicians, soldiers, horses, dogs or monkeys, set within monumental architecture or against verdant landscapes. As his name implies, Veronese originally came from Verona, but he settled in Venice where he was particularly influenced by the work of Titian.

► Giorgione, Tiepolo, Tintoretto, Titian

Veronese (Paolo Caliari). b Verona, 1528. **d** Venice, 1588. **The Finding of Moses**. c1580. Oil on canvas. **h**57 × **w**43 cm. **h**22½ × **w**17 in. Museo del Prado, Madrid

Verrocchio Andrea del

Bust of a Woman Holding a Nosegay

The crisply carved folds of this woman's dress have been created by the hand of a master sculptor. The head looks out and slightly upwards and the hands, which were the first to be shown in a portrait bust, are placed irregularly on the breast. Although Florentine artists of the Renaissance were proficient in most media and techniques, Verrocchio's versatility was exceptional. Trained as a goldsmith, he was also a painter, a sculptor and one of the most accomplished draughtsmen of the Renaissance. He led an extremely active workshop in Florence which trained a number of artists to be goldsmiths, sculptors and painters. These included Perugino amongst others, but the most famous product of Verrocchio's tutelage was Leonardo da Vinci. Leonardo's famous drawings and paintings are founded on his master's style and his hand can be recognized in some of Verrocchio's own paintings and sculpture.

▶ Algardi, Donatello, Ghirlandaio, Leonardo, Perugino

Andrea del Verrocchio. b Florence, 1435. **d** Venice, 1488. **Bust of a Woman Holding a Nosegay.** c1480. Marble. **h**60 cm. **h**23⅔ in.
Museo Nazionale del Bargello, Florence

Vieira da Silva Maria Elena

Checkmate

Juxtaposed squares, rectangles and lozenges in soft muted colours and random diagonal formations have been woven together to form a net-like pattern. A system of perspective has been employed so that the central chessboard pattern slowly recedes into the distance. The surface of the canvas appears to twist and turn but the painting is not disturbing. Instead, the use of gentle light and soft colours creates a peaceful and mysterious atmosphere. Vieira da Silva was a French painter of Portuguese origin. She initially worked as a sculptor with Émile Bourdelle and then after moving to Paris studied painting under Fernand Léger and engraving with Stanley William Hayter. During the 1930s she developed into an abstract painter and produced a multitude of works which are characterized by a use of muted colour contrasts, often dominated by tones of greys and whites, and of linear structures placed against amorphous grounds.

► Bourdelle, Hayter, Léger, Poliakoff, Riopelle, Vasarely

Maria Elena Vieira da Silva. b Lisbon, 1908. **d** Paris, 1992. **Checkmate.** 1949–50. Oil on canvas. **h**89 × **w**116 cm. **h**35 × **w**45⅝ in.
Private collection

Vigée-Lebrun Marie-Louise-Élisabeth   Self-portrait

The artist sits holding a handful of paintbrushes and a palette, her right hand at work on one of the portraits which made her famous. Painted on a neutral ground, this self-portrait is brought to life by the artist's radiant features and the rich, triumphant red of the material around her waist, which is repeated on the tip of one of the brushes. Vigée-Lebrun was noted for her wit and beauty and a sense of her charming personality is evoked by her peaceful gaze and engaging smile. Although she was aged 35 at the time of this painting, she has painted a somewhat idealized image of herself in the full bloom of innocent youth. This soft, flattering style of portraiture made Vigée-Lebrun highly sought-after throughout Europe. She excelled in portraits of women and children; her reputation as an artist was confirmed when she executed a portrait of Queen Marie-Antoinette who she is said to have painted 25 times.

► Anguissola, Greuze, Mengs, Ramsay, Sherman

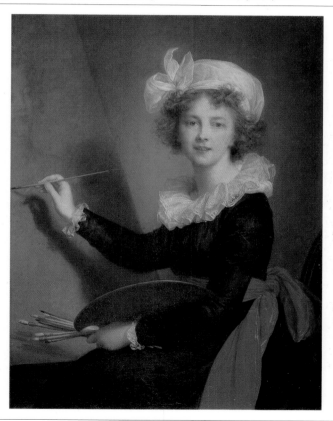

Viola **Bill**

The cycle of life – from the birth to the death of man, from the explosion of the universe to total darkness – is condensed into the space of a day in this video installation. A sequence of images flows across a TV screen in 12-hour cycles, computer programmed to repeat twice a day, seven days a week. A disembodied voice can also be heard reciting excerpts from Walt Whitman's poem *Song of Myself*. The images are strongest at night but washed out by daylight when only the voice can be discerned. Projecting itself like a glowing icon,

the work's title further suggests that this is a devotional object: it is almost a contemporary Book of Hours, as each image relates to a specific time of day. Viola takes state-of-the-art video, audio and information technology into visionary realms, drawing on sources ranging from ancient mystic teachings to the LA riots of 1992 in an exploration of the unconscious mind.

▶ Beauneveu, Flavin, Limbourg, Marclay, Merz, Nauman, Rist

Bill Viola. b New York, NY, 1951. **To Pray Without Ceasing**. 1992. Video/sound installation. Colour video image rear-projected on translucent screen, projected in two 12-hour cycles, 24 hours a day. Private collection

Vlaminck Maurice de

The Circus

Sweeping brushstrokes of blues, oranges and pinks have reduced the circus tent and the surrounding houses to their most basic shapes. The perspective has been distorted to create a highly expressive and turbulent scene. Largely self-taught, Vlaminck was a professional racing cyclist until he met the artist André Derain in 1900 and began to paint seriously. In 1905 he became a member of the Fauve movement, a group of artists including Derain, Henri Matisse and Georges Rouault who exhibited together at the Paris Salon. With its distorted forms and flat patterns painted in violent colours, their work created such a furore that a critic dubbed them *les fauves* ('the wild beasts'). Some of Vlaminck's best work dates from the Fauve period. Initially influenced by the expressive quality of Vincent van Gogh, from 1907 Vlaminck became interested in the work of Paul Cézanne and he rejected bright colours in favour of sombre tones and more traditional subjects.

► Derain, Van Gogh, Heckel, Kirchner, Pechstein

Maurice de Vlaminck. b Paris, 1876. d Rueil-la-Gadelière, 1958. **The Circus**. 1906. Oil on canvas. h60 × w73 cm. h23⅔ × w28¾ in. Private collection

Vouet Simon

Time Overcome by Hope, Love and Beauty

Two young women with deadly looking weapons threaten an old man who desperately tries to protect himself. The scythe that lies beneath him and the hourglass that he holds in his left hand tell us that he is Time. The two women are personifications of Hope (on the left) and Beauty (on the right); together with Love (the cherub Cupid) they are seen triumphing over Old Man Time, suggesting that Youth, Beauty and Love are eternal and immutable values. The extravagant gestures of all three figures, and the billowing

movement of the draperies as the figures push and pull against each other, are hallmarks of Vouet's classicized Baroque style of painting. His richly coloured and highly dramatic compositions, mostly of religious and allegorical works, set the artistic fashion in seventeenth-century Paris. He painted many large decorative paintings, most of which have unfortunately been destroyed.

► Bronzino, Caravaggio, Carracci, Domenichino, Poussin

Simon Vouet. b Paris, 1590. **d** Paris, 1649. **Time Overcome by Hope, Love and Beauty**. 1627. Oil on canvas. **h**107 × **w**142 cm. **h**42⅛ × **w**55⅞ in. Museo del Prado, Madrid

Vuillard Édouard

Two Schoolboys

Two young boys play in a public garden which Vuillard has turned into a magical dream world. The mottled bands of chalky browns and greens create speckled harmonies of colour, giving a delicately vibrant effect to the surface. Vuillard was commissioned to paint a series of nine large panels for the dining-room of a smart Parisian town house. The panels were an amalgam of his impressions of the parks of Paris, where he sketched children playing and recorded the patterns of shadow and light. Vuillard was inspired by the shimmering techniques of Georges Seurat and Claude Monet and these panels in particular recall the paintings Monet executed of his garden at Giverny. Vuillard is renowned for his use of bold but sensual colour harmonies, a feeling for textures and patterned shapes, and for having the rare ability to evoke atmosphere and reveal the mysterious charm of everyday life.

► Bonnard, Denis, Homer, Monet, Seurat, Vallotton

Édouard Vuillard. b Cuiseaux, 1868. **d** La Baule, 1940. **Two Schoolboys**. 1894. Distemper on canvas. **h**212 × **w**96 cm. **h**83½ × **w**37¾ in. 551
Musées Royaux des Beaux-Arts de Belgique, Brussels

Wadsworth Edward

The Beached Margin

Nautical objects are assembled in bold relief against a marine background of sea and sand. The painting displays Wadsworth's technical ability and meticulous draughtsmanship: the minutest details are depicted with startling detail and the difficult medium of egg tempera (which he mixed himself) is handled skilfully. The imaginative quality of these fantastic geometric creations gives an intellectual pleasure much greater than is offered by the usual still life. The painting comes close to Surrealism in its use of unexpected juxtapositions and in its hyper-real clarity. During the First World War, Wadsworth joined the Royal Navy and designed and painted camouflage for ships. This led to an overriding passion for the sea and ships, recurrent subjects in his work. As well as his paintings and engravings, Wadsworth also executed a number of mural decorations, notably for the liner *Queen Mary*.

► Carrà, De Chirico, Dali, Lewis, Nash

Edward Wadsworth. b Cleckheaton, 1889. **d** London, 1949. **The Beached Margin**. 1937. Tempera on linen. **h**71.1 × **w**101.6 cm. **h**28 × **w**40 in. Tate, London

The complete title of this work is *Slavery! Slavery! Presenting a GRAND and LIFELIKE Panoramic Journey into the Picturesque South. Slavery of 'Life at "Ol" Virginny's Hole" (sketches from Plantation Life)'. See the Peculiar Institution as Never Before! All Cut from Black Paper by the Able Hand of Kara Elizabeth Walker, an Emancipated Negress and Leader of her Cause.* The paper cut-outs have a cartoon-like prettiness at first glance, until a closer look reveals a hellish world of sex, slavery and sadism under a crescent moon and dripping Spanish moss. Racism dominates Walker's work, and she draws inspiration from historical fiction, actual slave narratives, minstrel shows and other artists, such as Adrian Piper. Yet within the story that she tells, whether in cut-out silhouettes, drawings or film, is a chaos of contradictory ideas. She plays with stereotypes, but the standard dualities – victim and predator, strong and weak, black and white – are unreliable and shifting, forcing the viewer to reconsider their own response.

► Frank, Perry, A Piper, Watteau

Kara Walker. b Stockton, CA, 1969. **Slavery! Slavery!** 1997. Paper cut-outs on wall. **h**3.7 × **w**25.9 m. **h**12 × **w**85 ft. As installed at the Hammer Museum, Los Angeles, CA

Wall Jeff

In a room sits a man. Above him, hanging from the ceiling, are hundreds of light bulbs (1,369 to be precise). Based on a close reading of the Prologue of Ralph Ellison's 1952 novel *Invisible Man*, Wall's photograph depicts the basement in Harlem to which the book's central character, overwhelmed by feelings of invisibility due to his race and social standing, retreats. Whilst this work is inspired by a fictional story, many of Wall's large-scale photographic tableaux are based on everyday events witnessed by the artist. The antithesis of the candid snapshot, Wall creates meticulously staged reconstructions, spending many months working with a cast of actors and assistants until he feels he has been able to capture accurately his experience of the original event. Before constructing the set for the current image in his Vancouver studio, Wall visited numerous basements in Harlem to ensure historical accuracy.

► Becher, Gursky, Richter, Wall

Jeff Wall. b Vancouver, BC, 1946. **After 'Invisible Man' by Ralph Ellison, the Prologue**. 1999–2000. Transparency in lightbox. **h**174 × **w**250.5 cm. **h**68½ × **w**98½ in. Öffentliche Kunstsammlung, Basel

Wallis Alfred

St Ives with Godrevy Lighthouse

A town with its harbour and lighthouse is depicted from a high vantage point. The work has a flat, naïve quality, recalling images created by children; it is completely free from optical mannerisms such as perspective or a vanishing point. Much of the brown card has been left visible, forming the colour-base of the painting to which only pale blue, green, white and black have been added. Wallis worked as a fisherman and only started to paint in his 60s. Discovered by Ben Nicholson, he became the most influential British 'primitive' artist through

his effect on the St Ives painters in Cornwall. His paintings, mainly of ships, coasts and harbours, were not drawn from life but were spontaneous responses to remembered or imagined experiences. Wallis often worked on pieces of cardboard cut into irregular shapes, a technique that was later emulated by the more sophisticated St Ives painters.

► Gontcharova, Lowry, B Nicholson, H Rousseau, Wadsworth

Alfred Wallis. b Devonport, 1855. **d** Madron, 1942. **St Ives with Godrevy Lighthouse.** c1935. Oil and pencil on card. **h**17 × **w**95 cm. **h**6⅔ × **w**37⅓ in. Private collection

555

Warhol Andy

Marilyn

Marilyn Monroe's face is presented as an impenetrable mask in bright luminous colours. Published in ten different colour combinations, using the impersonal screenprinting process, the multi-coloured surface portrays her image in a startlingly lurid manner. Monroe is probably Warhol's most famous subject. He used a publicity still as the basis for this and other pictures of her, presenting us with a frozen image that reinforces the universal power of the most tragic of all Hollywood's personae. The portrayal of Monroe as a product of mass culture, packaged for the public as if a consumer item, connects this work to the American Pop Art movement. Warhol, a painter, graphic artist and film-maker, was a cult figure during the 1960s. He remained, however, an intensely private man, saying: 'If you want to know everything about me, just look at the surface of my paintings, it's all there, there's nothing more.'

► De Kooning, Lichtenstein, Neel, Oldenburg, Rosenquist

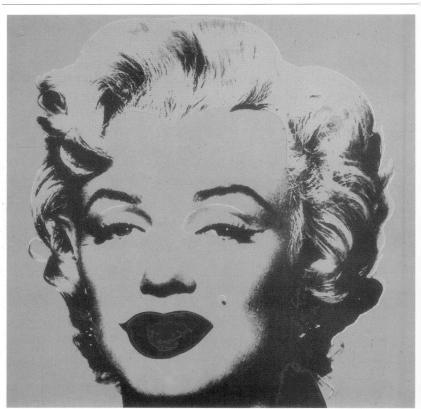

Andy Warhol. b Pittsburgh, PA, 1928. **d** New York, NY, 1987. **Marilyn.** 1967. Screenprint on paper. **h**91.5 × **w**91.5 cm. **h**36 × **w**36 in. Museum of Modern Art, New York, NY

Waterhouse John William

The Lady of Shalott

The luminosity of this painting and its careful attention to detail heighten the emotion in this episode from Tennyson's poem. One can almost feel the cool of the day as the doomed girl begins her final journey, her haunting beauty dominating the scene. Apart from telling a tragic story, this work is an exercise in closely observed landscape painting – each rush and reed has been painstakingly depicted and the same attention has been paid to rendering the reflections on the water. Waterhouse was a follower of the Pre-Raphaelite artists and continued their interest in depicting scenes from poetry and mythology. He displayed an unerring feel for the dramatic moment, combined with a fine sense of composition and superb painting technique. Above all, though, it is the beauty of his wistful female models (in this instance believed to be the artist's wife) that has ensured the artist's lasting popularity.

▶ Alma-Tadema, Burne-Jones, Leighton, Martini, Millais

John William Waterhouse. b Rome, 1849. **d** London, 1917. **The Lady of Shalott**. 1888. Oil on canvas. **h**153 × **w**200 cm. **h**60½ × **w**78¾ in. Tate, London

Watteau Antoine

The Embarkation for Cythera

Verdant trees, plump cherubs, amorous couples and sumptuous silks grace this vision of graceful gallantry. The festooned statue of Venus and Cupid emphasizes that this Arcadia is devoted to the pursuit of love. There is nothing overtly erotic about the painting, but it has an undeniable sensuousness. Like many of Watteau's paintings, its magical frivolity contains an undercurrent of melancholy – the wistful backward glance of the central figure seems to hint at the transitoriness of pleasure. Watteau championed this type

of idyllic, festive landscape and brought the genre, which is typical of the Rococo style, to a height never reached before. He held a great admiration for the work of Peter Paul Rubens, who was the main influence on his work. Watteau's sophistication and elegance are inherently French and reflect the pomp and extravagance of the Court of Louis XIV at Versailles.

► Boucher, Fragonard, Giorgione, Lancret, Rubens

Antoine Watteau. b Valenciennes, 1684. **d** Nogent-sur-Marne, 1721. **The Embarkation for Cythera**. 1718. Oil on canvas. **h**130 × **w**192 cm. **h**51¼ × **w**75½ in. Schloss Charlottenburg, Berlin

Weight Carel

Daisy in the Garden

The mundane and depressing atmosphere of a typical urban back garden in south-west London on an overcast day has been effectively captured in this precisely painted work. Weight's open brushwork heightens the intensity of the scene; in a mysterious way the bleak and dingy surroundings appear to amplify the loneliness of the human figure as she walks through the garden towards us. The originality of the painting is demonstrated by Weight's instinctive feeling for the subject. An individualist who avoided the commercial art world, Weight painted personal visions of everyday life imbued with an uneasy feeling. His figures are painted in urban and rural environments and are often running or walking briskly towards the edge of the painting, as if escaping. His compositions sometimes include spirits, ghosts and witches. Most of his scenes are set in south London where he lived and worked.

▶ Freud, Rego, Sickert, Spencer

Carel Weight. b London, 1908. **d** London, 1997. **Daisy in the Garden**. c1962. Oil on canvas. **h**76.2 × **w**101.6 cm. **h**30 × **w**40 in.
Private collection

Wesselmann Tom

Great American Nude No. 27

The erotic image of the spread-legged nude, her features left blank to avoid any suggestion of a portrait, is juxtaposed with cut-out images of milkshakes and ice-creams. This was one of a series of works created by Wesselmann in the early 1960s in which he combined nudes depicted in flat, clear colours with collage elements taken from brochures or posters. The painting's importance lies in its conspicuous demonstration of sexual freedom, painted at a time when nudity in the American media was still rare, and its inclusion of the direct imagery of the new consumer age. This manipulation of erotic symbols and the popular culture of a consumer society connects the painting to the American Pop Art movement. From 1983 Wesselmann abandoned painting on canvas and turned to the construction of cut-out metal wall-pieces derived from felt-tip or ink drawings.

► Boucher, Hamilton, Jones, Polke, Rosenquist, Warhol

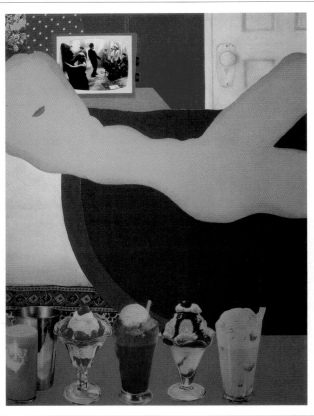

Tom Wesselmann. b Cincinnati, OH, 1931. **d** New York, NY, 2004. **Great American Nude No. 27.** 1962. Enamel paint and collage on panel. **h**122 × **w**91.4 cm. **h**48 × **w**36 in. Mayor Gallery, London

West Benjamin

William Penn's Treaty with the Indians

William Penn is depicted making peace with the Lenape Indians, a landmark in the creation of the Pennsylvania colony. This somewhat romanticized and inaccurate representation of a documented event, in which West has imposed a Classical composition on figures in contemporary dress, is typical of the historical paintings which earned West his international reputation. West was born in North America and studied in Italy before setting up as a portraitist in London in 1763. He had enormous flair and versatility

and achieved great popularity. He was appointed Historical Painter to George III and later replaced Sir Joshua Reynolds as President of the Royal Academy. West was an extremely influential figure in the development of American art. His studio in London was the training ground for some of the most important American artists of the period, including Gilbert Stuart.

► Cole, Hicks, Reynolds, Stuart

Benjamin West. b Swarthmore, PA, 1738. **d** London, 1820. **William Penn's Treaty with the Indians**. 177½. Oil on canvas.
h192 × **w**273 cm. **h**75½ × **w**107¾ in. Pennsylvania Academy of the Fine Arts, Philadelphia, PA

Weston Edward

Shells

Two shells have been arranged to create a sensuous sculptural form. The intensely lit photograph marries an almost scientific scrutinizing of the shells with a suggestive, poetic play on the sinuous lines and the subtly contrasting textures. Famed for his images of the female nude, Weston's still lifes of shells and vegetables are often suggestive of parts of the naked body, their biomorphic forms taking on a barely veiled eroticism. In turn, the contorted and truncated positioning of the model in some of his nude studies appears to be based on the natural forms captured in his still lifes. Weston claimed that subject matter was immaterial. Born in Chicago, at the age of twenty-one Weston moved to California. His cool, clean-edged photographs of the landscape and fauna of the region were recognized as epitomizing a modern, specifically West Coast, aesthetic. In the current work there are obvious formal similarities with the abstract sculptures of Constantin Brancusi and Jean Arp.

► Arp, Celmins, Kertész, Hepworth

Edward Weston. b Highland Park, IL, 1886. d Carmel, CA, 1958. **Shells**. 1927. Gelatin silver print. h25.4 × w20.3 cm. h10 × w8 in.
Center for Creative Photography, University of Arizona

Van der Weyden Rogier

The Descent from the Cross

The sorrowful demeanour of these figures makes this one of the most moving paintings in the history of art and one of the masterpieces of fifteenth-century painting. Details such as the tears falling from Mary Magdalene's nose and the way the fabric of her dress pulls across her back as she clasps her hands in sorrow show that Van der Weyden was a keen observer of life. Yet the overall composition, with the figures crowded into the front of the picture frame as if they were standing in a shallow box, looks more like a tableau in a Christmas pageant than an accurate description of a real event. Van der Weyden's early work shows the influence of Jan van Eyck and Robert Campin. He achieved great success during his lifetime and his influence was extremely profound for a long time after his death, not only on painting in northern Europe but throughout the Continent.

► Bouts, Campin, Van Eyck, Grünewald, Memling

Rogier van der Weyden. b Tournai, c1399. **d** Brussels, 1464. **The Descent from the Cross**. c1435/8. Oil on panel. **h**220 × **w**262 cm. **h**86⅝ × **w**103⅛ in. Museo del Prado, Madrid

Whistler James Abbott McNeill

Symphony in White No. 2: Little White Girl

This beautiful, sultry portrait of Whistler's mistress Joanna Hiffernan is a study in the arrangement of closely related shades of white. The asymmetrical composition with its off-centre, cropped figure, and the direct lighting which reduces the painting to a coloured pattern, clearly shows Whistler's interest in Japanese art. This influence, which was most marked in the 1860s when Japanese art was finding its way into Europe, is also alluded to in the depiction of the fan, the porcelain jar on the mantelpiece and the cherry blossom.

The technique of silhouetting a figure against an almost blank ground remained Whistler's standard practice. In a reaction against the domination of subject matter in Victorian painting, Whistler emphasized the aesthetic nature of his work by calling his paintings 'nocturnes' and 'symphonies'. Whistler's growing fame as a wit and eccentric coincided with his decline as a painter.

► Chase, Degas, Goya, Hiroshige, Hokusai, Manet

James Abbott McNeill Whistler. b Lowell, MA, 1834. **d** London, 1903. **Symphony in White No. 2: Little White Girl.** 1864. Oil on canvas. **h**76 × **w**51 cm. **h**30 × **w**20 in. Tate, London

Whiteread Rachel

Ghost

This is a plaster-cast of a room from a Victorian London town house. The negative space of the interior has taken on a solid form as everything has been inverted – the soot-stained cavity of the fireplace has become a protrusion; light-switch and door-handle sink into the dusty surface. Created by taking a series of moulds from sections of the room's walls and then assembling them on a steel frame, Whiteread has created a striking memorial to a once-inhabited space. Evocative of the paired-down forms of Minimalism, as well as the monumental presence of a nineteenth-century mausoleum, *Ghost* transforms the specific and recognizable features of a domestic room into a poetic monolith. In 1993 Whiteread developed the theme of *Ghost* further, producing a concrete cast of the interior of a complete house in East London. A public debate ensued when local authorities demolished the work in the following year.

► Becher, Christo, LeWitt, Matta-Clark, Segal

Rachel Whiteread. b London, 1963. **Ghost.** 1990. Plaster on steel frame. **h**269 × **w**355.5 × **d**317.5 cm. **h**105⅞ × **w**139⅞ × **d**125 in.
National Gallery of Art, Washington, DC

Wilkie Sir David

The Letter of Introduction

A young man presents a letter of introduction to an elderly gentleman who regards him with suspicion, an attitude reflected also by his dog. This subtle painting appeals to our emotions by juxtaposing the lad's ruddy, innocent country candour with the old man's sidelong glance of sceptical distrust, redolent of a life spent in the corrupt city. Wilkie specialized in painting moralizing domestic scenes in the manner of seventeenth-century Dutch genre painters such as Adriaen van Ostade and Gerard ter Borch. Much of Wilkie's art found its parallel in the poetry of Robert Burns and Sir Walter Scott. The son of a minister in Fife, Wilkie forms with Henry Raeburn and Allan Ramsay the great triumvirate of Scottish art. Perhaps the greatest eulogy given to him was when J M W Turner painted *Burial at Sea* to express his grief at learning about Wilkie's death while coming home from a trip to the Middle East.

► Ter Borch, Lely, Van Ostade, Raeburn, Ramsay, Turner

Sir David Wilkie. b Cults, Fife, 1785. **d** At sea (off Malta), 1841. **The Letter of Introduction.** 1813. Oil on panel. **h**61 × **w**50 cm. **h**24 × **w**19¾ in. National Gallery of Scotland, Edinburgh

Wilson Richard

View in Windsor Great Park

Bucolic hills inhabited by cattle and deer contribute to this pastoral scene. The horizon is so low the clouded sky has become as important to the picture as the land below. The rustic peasants are not here to tell a story but, like the livestock, are an integral part of the landscape. Wilson worked in London before travelling to Italy where he studied landscapes with imaginary Classical ruins and was greatly inspired by the Italian paintings of Claude Lorrain and Nicolas Poussin. Upon returning home, he continued to paint Italianate landscapes but used the scenery of England and Wales and views of country houses (he received many commissions) as the subjects of his paintings. These paralleled the grand schemes of the landscape designer Capability Brown. Wilson was one of the Founder-Members of the Royal Academy in London, but he never achieved commercial success in England and died in obscurity.

► Agasse, Claude, Pannini, Poussin, Zuccarelli

Witz Konrad

The Miraculous Draught of Fishes

The rather ungainly but solid and meticulously depicted figures animate the sun-lit landscape of the shores around Lake Geneva. Close attention has been paid to the naturalistic detailing of the rocks and plants in the shallows (visible through the water) and the trees and houses in the background. The scene is striking for its clarity and is especially important in the history of art for containing one of the first attempts by a painter to record faithfully the landscape before him. Witz is considered to be one of

the greatest of the pre-Renaissance German artists. Little is known of his life although his strongly realistic style suggests that he must have been familiar with the work of the Flemish painter Jan van Eyck. The luminous spaciousness of the hills which recede into the distance show that Witz was capable of rendering perspective, although this was not achieved by mathematical calculation.

► Van Eyck, Master of Moulins, Patinir, Schongauer

Konrad Witz. b Rottweil, c1410. **d** Basel, c1446. **The Miraculous Draught of Fishes.** 1444. Oil on panel. **h**132.1 × **w**153.7 cm. **h**52 × **w**60½ in. Musée d'Art et d'Histoire, Geneva

Wood Grant

American Gothic

Wood was captivated by a simple Gothic-style cottage he saw in a small town in southern Iowa and created this picture around the image which it evoked in his mind. He used his sister and his dentist as models for the couple standing in front of the plain white house. Wood was accused of satirizing Midwestern values, but he insisted that he made the work as a homage to the down-to-earth, Puritan dignity found in small-town America. A lifelong resident of Iowa, Wood was one of the exponents of Regionalism, a form of realism common in North America during the 1930s and based on the desire that American artists should end their cultural dependence on Europe by finding inspiration for their art in their local surroundings. His crisp, firmly delineated and precisely modelled style was derived from the Gothic and early Renaissance masters Wood had studied in Europe in the 1920s.

▶ Van Eyck, Hopper, Martini, Wyeth

Grant Wood. b Anamosa, IA, 1892. d Anamosa, IA, 1942. **American Gothic**. 1930. Oil on board. **h**74.3 × **w**62.4 cm. **h**29¼ × **w**24½ in.
Art Institute of Chicago, Chicago, IL

Wool Christopher

Apocalypse Now

'Sell the house. Sell the car. Sell the kids. Find someone else. Forget it. I'm never coming back. Forget it.' Captain Colby writes this final letter to his wife in the Vietnam War film *Apocalypse Now*. The message evokes a bleak vision – no family, no home, none of the attachments of normal life. The lines became a mantra in the late 1980s (a time of recession and decline in America), a simple, reductive hymn to moving on, leaving the past behind. But for Wool, the work was not just a statement, but also a painting. He breaks up the words so that reading them requires decipherment, like the forms and colours and textures of a painting. He deliberately reveals the process of the work's creation through the drips and splashes left by painting through stencils, and the patterning of the letters and spaces. Even the act of reading the message is part of the process – a confrontation of the grammatical, visual, emotional and imaginary.

► Holzer, Kruger, Nauman, Warhol

Christopher Wool. b Chicago, IL, 1955. Apocalypse Now. 1988. Alkyd and flashe on aluminium and steel. h213.4 × w182.9 cm. h84 × w72 in. Museum of Modern Art, New York, NY

Wright of Derby Joseph

An Experiment on a Bird in the Air Pump

A group gathers to watch an experiment in which a white cockatoo is slowly starved of oxygen in a vacuum pump. The emotions of those present are mixed. Whilst the couple to the left appear indifferent to the events unfolding – being more engrossed in each other – the sight of the bird suffocating is all too distressing for the two young girls towards the right of the composition. In contrast, the scientist in the centre confronts the viewer, challenging them to watch further. Such demonstrations were fairly common during the late eighteenth century, often touring town halls, or as is perhaps the case with the present painting, taking place in the homes of the inquisitive wealthy. By intensely illuminating the scene, Wright creates a dramatic *chiaroscuro* effect, more often found with religious or historical subject matter. The artist produced numerous paintings depicting the industrial and scientific advancements of his day.

► Brown, Caravaggio, Correggio, Honthorst

Joseph Wright of Derby. b Derby, 1734. d Derby, 1797. **An Experiment on a Bird in the Air Pump**. 1768. Oil on canvas. h183 × w244 cm. h72 × w94½ in. National Gallery, London

Wyeth Andrew

Christina's World

A young girl, seen from behind, sits in a field and gazes up at a farmhouse on top of the hill. A sense of melancholy and desolation is emphasized by the vast space between the figure and the distant houses. The finely depicted surface, executed in subdued tones but with a warm glow of bright sunlight, is typical of Wyeth's style which is characterized by a minute, precise realism, undoubtedly influenced by photography in its exactness of detail and the use of unusual viewpoints. His usual subjects are deserted landscapes and scenes conveying the conflicts of solitude but Wyeth adds a disturbing element by depicting such emotional themes in a highly detailed manner reminiscent of magazine illustration. Wyeth worked predominantly in the areas around Pennsylvania and Maine where he lived for most of his life. His work has tremendous popular appeal.

► Estes, Hopper, Richter, Sheeler, Wood

Andrew Wyeth. b Chadds Ford, PA, 1917. d Chadds Ford, PA, 2009. **Christina's World**. 1948. Tempera and gesso on panel. **h**82 × **w**121 cm.
h32¼ × **w**47¾ in. Museum of Modern Art, New York, NY

Yeats Jack Butler

The Basin in Which Pilate Washed his Hands

Slashing strokes of bright colour have been spontaneously applied in a loose, expressionistic manner. The passionate freedom of the artist's style and the bold approach to the subject are striking. The forms emerge and dissolve simultaneously from the indiscernible mass of the landscape background. Yeats was the son of a painter and the brother of the poet W B Yeats. He began his career as an illustrator and watercolour artist and did not begin painting in oils until 1915 at the age of 44. His style became increasingly

free and more violent in its use of colour. Yeats was greatly influenced by the Irish Troubles which were reflected in the subject matter of his later work. He was admired by his friend Oskar Kokoschka and his Expressionistic work draws a close parallel with that of the Austrian-born painter. Yeats' subject matter, however, remains entirely Irish.

► Appel, Gorky, Kokoschka, De Kooning, Kossoff, Pollock

ack Butler Yeats. b London, 1871. d Dublin, 1957. **The Basin in Which Pilate Washed his Hands**. 1951. Oil on canvas. 101.6 × w152.4 cm. **h**40 × **w**60 in. Waddington Galleries Ltd, London

Zhang Huan

Family Tree

From six separate photographs Zhang Huan stares out at the viewer. In each, the artist's expressionless face is adorned with Chinese writing. As we progress through the images his face becomes covered in more and more text, until eventually it is completely black with ink, his eyes made more intense in the process. In 2000 the Chinese-born artist invited three calligraphers to write text on his face. He told them what they should write – mainly extracts from traditional stories – and informed them that they must at all times 'keep a serious attitude'. The process lasted from morning to night, his face slowly following the shift from daylight to darkness. The artist notes that the work, a self-portrait, 'speaks about a family story' and pertains to ideas of determination and fate. Based in Shanghai and New York, Zhang Huan works across a wide range of media. The materials and symbols employed in his art often evoke spiritual and philosophical ideas associated with Buddhism.

► Abramović, Beuys, Cahun, Close

Zhang Huan. b Anyang, Henan Province, 1965. **Family Tree**. 2000. Serial self-portrait performance and calligraphy, New York, NY

Zhang Xiaogang

A Big Family

Resembling an old-fashioned studio portrait photograph, Zhang's painting includes a red-faced figure – an assertion of individuality among family members linked from heart to heart by blood-red drops. A splodge of colour tracks across all three faces and brings to mind a birthmark, with its social stigma, or the deterioration of aging film. Zhang grew up during China's Cultural Revolution (1966–76), and his *Family* paintings are inspired by the studio portraits of the time, which were typically laden with ideology (Mao jackets,

workmen's caps). His timeless figures, with their very subtle personal differences, illustrate the hugely important Chinese concept of family – immediate, extended, professional and social – and comment on the interaction of collective society, blood family and the individual. His look-alike figures allude to the mass-psychology of the Cultural Revolution, while the dreamy distortions, inspired by European Surrealism, impart a disturbing and complex emotional dimension to the work.

► Foujita, Katz, Laurencin, Ray

Zhang Xiaogang. b Kunming, Yunan Province, 1958. **A Big Family**. 1995. Oil on canvas. h179 × w229 cm. h70½ × w90 in.
Saatchi Gallery, London

Zoffany Johann

Marble athletes, nymphs, gods, goddesses and portrait busts are crammed into the library of this collector. Towneley, seated in the chair on the right, his faithful dog at his feet, is surrounded by fellow antiquaries and connoisseurs. The elegant library contains all the accoutrements of the cultured eighteenth-century gentleman with highly refined tastes. The bust of Clytie on the desk is said to have been such a favourite of Towneley's that he referred to it as his wife. German by birth, Zoffany travelled and studied extensively in

Italy. He met Towneley in Florence and the two men became close friends. Zoffany arrived in London in 1760 and set up as a painter of portraits, interiors and theatrical scenes. He was commissioned by the actor David Garrick to paint a number of conversation pieces and attracted the attention of King George III. In 1783 he went to India where he made his fortune painting portraits.

► Gainsborough, Hogarth, Kauffmann, Teniers

Johann Zoffany. b Frankfurt-am-Main, 1733. **d** London, 1810. **Charles Towneley's Library in Park Street.** 1783. Oil on canvas. **h**127 × **w**99 cm. **h**50 × **w**39 in. Towneley Hall Art Gallery, Burnley

Zorn Anders

Dagmar

Like a nymph watching her reflection in the rippled surface of a lake, this nude perches at the edge of the water absorbed in quiet thought. Her pink skin is echoed by the soft hues of the rocks and the greens of nature beyond. Although there is nothing overtly erotic about the figure, her voluptuous body beckons the viewer to look at the painting and there is something innocently sensuous about her pose. Zorn was also interested in printmaking; he made an etching of this composition and created prints of his paintings and sculpture.

One of the most cosmopolitan Swedish artists of his time, he travelled extensively in Europe and North America. Although his dancing brush and moving light and colour ally him to the Impressionists, his solid forms and the luminosity and natural feeling that can be seen in this work are characteristic of Scandinavian painting at the turn of the century.

► Boucher, Krøyer, Manet, Schiele

Anders Zorn. b Mora, 1860. d Mora, 1920. **Dagmar**. 1911. Oil on canvas. **h**88 × **w**63 cm. **h**34½ × **w**24¾ in. Private collection

Zuccarelli Francesco

Landscape with the Rape of Europa

A great softness and delicacy pervade this picturesque landscape animated with elegant female figures and playful putti. Zuccarelli has used the motifs of a Roman town and the story of the rape of Europa to evoke an Arcadian, pastoral landscape in the manner of the French landscape painter Claude Lorrain. Zeus, who has disguised himself as a bull, swims ashore to where Europa is playing. He entices her to climb onto his back and carries her away to Crete. This narrative scene has deliberately been relegated to the background and is almost incidental to the composition. Zuccarelli, a Florentine landscape painter, worked principally in Venice and London where he stayed for 17 years. His light and pleasing style of landscape painting inhabited by joyful peasantry was very popular in England. Zuccarelli was one of the Founder-Members of the Royal Academy in London.

► Allston, Claude, Piero di Cosimo, Wilson

Francesco Zuccarelli. b Pitigliano, 1702. d Florence, 1788. **Landscape with the Rape of Europa**. c1750. Oil on canvas. **h**131 × **w**168 cm. **h**51¼ × **w**66 in. Private collection

Zurbarán Francisco de

The Martyrdom of St Serapion

The unconscious body of the thirteenth-century British martyr Serapion hangs limply – roped, it seems, to the corners of the picture. He was said to have been crucified, dismembered and disembowelled, but Zurbarán portrays him without violence. Filling the canvas, his spotless white monk's habit hangs like a sheet, radiating a sublime light, while the human body just glimpsed underneath fades into the shadows. The artist's keen sense of the duality between the corporeal world and the realm of the spirit can be seen also in the fallen head, shadowed in death like his body, and yet supported, almost cradled, by the transcendent white habit. Zurbarán's use of a strong *chiaroscuro*, and the closeness of the figure to the picture plane, both heighten the emotional impact of the image. This artist's ascetic religious scenes were much in demand by churches and monasteries, but with the rise in popularity of a softer, sweeter style around mid-century, his reputation declined, and he died in poverty.

► Caravaggio, Murillo, Velázquez

Glossary of technical terms

Abstract

A form of art which does not seek to represent the world around us. The term is applicable to any art that does not represent recognizable objects, but refers particularly to forms of twentieth-century art in which the idea of art as imitation of nature has been abandoned. Piet Mondrian and Kasimir Malevich were among abstraction's early pioneers.

Acrylic

A synthetic paint, first used in the 1940s, combining some of the properties of oil and watercolour. It can be used to create a variety of effects from thin washes (see Morris Louis) to thick brushwork (see David Alfaro Siqueiros).

Anti-art

A term allegedly invented by Marcel Duchamp around 1914 to describe revolutionary forms of art. His addition of an obscene caption and a moustache to a copy of Leonardo da Vinci's *Mona Lisa* is an example of anti-art. The term also sums up many of the anarchic experiments of the Dadaists. It was later used by the Conceptual artists of the 1960s to describe the work of those who claimed to have retired altogether from the practice of art, or at least from the production of

works which could be sold. John Baldessari's exhibition of the ashes of his burnt paintings was seen as a typical anti-art gesture.

Antique, Classical

Terms referring to the civilizations of Ancient Greece and Rome, and their influence on the arts. Although sometimes considered interchangeable, the terms have slightly different meanings. 'The Antique' generally refers to the physical remains of the Greek and Roman world, such as architecture and sculpture; this was a particularly popular theme in the eighteenth century (see Giovanni Paolo Pannini and Francesco Zuccarelli). 'Classical' suggests a continuation of style or approach which can be traced directly to the Ancient world (see Jacques-Louis David and Hiram Powers).

Art Brut, Outsider Art

A French term, coined by Jean Dubuffet in 1947, which translates as 'Crude Art' but is often referred to as 'Outsider Art'. It is used to describe work produced outside the established art scene by the untutored (see Alfred Wallis), such as children, the insane and criminals. It is sometimes considered to be a more authentic form of expression.

Assemblage

The incorporation of three-dimensional, non-art materials and **found objects** into a work, originally inspired by the techniques of **collage**. The roots of assemblage lie in the early part of the twentieth century when Pablo Picasso began using real objects in his Cubist constructions – adding, for example, a spoon to his witty sculpture, *Glass of Absinthe* (1914). One of the earliest and most famous antecedents of assemblage was Marcel Duchamp's bicycle wheel attached to a stool, which he labelled the **'ready-made'**. Later, the Dadaists and Surrealists based their work on surprising conjunctions of disparate objects and images. The technique was particularly popular in the late 1950s, when artists such as Jim Dine made assemblage works, assimilating various materials, which included food and junk, into painting and sculpture. The growth of the use of assemblage in twentieth-century art reflects an anarchic approach to formal artistic practice.

Body Art

The use of the body itself as the raw material for art. This prime means of expression became widespread during the 1960s and 1970s and became one of the most direct ways of exploring issues of gender, sexuality and identity. Often it has tested the limits

of human endurance, as exemplified by artists such as Marina Abramovi'c and Zhang Huan. At times, it has involved gruesome acts of self-mutilation. Alongside **Performance**, **Land** and Conceptual art, it has taken art beyond the confines of the gallery and raised questions of ownership and permanence.

Chiaroscuro

Chiaroscuro means 'light-dark' in Italian and is used to describe the use of light and shade in a work of art, particularly when they are strongly contrasting. Caravaggio and Rembrandt are well known for their use of this technique, which they used for dramatic effect. The technique was particularly popular in the seventeenth century.

Cibachrome

Cibachromes are made from colour transparencies. The paper used has three silver-halide emulsion layers, each one of which is dedicated to one primary colour with its complementary. In the printing process, dyes are destroyed by chemical bleaching, leaving only those colours which make up the final image. Cibachrome is an Ilford product, marketed from 1963 onwards.

Classical see Antique

Collage, Photomontage

Collage, coming from the French world *coller* (meaning 'to stick'), is a technique in which pieces of paper, cloth and other miscellaneous objects are pasted onto a flat surface. The Cubists were the first to use collage as a serious artistic technique (see Juan Gris). Photomontage applies the same principles to the use of photographs; it was an important technique in Dadaism (see Raoul Hausmann and Hannah Höch) and Surrealism, and has also been used in Pop Art by artists such as Richard Hamilton.

Chromogenic colour print

Chromogenic colour prints are also known as C-type or dye-coupler prints (see Cindy Sherman and Stephen Shore). The chromogenic process was introduced in the 1950s and was, for most of the later twentieth and early twenty-first centuries the most common type of colour photographic printing. Chromogenic paper is coated with three emulsion layers sensitized to primary colours and protected by filters. The images are made from cyan, magenta and yellow dyes.

Dye-transfer print

A complex form of early colour printing in which a colour transparency was

photographed three times, in each case through a different filter. These new negatives were used to prepare further surfaces sensitive to the three subtractive primary colours: cyan, magenta and yellow. The dyes from these surfaces were then transferred one at a time onto gelatin-coated paper, producing very stable results (see William Eggleston). The process was introduced by the Jos Pé Company in 1925.

Figurative

Art which depicts recognizable images of the world around us. These images may be acutely accurate (see Chuck Close and Richard Estes) or heavily distorted (see Georges Braque). The term 'representational art' is used synonymously with figurative art.

Found Object

An everyday object, found by the artist and incorporated into a work of art. Also known as an *objet trouvé*, a found object often forms part of an **assemblage**, or is displayed on its own in an art context as a **ready-made**. Duchamp's exhibition of a real bicycle wheel attached to a stool is the original example of this art form, which was later taken up by the Dadaists (see Kurt Schwitters), the Surrealists (see Salvador Dalí), the Pop

artists (see Jim Dine) and the Nouveaux Réalistes (see Jean Tinguely). By elevating ordinary objects to the status of art, these artists challenged accepted ideas about what constitutes art.

Fresco

Meaning 'fresh' in Italian, fresco is a particular kind of wall painting in which pure pigment (colour) in powdered form is mixed with water and applied to a surface of wet, freshly laid lime plaster. This technique is known as *buon fresco*, or true fresco, to distinguish it from painting on dry plaster, known as *fresco secco*, which is far less durable as the pigment does not penetrate the substance of the plaster. Fresco painting is particularly appropriate to dry climates and was widely used in Italy from the late Middle Ages (see Fra Angelico and Giotto) up to the seventeenth century (see Pietro da Cortona).

Gelatin silver print

The standard contemporary monochrome print (see Ansel Adams and Eugène Atget). The paper (first introduced in 1882) is treated with the same gelatin silver emulsion used in the gelatin dry-plate process. By 1895 the gelatin silver print had replaced the albumen print.

Genre Painting

Painting that depicts scenes of everyday life rather than idealized or religious subjects. Genre painting was particularly popular in Holland in the seventeenth century, and artists often specialized in subjects such as tavern scenes (see Jan Steen), musical parties or simple interiors (see Jan Vermeer). The style became more prevalent elsewhere in the eighteenth century with the work of Jean-Baptiste-Siméon Chardin in France, Pietro Longhi in Italy and William Hogarth in England.

Gouache

Opaque **watercolour**, also known as body colour. The pigments (particles of colour) are bound together with glue; lighter tones are achieved by adding white (see Wifredo Lam). Gouache thus differs from transparent **watercolour**, where tone can be lightened simply by adding water. The thick texture of gouache can produce the same effects as oil paint, but it has the disadvantage of producing a final tone which, when dry, is lighter than it appears during application.

Happening

A fusion of art, theatre, and dance performed in front of an audience, and often involving participation.

The term was coined by the artist Allan Kaprow in 1959 and comes from the title of his multimedia event at the Reuben Gallery in New York, which was called 18 *Happenings in 6 Parts*. Originating in the Dadaist performances at the Cabaret Voltaire, Happenings attempted to bring art to the attention of a wider public. They were particularly used by the Fluxus group and some of the Pop artists, including Jim Dine, Claes Oldenburg, and Andy Warhol.

History Painting

A term identifying paintings that depict both actual and legendary events and figures of the past, particularly those of Classical antiquity and the Italian Renaissance. In Europe it was considered by the Academies to be the highest form of painting, a position reasserted by Sir Joshua Reynolds in his *Discourses* of the late-eighteenth century. The paintings often served as models for engravings that were reproduced in periodicals, which were a popular medium for conveying these historical themes to a wider public. Many of the paintings were executed on large canvases, the scale an appropriate expression of the subject's grandeur (see Eugène Delacroix). In American art, History Painting reached

its zenith in the early to mid-nineteenth century, paralleling the vogue for the European Grand Tour as a way to augment one's cultural and artistic education. While some artists concentrated on scenes from mythology, others adopted the grand format for paintings of specific scenes from recent American history (see John Singleton Copley and Benjamin West).

Illumination

Refers to the colourful decoration of manuscripts which was particularly popular from Medieval times to the Renaissance. The term is derived from the Latin word *illuminare*, meaning 'to adorn'. The manuscripts, made from parchment or vellum (treated animal skin), were written by hand and colourfully painted with miniatures, ornate capital letters and borders (see André Beauneveu, Pol, Jean and Herman de Limbourg). With the invention of printing the illuminated manuscript gradually went out of fashion and by the early sixteenth century relatively few were produced.

Impasto

This term has two meanings. It can refer to thickly applied pigment such as oil or acrylic, which often carries a visible brushstroke, or the marks of a palette knife. It also

refers to the technique of application, which artists have used to evoke emotion, to create drama through texture or emphasize their struggle with paint.

Installation

Originally used to describe the process of positioning works in the gallery setting, installation has also come to denote a distinct kind of art-making. In Installation Art, the individual elements arranged within a given space can be viewed as a single work and are often designed for a particular gallery (see Olafur Eliasson). Such works are known as **site-specific** and cannot be reconstructed anywhere else: the setting is as much part of the work as the things it contains. First appearing in the late 1950s and the early 1960s, when Pop artists such as Warhol began to design environments for **Happenings**, Installation Art typically involves theatrical dramatizations of space (see Ilya and Emilia Kabakov). Installations are frequently temporary, and, due to the fact that they are often unsaleable, most permanent installations are created specifically for major private collections.

Land Art, Earth Art

A form of art which uses natural elements. Arising in the mid-1960s as a

reaction against the growing commercialization of art, and the traditional context of the gallery or museum, Land Art (also known as Earth Art) entered into a direct dialogue with the environment. Some artists brought nature into the gallery, while others worked in the landscape, transforming it into **abstract** formations through ploughing, digging, levelling out and cutting away, which often required the use of bulldozers and mechanical excavators (see Michael Heizer). Often large-scale and situated in remote places, Land Art is frequently impermanent and subject to the erosive forces of nature. It therefore relies on photography as a means of documentation (see Robert Smithson).

Oeuvre

French word meaning the accumulated body of works produced by an artist over the course of his or her career.

Oil, Oilstick

Oil paint consists of pigment (colour) bound together with an oil medium, usually linseed oil. Its invention is usually credited to Jan van Eyck in the fifteenth century. Oil has the advantage over **tempera** of being slow to dry and therefore reworkable. It can be applied with a brush (see Anton Raphael Mengs) or a palette knife (see Jean-Paul

Riopelle), generally onto canvas, though certain woods (particularly poplar) were used in earlier periods. Oilsticks are a more recent invention, combining some of the properties of oil paint with those of **pastel** crayons (see Jean Michel Basquiat). They come in various sizes and can either be gripped in the hand like a pencil and applied 'neat', or diluted with a suitable medium.

Outsider Art see Art Brut

Pastel

A drawing material consisting of a stick of pigment (colour) bound together with resin or gum. It is generally used on paper and a variety of effects can be achieved, from sharply defined lines to soft shading. The powdery nature of pastel means that without careful handling the drawn image can quickly deteriorate. Pastel dates back to sixteenth-century Italy when colours were limited to black, white and terracotta red. Its heyday was in the eighteenth century when it became popular in portraiture; the medium underwent a revival in the nineteenth century with the work of the Impressionists see Jean-Étienne Liotard and Edgar Degas).

Performance Art

Closely related to dance and theatre, Performance Art is also linked to **Happenings** and **Body Art**. Its origins lie in the New York **Happenings** of the late 1950s, in which artists concocted theatrical contexts for their work in order to interact more immediately with their audiences. Performance Art was characterized in the 1960s by its use of the body as a sculptural element in work which took place over a period of time before a live audience. In the 1970s, artists influenced by popular culture, stand-up comedy and video began taking Performance Art out of the gallery and into theatres and clubs. Today the distinctions between Performance Art and other kinds of theatrical manifestations, whether they take place in the gallery or elsewhere, have blurred and they all come under the umbrella term of 'live art'.

Prints

A variety of techniques can be used to make prints, including woodblock, woodcut, engraving, etching, silkscreen, screenprint, and lithography. Woodblock and woodcut are known as 'relief methods' because the parts of the block which are to print black are left

in relief while the rest is cut away (see Katsushika Hokusai). Engraving and etching are 'intaglio methods', in which the design is engraved on a metal plate, or in the case of etching bitten into the plate by means of acid (see Stanley William Hayter). In silkscreen and other forms of screen printing, a stencil is attached to a screen (traditionally made from silk) stretched on a frame, and colour is forced through the unmasked areas of the screen (see Andy Warhol). With lithography, the design is drawn with wax onto a slab of stone and through the opposition of grease and water, areas which receive and reject the printing ink are separated (see Alphonse Mucha).

Psychoanalysis

A method of studying the mind through an exploration of the subconscious, psychoanalysis was developed by the Austrian psychiatrist Sigmund Freud in the early twentieth century, and focuses on dreams or slips of the tongue – moments when the mind expresses its true desires and fears. Psychoanalysis has been used in the visual arts to analyse the hidden meanings of images – meanings which may be different from the creator's

conscious intentions. Freud's ideas were particularly important to Dalí and the Surrealists, who attempted to free themselves from rational thought, creating works which sprang from the impulses of their subconscious.

Ready-made

A term originally coined by Duchamp to describe a **found object** selected by the artist and placed on its own in an art context. The most famous example is the urinal which Duchamp exhibited in its original state, calling it *Fountain*. His intention was to challenge the viewer's preconceptions about what created 'value' in art. He implied that it was not the object itself which carried artistic content, but the context in which the object was displayed. Many subsequent artists have incorporated ready-mades into their work, including Joseph Beuys and Mike Kelley, among others.

Sfumato

From the Italian word *fumo*, meaning smoke, 'sfumato' describes the blending of tones or colours so subtly that they melt into one another to produce a 'misty' effect, as Leonardo da Vinci put it, 'without lines or borders, in the manner of smoke'. Leonardo was himself one of the greatest exponents of this method, as can be seen in the soft gradations between light and shade in the *Mona Lisa*.

Site-specific

Art which is conceived and produced for a particular location or environment. The meaning of a site-specific work is often closely related to the place in which it is situated. Political, social or geographical aspects are taken into consideration and are intended by the artist to frame the viewer's experience and interpretation of the work (see Gordon Matta-Clark). In some cases, the intention of this approach has been an explicit rejection of the traditional context of the museum and other institutional spaces (see Jenny Holzer). It often takes the form of **installation**, **Land Art** (see Robert Smithson) and Public Art (see Richard Serra).

Stucco

A light plaster, mixed with powdered marble and glue and sometimes reinforced with hair or wire, used for sculpture and architectural decoration. It was most widely used from the sixteenth to the eighteenth centuries and is particularly suited to the ornate decorations of the Baroque and Rococo styles (see Francesco Primaticcio). Workers in stucco could produce a material similar

to marble by adding large quantities of glue and colour to the mixture. Good stucco is only distinguishable from marble in that it is warmer to the touch.

Sublime

An aesthetic value that describes the separate sensations of pleasure and awe combined with the feeling of personal vulnerability in the natural world. First set out by Edmund Burke in *A Philosophical Enquiry into the Origin of the Sublime and Beautiful*, published in 1757, the Sublime is most often associated with the Romantic spirit in art (see Caspar David Friedrich). At times evoked by showing nature at its most dramatic (see John Martin and J M W Turner), in the nineteenth-century the Sublime became a central theme in paintings of the expansive terrains of North America (see Albert Bierstadt and Thomas Cole).

Tempera

A paint made from ground pigment (colour) bound together with egg-yolk and water. This was the most common technique for the production of easel paintings until the late fifteenth century (see Cimabue and Jean Fouquet). Tempera was generally painted on a white chalky substance called 'gesso' which had been applied in layers to a wooden

support. The absorbent nature of gesso and the quick-drying qualities of tempera meant that the artist had to work quickly and accurately; reworking the image was virtually impossible. Despite the medium's decreased popularity in comparison to oil there have been twentieth-century practitioners (see Giacomo Balla and Edward Wadsworth).

Video Art

Artists have used video since the 1960s, both to make a record of performances and other impermanent works, and as a medium in its own right. The growth of Video Art coincides with the development and availability of video technology, and its use is historically linked to artists' forays into filmmaking. While some Video Art is made for television programs, much is designed for galleries and other spaces, often in the form of **installations**. Video Art is not constrained by the small screen – artists have projected videos onto buildings or other objects, worked with multiple screens (see Pipilotti Rist), or made complex juxtapositions of video with lighting, sound, and sculptural elements (see Francis Alÿs, Matthew Barney and Bill Viola).

Watercolour

Pigment (colour) bound by a water-soluble medium such as gum arabic. This is usually diluted with water to the point where it is translucent, and applied to paper in broad areas known as washes. White paper is often left exposed to create highlights and washes applied over one another to achieve gradations of tone (see Emil Nolde). Watercolour lends itself well to the creation of atmospheric effects and was particularly popular with English eighteenth- and nineteenth-century landscape painters such as John Robert Cozens and JMW Turner.

Glossary of artistic movements

Abstract Expressionism

A movement in American painting that developed in New York in the 1940s. Most Abstract Expressionists were energetic (or 'gestural') painters. They invariably used large canvases and applied paint rapidly and with force, sometimes using large brushes, sometimes dripping or even throwing paint directly onto the canvas. This expressive method of painting was often considered as important as the painting itself. Other Abstract Expressionist artists were concerned with adopting a peaceful and mystical approach to a purely abstract image. Not all the work from this movement was abstract (see Willem de Kooning and Philip Guston) or expressive (see Barnett Newman and Mark Rothko), but it was generally believed that the spontaneity of the artists' approach to their work would draw from and release the creativity of their unconscious minds.

☞ Francis, Frankenthaler, Guston, Hofmann, Kline, De Kooning, Motherwell, Newman, Pollock, Rothko, Still

Anthropological photography

Photographs of country people, slum dwellers and non-Europeans were taken during the nineteenth century to introduce such 'outsiders' to educated audiences in London, Paris, Berlin and the other major centres of learning. It was generally believed that tribespeople were doomed to extinction and ought to be recorded for posterity while it was still possible. Towards 1920, a new interest in cultural relativism began to make the old specimen photography look archaic. Anthropologists also started to take the view that the truth lay in social patterns and habits too subtle to be recorded by the camera.

☞ Adams, Sander

Art Informel

The French word *informel* means 'without form' rather than 'informal'. In the 1950s Art Informel artists were looking for a new way to create images without adopting the recognizable forms used by their predecessors (see **Cubism** and **Expressionism**). Their aim was to abandon geometrical and figurative forms and to discover a new artistic language. They invented shapes and methods that came about by improvisation. The work of Art Informel artists is extremely varied but they often used free brushstrokes and thick layering of paint. Like **Abstract Expressionism**, which developed simultaneously in the USA, Art Informel is a very broad label and includes figurative (see Jean Fautrier) and non-figurative (see Hans Hartung) painters. Although centred mainly on Paris, its influence reached other parts of Europe, notably Spain, Italy and Germany.

☞ Burri, Dubuffet, Fautrier, Hartung, Hesse, Riopelle, Soulages, De Staël, Tàpies

Art Nouveau

A French term which translates as 'new art', Art Nouveau was a decorative style of architecture and interior design that appeared in Europe and the USA in the 1890s and transformed art and design. The movement was characterized by stylized, sinuous lines and curving, organic forms such as tendrils and leaves. Art Nouveau painting is typified by extravagant patterns and elegant female figures with long, flowing hair (see Gustav Klimt). The sophisticated graphic work of Aubrey Beardsley represents its tendencies to eroticism and decadence (see also Egon Schiele), while the designs of Charles Rennie Mackintosh present a more restrained, geometric version. The style was taken to new heights of fantasy by the Spanish architect Antonio Gaudí.

☞ Klimt, Munch, Schiele

Arte Povera

Arte Povera – literally 'Poor Art' – was first defined as a movement in 1967 by the Italian critic Germano Celant, who became its main propagandist. Predominantly an Italian tendency, it remained influential until the late 1970s. The works, which were primarily three-dimensional sculptures, were made from the simplest of materials and natural elements. Mud, twigs, cloth, rags, paper, felt and cement were all used in an attempt to fuse nature and culture in a reflection of contemporary life. The artists were like alchemists, extracting metaphysical truths from these basic materials. Opposed to the cold detachment of **Minimalism**, they desired a more sensory and impassioned type of art.

☞ Boetti, Merz

Bauhaus

The Bauhaus school was founded by the architect Walter Gropius at Weimar in 1919 and became the centre of modern design in Germany in the 1920s. Reflecting some of the socialist currents in Europe at the time, its philosophy was to bring art and design into the domain of daily life. Gropius believed that artists and architects should be considered as craftsmen and that their creations should be practical and affordable. Bauhaus students included artists, architects, potters, weavers, sculptors and designers who studied together in workshops as had the artists and artisans of the **Renaissance**. The characteristic Bauhaus style was simple, geometrical and highly refined. In 1933 the school was closed by the Nazi government claiming that it was a centre of communist intellectualism.

☞ Albers, Kandinsky, Klee, Moholy-Nagy

Barbizon

In the early to mid-nineteenth century a number of French artists travelled to a small village 40 miles south-west of Paris. The village is called Barbizon and lies on the outskirts of the Forest of Fontainebleau. Far from the pressures of city life, these artists were able to take their easels into the countryside and paint from nature in the open air. They painted gentle landscapes and people at work in the fields, and studied the fleeting effects of light and atmospheric effects on the world around them.

☛ Corot, Courbet, Daubigny, Millet, T Rousseau

Baroque

The Baroque style flourished in Rome in the early 1600s and persisted in varying degrees throughout Europe until the eighteenth century. The name comes from the Italian word *barocco*, meaning bizarre or zany. Baroque art is generally defined by its dramatic exuberance and emotive appeal to the viewer. The archetypal Baroque religious picture might show the saints or the Madonna in a swirl of billowing draperies and fleecy clouds surrounded by cherubs. Themes such as subjects from Ancient mythology were also popular, and were treated in the same exaggerated manner. Not all art of the period was so

luxuriant, however, and the sombre dramaticism of artists such as Caravaggio is equally termed Baroque.

☛ Bernini, Caravaggio, Cuyp, Gentileschi, Guercino, Kalf, Rembrandt, Reni, Rubens, Sánchez-Cotan, Velázquez, Zurbarán

Der Blaue Reiter

A group of German Expressionists founded in Munich in 1911. The name translates as 'The Blue Rider' and was taken from a painting by Kandinsky. Although not strictly a movement with a defined programme, the group did veer more towards mysticism and spirituality than the other major **Expressionist** organization, **Die Brücke**. Key artists included Marc and August Macke, who were joined by Klee and Delaunay in 1912.

☛ Delaunay, Kandinsky, Klee, Marc

Die Brücke

A group of **Expressionist** artists formed in Dresden in 1905. The name translates as 'The Bridge', and suggests that they saw their art as a bridge between that of the past and the future. A loose association rather than a coherent group, Die Brücke artists favoured vibrant colours (influenced in part by the **Fauvists**), simplified, natural forms and an expressive use of line,

which lent itself particularly well to graphic work. Artists associated with the group included Kirchner, Nolde and Pechstein. The group moved to Berlin in 1910, and was disbanded in 1913.

☛ Heckel, Kirchner, Nolde, Pechstein

The Camden Town Group

An English group of painters formed in 1911. The group often met in Walter Sickert's studio in north London. They took much of their subject matter from urban working-class life and were influenced by the strong forms and colours used by artists such as Vincent van Gogh and Paul Gauguin. In 1913 it amalgamated with other groups to become the London Group.

☛ Gilman, Sickert

Cobra

An international association of artists that existed in Europe typified from 1948 to 1951. The name Cobra was made up from the initials of the cities in which the original members of the association were living (Copenhagen, Brussels and Amsterdam). The aim of the Cobra artists was to promote free expression of the unconscious and they used thick free handling of paint and striking colours to give their work vitality and force. They put particular

emphasis on the development of fantastical imagery derived from Nordic folklore, and from mystical symbols of the unconscious rather than purely abstract forms.

☛ Appel

Conceptual Art

In Conceptual Art it is the 'concept' behind the work, rather than the technical skill of the artist in making it, that is important. Conceptual Art became a major international phenomenon in the 1960s and its manifestations have been very diverse. The ideas or 'concepts' may be communicated using a variety of different media, including texts, maps, diagrams, film/video, photographs and performances, and displayed in a gallery or designed for a specific site. In some cases the landscape itself becomes an integral part of the artist's work, as in the 'land art' of Richard Long or the 'environmental sculptures' of Christo and Jeanne-Claude. The ideas expressed through Conceptual work have been drawn from philosophy, **feminism**, psychoanalysis, film studies and political activism. The notion of the Conceptual artist as a maker of ideas rather than objects undermines traditional ideas about the status of the artist and the art object. **'Arte Povera'**, a Conceptual tendency that established itself in Italy in the 1960s, developed this idea by using banal and worthless materials (see Joseph Beuys and Mario Merz).

☞ Baldessari, Beuys, Buren, Calle, Gonzalez-Torres, Graham, Holzer, Kawara, Long, Merz, Nauman, A Piper, Viola

Constructivism

An abstract art movement that was founded in Russia in 1913. Constructivism swept away traditional notions about art, believing that it should imitate the forms and processes of modern technology. This was especially true of sculpture, which was 'constructed' out of component parts using industrial materials and techniques. In painting, the same principles were applied within a two-dimensional format; abstract forms were used to create structures reminiscent of machine technology and were suspended in space in almost architectural fashion. Although 'pure' Constructivism was current in Russia during the early years of the Revolution, its aims and ideals have been used by artists throughout the twentieth century.

☞ Gabo, Lissitzky, Moholy-Nagy, Rodchenko, Tatlin

Cubism

This revolutionary method of representation was invented by Pablo Picasso and Georges Braque in the first decade of the twentieth century. Although it may appear abstract and geometrical, Cubist art does depict real objects. These are 'flattened' onto the canvas so that different sides of each shape can be shown simultaneously. Instead of creating the illusion of an object in space, as artists had endeavoured to do since the **Renaissance**, Cubist art defines objects in the two-dimensional terms of the canvas. This innovation gave rise to an extraordinary reassessment of the interaction between form and space, changing the course of Western art forever.

☞ Archipenko, Braque, Gris, Léger, Picasso

Dada

The name Dada is deliberately meaningless and was given to an international 'anti-art' movement that flourished from 1915 to 1922. Its main centre of activity was the Cabaret Voltaire in Zurich, where like-minded poets, artists, writers and musicians would participate in experimental activities such as nonsense poetry, 'noise music' and automatic drawing. Dada was a violent reaction to the snobbery and traditionalism of the art establishment: its members were ready to use any means to cause outrage amongst the bourgeoisie. A typical Dada work of art was the 'ready-made', essentially an ordinary object taken from its original context and put on exhibit as 'art'. The Dada movement, with its cult of the irrational, was important in preparing the ground for the advent of **Surrealism** in the 1920s.

☞ Arp, Duchamp, Hausmann, Höch, Man Ray, Schwitters

De Stijl

An artistic movement and magazine founded in Holland in 1917 by Theo van Doesburg and Piet Mondrian. These men believed that art should strive towards complete harmony, order and clarity in a constant process of refinement. The work of De Stijl was therefore austere and geometrical, using mainly square forms. It was composed of the simplest elements: straight lines and pure primary colours. The movement's aims were deeply philosophical and were rooted in the idea that art should in some way reflect the mystery and order of the universe. The movement came to an end in 1931 after Van Doesburg's death, but had a profound effect on architecture and the applied arts in Europe.

☞ Van Doesburg, Mondrian

Documentary photography

Photographers have been documentarists since the invention of the medium. Government agencies, such as the French Commission des monuments historiques in the early 1850s, tended to think of photographic records as potentially valuable and as supplements to written records. Documentary was always undertaken on behalf of posterity, as opposed to reportage which involves news for contemporaries. Roy Stryker's Farm Security Administration (FSA) project in the USA in the 1930s is the most celebrated of all documentary undertakings.

☞ Atget, Cartier-Bresson, W. Evans, Frank, Kertész, Le Gray, Sander

Expressionism

An artistic force concentrated mainly in Germany from 1905 to 1930. Expressionist artists sought to develop pictorial forms which would express their innermost feelings rather than represent the external world. Expressionist painting is intense, passionate and highly personal, based on the concept of the painter's canvas as a vehicle for demonstrating emotions. Violent, unreal colour and dramatic brushwork make the typical Expressionist painting quiver with vitality. It is not surprising that Vincent van Gogh, with his frenzied painting technique and extraordinary use of colour, was the inspiration for many Expressionist painters.

☛ Beckman, Van Gogh, Heckel, Jawlensky, Kirchner, Kokoschka, Marc, Munch, Nolde, Pechstein, Rouault, Schiele, Schmidt-Rottluff, Soutine

Fauvism

In 1905 an exhibition was held in Paris which included a room full of paintings that blazed with pure, highly contrasting colours. They seemed to have been painted with great enthusiasm and passion. One critic dubbed the creators of these paintings '*les fauves*' – French for 'wild beasts' – and the name stuck. This 'wildness' manifested itself mainly in the strong colours, dynamic brushwork and expressive depth of their pictures, which evoke a fantastical, joyous world of heightened emotion and colour.

☛ Derain, Van Dongen, Matisse, Vlaminck

Feminism

Primarily a political movement, feminism has had a huge impact on twentieth-century art. Its rejection of the notion that a heterosexual, white, male view of the world is a universal one has influenced not only artists but also art historians and critics. The term 'feminist art' emerged only in the 1960s, but women artists have been fighting for, and winning, increased visibility since

the start of the twentieth century. As a move away from male-dominated traditions of painting, they have been experimenting with crafts, film, video, performance, installation and text-based art. By changing the ground rules of how art is both made and perceived, feminism has influenced the work of a number of artists such as Sophie Calle, Barbara Kruger, and Cindy Sherman, who examine the way in which women have been represented by men. Feminists have also questioned the accepted orthodoxies of art history, initiating research into women artists who had been overlooked by generations of scholars.

☛ Calle, Holzer, Kruger, Sherman

Fluxus

Active between the early 1960s and the mid-1970s, Fluxus was as much a state of mind as a particular style. The term was first used in 1961 by George Manciunas, and was intended to describe a condition of perpetual activity and change. Fluxus had a similar iconoclastic ideology to **Dada** and was focused on a loosely interconnected, revolutionary group of artists in Europe and the USA, who reacted against traditional art forms. The style manifested itself in Happenings, interactive performances, videos, poetry

and found objects, and was important in paving the way for Performance and **Conceptual Art**.

☛ Beuys

Futurism

An avant-garde movement founded in Milan in 1909. Its members aimed to liberate Italy from the weight of its past and to glorify modernity. The Futurists were fascinated by modern machinery, transport and communications. In painting and sculpture, angular forms and powerful lines were used to convey a sense of dynamism. One of the main features of Futurist art was its attempt to capture movement and speed: this was usually achieved by depicting several images of the same object or figure in slightly differing positions at the same time, giving the impression of a flurry of movement.

☛ Balla, Boccioni

Gothic

Predominant in the Middle Ages (from around 1150 to 1500), this is the style of the great cathedrals of Europe. Altarpieces made during this time had elaborate crenellations which mimicked church architecture. Gothic paintings and sculptures are characterized by elongated figures which are highly patterned. In painting, there is

often little attempt to depict three-dimensional space. The perspective that was employed is usually random and unconvincing. At the end of the fourteenth century there was a move towards greater elegance and refinement, and an increased interest in natural themes. Minutely detailed depictions of plants and animals became a common feature in paintings. Because this later style was not confined to one country, it is often called International Gothic.

☛ Beauneveu, Cimabue, Duccio, Fouquet, Gaddi, Gentile da Fabriano, Limbourg, Lorenzetti, Lorenzo Monaco, Martini, Della Quercia

Impressionism

A movement in painting that originated in France in the 1860s. Impressionist painters celebrated the overwhelming vision of nature seen in the splendour of natural light – whether dawn, daylight or twilight. They were fascinated by the relationship between light and colour, painting in pure pigment using free brushstrokes. They were also radical in their choice of subject matter, avoiding traditional historical, religious or romantic themes to concentrate on landscapes and scenes of everyday life. The movement's name, initially coined in derision by a journalist, was inspired by one of Claude Monet's paintings entitled *Impression – Sunrise*.

☛ Caillebotte, Cassatt, Degas, Manet, Monet, Morisot, Pissarro, Renoir, Sisley

Kinetic Art

Term used to describe art incorporating real or apparent movement. The idea was first introduced in the 1920s but reached its height of popularity during the 1950s and 1960s. Kinetic art may be quite simple (such as Alexander Calder's wind-driven mobiles) or complex (such as Jean Tinguely's motor-operated sculptures). The term may also be applied to works of art that use light effects to give the viewer the illusion of movement.

☛ Calder, Tinguely

Mannerism

A development of the **Renaissance** style, Mannerism is generally seen as a reaction against the harmony, order and perfection of the fifteenth and early sixteenth centuries. The style was prevalent in Italy between 1520 and 1600. It is characterized by a use of bright, almost garish colours, elaborate compositions, exaggerated forms and dramatic movement. The term originates in the use of the word *maniera*, meaning 'stylishness' and signifying grace, poise and harmony.

The word has developed a variety of meanings over the centuries; however, it is generally associated with art and artists who openly demonstrated excessive skill, virtuosity and caprice.

☛ Bronzino, Cellini, Giambologna, Giulio Romano, El Greco, Parmigianino, Pontormo, Rosso, Tintoretto

Minimalism

A trend in painting and sculpture that developed primarily in the USA during the 1960s and 1970s. As the name implies, Minimalist Art is pared down to its essentials; it is purely abstract, objective and anonymous, free of surface decoration or expressive gesture. Minimalist painting and drawing is monochromatic and often draws on mathematically derived grids and linear matrices; yet it can also evoke a sensation of the sublime and of states of being. Sculptors used industrial processes and materials, such as steel, Perspex, even fluorescent tubes, to produce geometric forms, often made in series. This sculpture has no illusionistic properties, relying instead on a bodily experience of the work by the spectator. Minimalism can be seen as a reaction against the emotionalism of **Abstract Expressionism**, which had dominated modern art through the 1950s.

☛ Andre, Flavin, Judd, Kelly, LeWitt, Mangold, Ryman, Serra, Stella

Nabis

A small group of French artists, active in the 1880s, who were inspired by Paul Gauguin's method of painting in pure colour. Their approach is epitomized by a statement by Maurice Denis, one of the group's members: 'Remember that a picture, before being a horse, a nude, or some kind of anecdote, is essentially a flat surface covered with colours.' As well as painting the group was interested in print-making, posters, book illustrations, textiles and theatre design.

☛ Bonnard, Denis, Maillol, Vallotton, Vuillard

Neo (-Classicism, -Expressionism, -Romanticism)

The prefix 'neo', meaning 'new', refers to a revival of trends or ideas. *Neo-Classicism*, for example, was a movement that developed in the latter half of the eighteenth century; its aims were a return to **Classical** values and a revival of the elegant styles of Ancient Greek and Roman art. In art and architecture it is characterized by a preference for line and symmetry, and by its frequent borrowing from Antique sources. *Neo-Expressionism* refers to the re-emergence of

Expressionist characteristics in the work of particular artists in the USA and Europe, especially Germany, in the late 1970s. Neo-Expressionist works tend to be highly personal, often executed with violent fervour. *Neo-Romanticism* refers to a strongly theatrical form of twentieth-century painting which combines both **Romantic** and **Surrealist** elements.

☛ (Neo-Classicism) Alma-Tadema, Canova, J-L David, Gérôme, Ingres, Leighton, Mengs, Powers, Prud'hon; (Neo-Expressionism) Auerbach, Baselitz, Bomberg, Boyd, Clemente, Frink, Kiefer, Schnabel; (Neo-Romanticism) Nash, Piper

Die Neue Sachlichkeit

A stylistic tendency within the German Expressionist movement in the 1920s which reflected the cynicism that pervaded Germany after the First World War. It translates as 'The New Objectivity'. Artists of the Neue Sachlichkeit group, who included Dix and Grosz, tended to put a greater emphasis on social criticism and political comment than other **Expressionists**, who dealt with more subjective and emotional themes.

☛ Dix, Grosz, Schad

New York School

Originally a term synonymous with **Abstract**

Expressionism, the New York School is used more generally now to signify the Western art world's shift – both physically and conceptually – to New York City in the years after World War II and continuing through the 1960s. The term originated with a 1965 Los Angeles County Museum of Art exhibition, 'The New York School: The First Generation Painting of the 1940s and 1950s,' which featured the work of Willem de Kooning, Philip Guston, Robert Motherwell, Jackson Pollock, and Mark Rothko, among others. Paintings by the first generation of New York School artists were large and abstract, and emphasized bold, aggressive brushstrokes; critic Harold Rosenberg coined the phrase 'action painting' to describe these works. Subjective and highly gestural, they addressed the theme of human impulse and desires, in addition to commenting on society's need to impose order on such expression and to define and control taboos through myth.

☛ Frankenthaler, Gorky, Kline, De Kooning, Newman, Pollock, Rauschenberg, Reinhardt, Rothko, D. Smith, Still

Op Art

A movement in abstract art that developed in the 1960s and continues today. Op Art (short for 'optical art') exploits the fallibility of the human eye. Although the work of art itself is static, the forms and colours used by the artist cause an optical illusion of movement.

☛ Riley, Vasarely

Pittura Metafisica (Metaphysical Painting)

Metaphysical Painting was founded in Italy in 1917 by Giorgio de Chirico and Carlo Carrà. It is characterized by distorted perspectives, unnatural lighting and strange imagery, often using tailors' dummies and statues instead of the human body. By placing objects in unlikely contexts, the Metaphysical Painters aimed to create a dreamlike, magical atmosphere. In this respect the movement has much in common with **Surrealism**, but it differs from **Surrealism** in its concern with rigid compositional structure and architectural values.

☛ Carrà, De Chirico, Delvaux

Pop Art

A movement in the USA and Britain that emerged in the 1950s and took its inspiration from the imagery of consumer society and pop culture. Comic strips, advertising and mass-produced objects all played a part in this movement, which was characterized by one of its members, Richard Hamilton, as 'popular, transient, expendable, low cost, mass-produced, young, witty, sexy, gimmicky, glamorous and Big Business'. The brashness of subject matter is often emphasized by hard-edged photograph-like techniques in painting and minute attention to detail in sculpture. Photomontage, collage and assemblage are also common in Pop Art.

☛ P Blake, Dine, Hamilton, Hockney, Johns, Jones, Katz, Kitaj, Lichtenstein, Oldenburg, Rauschenberg, Rosenquist, Ruscha, Segal, Thiebaud, Warhol, Wesselmann

Pre-Raphaelite Brotherhood

An association of young English artists formed in 1848. Dismayed at what they saw as the decadent state of British painting, the Pre-Raphaelites sought to evoke the sincerity of early Italian art before the High **Renaissance** master Raphael, as exemplified by artists such as Sandro Botticelli and Filippo Lippi. Pre-Raphaelite pictures frequently depict literary, historical and religious scenes and often make moralizing comments on social behaviour and relationships. The artists painted richly textured and minutely detailed pictures which show particular interest in the decorative qualities of flowers and fabric.

☛ Brown, Burne-Jones, Hunt, Millais, Rossetti, Waterhouse

Renaissance

Throughout the Middle Ages man lived in fear of God and within the omnipresence of the Church. Art generally showed the heavens and saints, and bore little relation to what was happening on earth. From the fourteenth century, however, man began to realize his importance and effect on the world. This rebirth (or 'renaissance') was reflected in art: figures became more life-like, space became more real and the Christian story began to be told from a human point of view. As the decades continued artists were able to recreate the world on panels, frescos and altarpieces with increasing ease. Beginning with the stylized works of Giotto and Masaccio, the Renaissance culminated in the monumental creations of Leonardo, Raphael and Michelangelo. Although generally associated with Italy, the Renaissance also developed independently north of the Alps in Germany and Flanders. While Italian Renaissance artists laid emphasis on perspective and the illusion of space, Flemish and German artists were more interested in a detailed, jewel-like depiction of the world around them.

☛ (Early Renaissance) Fra Angelico, Botticelli, Donatello, Ghiberti, Ghirlandaio, Giotto, Giovanni di Paolo, Filippino Lippi, Mantegna,

Masaccio, Perugino, Piero della Francesca, Pollaiuolo, Signorelli, Verrocchio; (High Renaissance) Andrea del Sarto, Fra Bartolommeo, Leonardo da Vinci, Michelangelo, Raphael, Titian; (Northern Renaissance) Altdorfer, Dürer, Elsheimer, Gossaert, Grünewald, Massys, Van der Weyden

Rococo

A light, playful and decorative style that emerged in France around 1700 and was disseminated throughout Europe in the eighteenth century. The term comes from the French word *rocaille*, meaning the fancy shell- and rockwork used to decorate fountains and grottoes. Predominantly a style of interior decoration, the Rococo is typified by charm and playfulness and a palette of pastel colours. Its subject matter frequently dealt with the leisurely pastimes of the aristocracy.

☛ Amigoni, Boucher, Fragonard, Tiepolo, Watteau

Romanticism

A movement in the arts that flourished in northern Europe and the USA during the late eighteenth and early nineteenth centuries. Romanticism is so varied in its manifestations that a single definition is almost impossible. Romantic

artists turned away from intellectual disciplines and placed importance on the imagination and individual expression. Their paintings often depict grand emotions such as fear, desolation, victory, and true love. The movement had officially died out by the mid-nineteenth century but romantic tendencies have survived into the twentieth century in artistic strains such as **Expressionism** and **Neo-Expressionism**.

☛ Allston, Bierstadt, Blake, Church, Cole, Constable, Cozens, Etty, Friedrich, Géricault, Goya, Martin, Turner

St Ives Group

A group of artists who lived and worked in the Cornish seaside town of St Ives in the early 1940s. Key members of the group were Hepworth and Nicholson, who moved to St Ives during the Second World War. Although each had their own individual style, they all worked in the abstract tradition, producing works influenced by the light, sea and landscape of their immediate surroundings.

☛ Hepworth, Heron, B Nicholson, Wallis

The Viennese Secession

An avant-garde group founded in 1897 by the artist Klimt. Its aim was to break

away from the established artistic bodies and raise the level of production of arts and crafts in Austria to that of other European countries. Many of the group were based at the movement's headquarters, the Viennese Workshop. The Secession style was close to Art Nouveau. Other Secession groups were formed in Munich and Berlin at around the same time.

☛ Klimt, Schiele

Surrealism

Surrealism originated in France in the 1920s. In the words of its main theorist, the writer André Breton, its aim was to 'resolve the previously contradictory conditions of dream and reality', and the ways in which this was achieved varied widely. Artists painted unnerving and illogical scenes with photographic precision, created strange creatures from collections of everyday objects, or developed techniques of painting which would allow the unconscious to express itself. Surrealist pictures, while figurative, represent an alien world, whose images range from dreamlike serenity to nightmarish fantasy.

☛ Bellmer, Brauner, Cahun, Dalí, Delvaux, Ernst, Kahlo, Gorky, Magritte, Matta, Miró, Tanguy, Wadsworth

Symbolism

A literary and artistic movement that flourished in France in the late nineteenth century. Symbolist artists rejected realism, believing that painting should convey ideas and states of mind rather than simply describe the visible world. Their styles varied from jewel-like richness to pale serenity but their common interest was in conveying a feeling of other-worldliness. Subjects of a religious or mythological flavour were popular, and eroticism, death and sin were common themes.

☛ Moreau, Redon

Vorticism

An English avant-garde movement founded by Wyndham Lewis in 1914. The name Vorticism came from the poet Ezra Pound, and was derived from his statement that the vortex is the point of maximum energy. Like **Futurism**, Vorticism employed a harsh, angular and highly dynamic style in both painting and sculpture and aimed at capturing activity and movement. Although Vorticism did not survive the First World War, it was significant as the first movement towards abstraction in British art.

☛ Bomberg, Lewis

Directory of museums and galleries

Australia

Art Gallery of New South Wales
Sydney NSW 2000

Boyd, *The Australian Scapegoat*

Austria

Kunsthistorisches Museum
Burgring 5
1010 Vienna

Giovanni Bellini, *Young Woman at her Toilet*
P Bruegel, *Peasant Wedding*
Cellini, *Salt Cellar*
Van der Goes, *The Fall of Man*
Gossaert, *Saint Luke Painting the Virgin*
Sittow, *Katherine of Aragon*

Österreichische Galerie
Prinz Eugen-strasse 27
1037 Vienna

Klimt, *The Kiss*

Belgium

Koninklijk Museum voor Schone Kunsten
Leopold de Waelplein
2000 Antwerp

Ensor, *Skeletons Fighting for the Body of a Hanged Man*
Fouquet, *Virgin and Child*

Memlingmuseum Het Sint-Janshospitaal
Mariastraat 38
Bruges

Memling, *Saint John Altarpiece*

Musées Royaux des Beaux-Arts de Belgique
9 rue du Musée
1000 Brussels

J-L David, *The Death of Marat*
Vuillard, *Two Schoolboys*

Canada

Art Gallery of Ontario
317 Dundas Street West
Toronto, ON, M5T 1G4

Oldenburg, *Giant Hamburger*

Czech Republic

Národní Galerie
Hradcanské nám 15
11904 Prague 1

Schiele, *Seated Woman with Bent Knee*

Denmark

Skagens Museum
Eröndumsvej
9990 Skagen

Krøyer, *Summer Evening on the Southern Beach*

France

Musée National Fernand Léger
Chemin du Val de Pome
06410 Biot

Léger, *The Builders*

Musée Condé
Château de Chantilly
BP 243, 60631 Chantilly

Limbourg, *January*
De Troy, *The Oyster Lunch*

Musée d'Unterlinden
1 place d'Unterlinden
68000 Colmar

Grünewald, *The Crucifixion*

Château de Fontainebleau
77300 Fontainebleau

Primaticcio, *Danaë*

Musée Fabre
39 boulevard Bonne Nouvelle
34000 Montpellier

Courbet, *Bonjour, Monsieur Courbet*

Musée des Beaux-Arts
10 rue Georges-Clémenceau
44000 Nantes

Greuze, *The Guitarist*

Bibliothèque Nationale
58 rue de Richelieu
75084 Paris

Beauneveu, *Saint Philip*

Centre National des Arts Plastiques
Tour Atlantique
1 place de la Pyramide
92911 Paris-La Défense

Orozco, *La DS*

Musée Bourdelle
16 rue Antoine-Bourdelle
75015 Paris

Bourdelle, *Herakles*

Musée d'Art Moderne de la Ville de Paris
11 ave du Président Wilson
75116 Paris

Delaunay, *Homage to Blériot*

Musée de l'Orangerie
Place de la Concorde
75001 Paris

Soutine, *The Little Pastry Cook*
Utrillo, *Flag Over the Town Hall*

Musée d'Orsay
1 rue de Bellechasse
75007 Paris

Bazille, *The Artist's Studio on the rue de la Condamine*
Boudin, *The Beach at Trouville*
Cassatt, *Woman Sewing*
Van Gogh, *Self-portrait*
Manet, *Le déjeuner sur l'herbe*
Millet, *The Gleaners*
Morisot, *The Cradle*
Orpen, *The Café Royal in London*
Pissarro, *Landscape at Chaponval*
Renoir, *Ball at the Moulin de la Galette*
Signac, *The Papal Palace, Avignon*
Sisley, *Snow at Louveciennes*

Musée du Louvre
Palais du Louvre
75001 Paris

Arcimboldo, *Summer*
Boucher, *Odalisque*
Canova, *Cupid and Psyche*
Champaigne, *The Last Supper*
G David, *The Marriage Feast at Cana*
Géricault, *Officer of the Hussars*

De Heem, *Still Life of Dessert*
Houdon, *Bust of Denis Diderot*
Ingres, *The Bather of Valpinçon*
Jordaens, *The Four Evangelists*
La Tour, *The Cheat with the Ace of Diamonds*
Leonardo da Vinci, *Mona Lisa*
Pisanello, *Ginevra d'Este*
Poussin, *The Arcadian Shepherds*
Prud'hon, *The Empress Josephine*
Rigaud, *Louis XIV*

Musée Marmottan Monet
2 rue Louis Boilly
75016 Paris

Monet, *Impression, Sunrise*

Musée National Auguste Rodin
79 rue de Varenne
75007 Paris

Rodin, *The Kiss*

Musée National d'Art Moderne
Centre National d'Art et de Culture Georges Pompidou
Place Georges Pompidou
75004 Paris

Dix, *Portrait of the Journalist Sylvia von Harden*
Graham, *Present Continuous Past(s)*
Tatlin, *Monument to the Third International*

Musée des Beaux-Arts
place Saint Corentin
29000 Quimper

Vallotton, *Landscape with Trees*

Musée des Beaux-Arts
26 bis rue Thiers
76000 Rouen

Daubigny, *The Lock at Optevoz*

Musée Départemental du Prieuré
2 bis rue Maurice Denis
78100 Saint-Germain-en-Laye

Denis, *Portrait of Yvonne Lerolle*

Musée National du Château de Versailles
78000 Versailles

Delacroix, *The Battle of Taillebourg*

Germany

Neue Nationalgalerie Staatliche Museen zu Berlin
Potsdamer Straße 50
10785 Berlin

Höch, *Cut with the Kitchen Knife…*

Schloss Charlottenburg
Luisenplatz
1000 Berlin 19

Watteau, *The Embarkation for Cythera*

Ludwig Roselius Sammlung
Böttcherstrasse 4
2800 Bremen 1

Modersohn-Becker, *Old Poorhouse Woman with a Glass Bottle*

Wallraf-Richartz Museum
Bischofsgartenstrasse 1
5000 Cologne 1

Lochner, *The Virgin and Child in a Rose Arbour*

Staatliche Kunstsammlungen Dresden
Georg-Treu-Platz 1
PSF 450
8012 Dresden

Correggio, *The Nativity*
Liotard, *The Chocolate Pot*

Wilhelm-Lehmbruck Museum
Düsseldorferstrasse 51
4100 Duisburg

Heckel, *Windmill, Dangast*

Städelsches Kunstinstitut und Städtische Galerie
Schaumainkai 63
6000 Frankfurt 70

Cranach, *Venus*

Hamburger Kunsthalle
Glockengiesserwall
2000 Hamburg 1

Friedrich, *The Wreck of the Hope*
Kirchner, *Self-portrait with Model*
Overbeck, *The Adoration of the Magi*

Staatliche Kunstsammlungen Kassel
Schloss Wilhelmshöhe
3500 Kassel

Ter Brugghen, *The Flute Player*

Alte Pinakothek
Barerstrasse 27
8000 Munich 40

Altdorfer, *Battle of Alexander at Issus*

Stiftung Schlösser und Gärten Potsdam-Sanssouci
Park Sanssouci
0-1500 Potsdam

Caravaggio, *Doubting Thomas*

Staatsgalerie Stuttgart
Konrad-Adenauer-Strasse
30-32, 7000 Stuttgart

Marc, *Little Yellow Horses*

Kunsthalle Tübingen
Philosophenweg 76
7400 Tübingen 1

Hamilton, *Just What is it That Makes Today's Homes So Different, So Appealing?*

Italy

Basilica di San Francesco d'Assisi
Piazza San Francesco, 2
06081 Assisi, Perugia

Piero della Francesca, *The Procession of the Queen of Sheba*

Pinacoteca Nazionale
Via Belle Arti 56
40100 Bologna

Perugino, *The Virgin and Child with Saints*

Palazzo Schifanoia
Via Scandiana 23
44100 Ferrara

Del Cossa, *May*

Galleria degli Uffizi
Piazzale degli Uffizi
50122 Florence

Andrea del Sarto, *Madonna of the Harpies*
Botticelli, *Spring*
Catena, *The Supper at Emmaus*
Cimabue, *The Santa Trinità Madonna*
Clouet, *Portrait of François I on Horseback*
Duccio, *The Rucellai Madonna*
Gentile da Fabriano, *The Adoration of the Magi*
Gentileschi, *Judith and Holofernes*
Filippino Lippi, *Portrait of an Old Man*
Filippo Lippi, *The Coronation of the Virgin*
Lorenzo Monaco, *The Coronation of the Virgin*
Luini, *The Executioner Presents John the Baptist's Head to Herod*
Martini, *The Annunciation*
Orcagna, *Saint Matthew and Stories from his Life*
Palma Vecchio, *The Holy Family with Mary Magdalene and the Infant Saint John*
Parmigianino, *The Madonna with the Long Neck*
Piero di Cosimo, *Perseus Freeing Andromeda*
Rosso Fiorentino, *Moses Defends the Daughters of Jethro*
Salviati, *Charity*
Sebastiano del Piombo, *The Death of Adonis*
Vigée-Lebrun, *Self-portrait*

Palazzo Pitti
Piazza Pitti 1
50100 Florence

Fra Bartolommeo, *Resurrected Christ with Saints*

Museo Nazionale del Bargello
Via del Proconsolo 4
50122 Florence

Algardi, *Bust of Cardinal Paolo Emilio Zacchia*
Donatello, *David*
Della Robbia, *Madonna and Child between Two Angels*
Verrocchio, *Bust of a Woman Holding a Nosegay*

Pinacoteca di Brera
Via Brera 28
20121 Milan

Carrà, *The Metaphysical Muse*
Signorelli, *The Flagellation of Christ*

Galleria e Museo Estense
Piazza Sant Agostino 109
41100 Modena

Dossi, *Alfonso I d'Este*

Casino dell'Aurora
Palazzo Pallavicini Rospigliosi
Via 24 Maggio, 43
00184 Rome

Reni, *Aurora*

Palazzo Barberini
Via Quattro Fontane 13
00184 Rome

Pietro da Cortona, *Glorification of the Rule of Urban VIII*

Palazzo del Vaticano
00120 Vatican City
Rome

Raphael, *The School of Athens*

Papal Basilica of Saint Peter
Piazza San Pietro
Vatican City
Rome

Michelangelo, *Pietà*

Palazzo Pubblico
Piazza del Campo
53100 Siena

Lorenzetti, *Allegory of Good Government*

Pinacoteca Nazionale di Siena
Via San Pietro 31
53100 Siena

Sodoma, *The Descent from the Cross*

Galleria Internazionale d'Arte Moderna di Ca' Pesaro
Santa Croce 2076
30100 Venice

Manzù, *The Cardinal*

Galleria dell'Accademia
Campo della Carità 1059A
30121 Venice

Gentile Bellini, *The Miracle of the True Cross near the San Lorenzo Bridge*
Bordone, *Presentation of the Ring to the Doge of Venice*
Giorgione, *The Tempest*

Museo Correr
Piazza San Marco 52
30100 Venice

Carpaccio, *Two Venetian Ladies on a Balcony*

Palazzo Labia
Cannaregio 275
Campo San Geremia
Venice

Tiepolo, *The Meeting of Antony and Cleopatra*

Mexico

Museo de Arte Alvar y Carmen T de Carillo
Avenida Revolución 1608
01000 Mexico City, DF

Siqueiros, *Death and Funeral of Cain*

The Netherlands

Stedelijk Museum
Paulus Potterstraat 13
1071 CX Amsterdam

Kienholz, *The Beanery*
Malevich, *Suprematism*
Merz, *Unreal City*

Rijksmuseum
Jan Luijkenstraat 1
1071 CJ, Amsterdam

Vermeer, *Woman in Blue Reading a Letter*

Mauritshuis
Korte Vijverberg 8
2513 AB The Hague

Fabritius, *The Goldfinch*

Rijksmuseum Kröller-Müller
Nationale Park de Hoge Veluwe
Houtkampweg 6
6731 AW Otterlo

Redon, *The Cyclops*

Museum Boymans-van Beuningen
Museumpark 18-20
3015 CB Rotterdam

Dou, *Maidservant at a Window*
Kippenberger, *The Happy End of Franz Kafka's 'Amerika'*
Severini, *Pierrot the Musician*

Norway

Nasjonalgalleriet
Universitetsgaten 13
0033 Oslo 1

Munch, *The Madonna*

Portugal

Museu Nacional de Arte Antiga
Rua das Janelas Verdes
1293 Lisbon

Bosch, *The Tribulations of St Anthony*

Romania

Muzeul de Arta
Calea Unirii 15, 1100 Craiova

Brancusi, *The Kiss*

Russia

Tretyakov Gallery
Lavrushensky Per 10
109017 Moscow

Chagall, *Above the Town*
Ivanov, *The Appearance of Christ to the People*

Hermitage Museum
Dvortsovaya nab 34
St Petersburg

Gros, *Napoleon Bonaparte on the Bridge at Arcole*
De Hooch, *Woman and a Maid with a Pail in a Courtyard*
Matisse, *The Dinner Table (Harmony in Red)*
Mengs, *Self-portrait*

Spain

Museo de Bellas Artes
Plaza del Museo 2
48011 Bilbao

Vasarely, *Pal-Ket*

Fundación Colección Thyssen-Bornemisza
Paseo del Prado 8
28014 Madrid

Constable, *The Lock*
Ghirlandaio, *Portrait of Giovanna Tornabuoni*
Schad, *Portrait of Doctor Haustein*

Museo Nacional del Prado
Paseo del Prado
28014 Madrid

Baldung, *The Three Ages of Man and Death*
Bassano, *The Animals Entering the Ark*
Domenichino, *The Sacrifice of Isaac*
Dürer, *Self-portrait with Gloves*
Gaddi, *Saint Eligius in the Goldsmith's Shop*
Giordano, *The Dream of Solomon*

Murillo, *The Immaculate Conception of the Escorial*
Ribera, *Saint Paul the Hermit*
Velázquez, *Las Meninas*
Veronese, *The Finding of Moses*
Vouet, *Time Overcome by Hope, Love and Beauty*
Van der Weyden, *The Descent from the Cross*

Switzerland

Öffentliche Kunstsammlung Kunstmuseum Basel
St Alban-Graben 16
CH-4010 Basel

Böcklin, *Centaur's Combat*
Klee, *Senecio*
Wall, *After 'Invisible Man' by Ralph Ellison, the Prologue*

Musée d'Art et d'Histoire
2 rue Charles Galland
1211 Geneva 3

Hodler, *Lake Thun*
Witz, *The Miraculous Draught of Fishes*

UK

Towneley Hall Art Gallery
Burnley, Lancashire
BB11 3RQ

Zoffany, *Charles Towneley's Library in Park Street*

The Fitzwilliam Museum
Trumpington Street
Cambridge CB2 1RB

Rosselli, *The Virgin and Child Enthroned with Saints*

National Museum of Wales
Cathays Park, Cardiff CF1 3NP

Wilson, *View in Windsor Great Park*

National Gallery of Scotland
The Mound
Edinburgh EH2 2EL

Bellotto, *View of the Ponte delle Navi, Verona*
Elsheimer, *The Stoning of Saint Stephen*
Massys, *Portrait of a Man*
Raeburn, *The Reverend Robert Walker Skating on Duddingston Loch*
Ramsay, *Lady Robert Manners*
Titian, *Diana and Actaeon*
Wilkie, *The Letter of Introduction*

Scottish National Gallery of Modern Art
Belford Road
Edinburgh EH4 3DR

Kitaj, *If Not, Not*
Kokoschka, *Portrait of a 'Degenerate Artist'*
Lichtenstein, *In the Car*
Nicholson, *The Lustre Bowl with Green Peas*

The Burrell Collection
Pollok Country Park
2060 Pollokshaws Road
Glasgow GA3 1AT

Degas, *The Rehearsal*

Jersey Museum and Art Gallery
The Weighbridge
St Helier, JE2 3NG

Cahun, *Untitled (Self-Portrait)*

Leeds City Art Gallery
The Headrow
Leeds LS1 3AA

Grimshaw, *Nightfall down the Thames*

British Museum
Great Russell Street
London WC1B 3DG

Bonington, *Rouen from the Quais*
Hiroshige, *Moonlight, Nagakubo*
Hokusai, *Mount Fuji in Clear Weather*

Courtauld Institute of Art Gallery
Somerset House
Strand, London
WC2R 0RN

Modigliani, *Female Nude*

Imperial War Museum
Lambeth Road
London SE1 6HZ

Lewis, *A Battery Shelled*

National Gallery
Trafalgar Square
London WC2N 5DN

Antonello da Messina, *Saint Jerome in his Study*
Avercamp, *A Scene on the Ice Near a Town*
Beccafumi, *Tanaquil, Wife of Lucomo*
Bronzino, *An Allegory with Venus and Cupid*
Campin, *The Virgin and Child before a Fire Screen*
Canaletto, *The Basin of San Marco on Ascension Day*
Carracci, *Christ Appearing to Saint Peter on the Appian Way*
Chardin, *The Young Schoolmistress*
Cuyp, *Peasants and Cattle by the River Merwede*

Drouais, *Madame de Pompadour at her Tambour Frame*
Van Dyck, *Charles I on Horseback*
Van Eyck, *The Arnolfini Portrait*
Gainsborough, *Mr and Mrs Andrews*
Guardi, *An Architectural Caprice*
Hals, *Portrait of a Young Man with a Skull*
Hogarth, *The Tête à Tête, from Marriage A la Mode*
Holbein, *The Ambassadors*
Honthorst, *Christ Before the High Priest*
Kalf, *Still Life with Lobster, Drinking Horn and Glasses*
Lancret, *A Lady in a Garden taking Coffee with some Children*
Longhi, *Exhibition of a Rhinoceros at Venice*
Lotto, *Portrait of a Woman inspired by Lucretia*
Mantegna, *The Agony in the Garden*
Metsu, *The Music Lesson*
Patinir, *Saint Jerome in a Rocky Landscape*
Pollaiuolo, *Apollo and Daphne*
Rembrandt, *Self Portrait at the Age of Sixty-Three*
Rosa, *Self-portrait*
Rubens, *The Judgement of Paris*
Sassetta, *Saint Francis of Assisi Renouncing his Earthly Father*
Savery, *Orpheus*
Uccello, *The Battle of San Romano*
Wright of Derby, *An Experiment on a Bird in the Air Pump*

National Portrait Gallery
2 Saint Martin's Place
London
WC2H 0HE

Organ, *Prince Charles*

Saatchi Gallery
Duke of York's HQ
King's Road
London SW3 4RY

Dumas, *Jule – The Woman*
Rego, *The Family*
Zhang Xiaogang, *A Big Family*

Tate
Millbank
London SW1P 4RG

Tate Modern
Bankside
London SE1 9TG

(Items in the Tate collection are occasionally moved, please contact the gallery before visiting to see a specific work)

Albers, *Homage to the Square*
Bellmer, *The Spinning Top*
P Blake, *On the Balcony*
W Blake, *Pity*
Bomberg, *The Mud Bath*
Broodthaers, *Casserole and Closed Mussels*
Burne-Jones, *King Cophetua and the Beggar Maid*
Caro, *Early One Morning*
De Chirico, *The Uncertainty of the Poet*
Copley, *The Death of Major Pierson*
Dali, *Lobster Telephone*
Delvaux, *Venus Asleep*
Derain, *The Pool of London*
Dobson, *Endymion Porter*
Ernst, *Forest and Dove*
Francis, *Around the Blues*
Gaudier-Brzeska, *Red Stone Dancer*
Gertler, *The Merry-Go-Round*
Gorky, *The Waterfall*
Hausmann, *The Art Critic*
Hockney, *A Bigger Splash*

Hunt, *The Awakening Conscience*
Jones, *Man Woman*
Kandinsky, *Cossacks*
Klein, *IKB 79*
Leighton, *The Bath of Psyche*
Lipchitz, *Half-standing Figure*
Louis, *Alpha-Phi*
Martin, *The Great Day of His Wrath*
Millais, *Ophelia*
Miró, *Women and Bird in the Moonlight*
Moore, *Recumbent Figure*
Nash, *Dead Sea*
Nicholson, *August 1956 (Val d'Orcia)*
Noland, *Gift*
Picasso, *Weeping Woman*
Rothko, *Untitled*
Sargent, *Carnation, Lily, Lily, Rose*
Schwitters, *Picture with Spatial Growths – Picture with Two Small Dogs*
Sickert, *Ennui*
Spencer, *Saint Francis and the Birds*
Stubbs, *Mares and Foals in a Landscape*
Sutherland, *Portrait of Somerset Maugham*
Tanguy, *The Invisibles*
Tàpies, *Grey Ochre*
Tissot, *Holiday (The Picnic)*
Turner, *Snowstorm*
Wadsworth, *The Beached Margin*
Waterhouse, *The Lady of Shalott*
Whistler, *Symphony in White No. 2: Little White Girl*

Victoria and Albert Museum
Cromwell Road
South Kensington
London SW7 2RL

J Bruegel, *The Garden of Eden*
Daumier, *The Print Collectors*
Hilliard, *Young Man Among Roses*

Le Gray, *Brig on the Water*
Rossetti, *The Day-dream*
Utamaro, *Lovers*

Wallace Collection
Hertford House
Manchester Square
London W1M 6BM

Fragonard, *The Swing*
Van Ostade, *Interior with Peasants*
Romney, *Mrs Mary Robinson, 'Perdita'*
T Rousseau, *The Forest of Fontainebleau, Morning*
Steen, *The Christening Feast*

Maidstone Museum and Art Gallery
Saint Faith's Street
Maidstone ME14 1LH

Pannini, *Roman Capriccio*

Manchester City Art Gallery
Corner of Mosley Street and Princess Street
Manchester M2 3JL

Brown, *Work*

Laing Art Gallery
Higham Place
Newcastle upon Tyne
NE1 8AG

Landseer, *Wild Cattle at Chillingham*

The Lowry
Pier 8
Salford Quays
M50 3AZ

Lowry, *Coming from the Mill*

Sheffield City Art Galleries
The Graves Art Gallery
Surrey Street
Sheffield S1 1XZ

Gilman, *An Eating House*

Winchester Cathedral
9 The Close
Winchester
Hampshire, SO23 9LS

Gormley, *Sound II*

The Royal Collection
The Royal Library
Windsor Castle
Berkshire SL4 1NJ

Agasse, *The Nubian Giraffe*

York City Art Gallery
Exhibition Square
York YO1 2EW

Snyders, *A Game Stall*

USA

Center for Creative Photography
1030 N Olive Road
AZ 85721

Weston, *Shells*

Baltimore Museum of Art
Art Museum Drive
Baltimore, MD 21218

Andre, *Zinc Magnesium Plain*

Indiana University Art Museum
Bloomington
IN 47405

Duchamp, *Fountain*

Museum of Fine Arts
465 Huntington Avenue
Boston
MA 02115

Allston, *Landscape with a Lake*

Art Institute of Chicago
Michigan Avenue
at Adams Street
Chicago
IL 60603

Hesse, *Sequel*
Seurat, *Sunday Afternoon on the Island of the Grande Jatte*
Wood, *American Gothic*

Museum of Contemporary Art Chicago
220 East Chicago Avenue
Chicago
IL 60611

Piper, *Cornered*

Cleveland Museum of Art
11150 East Boulevard
Cleveland
OH 44106

Church, *Twilight in the Wilderness*

Des Moines Art Center
4700 Grand Avenue
Des Moines
IA 50312

Bacon, *Study after Velázquez's Portrait of Pope Innocent X*

Detroit Institute of Arts
5200 Woodward Avenue
Detroit,
MI 48202

Feininger, *Sailing Boats*

Wadsworth Atheneum
600 Main Street
Hartford
CT 06103

Cole, *Scene from Last of the Mohicans*

Zurbarán, *The Martyrdom of St Serapion*

Hammer Museum
10899 Wilshire Boulevard
Los Angeles
CA 90024

Walker, *Slavery! Slavery! …*

Los Angeles County Museum of Art
5905 Wilshire Boulevard
Los Angeles
CA 90036

Magritte, *The Treachery of Images*

Museum of Contemporary Art
250 South Grand Avenue
Los Angeles
CA 90012

Doig, *100 Years Ago*

Barnes Foundation
300 North Latch's Lane
Merion
PA 19066

Cézanne, *Mont Sainte-Victoire*

Walker Art Center
1750 Hennepin Avenue
Minneapolis
MN 55403

Close, *Big Self-Portrait*

Yale University Art Gallery
1111 Chapel Street at
York Street
New Haven
CT 06520

Powers, *The Greek Slave*

Solomon R Guggenheim Museum
1071 Fifth Avenue
New York
NY 10128

Becher, *Water Towers*
Mondrian, *Composition*

Hispanic Society of America Museum
Broadway between 155
and 156 Streets
New York
NY 10032

Goya, *Portrait of the Duchess of Alba*

Metropolitan Museum of Art
Fifth Avenue at 82nd Street
New York
NY 10028

Bierstadt, *The Rocky Mountains*
Bingham, *Fur Traders Descending the Missouri*
Evans, *Kitchen Corner, Tenant Farmhouse, Hale County, Alabama*
Gauguin, *Ia Orana Maria (Hail Mary)*
Gérôme, *Bashi-Bazouk*
Giovanni di Paolo, *The Creation and the Expulsion from Paradise*
Shore, *US 97, South of Klamath Falls, Oregon, July 21, 1973*
Stuart, *George Washington*

Museum of Modern Art
11 West 53rd Street
New York
NY 10019

Arp, *Leaves and Navels, 1*
Balla, *Flight of the Swallows*
Beckmann, *Departure*
Calder, *Lobster Trap and Fish Tail*
Cartier-Bresson, *Juvisy, France*
Celmins, *Web #1*
Eggleston, *Greenwood, Mississippi*
Gonzalez-Torres, *Untitled (Perfect Lovers)*
Lam, *The Jungle*
Marini, *Horseman*
Noguchi, *Stone of Spiritual Understanding*
Pollock, *Number 1A, 1948*
Ray, *Family Romance*
Rist, *Ever is Over All*
Smith, *Australia*
Steichen, *The Pond – Moonlight*
Stieglitz, *The Flatiron Building*
Stella, *Kastura*
Still, *Painting, 1944*
Tuymans, *Lumumba*
Warhol, *Marilyn*
Wool, *Apocalypse Now*
Wyeth, *Christina's World*

Whitney Museum of American Art
945 Madison Avenue
New York
NY 10021

Johns, *Three Flags*
Neel, *Andy Warhol*

George Eastman House
900 East Avenue
Rochester
NY 14607

Atget, *Saint-Cloud*

Pennsylvania Academy of the Fine Arts
118 North Broad Street
Philadelphia
PA 19102

West, *William Penn's Treaty with the Indians*

Philadelphia Museum of Art
26th Street at Benjamin
Franklin Parkway
Philadelphia
PA 19101

Eakins, *Between Rounds*
Hicks, *The Peaceable Kingdom*
Masolino, *Saint Peter and Saint Paul*
H Rousseau, *The Monkeys*
Toulouse-Lautrec, *Dance at the Moulin Rouge*

Carnegie Museum of Art
4400 Forbes Avenue
Pittsburgh
PA 15213

Catlin, *Ambush for Flamingoes*
Kelley, *Craft Morphology Flow Chart*

Corcoran Gallery of Art
500 17th Street NW
Washington DC 20006

Bellows, *Forty-two Kids*

Hirshhorn Museum and Sculpture Garden
Independence Avenue at 7th
Street SW
Washington DC 20560

Deacon, *Fish Out of Water*
Newman, *Covenant*
Segal, *Bus Riders*

Library of Congress
Thomas Jefferson Building
10 First Street, SE
Washington, DC 20540

Adams, *View South from Manzanar to Alabama Hills*

National Gallery of Art
6th Street at Constitution
Avenue NW
Washington DC 20565

Castagno, *The Young David*
Chase, *A Friendly Visit*
Corot, *Ville d'Avray*
Frankenthaler, *Mountains and Sea*
Homer, *Breezing Up*
Hopper, *Cape Cod Evening*
Leyster, *Self-portrait*
Whiteread, *Ghost*

National Museum of American Art
Eighth and G Streets NW
Washington DC 20560

Rauschenberg, *Reservoir*

Phillips Collection
1600 21st Street NW
Washington DC 20009-1090

Bonnard, *The Open Window*
Braque, *The Round Table*
Davis, *Egg Beater No. 4*
Dove, *Me and the Moon*
Marin, *Maine Islands*

Acknowledgements

Authors

Lee Beard, Adam Butler, Claire Van Cleave, Diane Fortenberry and Susan Stirling

Design

The publishers wish to thank Javier Mariscal for his jacket design for this new edition

Photographic Acknowledgements

All copyright works are © the artists

© Marina Abramovic/DACS 2012, photograph by Stephen P. Harris: 4; Courtesy Ai Weiwei, Leister Foundation, Switzerland, Erlenmeyer Stiftung, Switzerland & Galerie Urs Meile, Beijing-Lucerne: 8; AKG-images: 543; Courtesy Salvatore Ala Gallery, NY: 368; Courtesy Francis Alÿs: 14; Courtesy Nobuyoshi Araki: 22; Art Gallery of Ontario, Toronto. Purchase, 1967 (Acc. No.66/ 19): 399; © John Baldessari, photograph courtesy Sprüth Magers Berlin London: 31; © Desmond Banks. Photograph courtesy National Galleries of Scotland: 393; © Matthew Barney, photograph courtesy Gladstone Gallery, NY & Brussels, photograph Michael James O'Brien: 35; © Bernd & Hilla Becher, Courtesy Sonnabend Gallery, NY: 45; Courtesy Galerie Bruno Bischofberger, Zurich: 121; Courtesy Marc Blondeau: 183; Galleria Blu,

Milan: 186; © Alighiero Boerti/ DACS, London 2012: 60; © Estate of Georges Braque/ DACS, London 2012. Photograph courtesy of the Phillips Collection, Washington DC: 77; Bridgeman Art Library: 12, 13, 19, 21, 27, 32, 33, 39, 42, 44, 47, 51, 59, 66, 74, 82, 83, 93, 98, 99, 104. 114, 115, 116, 119, 129, 134, 138, 152, 156, 157, 158, 159, 160, 164, 169, 170, 173, 182, 188, 189, 198, 199, 200, 202, 203, 206, 213, 214, 215, 217, 218, 226, 232, 233, 237, 247, 272, 274, 276, 277, 279, 284, 287, 292, 301, 303, 308, 316, 318, 319, 325, 329, 335, 336, 337, 338, 340, 341, 344, 349, 350, 353, 366, 374, 379, 382, 383, 387, 395, 400, 403, 406, 407, 408, 414, 417, 418, 421, 438, 447, 459, 460, 461, 462, 464, 465, 466, 468, 469, 471, 473, 480, 485, 486, 490, 494, 497, 500, 504, 517, 518, 526, 528, 529, 536, 541, 544, 545, 547, 550, 564, 569, 576, 577, 578, 579; Galerie Jeanne Bucher, Paris: 510, 546; © Daniel Buren/ Corbis: 85; © Claude Cahun/ Jersey Heritage Collections: 89; © Sophie Calle/ DACS, London 2012, photograph courtesy Paula Cooper Gallery, NY: 92; © Anthony Caro/ Barford Sculptures Ltd/ photograph Tate, London: 97; © Henri Cartier-Bresson/ Magnum Photos: 101; Leo Castelli Gallery, NY / photo © 1989 Dorothy Zeidman: 185; © Maurizio Cattelan, photograph courtesy Marian Goodman Gallery: 106; © Vija Celmins, courtesy McKee Galley, NY, digital image © 2012 The

Museum of Modern Art, NY/ Scala, Florence: 108; Collection Center for Creative Photography © 1981 Arizona Board of Regents: 562; © John Chamberlain/ DACS, London 2012, photograph courtesy of the Pace Gallery, NY: 111; Christie's, NY: 110, 187, 520; The Cleveland Museum of Art, Mr & Mrs William H Marlatt Fund: 117; © Chuck Close, photograph courtesy the Pace Gallery: 122; Courtesy Paula Cooper Gallery, NY/ photograph © 1989 D James Dee: 16; Crane Kalman Gallery Ltd, London: 262; © Salvador Dalí, Fundació Gala-Salvador Dalí, DACS, London 2012/ photograph Tate, London: 136; © Thomas Demand/ DACS London 2012. Photograph courtesy Sprüth Magers Berlin London: 147; Patrick Derom Gallery, Brussels/ photo Vincent Everarts: 509; © Peter Doig. Courtesy of Victoria Miro Gallery: 155; © Marlene Dumas, photograph courtesy Zeno X Gallery: 167; Courtesy of the Eggleston Artistic Trust, digital image © 2012 The Museum of Modern Art, NY/ Scala, Florence: 171; Courtesy Fischer Fine Art, London: 75; © Robert Frank, from 'The Americans'. Collection of the artist, Courtesy Pace/ MacGill Gallery, NY: 191; © The Lucian Freud Archive, photograph © Christie's Images/ The Bridgeman Art Library: 193; Gimpel Fils, London: 250, 527; Giraudon/ Bridgeman Art Library: 64, 70, 71, 95, 112, 123, 137, 139, 140, 144, 145, 163, 196, 207, 230, 248, 310, 326,

327, 371, 381, 404, 430, 433, 496, 507, 533, 539, 540; Marian Goodman Gallery, NY/ photo Michael Goodman: 61; © The Felix Gonzalez-Torres Foundation / digital image © 2012 The Museum of Modern Art, NY / Scala, Florence: 221 © Anthony Gormley, photograph by Louis Bustamante: 223; © Dan Graham, image Courtesy Marian Goodman Gallery: 228; Courtesy Greengrassi, London, photograph by Marcus Leith: 5; Galerie Karsten Greve, Cologne / photograph by Georges Poncet: 73; © Andreas Gursky/ DACS, London 2012: 238; © The Estate of Eva Hesse. Courtesy Hauser & Wirth. Photocredit: Susan Einstein: 252; Photo Credit: Michael Heizer. © Triple Aught Foundation 2010: 249; Hirschl & Adler Galleries Inc., NY: 491; Hirshhorn Museum & Sculpture Garden, Smithsonian Institution, Gift of Joseph H Hirshhorn, 1966/ photo Lee Stalsworth: 487; © Damien Hirst & Science Ltd. All rights reserved/ DACS, London 2012: 256; © Estate of Hannah Höch / DACS, London 2012: 258; © David Hockney, photograph Tate, London: 259; © 1977–9 Jenny Holzer/ DACS, London 2012: 266; © Estate of Edward Hopper: 270; Courtesy Leonard Hutton Galleries, NY: 220, 481; Courtesy Leonard Hutton Galleries, NY / © Nolde-Stiftung Seebüll: 397; Index/ Bridgeman Art Library: 229, 453; Indiana University Art Museum, Partial Gift of